SCOTLAND IN DEFINITION:
A HISTORY OF SCOTTISH DICTIONARIES

SCOTLAND IN DEFINITION

A History of Scottish Dictionaries

Edited by
Iseabail Macleod and
J. Derrick McClure

First published in 2012 by
John Donald, an imprint of Birlinn Ltd

West Newington House
10 Newington Road
Edinburgh
EH9 1QS
www.birlinn.co.uk

ISBN 978 1 906566 49 4

The publishers gratefully acknowledge
the support of
the Scotland Inheritance Fund
and the Strathmartine Trust
towards the publication of this book

British Library Cataloguing-in-Publication Data
A catalogue record for this book is available on request
from the British Library

Typeset in Arno by
Koinonia, Manchester
Printed and bound in Britain by
TJ International Ltd, Padstow, Cornwall

To the memory of A. J. Aitken,
whose contribution to Scottish lexicography is immeasurable

Contents

PART II Gaelic Lexicography

PART III The Scottish Contribution to English Dictionaries

Contributors

Margaret Grace (Marace) Dareau was born in Dumfriesshire and attended Annan Academy. She graduated from Edinburgh University with first class honours in English Language and Linguistics in 1966 and commenced her career on the *Dictionary of the Older Scottish Tongue* (*DOST*) in 1969. She was Senior Editor of the *DOST*, then Editorial Director, (1987–2001). She was Editorial Director of Scottish Language Dictionaries (2002–5), Principal Editor (2005–12) and now consultant. She is Lexicographical Consultant of Faclair na Gàidhlig. She was an editor of the *Concise Scots Dictionary* (1979–84) and author of the Glossary of the *Encyclopedia of Language and Linguistics* (1994).

William Gillies was Professor of Celtic at the University of Edinburgh 1979–2009 and Visiting Professor of Celtic Languages and Literatures at Harvard University 2009–10. He has published extensively on Scottish Gaelic, Irish and Celtic subjects, and has special research interests in the Books of Clanranald and the Book of the Dean of Lismore. He was Manager of the *Dictionary of the Older Scottish Tongue* 1994–2001 and is General Editor of the Survey of the Gaelic Dialects of Scotland. He is currently involved with the inter-University historical dictionary *Faclair na Gàidhlig* and the Alexander Carmichael project at Edinburgh University.

J. Derrick McClure, educated at Ayr Academy, Glasgow University and Edinburgh University, has recently retired after nearly forty years of lecturing in the English Department at the University of Aberdeen. He has published four monographs and over a hundred articles on Scottish literary and linguistic topics, as well as numerous Scots poetic translations from Gaelic, Italian and other languages. He has at different times chaired the Association for Scottish Literary Studies (ASLS) Language Committee, the Forum for Research in the Languages of Scotland and Ulster, and the Scottish Government's Ministerial Advisory Group on the Scots Language. In 2002 he was awarded an MBE for services to Scottish culture.

Iseabail Macleod spent some years as a dictionaries editor with Collins and later Chambers. From 1979 she worked for the Scottish National Dictionary Association – from 1986 until 2002 as Editorial Director – and she was joint editor of several of their dictionaries. She was joint editor with Caroline Macafee of *The Nuttis Schell: Essays on the Scots Language* (1988) and her other publications include *The Pocket Guide to Scottish Words* (1986, 2006). She was General Editor of the *Illustrated Encyclopedia of Scotland* (2004), and of *About Scotland: People, Places, Heritage* (2007).

Michael Montgomery is Distinguished Professor Emeritus of English and Linguistics at the University of South Carolina, where he taught until he retired in 1999. He is currently revising his comprehensive *Dictionary of Smoky Mountain English* (2004, based partly on the collections of J. S. Hall). His study of Appalachian English has included detailed examination of its Scots and Irish English roots; and his findings have been published in numerous books and articles including *From Ulster to America: The Scotch–Irish Heritage of American English* (2006, 2007). He has served as President of the American Dialect Society and he is President of Ulster Scots Language Society.

Mary O'Neill is a lexicographer and editor. She graduated from Glasgow University in 1992 with an MA in English Language and Literature. For a number of years she was a lexicographer with Collins in Glasgow, where she worked on a number of dictionaries, including *Collins English Dictionary* and the *Gem Scots Dictionary*. From 2000 she was an editor at Chambers in Edinburgh, where she was editor-in-chief of *The Chambers Dictionary* in 2008–9.

Lorna Pike was born in Fort William, Inverness-shire. She graduated from Edinburgh University in 1978 with an MA in English Language and Linguistics. Her career in lexicography began on the *Concise Scots Dictionary* (Editor, 1979–83). She subsequently joined the staff of the *Dictionary of the Older Scottish Tongue* and was part of the editorial team which brought the project to completion. She has also worked as Senior Editor with the Scottish National Dictionary Association and its successor, Scottish Language Dictionaries. She is currently Project Co-ordinator with *Faclair na Gàidhlig* working towards transferring skills in historical lexicography from Scots to Gaelic.

Susan Rennie is a lexicographer and author. A former Senior Editor with Scottish Language Dictionaries, she edited and managed the online *Dictionary of the Scots Language* at the University of Dundee in 2001–4. She has worked on both Scots and English dictionaries, including *The New Shorter Oxford English Dictionary* and *Chambers Dictionary*, and is the author of *The Oxford English*

Thesaurus for Schools and *The Oxford Primary Thesaurus*. She was a co-founder of Itchy Coo Books, and has written several books for children in Scots, including the award-winning *Animal ABC: A Scots Alphabet*.

Keith Williamson is a Research Fellow in the Institute for Historical Dialectology, University of Edinburgh. He is compiling the first phase of a Linguistic Atlas of Older Scots and has published articles on spatio-temporal variation in Older Scots, and on theory and methodology for historical dialectology.

Acknowledgements

The authors' thanks are due to many people who have advised and informed at various stages of the book's creation. Particular gratitude is owed to Caroline Macafee for help with so many chapters, and to the late Richard Bailey, whose advice was so much missed in the late stages.

They are also very grateful to the Strathmartine Trust and the Scotland Inheritance Fund for their generous financial contributions to the publication of the book.

Finally, they would like to thank the following for permission to use illustrations:

Faroes National Library and the University of the Faroes (p. 89)
National Library of Scotland (pp. 155, 157, 165)
School of Scottish Studies Archives, University of Edinburgh (pp. 124, 149)
Scottish Language Dictionaries (pp. 117, 134, 139)
Special Collections, Aberdeen University Library (pp. 41, 51)
Donald Meek Collection (p. 225)
Sabhal Mòr Ostaig UHI (p. 255)

Abbreviations

AUP	Aberdeen University Press
CESD	*Concise English–Scots Dictionary*
CSD	*Concise Scots Dictionary*
DASG	Digital Archive of Scottish Gaelic
DIL	*Dictionary of the Irish Language*
DOST	*Dictionary of the Older Scottish Tongue*
EDD	*English Dialect Dictionary*
EME	Early Middle English
EUL	Edinburgh University Library
EUP	Edinburgh University Press
FnaG	Faclair na Gàidhlig
GOC	Gaelic Orthographic Conventions
HDSG	Historical Dictionary of Scottish Gaelic
HDSG-A	Historical Dictionary of Scottish Gaelic Archive
IPA	International Phonetic Association
ME	Middle English
MSc	Middle Scots
ModSc	Modern Scots
NLS	National Library of Scotland
ODNB	*Oxford Dictionary of National Biography*
OE	Old English
OED	*Oxford English Dictionary*
ON	Old Norse
OSc	Older Scots
OUP	Oxford University Press
PSD	*Pocket Scots Dictionary*
SGTS	Scottish Gaelic Texts Society
SLD	Scottish Language Dictionaries
SLS	Scots Language Society

SND	*Scottish National Dictionary*
SNDA	Scottish National Dictionaries Association
SSD	*Scots Schools Dictionary*
SSPCK	Society in Scotland for Propagating Christian Knowledge
STS	Scottish Text Society
TGSI	*Transactions of the Gaelic Society of Inverness*

Introduction

ISEABAIL MACLEOD AND J. DERRICK MCCLURE

Lexicography – defined by one of its greatest exponents, Dr Samuel Johnson, as 'the art or practice of writing dictionaries' – has a long and distinguished history in Scotland. Not only have the indigenous languages, Scots and Gaelic, been examined in dictionaries of outstanding quality, but Scottish scholars have also made important contributions to the lexicography of English. *Scotland in Definition* is a tribute to the *literati* and academics through the centuries who have developed lexicography as a field of study and applied it to describing their national languages.

The authors and editors of this book had a twofold aim: to provide scholars with descriptions and assessments of the dictionaries and word lists produced in Scotland for Scots, Gaelic and English; and to bring the interest and importance of lexicography to the attention of the general reader. In particular, we hope to have shown that the subject has a significance that is far from merely historical: dictionaries have a key part to play in the maintenance and development of the living languages which we speak. The various chapters range from the earliest medieval glossaries to the electronic projects of the twenty-first century; and examine the actual content of the dictionaries, the lives of the people who made them, and the ways in which the changing cultural and intellectual background motivated the lexicographers and led them to produce their distinctive individual works.

Scotland in the twenty-first century has three indigenous languages: English, Scots and Gaelic (in ascending order of antiquity, and descending order of contemporary demographic strength). This situation is fraught with tensions of various kinds; but the historical background is more complex still. In early times much of what is now Scotland was P-Celtic in speech (the language group which has given rise to modern Welsh): though the evidence is far from sufficient to warrant any degree of certainty, it suggests that some dialect differences existed between the Pictish of the north-east and the Cumbric of the south-west. Gaelic, a Q-Celtic language, arrived from Ireland, beginning possibly as early as the third century AD, and gradually spread eastwards, gaining importance with the rise of the kings of Dal Riada and the eventual dynastic union of Scots and Picts in the ninth century to form the beginning of the medieval Scottish kingdom. In Scotland, as in other European countries (and for a longer period than in most of them), Latin played a key part as the international language of law, diplomacy and scholarship. Other languages arrived from overseas, further complicating the language map of Scotland. Viking settlements beginning in the ninth century brought the Old Norse tongue to the Northern and Western Isles and much of the northern mainland: its descendant Norn survived in Orkney and Shetland until the eighteenth or even the nineteenth century, and has left its mark on the dialects still spoken in the Northern Isles. The landowners who arrived in the twelfth century from Normandy or Norman England, as the Scottish kings remodelled their realm as a European state, brought Norman French as a language of the ruling class. Their servants and followers, by contrast, in many cases spoke the strongly Norse-influenced English dialect of what had once been the Danelaw, thus reinforcing the Anglo-Saxon tongue spoken in south-east Scotland (part of the kingdom of Northumbria until annexed by Malcolm II, the grandfather of Macbeth, in 1018) since the seventh century. This was the language which was later to develop into Scots. Another language that influenced Scots as the kingdom established its place among the nations of Europe was Dutch, through trading links with the Low Countries; Gaelic too, despite the long-standing cultural and political antagonism between Highlands and Lowlands, exerted an influence on the Scots tongue which is more pervasive than is often admitted.

The reign of Alexander III (r. 1249–1286) represents the high-water mark of this stage of Scotland's development into a fully fledged, mainstream European monarchy. Though French had been adopted as a court language, the king's native tongue was Gaelic, as that of his predecessors had been; and Gaelic was still spoken over more than half the land area of the kingdom. However, the Anglo-Saxon dialect which we may now call Scots (although two centuries were to pass before it came to be called that by its speakers) had spread far beyond its original boundaries, at the expense of Gaelic and Cumbric, and had grown enormously in social importance through being the speech of the burghs. Its demographic strength had been increased to some extent, as already noted, by the households of the Norman lords; but also, and much more importantly, by the influx of refugees from England during the oppressions of the first Norman kings and the anarchy of Stephen's reign. Incomers from Scandinavia and the Low Countries, speaking closely related languages, found it easier to learn than Gaelic. Relations between the two communities were relatively peaceful

– there was as yet no sign of the polarisation of Scotland into mutually hostile 'Highlands' and 'Lowlands', which is a prevalent and often tragic feature of its later history – and had the steady cultural, commercial and political progress of the reigns of Alexander and his immediate predecessors been maintained, it is permissible to imagine that the linguistic history of Scotland, particularly in respect of Gaelic, might have been very different.

The course of Scottish history was radically altered, however, by the deaths of Alexander and his granddaughter and heir. This extinction of the ancient royal line led not only to the Wars of Independence (which are not our present concern) but to a decisive shifting of the kingdom's social and political centre of gravity from the Gaelic-speaking to the Scots-speaking area. Robert Bruce was Gaelic-speaking, as was his earldom of Carrick; but the Stewarts located their power base firmly in the Lowlands, with Edinburgh as the capital. It was in Scots that John Barbour in 1375 wrote his epic of Robert Bruce; and when James I had the Acts of Parliament of earlier reigns translated into the vernacular, he chose Scots and not Gaelic. The Gàidhealtachd, increasingly neglected by the monarchy, came to regard the Lord of the Isles and not the king as its leader; and James IV, though the only Stewart to learn Gaelic and make active efforts to regain the allegiance of its speakers, also made the disastrous move (for the Highlands) of forfeiting the Lordship of the Isles, thus depriving the region of a political focus.

Scots, as the language of the confident and dynamic Stewart monarchy, entered on what is arguably its greatest period of cultural and literary development: writers of the calibre of Barbour, James I, Blind Harry, Henryson and Dunbar made it one of Europe's great poetic languages; Gavin Douglas set the seal on its development by using it for the first (and by some estimates the greatest) complete poetic translation ever made of Virgil's *Aeneid*;[1] its potential as a prose medium was exploited by, among others, John Bellenden and Robert Lyndsay of Pitscottie, and its aptitude for drama by David Lyndsay in *Ane Satyre of the Thrie Estaitis*, a play still capable, as several recent revivals have confirmed, of appealing to theatre audiences. The advent of printing, however, signalled its death warrant, although it was some time before this became apparent. Some of Scotland's first printers were English or had previously worked in England, and began, no doubt at first quite unthinkingly, to assimilate the spelling and grammar of Scots texts to English norms. The contribution made by the Reformation and the Union of the Crowns to this process was very real; but it is difficult to conceive of *any* historical circumstances under which the change would not have occurred, if only for the fundamental reason that the language of English printed texts was bound to influence that of Scottish ones by simple weight of numbers. In the course of the seventeenth century, bilingualism in Scots and English became the norm among Scotland's educated populace; and in the eighteenth, notoriously, a determined effort was made to excise all 'Scotticisms' from speech. Vigorous efforts to counter this by the poets of the Vernacular Revival had a measure of success; but the perception of Scots as a mere rustic dialect, and as such a social and educational handicap, has persisted into our own time and has not been fully outgrown even yet. Scots, nonetheless, has shown remarkable powers of survival: today there are still communities where the language is spoken in its pristine purity (though all its speakers are bilingual and all are literate in English), and the feature of 'style-drifting' – modulating on a continuous plane extending from full Scots to Scottish Standard English – is frequently encountered. A recent development has been the rise of distinctive urban basilects (in Glasgow and Dundee this is long-established; in Aberdeen it is visibly happening at the moment); and a much more recent one has been the recognition that these are not mere 'slovenly speech' or 'bad English' but distinctive Scottish examples of a common sociolinguistic development and as such worthy of respect.

Gaelic, for its part, had seen a similar rise to high literary distinction followed by a period of oppression and consequent decline. It was in the sixteenth century that modern Scottish Gaelic began to emerge as an independent language (until then a common form referred to as Classical Gaelic had been used in both Scotland and Ireland); and the rapidity with which it developed its own literary tradition, and the scope and quality of its poetic achievement over the next two-and-a-half centuries, are remarkable by any standards: the stature of such poets as Iain Lom, Rob Donn, Silis na Ceapaich, Donnchadh Bàn Mac an t-Saoir and, above all, Alasdair Mac Mhaighistir Alasdair is unmistakeable to anyone who reads their work with even an imperfect knowledge of Gaelic. Over precisely the same period, however, political events were undercutting the status of the language: James VI's Statutes of Iona of 1609, obliging all Highland chiefs to send their sons to be educated in the Lowlands; the Society in Scotland for Propagating Christian Knowledge (SSPCK) founded in 1709 for 'the extirpation of the Irish language and other pious usages'; the vicious repression of the Highlands after the defeat of the Jacobite cause; and finally the infamous Clearances, had the effect intended by their perpetrators of reducing both the social and educational status of the language and its demographic strength. The 1872 Education Act, by simply ignoring the existence of Gaelic, effectively placed the language beyond the pale; and the First World War was a further devastating blow, diminishing the number of Gaelic speakers still further and destroying many long-established communities. In the twentieth century the rate of decline became catastrophic, and though official policy towards the language has been reversed in recent times and several important measures have been taken for its preservation, it is still in a critical state.

How the developing science of lexicography in Scotland has been applied to the events in this complex story will be illustrated by the chapters of this book. Lexicography in most European languages has its origin in marginal glosses in Latin texts. Some of the earliest Scottish examples are the *Thesaurus Palaeohibernica* and notes in early religious, legal and literary documents from the Gàidhealtachd; and for Scots, the Scone Gloss, a set of marginal notes in a mid-fourteenth-century document relating to land leased by the Hay family from the monastery of Scone, in which many words and phrases in the Latin text are provided with Scots equivalents. These nonce and random notes were gradually collected and arranged systematically, developing into dictionaries in which Latin words were glossed by their vernacular equivalents. Lists in which one vernacular language was translated into another (e.g. French or Italian into English) were also compiled, at a somewhat later date. Monolingual dictionaries took longer still to appear, and at first were little more than individually selected lists of 'difficult' words. The first work in English to be recognisable as a dictionary in the modern sense is Robert Cawdrey's *A Table Alphabeticall* of 1604. As the vernacular languages triumphed in their long struggle for parity with Latin, the perceived need for prestigious scholarly dictionaries, designed to establish and preserve canonical forms for the languages, led to the production of such works by the Accademia della Crusca in Florence and the Académie Française in Paris: Dr Samuel Johnson's *Dictionary of the English Language* of 1755 was a belated attempt to provide a reference work of similar stature for English. By the nineteenth century the function of lexicography had come to be seen as descriptive rather than prescriptive, and the aim of the *New English Dictionary*, later the *Oxford English Dictionary* (*OED*), was to give as detailed a record of the language as could be attained.

The *OED* is one of the great historical dictionaries of the world. As it approached completion, however, Sir William Craigie, one of its editors, put forward a plan for a series of supplements in the form of 'period dictionaries', designed to cover specific geographical or chronological forms of the language in more detail than had been possible in the parent dictionary. Not all of Craigie's proposed 'period dictionaries' have been completed and some were never even begun; but his suggestion of dictionaries for Older and Modern Scots have come to fruition in *A Dictionary of the Older Scottish Tongue* (*DOST*) and *The Scottish National Dictionary* (*SND*). The value of Craigie's conception is readily illustrated by those two dictionaries: Scots is very far from being ignored in the

OED itself, no doubt partly because both Craigie and Sir James Murray, the chief editor, were Scottish; but although the Scots words found in, say, Burns, Scott and Stevenson are in most cases present in the *OED*, the range of its Scots coverage is only a fraction of the lexicographical information contained in the *DOST* and *SND*.

The development of Scots lexicography is intimately related to, and latterly an integral part of, the development of lexicography in English. The story of Gaelic is somewhat different. Beginning, as did Scots, with Old Irish glosses in Latin texts and developing along similar lines in the medieval period, Gaelic lexicography entered the modern age with Alasdair Mac Mhaighistir Alasdair, whose *A Galick and English Vocabulary* of 1741 was the first of its kind. Besides being by some estimates the greatest poet ever to write in the language, Mac Mhaighistir Alasdair was a staunch Jacobite and an ardent defender of Highland culture against what he called *mi-rùn mór nan Gall*, 'the great ill-will of the Lowlanders'; and his dictionary appeared at a time when the established Church of Scotland was no less hostile than the secular state towards Gaelic, seeing the supersession of the language as a necessary means towards 'civilising' the Highlands and bringing them into the ambit of the Kirk. Several compilers of the first Gaelic dictionaries were ministers or priests: Mac Mhaighistir Alasdair, however, was diametrically opposed to this stance, and his dictionary may well have been conceived as an attempt to prepare his compatriots for the cultural onslaught and enable them to withstand it. The element of religious proselytising which had marked eighteenth-century Gaelic lexicography faded somewhat in the nineteenth; and the continuing work in the field culminated in two remarkable dictionaries: Alexander MacBain's ground-breaking *An Etymological Dictionary of the Gaelic Language* of 1896, still a valuable work though partly superseded by later research; and the *Illustrated Gaelic-English Dictionary* (1901–11) by Edward Dwelly (born near Arundel but married to a Gaelic speaker), the fruit of a lifetime's research into the language in all its forms and among the great one-man achievements in the history of lexicography. The twentieth century was less productive: scandalously, even in the 1950s and 1960s Dwelly's was still the most complete and authoritative Gaelic dictionary available, but progress resumed in the late twentieth and twenty-first centuries, and the planned *Faclair na Gàidhlig*, a historical dictionary on modern lexicographical lines, will when complete not only bring Gaelic lexicography back to the cutting edge but be a major step forward in the preservation and maintenance of the language.

This volume is divided into three parts. The first covers the lexicography of Scots from the medieval glossaries to the massive historical works of the twentieth century, and the results of more recent efforts to build on these great foundations. This section opens with Keith Williamson's discussion of the earliest Scots glossaries, and of the ways in which they illustrate the pattern of development from textual glossary to bilingual word list. J. Derrick McClure in Chapter 2 notes how conflicting attitudes to the Scots tongue in the eighteenth century influenced descriptions of the language: almost paradoxically, the lists of Scotticisms compiled to show people how *not* to speak and the glossaries to Scots literary texts compiled in a spirit of cultural and linguistic patriotism are equally valuable as sources of information, both on what the language was like and how it was perceived. Chapter 3, by Susan Rennie, is devoted to what is by far the most important work of Scots lexicography before the twentieth century, John Jamieson's landmark *Etymological Dictionary of the Scottish Language*. It examines both the *Dictionary* itself, in the light of the intellectual context in which it appeared, and its status as the groundwork for all subsequent projects in the field. The growing realisation of the interest and value of the various regional dialects of Scots, still one of the most fascinating features of the language, led from the nineteenth century to the appearance of a number of word lists for the individual dialects – a development examined by Iseabail Macleod in Chapter 4. The last three chapters of the Scots section deal with the two major historical dictionaries and their successors: *A Dictionary of the Older Scottish Tongue* and, for the modern period, *The Scottish National Dictionary*. In Chapter 5, Margaret G. Dareau recounts the history of the *DOST*, showing how its enormous range of material, far exceeding the Scottish component of the *OED*, illustrates the scope of the language in the Older Scots period. The next two chapters, both by Iseabail Macleod, deal with the *SND* and its successors. Chapter 6 describes the need for a dictionary of modern Scots and recounts the story of the great struggle that went into producing it, brought to a successful conclusion by the 1970s. Chapter 7 shows how the riches of the historical dictionaries were made accessible to a wider public by derived works, and outlines other, smaller Scots dictionaries of the last century.

Part 2 (Chapters 8 and 9), by Lorna Pike and William Gillies, gives a wide-ranging account of Gaelic lexicography, from glosses in Old Irish texts to the latest plans for a historical dictionary of Scottish Gaelic, Faclair na Gàidhlig. Chapter 8 charts the gradual emergence of a lexicographical tradition in the eighteenth and nineteenth centuries, culminating in the comprehensive Gaelic–English dictionary of the Londoner Edward Dwelly. Chapter 9 examines how educational, political and demographic developments in the twentieth century have been reflected in Gaelic lexicography. Finally, Part 3 deals with the enormous contributions made by Scottish scholars to the lexicography of English. Long before the work of Sir James Murray and Sir William Craigie on the *OED*, Scotsmen had played their part in producing the many educational works designed to encourage the use of 'correct' English; and, in more recent times, some of the most widely used general-purpose dictionaries have come from Chambers in Edinburgh and Collins in Glasgow. Mary O'Neill in Chapter 10 provides a full account of these contributions.

That the efforts of lexicographers have contributed vastly to the understanding, development and latterly preservation of Scots and Gaelic will be amply demonstrated in this book; yet it will also show that lexicographers are no more immune than the rest of us to being affected by the attitudes of their times. The steady rise in importance of English in Scotland in the seventeenth and eighteenth centuries was inevitably linked, as already noted, to negative attitudes towards both Scots and Gaelic. Even today, though outright hostility to the languages, and efforts to extirpate them, have largely disappeared, the long-term neglect which they have endured, especially in the field of education, has probably been no less damaging, and has yet to be completely eliminated. Scots and Gaelic dictionaries, with some exceptions, may be seen partly as counterweights to these attitudes, especially those designed specifically for school use. Dwelly's Gaelic dictionary and the ten-volume *SND* give a vivid picture of the languages' range and breadth in the modern period. At times, however, dictionaries can reflect negative attitudes: the *SND*'s neglect of urban dialects, especially that of Glasgow (famously described as 'hopelessly corrupt' in its Introduction), was symptomatic of the then (and to some extent still) current view that only the rural dialects are 'real' or 'good' Scots, urban speech being merely bad or slovenly. In our days, when the rural dialects have been weakened by the decline in rural populations and diluted by the increasing presence of incomers, it is arguably the urban dialects that represent the strongest and most vital side of Scots. Authors such as Irvine Welsh and James Kelman will feature in future editions of the *SND*. And while both Scots and Gaelic compete against the common enemy that is English, the ancient antagonism between the speakers of the two languages also surfaces in lexicographical works. Some otherwise admirable Scots lexicographers of the eighteenth century, such as Sibbald, visibly flout the Gaelic contribution to the language; and in the other direction, the use of Scots words in the definitions of some Gaelic–English dictionaries fluctuates for reasons on which it is tempting to speculate, as in Ewen MacEachen's *Faclair Gàidhlig us Beurla*. This aspect of lexicography is an integral part of the history of the topic, and as such is referred to in the book.

Scotland in Definition aims to give a broad view of the current state of play in Scottish lexicography, offering a comprehensive and detailed overview of the field, and showing how dictionaries can influence the development of the languages and their status in the social, cultural and other fields. But linguistic research is by no means confined to lexicography; and though this is beyond the scope of this book, it is worth noting as a final reflection that research in other fields has a distinguished history in Scotland, and continues to flourish. The Linguistic Survey of Scotland, dealing with the spoken forms of Scots and Gaelic, conducted extensive fieldwork from the 1950s to the 1970s, and its most important outcomes have been the three-volume *Linguistic Atlas of Scotland* and the five-volume *Survey of the Gaelic Dialects of Scotland* (1994–7). The study of place-names, besides its intrinsic interest, can illuminate wide-ranging issues of demographic, social and linguistic history; and the published and ongoing work of the Place-Name Survey testifies to the quality of the research conducted in this field in Scotland. Simon Taylor's series of volumes *The Place-names of Fife*, of which three have appeared at the time of writing, is an outstanding example.

Both Scots and Gaelic have suffered in the past from antagonistic attitudes, but there is no doubt that enormous progress has been made in recent years: not only in the scholarly study of the languages, but in recognition of their value and importance and consequent changes to long-standing assumptions regarding their place in education and in the social and cultural life of the nation. Since the establishment of the Scottish Parliament, the rate of this progress has markedly increased – one example is the recent welcome increase in support for both Scots and Gaelic dictionaries, and further developments are confidently awaited. If this book alerts readers not only to what has been achieved in the field but what still remains to be done, it will have served a useful purpose.

PART I

Scots Dictionaries

ONE

Lexicography of Scots before 1700

KEITH WILLIAMSON

Introduction

On 22 June 1900, James A.H. Murray gave Oxford University's Romanes Lecture, entitled *The Evolution of English Lexicography*. Murray was then chief editor of the 'New English Dictionary', now the *Oxford English Dictionary* (*OED*) (see Chapter 10). In his lecture he outlined the history of English lexicography from its distant roots in the Old English glosses up to the *OED* itself, a work founded on clear 'scientific' principles. Though himself a Scot and well acquainted with Scots as both native speaker and philologist, he makes no mention in his lecture of Scotland or Scottish works. He had no need to do so, of course. His focus was the developments in lexicographical practice that were to lead to the *OED*, and that is what would have interested his Oxford audience.

Murray summarises the evolution of English lexicography thus:

> ... the glossing of difficult words in Latin manuscripts by easier Latin and at length by English words; the collection of English glosses into Glossaries and the elaboration of Latin-English Vocabularies; the production of Dictionaries of English and another modern language; the compilation of Glossaries and Dictionaries of 'hard' English words; the extension of these by Bailey,[1] for etymological purposes, to include words in general; the idea of a Standard Dictionary, and its realisation by Dr. Johnson with illustrative quotations; the notion that a Dictionary should also show the pronunciation of the living word; the extension of the function of quotations by Richardson;[2] the idea that the Dictionary should be a biography of every word, and should set forth every fact connected with its origin, history and use, on a strictly historical method.[3]

With respect to the earlier stages, he outlines what was the typical path in the development of lexicography in the Western European languages.

This chapter is concerned with the origins of what I will call *lexicographical activity* in relation to Scots. The early developments – *pace* Murray's understandable silence – ought to be seen in the wider European context. Dictionary-making proper in relation to the vernacular languages was well under way in

Continental Europe by the sixteenth century. The Frenchman Robert Estienne (or Robertus Stephanus, c.1503–1559) had published Latin–French dictionaries – *Dictionarium Latino–Gallicum* (1538) and the *Dictionnaire françois–latin* (1539) – as well as a monolingual Latin dictionary, *Thesaurus Linguae Latinae* (1543).[4] Bilingual and multilingual dictionaries were also produced in France by A. Calepino. G. Meurieur's *Dictionnaire françois–flamand* (1562) was innovative in that it related two vernacular languages, rather than Latin exclusively or Latin and a vernacular.[5] England lagged somewhat behind and drew at first on the Continental works, but dictionary-making was under way before 1700, beginning with Robert Cawdrey's *A Table Alphabeticall, Conteyning and Teaching the True Writing, and Understanding of Hard Usuall English Wordes . . .*, published in 1604.

So far as Scotland is concerned, before 1700 nothing was produced that can be called a 'dictionary' in the sense of a work which set out exclusively to list Scots words and define them. For certain there was lexicographical activity, but it was always the product of an ulterior aim, and the focus was not usually the vernacular itself but Latin. By 'lexicographical activity' I mean 'the explanation of words or phrases through other words or phrases'. This is the core task of any dictionary, whether monolingual or multilingual. At a basic level, the explanation will be an attempt to render simple equivalence of sense, or it may involve adding detail about the provenance, pronunciation or history of the word. As a corollary to the idea of explanation, one could add 'in a systematic manner'. If we apply this to the activity we find in our period, we will find that there are degrees of systematicity.

Lexicographical activity, in the broad sense of 'explanation through other words', is certainly to be found in Scotland in the medieval and late modern periods. The focus is on Latin and the teaching and learning of Latin. Latin words are explained by Scots words. We also find another type of lexicographical activity in the explanation of words within specialised discourses, notably in the law.

We are concerned with the history of 'lexicographical activity' with respect to Scots. We may take 1150 to be the start of the Older Scots period. The first sign of lexicographical activity with respect to Scots appears in the form of glosses.

Glosses

The 'glossing' of texts goes back to antiquity. There is extant a considerable number of texts from the Old English period which contain glosses.

> Interlinear (and marginal) glosses to texts were intended as explanations of the words in the texts they gloss and not as independent texts in their own right.[6]

Glosses 'indicate how Latin texts were read and interpreted and how Latin words were understood and rendered'.[7]

Internal glosses

Internal glosses, unlike interlinear or marginal glosses, form part of a text itself and are products of the author, or perhaps copyist, of a text. Unlike interlinear glosses, they are not addenda by a reader or other interpreter of the text. An internal gloss is created where in a Latin text a word is given a vernacular explanation, usually flagged by such words or phrases as *vulgariter, nuncupatus, vulgariter nuncupatus, appelatus, vulgo, anglice*. This kind of gloss can be found particularly in record texts throughout the Older Scots period. The aim would seem to be to make clear to a reader the sense of words that might be less well known to a reader of Latin and/or whose referents were more commonly expressed in the vernacular. Examples, culled from the quotations in the *Dictionary of the Older Scottish Tongue (DOST)*, are:

> In brasina . . . algeam wlgariter le trowch i fattum et i sa et i barell; c1350 *Reg. Episc. Morav.* 367.; c1350 *Reg. Episc. Morav.* 367. [s.v. Tro(u)ch, *n.*]
>
> Quæ lacunar ['ceiling'] sive testudo ['vault'], vulgariter autem To-fall . . . nuncupatur; a1447 *Bower Chron.* II 398. [s.v. To-fal(l, *n.*]
>
> Per traditionem aspersorii, wlgariter le haly water styk, in manibus . . . fratris Willelmi Howstoun; 1498 *Glasgow Dioc. Reg.* II. 67. [s.v. Haly water, *n.*]
>
> Vnam peluem et lauacrum argenti . . . deaurata, vulgariter giltet about the eggis and extremeteis; 1547–9 *Liber Offic. S. Andree* 140. [s.v. Extremité, -itie, *n.*]
>
> Duas ampullas stanneas lie flakkettis nuncupatas; 1550 *Reg. Great S.* 102/2. [s.v. Flak(k)et, Flacat, *n.*]
>
> Sexdecim marcarum victualium, vulgo coist nuncupatarum; 1564 *Orkney & Shet. Rec.* I.150. [s.v. Cost, Coist, *n.*]

Here, arguably, the Latin is defining the vernacular word. According to *DOST coist* here is 'ON. *kost-r* (Norw. *kost*), food, victuals, corn'. It would seem to have been a term peculiar to Orkney and might well require explanation for Lowland incomers.

> Et quatuor oneribus equorum straminum vulgariter nuncupatis four kimples of stray; 1629 *Byrehills (Fife) Chart. MS. (OED.)*. [s.v. Kimpill, *n.*]

> Avis quaedam rarissima capercalze, id est sylvester equus vulgo dicta; Leslie *De Orig. Scot.* (1675) 24. [s.v. Capercailȝe, -calȝe, *n.*]

In this example, 'vulgo' applies to sense and not form: 'sylvester equus' is a Latin calque on 'capercalze', 'wood horse' (Sc. Gael. *capull coille* = lit. 'horse of the wood').

An Interlinear Gloss

An important early example of an interlinear gloss is a bipartite chirograph of which a copy is in Register House.[8] The text is an agreement, dated 1312, made between (i) the abbot and convent of Scone and (ii) Sir Edmund de Hay 'del Leys' and William, his son. The terms of the charter concern the lease of the abbey's land of 'Balgarvi',[9] with its pertinences,[10] to Edmund, William and William's heirs for thirty years. About a half century after the date of making the charter, on this copy, someone has written interlinear Scots translations of some of the Latin words and phrases. This addition is known as the 'Scone Gloss' (SG). It is possible that the gloss was written in more than one stint. There are changes in the size and thickness of writing, which are probably the result of change of pen.

Written on the verso of the document, in the same hand as the gloss, is what seems to be the draft of a letter (in Latin) concerning the appointment of a nominee to the vicarage of Echt (Aberdeenshire). The draft claims to be written at Scone: 'ad mon[asterium] n[ost]r[u]m de Sco[na]'. There are other jottings on the verso. The date of the addition of the gloss cannot be determined with precision. A piece of evidence for an approximate dating of the gloss is to be found in one manuscript of the 'Liber Ecclesie de Scon', which contains the cartulary of the abbey of Scone. The 'Liber' survives in two National Library of Scotland manuscripts, one made in the middle of the fourteenth century and the other a mid-fifteenth-century production (1450–60).[11] Both manuscripts contain copies of early charters relating to the abbey of Scone, but no copy of the charter in the Scone Gloss appears in either version. However, the distinctive hand of the SG can be identified in the mid-fourteenth-century MS. On ff. 30–1, beginning a little more than halfway down f. 30r, the hand contributes a memorandum concerning a visitation of the bishop of St Andrews. The entry, the last in the manuscript, begins:

> Ad memoria[m] r[e]ducim[us] q[uod] Nos Will[ielmus] d[e]i gr[aci]a Ep[iscopu]s S[anc]ti Andr[e][12] in ulti[m]a visitac[i]one m[e]a / ap[ud] mon[asterium] de Scona f[a]ct[a] vicesi[m]o die Januar[e] cu[m] [con]tinuac[i]o[n]e dier[um] Anno gr[aci]e mill[esim]o t[ri]ce[n]tesi[m]o / sexage[s]i[m]o q[ui]nto . . .

> [We bring back to memory that We William by the grace of God, Bishop of St Andrews, in my last visitation at the monastery of Scone, made on the 20th day of January with continuation of days in the year of grace 1365 . . .]

The SG scribe, then, was active in the abbey of Scone around 1365/6.[13] The use of the verso of the charter to write the style and the other annotations show that the charter had become, if not 'scrap' parchment, then 'recycled' parchment. As the charter would have ceased to have any legal effect after 1342, the date of expiry of the lease, it is most likely that the gloss, the other jottings and the style letter were added after this date.

Below is the opening of the charter text with glosses interpolated following the lemmata that they gloss.

> Anno gr*acie* · M^{o} · CC^{o}C · Duodecimo · F*act*a e*st* *con*uenci*o* hec int*er* Religiosos viros D*omi*nu*m* Thoma*m* dei gr*aci*a Abb*at*em de Scon*a* · & ei*us*dem loci co*n*uentu*m* ex vna / p*a*rte · et Edmu*n*dum de Haya del Leys · & Will*elmu*m filiu*m* ei*us* ex alt*era* p*a*rte · videl*icet* q*uod* di*c*ti Abb*as* & *con*uent*us* **conceseru*n*t** [**has gr*a*ntit**] & ad f*er*ma*m* **dimiseru*n*t** [**has letin**] / tota*m* t*er*ram sua*m* de Balgarvi cu*m* om*n*ib*us* **pertinencijs** [**purtenauncis**]· & suis **rectis** [**rithwis**] **diuisis** [**diuisis**] · cum **q*u*i*bus*** [**diuisis**] Husbandi eande*m* t*er*ra*m* ad f*er*ma*m* tenere **soleba*n*t** [**was wont**] d*ic*tis Edmundo & Will*elm*o / filio suo · & h*er*edib*us* d*ic*ti Will*elm*i de corp*o*re suo p*ro*pr*i*o legitime · dir*e*cte · inmediate · **linialit*er*** [**euin in line**] · & n*on* **ex lat*e*re** [**on side**] **p*ro*cr*e*andis** [**to be to gett**] & **descendentib*us*** [**desce*n*da*n*t**] vsque ad terminum **t*ri*ginta** [**yritti**] Annor*um* / s*u*bseq*u*encium plene co*m*plendor*um* . . .

The lemmata and the glosses are in bold type, and the glosses are placed inside [ ] following the lemmata rather than interlinearly.

The SG has attracted the attention of scholars of the Scots language because of the date, mid-fourteenth century, which makes it the earliest record of Scots forms not an integral part of a Latin text. But they cannot be considered as an independent writing. While the text of the charter might stand as an independent text, the glosses depend, for proper interpretation, on their relation not only to their lemmata but to the whole Latin text to which they are an addition. Only in that context do they make sense both individually and as an assemblage.

The section quoted reveals a concern with grammar as well as definition: 'co*n*cesseru*n*t' and 'dimiseru*n*t' are both given translations as perfectives translated as HAVE + past participle, 'has gr*a*ntit' and 'has letin'. Note that the form of HAVE is 'has'. The subject of the Latin verbs is plural and non-pronominal, and we might interpret the use of the 'has' form as being influenced by the Latin subject. The Scots glosses would then be in accord with the Northern Present

Tense Rule (NPTR). The glosses in 'suis rectis [rithwis] diuiisis [diuisis] · cum q*ui*b*us* [diuisis]', seem to be motivated by specifying the antecedent of the relative pronoun 'quibus'. In the gloss, '**kynd o'** for '**gen*ere*** bladi' reflects that the lemma is a genitive construction; although 'bladi' is not glossed, its grammatical category is.

That NPTR was part of the glosser's grammar is further supported by the gloss to 'successorib*us*' later on:

> Saluo di*c*tis Abb*at*i & *con*uentui & eor*um* **successorib*us*** [**ya y^t^ comis in yair stede**] in co*m*muni pastura di*c*te te*r*re **vsufructu** [***gres* wat*er* a*nd* oy*er* pro*fitis**] *pro* suis a*n*i*m*alib*us*

In the gloss, 'ya y^t^ comis in yair stede', the inflected form 'comis' is consonant with NPTR, where (within the gloss) the immediate subject is a relative pronoun 'y^t^' with a plural personal pronoun as antecedent. The intent of the gloss seems to be to spell out carefully the sense of 'succesori*bus*'. The vernacular word SUCCESSOR (originally, of course, a Romance borrowing) is recorded for Scots in the late fourteenth century. It is not unreasonable, therefore, to propose that it might well have been known to the glosser and equatable with the form in the Latin text of the charter. 'Vsufructu' is glossed as '*gre*s wat*er* a*n*d oy*er* p*ro*fitis'. Properly 'usufructus' is 'The right of temporary possession, use, or enjoyment of the advantages of property belonging to another, so far as may be had without causing damage or prejudice to this' (*OED*, s.v. *usufruct*), i.e. enjoyment of the fruits, but without actual possession of the property itself. Here the glosser is specifying characteristics of the 'right' – the use of pasturage, water and other unspecified fruits of the land.

In the orthography of the gloss, there are interesting indications of early forms, some of which are never or hardly ever recorded later, or there is a hiatus in their appearance, in Scots texts at least. 'Annuatim' is glossed as 'iere bi iere'. The 'i' for /j/ initially is curious. We might have expected 'ȝh' or 'yh' in an early text. But 'i' might simply be the influence of Latin orthography on the vernacular form, as 'i' for /j/ in Latin would be normal. 'Lau[er]dscape' 'lordship' glosses 'dominio'. The gloss not only records an unsyncopated form of LORD (< OE *hlāford, hlāfweard*), but also a Scandinavian suffix, a reflex of OScand. *skáp*. We might have expected a reflex of OE *-scip*, as is to be found in later Older Scots texts. A similar kind of Anglo-Scandinavian hybrid is to be found in 'four a*n*d tuentia*n*d fat', glossing 'vicesimu*m* q*u*artu*m* vas'. Here the ordinal suffix in 'tuentia*n*d' is of Scandinavian origin, viz. OScan. *-andi* where the stem is a reflex of OE *twenti(g)* and the inflexion a reflex of an OScand. ending (cf. OScand. *tuttugandi* 'twentieth'). Later reflexes of *-skáp* and *-andi* are rare. Apparent reflexes of *-andi* are noted in two

DOST quotations s.v. (Twentieth), Tuentieth, *adj.* 'the twentiand corne; 1553 *Prot. Bk. M. Carruthers* 57' and 'The four and twentiend pek of shilling of multour; 1644 *Kirkcudbr. B. Rec.* II 705'. Perhaps significant here is that both these sources are South-Western. Mark Carruthers was a notary working in Dumfries and Kirkcudbright, an area earlier settled by Scandinavian speakers.

'Jure Seruientis' is glossed 'cnaueschipe'. KNAVESCHIP does not appear again in Older Scots texts until much later. The next earliest example that *DOST* cites is in Peebles Burgh Records for 1476. Thereafter, all the quotations citing the word are from sixteenth- and seventeenth-century texts. The Scone Gloss thus provides the earliest Scots evidence for this word. The sense is 'Chiefly, a small quantity of corn or meal in addition to the multure, levied on each lot of corn ground at a mill, as payment for the miller's servants' (*DOST*, s.v. Knave-, Knaifschip 1.b (and also s.v. Knaschip). *DOST* also notes regarding sense 1.b: 'After *c* 1550, found commonly in grants or leases of lands, as one of the customary emoluments of a mill.' This word also finds a place for discussion in Sir John Skene's *De Verborum* (see below).

The Scone Gloss would seem to be a piece of private lexicographical activity. It shows interest in points of Latin grammar and with explanation of legal terms. It was probably made by someone at the abbey of Scone using a copy of a charter no longer required to aid his understanding of the vocabulary and forms of charter-making in Latin. Some of the forms – the Scandinavian elements in the inflexions – might suggest that the glosser was not from the Perth area, but had learned to write a more Scandinavianised form of Scots.

A glossa collecta

The 'Makculloch MS' (Edinburgh University Library MS 205) mainly comprises material from lectures written down in 1477 by Magnus Makculloch (d.1484) when he was a student at the University of Louvain. These 'lecture notes' are from his classes in Logic and they are, of course, in Latin. The Makculloch MS has significance for scholars of Older Scots literature not for any material in the manuscript by Makculloch himself, but because a later hand copied onto the opening flyleaves and some blank folios a number of poems written in Older Scots, including a copy of the 'Prologue' to Robert Henryson's *Fables* and *The Tale of the Cock and the Jasp*. This later hand has been ascribed either to the late fifteenth century or early sixteenth century.[14] Of interest here is that on ff. 187v–188r is a Latin–Older Scots *glossa collecta* of 106 items (including one repetition). This glossary is in the same hand as that of the poems.[15]

The glossary gives first a Latin word then a Scots equivalent. The Latin words are ordered to give first nouns, eighty-five in number; and then verbs, of which there are twenty-one. The nouns are arranged in three columns on f. 187v: thirty-six in the first column, forty-four in the second and five in the third. The nouns are grouped broadly according to their grammatical gender. The gender of the Latin noun in each case is indicated by prefixing 'hic', 'hec' or 'hoc' as appropriate. First come thirty-six neuter nouns, followed by forty-nine masculine and feminine intermixed. For example:

hoc ydeoma	a leid
hoc numisma	cugȝe
hoc crepusculu*m*	a ewintyd
:	
hic croc*us*	safferoñ
hic Fustis	a staf
hic polipus	a lopstar*e*
hic conca	wilk
hec Facicula	a syth
hec calendula	a guld
hec salgea	sag*e*
hic ysopus	ysop
⋮	
hoc alabru*m*	a reill
hoc depletoriu*m*	a ladill
hic wncul*us*	a nok
hec armelausa	clok
hec sagana	surplis

In three cases – 'forfex', 'forpex' and 'ganneta' – the gloss-maker/copyist failed to specify the gender. In 'forfex' and 'forpex', he has written simply 'h.', and to the left of 'ganneta' is a partly erased 'h'. In the Scots equivalents, forty-two out of the eighty-five nouns are preceded by the indefinite article, 'a'. The verbs are listed separately on f. 188r. The Latin verbs are given in the first person singular indicative form. In the Scots equivalents, they are presented as infinitives, marked usually by 'as to', but also simple 'to' . 'As to' would seem to mean 'like' or perhaps 'as [if it were]'. For example:

mino	as to dryf
matro	as to ryp
occo	as to cloid
ampulo	as to spred
scaturiso	to spring
amputo	to cut

The Makculloch glossary seems to be an abbreviated version of a type to be found in fifteenth-century and earlier English manuscripts. Examples of these from manuscripts dating from the eighth to the fifteenth century have been collected and edited by Wright-Wülcker (1884). These examples are all arranged (like the Makculloch glossary) with the Latin word given first, followed by the vernacular (English) equivalent. However, the opposite arrangement is to be found in Galfridus' *Promptorium Parvulorum*, which also provides additional morphological information, for example the declension and the gender of nouns. Many of the words found in the Makculloch glossary are to be found among other medieval glossaries, some recurring even from the Latin–Old English glossaries. It seems plausible, therefore, that the items in the Makculloch glossary were copied from a source (perhaps more than one) which was itself a glossary, and that the blank leaves of the manuscript were a convenient place to record the items.

There are a number of apparent errors in the translations of the Latin. For example, 'hec sagana' is rendered in Scots 'surplis' = 'gown; loose garment'. *DOST* s.v. Surples, Surplice *n.* quotes the Makculloch manuscript and notes: 'L. *sagana* (= a female soothsayer, a witch) seems to have been confused with *sagum* or *sagus* a coarse woollen blanket or mantle; a garment, or *sagulum* a small military cloak.' And puzzling is 'hoc antipodium' translated as 'fordel'. 'Antipodium' could be for *antepedia* or *antepedale* 'the vamp or upper part of a shoe'; 'fordel' does not seem to match this at all. Cf. *DOST* s.v. Fordell *n.* 1 '?precedence, lead; advantage, profit'. If 'antipodium' does mean 'vamp or upper of a shoe', then 'fordell' might be interpreted as *fore-* 'before, forward'+ *deal* 'part' (cf. OSc *dele* 'bit, part').[16]

The individual forms of the vernacular words in the glossary are cognates of many of the vernacular words to be found in the surviving English glossaries, but the forms themselves are Scots, and the whole assemblage must be taken as Scots. However, a small set of the lexical items seem to be examples of distinctively Scots lexis: 'leid', 'soland', 'castok', 'to brank', although, excluding 'soland', these have recorded forms in earlier English (see *OED*). 'Soland' seems to have become known among English writers from the seventeenth century (see *OED*, s.v. solan). Since we are reliant on the survivals of written records for the medieval period, it cannot be said for sure that these words had been lost in *spoken* (Northern) English coevally with the time of the Mackulloch text.

While much of the lexis in the Makculloch glossary is to be found in other non-Scottish glossaries, was there a purpose in the assembling of this particular subset of words? Does the content of the glossary suggest anything about the compiler or his interests? By its nature, the glossary implies acquisition of Latin vocabulary, and it is fair to conjecture that was the purpose of the glossary – essentially a small, personal dictionary. The Scots poems in the manuscript are of a strongly religious character, and include verse versions of a 'Paternoster', a 'hail Mary' and a 'creed'. A number of glosses refer to ecclesiastical items: 'hoc mortuarum = a cors presend'; 'hoc aspersorium = a water styk'; 'hoc preconium = honowre'; 'hic ysopus = ysop'. To this list might be added 'hoc pedum = a schipcruk', taking the sense as 'crozier'. That the glossary compiler had an association with some religious establishment is an obvious inference. He may have belonged to some kind of clergy, or have been in training towards becoming so.

There is an emphasis on 'textiles' – thirty-one of the glosses can be interpreted as having to do with textiles, their preparation and manufacture, and in items of clothing. If one were to consider the whole collection of glosses as conscious choice, then one might infer that the glossary-maker was connected with a religious house with agricultural interests and with a connection to textile manufacture.

A number of lexical items refer to aquatic creatures or parts of their anatomy: otter, octopus (albeit incorrectly glossed as 'a lopstare'), whelk or buckie, gannet, fish fin, gill. The solan goose or gannet was hunted (cf. the reference to fowling in the glossary) for its meat and feathers, and the oil that could be rendered from it. One might cite the comment in an Act of Parliament (1592): 'How proffitable the solane geis . . . quhilkis hantis . . . within the Ile of bas . . . ar to the commoun weill of this realme.'[17] Otters were hunted for their pelts and were a luxury item. The Perth Guildry records (1530) refer to 'All vther costly geir mertrik tod or ottir'.[18] Fish was important to the medieval Scottish economy. The references to sea creatures is not therefore surprising, as testify numerous references to fish in civil and ecclesiastical as well as the parliamentary records. *Wilks* 'whelks' (also known as *buckies*) were gathered for food and to bait fishing lines. Their shells were used to make buttons: 'Ane gros & ane string of buckie buttones; 1592 *Edinb. Test.* XXV.25' (*DOST* s.v. Buckie); '12 dusson of wilke buttones; 1684 *Oliphants* 287' (*DOST* s.v. Wilk).[19]

Glossaries in Latin Grammars

In late medieval and Renaissance Europe, Latin was the principal medium for transmitting education and scholarship. National and regional vernaculars were coming to be used more and more for a wider variety of functions, but Latinity still held sway in the schools and universities. If anything, the revival of interest in classical learning that characterises the Renaissance gave the teaching and learning of Latin fresh impetus. Greek and Hebrew too were added to the curriculum of the universities as Biblical scholars searched for greater understanding in the scriptures. Philological scholarship was enlivened by the study of new versions of texts of classical authors. Printing hugely expanded the availability of texts. As scientific enquiry widened and deepened, so Latin developed with it, acquiring new vocabulary. Poetry in Latin flourished, with Scots as notable contributors, the pre-eminent name among Scots intellectuals being George Buchanan. Ancient philosophy was being rediscovered and explored in the light of contemporary problems of living in an age of political and religious strife. Many Scots developed an intense interest in Stoicism, for example.[20]

The importance of Latin provoked the desire for better methods of instruction. The long-used grammars of Donatus and Despauter were to be superseded by better textbooks. For the Scottish Reformers, education was the means to social and moral progress. Literacy in the vernacular (Scots, but mediated partly through an English translation of the Bible) was a basic goal. But for the scholar who wanted to advance, competence in Latin was a necessity. From the latter part of the sixteenth century appeared a new crop of Latin grammars, promoted by presbyteries, town councils and individuals. The teaching of Latin and the character of the grammars per se has been discussed elsewhere.[21] The grammars had much the same structure. The text of the grammars is in Latin from the start, including the explanation of letters and sounds. The teaching of Latin was done mainly through the medium of Latin. There is a lexicographical aspect to some of these grammars: in some cases their authors have provided glossaries or glosses which give vernacular translation of Latin words. These may occur as a separate section at the end, or words used as examples in the main text may be given a vernacular translation. The orthographic form of these glossaries and glosses may vary: in some cases the translation equivalent is clearly Scots; in others it is English. But often the orthography is mixed, i.e., there is a deployment of English spellings, albeit not always distributed in the lexis in the same way as in a typical contemporary English text. This is not necessarily an indication of anglicisation of the language. In some cases it may reflect changes in the phonology of Scots, where the 'English' adoptions are borrowed to reflect this. A number of other factors come into play: the date of the edition of the grammar (some went through a number of editions, not always with the same printer), the aims of the author, and the target readership (Scottish or 'British').

Given the importance of education for the Scottish Reformers, it is no surprise to find Church of Scotland ministers at the forefront of grammar production.

Andrew Duncan

Andrew Duncan was minister at Crail. He had been a regent at St Leonard's College, where initially he opposed the curricular reforms of Principal Andrew Melville and Melville's rejection of the traditional teaching of Aristotle's philosophy. However, Duncan became a convert to Melville's cause and was thenceforth associated with his party in religion and politics.[22] In 1595 was published

Duncan's *Latinae Grammaticae pars prior, sive Etymologia Latina in usum rudiorum,* printed in Edinburgh by Robert Waldgrave. He appended to his grammar INDEX VOCUM TVM QVÆ IN ÆTYMOLOGIA sparsim occurrunt, tum quæ ad *calcem adiectæ sunt, Inter*pres Scot.[23]

In the Waldgrave edition, the index is laid out with the Latin word as headword. The Scots gloss is in a different (gothic-style) typeface. Each entry ends with a stop. Words and phrases are separated with commas. The Scots equivalent may be separated from the Latin by a colon, or alternative Scots senses may be separated by a colon. The usage of colon or comma is inconsistent.

That a final vowel is to be pronounced is indicated by a grave accent, e.g.:

> Ægrè, **skarcely**

There may be more than one Latin headword assigned the same meaning, e.g.:

> Abluo, expurgo, **To wash away**.

But 'expurgo' does not occur separately.

> Adhuc, **ȝet, hithertils**.

A sample of the entries is given below:

> Demulceo, **to clap: to / straike with the hand.**
> Dentale, **the plowgh / culter.**
> Dilanio, dialcero: **to / rent in sundry peeces.**
> Falx, **a huik, or syith**
> Fulmen, **fyreflaught.**
> Hebdomas, hebdomada, septimana, **an oulke.**
> Horizon, **The circle / bounding our sicht.**
> Litigo, **to flyte, to be at / the Lawe.**
> pinso, **to baik.**
> pugno, dimico, **To fecht.**
> Scæva, **carhanded.**
> Spatha, **a twa handed / sword, a ladle.**
> Tabes, vel, um : **a con=/suming sicknes.**
> Vappa, **spilt wine: a / slicht man.**
> Vortex, **a whirle-pule, / or whirle-winde.**

In a glossary such as this it is not possible to give all the ranges of sense that the headword might have. Occasionally, Duncan's definition seems to miss the mark. For example, 'Excors, insanus' he defines as 'mad: a sot'. Lewis and Short's *Latin Dictionary*[24] defines *ex-cors* (s.v. ibid.) 'without intelligence, without understanding, senseless, silly, stupid' and *in-sānus* (s.v. ibid.) as 'mad, insane' with the transferred sense 'that acts like a madman, raging, raving, foolish, frantic'. *DOST* defines *sot* (s.v. ibid.) as 'A foolish or contemptible person, fool, idiot. b. specif. In collocation with drunken: One who behaves foolishly on account of excessive drinking.' The collocation of 'ex-cors' with 'in-sānus' is not then really apt, the former word implying something milder than 'insane' or 'mad' behaviour.

James Carmichael

James Carmichael (1542/3–1628) was a Church of Scotland minister and grammar school teacher. He was master of the grammar school of St Andrews until he was appointed minister in Haddington in 1570. Between 1572 and 1576 he was also burgh schoolmaster in the town.[25]

It was while he was in political exile in England that his *Grammaticae Latinae, de etymologia, liber secondus* was published through the Cambridge University printer, Thomas Thomas, in 1587. Although this work is a grammar, the Latin lexis used to exemplify the grammatical categories is heavily glossed in Scots. The layout seems untidy to a modern reader, with the Scots senses sometimes above their lemmata, sometimes following:

		Caſt r.i.fiber, *a Beuer*	*Maſc.*
		Vulpeſ, *a Fox.*	*Fæm.*
	Ferarum:	Dama, *A Buck, or a Dea*	*modo m.*
		Talpa, *A Modiwart*	*modo fæ.*
Epi-cœna. i. *prom:ſena:*		Paſſer, *A Sparrow*	*maſ.*
nomina animalium		Aquila, *An Egle.*	*maſ.*
in quibuſ obſcurior	< Avium:	Bubo, *An Howlet.*	*modo maſ.*
est sexuſ discretio,		Grus, *A Cran*	
ſub una terminatione		Perdix ( ) *A Pertrick*	*modo fæm.*
uttunq; ſexum com-		Salmo, *A Salmond*	*M.*
plectuntur:	Piſcium	Perca ( ) *A Pearch*	*fæ.*
		Pulex, *A flea.* Culex, *a mige*	*M.*
	Insectorú:	Musca, *a Flie.* Vipera, *a Viper.*	*fæ.*

Thus, the learner has reference to the vernacular as he works through the grammar.

David Wedderburn

David Wedderburn (bap. 1580–1646) was master at Aberdeen Grammar School, where he became rector. He also taught humanities at Marischal College from 1614 to 1624.[26] As well as being an instructor of Latin, Wedderburn was also an accomplished Latin poet. His *A Short Introduction to Grammar Compyled for the Instruction of Youth* was first published in 1632 and found considerable success as a textbook.[27] This is a bilingual work, using Latin and English (not Scots). The main text is in English, but it is partly 'glossed', one might call it, in Latin (in italic type). For example, under the heading '*Of Comparison*' translated '*De* comparatione', the English text begins:

> Some Adjectives are compared: to wit, those whose significations may increase, or be diminished: as *doctus*, learned for we may say, *doctior*, more learned: *doctissimus*, most learned: but in those *Adjectives, omnis*, all : *Nullus*, none: and such like this is not to be found.[28]

The Latin version is:

> *Adjective comparuntur quorum significatio potest augeri vel minui.*

The Latin does not duplicate the examples. The lexicographical element here is in the copious examples of Latin with English translation to illustrate the points of the grammar.

But the main lexicographical work from David Wedderburn is his *Vocabula Cum aliis nonnullis Latinæ Linguæ Subsidiis. In eorum gratiam, qui prima Latini Sermonis tyrocinia faciunt* (title from the 1685 edition printed in Edinburgh by Heirs of Andrew Anderson). This was first published in 1636. It was still being produced at the end of the seventeenth century: the *Vocabula* went through four editions between 1685 and 1700, printed successively by Heirs of Andrew Anderson (Glasgow, 1685); Robert Sanders (Glasgow, 1691); and Heirs of Andrew Anderson (Edinburgh, 1695 and 1700).

The *Vocabula* is laid out more like a phrasebook than a dictionary. It is divided into five sections, with sub-sections. The *Sectio Prima* perhaps gives some indication of how Latin was taught in its early stages. Many contemporary grammars were entirely in Latin, but there must have been oral input in the vernacular from the teachers until the students had learned sufficient material to be able to understand and use simple Latin. In the *Sectio Prima* Wedderburn gives first a list of words, beginning (perhaps not surprisingly) with DEUS, GOD. Then follows:

> *Templum*, the Church
> *Pater*, a father
> *Mater*, a mother
> *Frater*, a brother
> *Soror*, a sister
> *Domus*, a house
> *Schola*, the School

Thus, the vocabulary for a student's spiritual, social and moral environment is set. Thereafter comes basic vocabulary for school (e.g., pen, ink, inkhorn) and clothing (e.g., hat, gown, hose). At the end of the section is *Hora prima*, followed by the other ordinals up to twelve *Secunda* . . . *Duodecima*, but curiously glossed as cardinals, 'one hour, two . . . twelve'.

The subsection that follows contains a list of phrases, *FORMULÆ*. The phrases are concerned with interaction in the class between student and teacher:

> *Da mihi librum meum*, Give me my book
> *Præforma mihi exemplum*, Write me a copy (p. 3)

The vocabulary is then arranged into sections to illustrate grammatical types and forms. Again, many of the illustrative phrases refer to activity in the schoolroom. Under *Partes indeclinabiles, Adverbia* (p. 6) come:

Semel repetivi lectionem	I have repeated my lesson
Diligenter vacat studiis	he is diligent at his book

Other phrases have more general use. Under *Præpositiones* is

Veni ante horam sextam	I am come before six a clock.
Non potest hoc fieri sine pecunia	this cannot be done without mone

The SECTIO SECUNDA *ubi substantiva usitatiora in suas quasdam classes redacta sunt* introduces grammatical forms. Here first is treated DE DEO (*Dominus* and *Angelus*), then *De Cœlo* (*Cœlum, Sol, Luna, Stella, Mundus*), then *De Ventis*. The *Vocabula* goes on to list words under headings such as *De vestibus, De cibi generibus, De potu* (p. 14) *De Insectis, De Piscibus, De Arboribus, De Fructibus, De Herbis* (pp. 26–7). The world about the student is translated into Latin. The latter part of the *Vocabula* contains sections arranged under different themes with phrases and expressions, some variations for saying the same thing. There is a section treating of Games and Sports, e.g. *ARCUS, GLOBI* (football) and *BACULUS*, which is mainly concerned with golf:

> Baculus, Pila clavaria, a goulfe ball: Fovea, a goat:[29] Percute pilam baculo . . . Procul excussisti pilam, that is a good stroak. Statumina pilam arena, Teaz your ball on the sand . . . Cedo baculum ferreum, let see the bunkard Club . . . Immissa est in paludem, it is in the mire . . . Baculi caput, the head of the Club. Baculi caulis, the shaft of the Club. Baculi manubrium, the handle where the wippen is. Baculi filum, the wippen. (pp. 37–8)

The *Vocabula* is a well thought-through work, carefully structured to introduce vocabulary and phrases describing the world with which the students would be familiar. It is very modern in its format, echoing closely the present-day vocabularies and phrasebooks used as aids for learning foreign languages.

Specialised Lexicographical Works

Heraldic

In the modern age we are accustomed to dictionaries of general lexis, either monolingual or bilingual, of varying sizes and scopes. There are also more specialised dictionaries, covering the terminology of some field of activity, for example, architecture, ships and sailing, cuisine or golf.[30]

One example of a specialist text from the fifteenth century is the *Deidis of Armorie*. This is a heraldic manual and bestiary.[31] The *Deidis* has a dictionary-like structure: it contains a set of terms which are to be explained. The text is not a Scots original, but a translation of a French original. It defines and explains the elements of heraldry, the metals, colours, devices and beasts that figure on coats of arms and banners. In the itemising of the heraldic bestiary, each section is introduced with the name of the animal to be described – in effect a headword – followed by its heraldic signification. The heraldic explanation is sometimes prefaced by a description of the animal's form and characteristics. Thus:

> The modewarp is a blind best haffand a gronȝe in form of a porc, eu*er* beand vorceland in þe erd. And Signifies þat he þat bur it first has been a thef and brigand hidand him daly in wodd*is* *and* cave*r*nis peillȝand *and* revand, ffor it is said co*m*monly he þat evil dois hattis þe licht.[32]

> The herichon, eftir Ysodre sais in his xi buk is a litill best armyt of al p*artis* wit*h* spines, thornys or pickand*is*; and þai ar his armys to defend him quhen his enemy ry*n*nis on him, and womplis him wit*h*in al round as esteur sua þat his enemy dar noch tuiche him; as Arestot sais in his Buke of Phisiqȝ , he has ma spinis or of poingnance þan othir best of fowr feit, for al þe substance of his mete or it þat noris him turnys noc*h*t in his body bot in þe spinis or pickand*is* of him. And signifies he þ*a*t first bur him in armes wes litil *and* waik, haffand mair confidens in his harnas *and* in þe power of men þan in defence of his body; and gat mair honour followand the cumpany of vailland men na be the vaillance and puissance of his body.[33]

The original source text for the *Deidis* at this point draws for authority, if not information, on the *Etymologiae* of Isidore of Seville, a work still much in favour as a source of information in the late medieval and Renaissance periods. Whether the reference to Aristotle came from his work independently or via Isidore is not clear. Nonetheless, we can see here, in Scots through translation, a systematically organised lexicon-like text. The *Deidis* is a specialised work, of course, for the use of heralds primarily, but it has some claim to membership of the lexicographical canon.

Legal glossaries

De Verborum Significatione

Sir John Skene of Curriehill (c.1540–1617), advocate and jurist, produced a dictionary of terms found in *Regiam Majestatem*, which was one of the principal texts in which the law of Scotland had been codified since the late fourteenth century.[34] Versions of the *Regiam* were to be found in both in Scots and Latin, with considerable variations in content and order. In 1575 Skene was appointed by the earl of Morton as regent to a commission tasked with reviewing the old laws. The objective was to formalise 'ane certain writtin law'.[35] In 1592, Skene was appointed to another commission whose task 'to review and print acts of parliament and other laws resulted in the publication in 1597 of *The Lawes and Actes of Parliament*, containing post-1424 statutes.'[36] As a spin-off from his juridical researches amongst the manuscripts of the *Regiam* and of the parliamentary records Skene produced *De Verborum Significatione*. This work and its proximate source, the editorial revisions of *Regiam*, can be viewed as an example of the application of humanistic learning to the study of law texts. 'L'intérêt du 16e siècle pour le sens précis et l'etymologie des mots était aussi reflèté par les commentaires au titre du Digeste 50.16 *De verborum significatione* qui devenaient de mode' (the sixteenth-century interest in the precise sense and etymology of words was also reflected by the commentaries to the title of the Digeste 50.16, *De verborum signifactione*, which became fashionable).[37] *De Verborum Significatione* was hardly an original title, then, but it places the work within a contemporary frame of scholarship, in particular 'the application of philological methods and grammar and style to the language of the texts' and 'the use of other historical sources to elucidate the texts with reference to their social and historical background'.[38] Skene, like many of his legal contemporaries, had studied on the Continent: 'He spent seven years in Europe (c.1567–1574), studying law in Paris and visiting Switzerland, Poland, and Scandinavia before settling in Germany, at the University of Wittenberg.'[39] No doubt it was through his education furth of Scotland – particularly during his sojourn in Paris[40] – that he became acquainted with the new methods of philological scholarship as applied to legal texts. The extended title of *De Verborum Significatione* gives Skene's precise intentions:

> The exposition of the termes and difficill wordes, conteined in the foure buikes of Regiam Majestatem, and uthers, in the Acts of Parliament, infeftments, and used in the practique of this realme, with diverse rules, and common places, or principalles of the lawes. Collected and exponed be M. John Skene, clerke of our Soveraine Lordis register, councell and rolles.

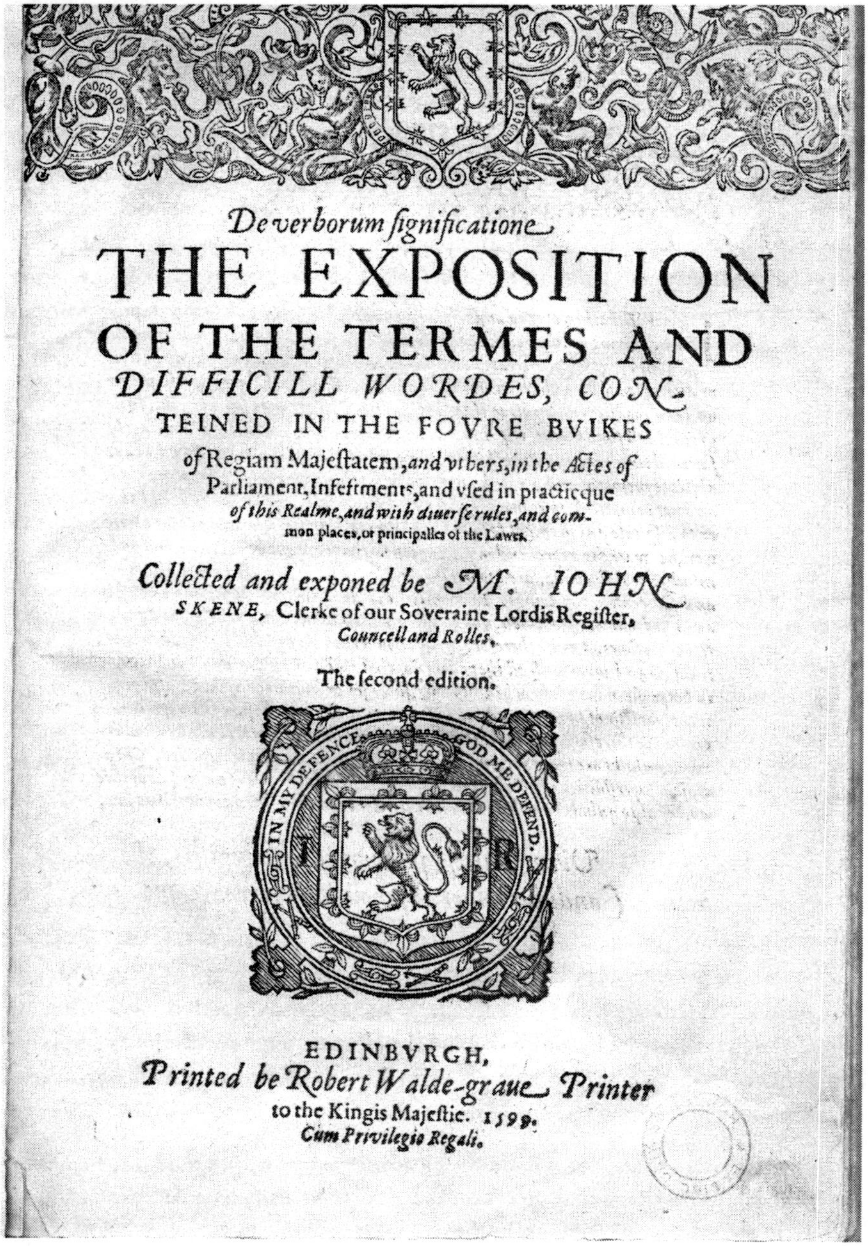

De verborum ſignificatione

THE EXPOSITION

OF THE TERMES AND

DIFFICILL WORDES, CON-

TEINED IN THE FOVRE BVIKES

of Regiam Majeſtatem, *and vthers, in the Actes of*

Parliament, Infeftments, and vſed in practicque

of this Realme, and with diuerſe rules, and com-

mon places, or principalles of the Lawes.

Collected and exponed be M. IOHN

SKENE, Clerke of our Soveraine Lordis Regiſter,

Councell and Rolles.

The ſecond edition.

IN MY DEFENCE GOD ME DEFEND.

I R

EDINBVRGH,

Printed be Robert Walde-graue Printer

to the Kingis Majeſtie. 1599.

Cum Privilegio Regali.

Title page of Sir John Skene's *De Verborum Significatione.*

The work is laid out with a headword followed by an explanation of the word. The explanations vary in length, some with sub-divisions dealing with phrases incorporating the main term. The entries may sometimes extend into encyclopedia-like articles. Often the source language of the words is indicated. Consider

> ASSISA, ane French word, Quhilk signifies properlie sitting, or Session, and hes divers uther significations in the Lawes of this Realme, for *assisa* is taken for ane constitution, ordinance or law.

He then goes on to cite instances and senses:

> *assisa terræ* is taken for the Law and constitution of the land . . .
>
> Item *assisa* is called ane measure, or certaine quantity, as the barrell bind of Salmond suld keepe and conteine the assise, and measure of fourteene gallons.

A good example of his method can be found under DYOUR

> DYOUR, Dyvour, utherwaies Bair-man, quha being involved and drowned in debtes, and not able to pay or satisfie the same: For eschewing of prison and uther paines makes cession and assignation of all his gudes and geare, in favoures of his creditoures: And dois his devour and dewtie to them, proclaimand himselfe Bair-man, and indigent, and becummand debt-bound to them, of all that he hes. *Leg. burg. ca.* Bair-man. 144. In Latine, *cedere bonis,* quhilk is most commonlie used amangst merchandes, to make *Bank-rout Bankrupt,* or *Bankrompue,* Because the doer thereof, as it were breaks his bank, stall, or seate, quhair he used his trafficque of before . . .

The term 'Bair-man' is explained thus:

> Bot to the effect that debtoures suld be feared to deceive their creditoures, and suld the mair willinglie pay their debtes in sindrie places, diverse shamefull formes of dyvourie, ar used and observed: for sum-times the debtour naked, sittis upon ane cauld stane, in presence of the people.

He considers changes in sense, so

> AVUNCULUS properly is the mother-brother, bot sumtime conform to the French maner of speach, it is taken for the father-brother, in Latin *patruus* . . .
>
> COLPINDACH, ane zoung beast, or Kow, of the age of an or twa zeires, quhilk now is called an *Cowdach,* or quoyach, quhairof the price was 30 d. . . . It is an *Irish* word, and properly signifies ane fut follower

It is not evident what methodology he used to identify a source language for a term. 'FERDINGMANNUS' he says is 'ane Dutch word, ane penni-master, or Thesaurar. *Stat. gild. c. 5.*'. In fact, this word has proved a puzzle for modern etymologists. The quotation is also cited in *DOST* s.v. Penny-maister. There the etymology refers to 'MDu. *penning-meester*, MLG. *pennincmeester*, treasurer'. The form 'ferding' suggests OE *féorðing*. Skene is perhaps making a semantic rather than a formal connection between the Scots and Dutch.[41]

Perhaps because of the form Skene claims that ARRENDARE 'is ane Spanish word', 'commonly used in chartoures and infeftments in this Realme …'. In fact, he makes a connection with French and defines it as 'to set and give, landes or tenements to onie man for an zeirlie duetie'. The likely source here is thus French *ar(r)enter* 'to arrent land; let to farm'.

In the entry s.v. PEDELLUS, we can see Skene's use of source law texts and his attempt at an etymology:

> PEDELLUS, *Leg. burg. c. citatio.* 109. The seriand or beddle of the burgh, quha suld execute summondes: make attachementes, or take poindes, *quon-attach-s. nullus* 57. quhairof they have na power, without their awin jurisdiction. *Ass.reg.Da.c nullus* 13. *Dicitur autem pedellus a pedo hoc est baculo*, because all sik serjandes suld use ane wand, staff, halbert. Ia. I.p.6.c. 99

He is drawing here on *Leges Quatuor Burgorum, Quoniam Attachiamenta* and the *Assisa*.

Skene's application of philological method is not always profound, but the compilation itself and the thoroughness in the editing of the texts on which he draws is clear evidence of humanistic influence.

Mackenzie's Institutions

Sir George Mackenzie of Rosehaugh (1636 or 1638–1691), advocate and jurist and on several occasions lord advocate, also contributed in a smaller way to the lexicography of Scots Law. Demonised in his lifetime, and in later popular and literary tradition, as a persecutor of Covenanters, Mackenzie was in fact a humane and cultured figure, belying his soubriquet of 'Bluidy Mackenzie'. He wrote a considerable number of works legal and non-legal, including a novel.[42] In his legal writings he was much concerned to make clear explications of the laws and constitution of Scotland for laymen as well as lawyers. The point of interest here is that his *Institutions of the Law of Scotland* (1694) was published 'With an Alphabetical Explanation of the most difficult Scots Words'.[43] Whether Mackenzie himself supplied the glossary is not clear. Doubts have been expressed.[44]

The glossary is in English. It is short (eight pages, following page 263 in the 1694 printing) and very basic in form and content. The terms to be defined are arranged alphabetically, grouped in blocks under the initial letter. A left-hand column contains the words or phrases to be defined, printed in italic type; a right-hand column contains the definitions, in roman type. For example:

> *Apprising,* The adjudging of an Estate to pay Debts
> *Diligence,* Putting a Legal Sentence in Execution
> *To Fence a court,* To hold a Court in the usual Formalities as in the King's name, *&c.*
> *Heritage,* Inheritance
> *Testament,* Will

Many of his terms are defined by what he deemed to have been their nearest English Law equivalents, e.g.:

> *Cautioner,* Bondsman
> *College of Justice,* Inns of Court
> *Escheat,* Forfeit
> *He libels,* He informs or says
> *Justice General,* Lord Chief Justice
> *Poynding,* Distraining or Seizing
> *Session,* Term
> *Wadset,* Mortgage

Other words are general vocabulary items, but are used within his work with a specific legal sense, or are the subjects of specific laws. These terms are included presumably for the benefit of a non-Scots reader, as these would not have been 'difficult' words for a Scots speaker. For example:

> *Bairns,* Children
> *Coalheugh,* Coal-mine
> *Divot,* Green Turf for covering Houses
> *Goods,* Cattle
> *Lint,* Flax
> *Moor,* Heath
> *Onerous,* Weighty
> *Thole,* Endure

Some words are formally similar to English terms, e.g.:

> *Forfaulture,* forfeiture
> *Habile,* Able
> *Notar,* Notary

Propone, Propose
Tailze, Entail

These were originally Latin or French borrowings which were adopted with different forms into Scots and English.

Mackenzie's motivation in including – if not compiling directly – the glossary is practical: an aid to the better understanding of his text for those not only untutored in Scots Law but perhaps also unfamiliar with the Scots tongue as one of the linguistic moulds in which that law was cast.

Conclusion

I have attempted to give some idea of the kind of 'lexicographical activity' that was carried out in Scotland before 1700. It is closely tied to the learning and interpretation of Latin texts, both generally and in specific fields of activity. Latin is rendered into Scots or English or some admixture, to aid the understanding of Latin. Scottish lexicography had not progressed beyond Murray's stage of 'the elaboration of Latin–English Vocabularies'. No one had yet turned a hand to the dictionary-making of Scots itself. It is only at the turn of the seventeenth century to the eighteenth century that we find a growing philological interest in Scots itself, and earlier Scots in particular. Provoked by the possibility of political union with England, Scottish literati were looking afresh at their own history, languages and literature. The Middle Scots poets were rediscovered and their works printed anew, notably in the anthologies of James Watson and Allan Ramsay. But the most significant lexicographical development to emerge from this activity was Thomas Ruddiman's edition (1710) of Gavin Douglas' *Eneados*. To this Ruddiman added an extensive and discursive glossary. It is in Ruddiman's work that we find the beginning of the lexicography of Scots (see Chapter 2). But Ruddiman was a classical scholar, author of a Latin grammar that was to be long used in Scottish schools. His lexicographical work on the *Eneados* can be seen as growing out of the lexicographical tradition described above.

TWO

Glossaries and Scotticisms: Lexicography in the Eighteenth Century

J. DERRICK McCLURE

Scots lexicography, like all great academic ventures, had its foundations in the work of scholars who would have been astounded to see the heights of achievement to which their own contributions would eventually lead; yet the cliché 'humble beginnings' is hardly appropriate. The scene for the development of a field which would eventually give rise to the great multi-volume dictionaries was set by a work which is by any standards impressive, and in its time could be not unfittingly described as revolutionary.

Thomas Ruddiman, born on a Banffshire farm in 1674, was trained at Aberdeen University, which throughout the seventeenth century had been renowned across Europe for the excellence of its Latin scholarship. Ruddiman, a conservative Jacobite, proved a worthy heir to the tradition: his reputation was first established by his editions of the Latin works of other Scottish scholars; and he proceeded to write *Rudiments of Latin Grammar* (a standard textbook for several generations of Scottish schoolchildren), a critical edition of the *Opera Omnia* of the great sixteenth-century scholar George Buchanan, and later an edition of Livy. His scholarly reputation assisted him in obtaining a place as first an assistant librarian in the Advocates' Library and eventually its keeper; and he was also a successful printer and publisher in Edinburgh, the outputs of his press including the journal *The Caledonian Mercury*.[1] And it was his edition of *Virgil's Æneis, Translated into Scottish Verse, by the Famous Gawin Douglas Bishop of Dunkeld*, published in Edinburgh in 1710, which laid the foundations for the scientific study of Scots by including 'A Large Glossary, Explaining the Difficult Words: Which may serve for a Dictionary to the old SCOTTISH language'. More than a century and a half had passed since the last printed edition of Douglas's great translation;[2] and Ruddiman's intention was to reanimate it by producing a version free of the 'innumerable and gross Errors, through the Incorrectness of the Copy, or Negligence of the Printers, or probably both' found in the 1553 text. This new edition was a central contribution to the reawakening of popular interest in the national literary achievements of earlier times, which had already

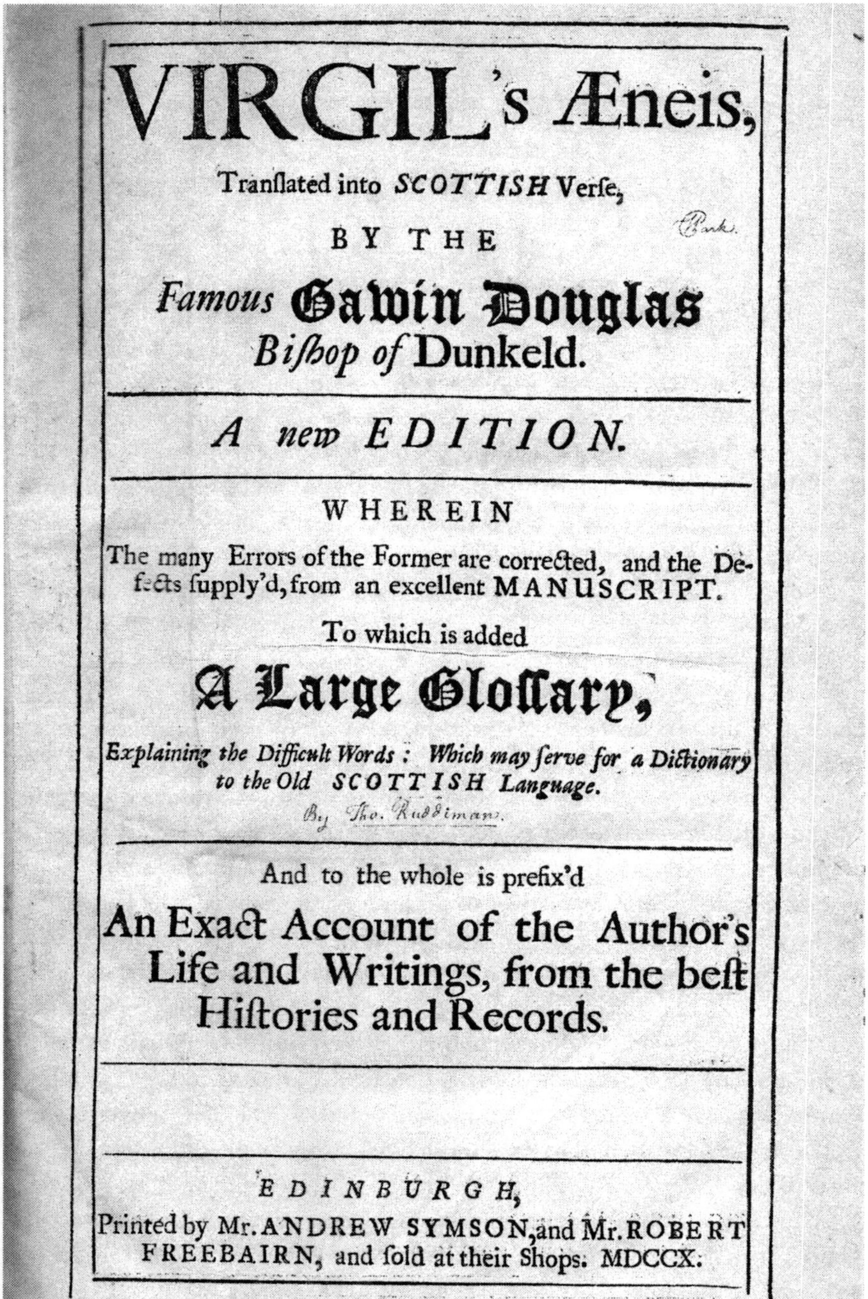

VIRGIL's Æneis,

Tranflated into *SCOTTISH* Verfe,

BY THE

Famous Gawin Douglas

Bifhop of Dunkeld.

A new EDITION.

WHEREIN

The many Errors of the Former are corrected, and the Defects fupply'd, from an excellent MANUSCRIPT.

To which is added

A Large Gloffary,

Explaining the Difficult Words: Which may ferve for a Dictionary to the Old SCOTTISH Language.

By Tho. Ruddiman.

And to the whole is prefix'd

An Exact Account of the Author's Life and Writings, from the beft Hiftories and Records.

EDINBURGH,

Printed by Mr. ANDREW SYMSON, and Mr. ROBERT FREEBAIRN, and fold at their Shops. MDCCX.

Title page of Ruddiman's edition of Gavin Douglas' translation of Virgil's *Aeneis*.

resulted in Watson's *Choice Collection* (which has no glossary nor annotations of any kind) and was soon to inspire Ramsay's *The Ever Green*. And though the practice of adding glossaries to editions of Chaucer and other Middle English texts had long been established, Ruddiman's 'large Glossary' was by far the most comprehensive yet produced for any late-medieval text.[3]

The Glossary, which includes not only definitions of the words but notes on 'their Rise and Etymology from other Languages', was clearly intended not merely as an adjunct to the text but as a major reference work in its own right. The compiler's approach is explained in the Preface, according to which it is much wider in scope than the *Eneados* and can therefore serve as a guide to other Scottish works: 'Yea Chaucer and the other English Writers about that time are rendreed more plain and easy by it.' A substantial list is given of scholarly authorities and published works consulted, including dictionaries of French and Italian as well as English and Latin (on occasions he uses a comparison with Virgil's text as evidence for the meaning which Douglas intended by a rare or obscure word). It is noted that since Scots contains many words 'most Significant and Emphatical' which have no exact translation in English, some entries consist of circumlocutions rather than single-word equivalents; and still more interestingly, not only because it testifies to the observed continuity of the Scots tongue from the early sixteenth to the early eighteenth century but also for what it reveals about the thoroughness of the research underlying the Glossary, information is said to have been sought on the actual uses of words in the living language:

> It was found necessary also to converse with People of the several Shires and Places, where some of the old Words are as yet used. This seem'd the best Method for discovering their true Meaning, next to the Comparing of Translations with the Originals; for though the Vulgar are not able to give the Etymology of a word, or any Reason why it signifies so, yet they cannot be ignorant what Idea they express by it.

'Words, which are to this day used in some parts of Scotland by the Common People' are marked by an S in the Glossary; SB ('Scotia Borealis') is used for words from northern dialects, often reflecting Ruddiman's own origins in Banffshire.

A set of 'General Rules for understanding the language of Bishop Dowglas's Translation of Virgil's Æneis', which precedes the Glossary proper, contains valid (though unsystematically presented) observations on MSc grammar and spelling and on Douglas' own style: several refer to features still present in the spoken Scots of Ruddiman's time (and in some cases still today), such as the use of *for to*, double negatives, and archaic past tense forms such as *clam* (climbed) and *keist* (cast). Observations which in an age when linguistic thought was more developed would come under the separate headings of orthography and phonology are arranged in alphabetical order, resulting in a promiscuous mixter-maxter: '*A* is in a very great number of words, where the *Eng.* now have *o*, as *ald, cald, aik, ait, airis, wame, blaw, lang, fame, snaw, saul, hame, ane*, &c. which are as yet much used in *Scotland* . . .' (where four distinct phonological developments are subsumed in a single list); '*C* is put before *h*, where now we use *g*, as *licht, richt, sich, enewch, teuch, socht*, &c.' (a feature marking an important phonological difference between Scots and English); '*T* is often omitted before *ch*, as *mache, cache, wreche* or *wrache, wache*, for *match, catch*, &c. But sometimes in our Author, & to this day *Scot.* the Eng. *tch* or *ch* is chang'd into *k*, as *pik, thak, steik, reik, streik, nokkis, sik, eik, beseik*, for *pitch, thatch* [etc.]' (again, associating a mere orthographic variant with a major phonological divergence – and mis-stating the latter, since it is of course an original [k] which has been changed in the English words to the affricate, not vice versa). Naïve though they are, however, Ruddiman's 'General Rules' collectively testify to a full recognition of the regular and consistent distinctions between MSc and English: i.e., though Ruddiman might not have expressed it in those terms, of the status of Scots as a language form with a self-contained structure rather than merely a set of random variants from the English norm.

The Glossary proper contains an impressive c.3,000 entries. Notably, as he progresses through the alphabet the coverage becomes more complete and the entries more detailed: letter A is covered in barely two pages; letter R has over six. Some are mere single-word glosses: most of these are for either words which differ only orthographically from their English equivalents (Dew: *due*, Goistis: *ghosts*, Irne: *iron*, Kene: *keen*, Schyppis: *ships*) or have obvious etymological relationships to them (Aith: *oath*, Fund: *found*, Pure: *poor*, Snaw: *snow*, Teuch: *tough*), or are in very common use (Abone: *above*, Bere: *barley*, Wit: *known*). At the opposite extreme, many entries amount to miniature essays on the meaning, usage, history and/or etymology of the words. Here is one such example:

> Deray, *merriment, jollity, solemnity*, 35, 12 [a page and line reference[4]]. It. *tumult, disorder, noise*, 288, 16. from the old F. word *desroyer*, which, according to *Pasquier*, signifies, *tirer hors de voye, ou de roye*, i.e. *to mislead, or turn out of the right way*: Hence comes the word, *arroy, array, order*, and it's [*sic*] compound *dissarroy*, disorder, confusion. *Desroyer* signifies also, as *Furetierie* shews us, *to become a fool*, because *fools* go *astray*, and have their spirits in *disorder*; and the same reason hold in the word *deray*; for when men are heated with wine, and begin to be merry, their words and actions are very often *roving* and *extravagant*. Thus the celebrated Poem, called *Christ's*

> *Kirk on the Green* (composed by *King James* V.) begins.
> Was ever in Scotland heard or seen
> Such Dancing and Deray.
> From the same *Desroyer* may be also derived the common Scots word Royed or Royet, Royit, *waggish or extravagant*, q. deroyed , by taking away the first syllable, which is very usual; as *skirmish*, for F. *escarmouche*, *sample*, for *example*, *oncle*, for *avunculus*, *spittle* for *hospital*, *fend* for *defend*, *&c.*

The detailed explanations, with frequent references to scholarly authorities, are characteristic: Ruddiman's erudition, and the care with which he has applied it, are manifest throughout.

Many entries in the Glossary are familiar to contemporary speakers of Scots, or at any rate to readers of more recent Scottish literature: such people will feel themselves to be on home territory on finding such entries as 'But *and* ben, *outer and inner room*'; 'Kowschot, *a ring-dove*, palumbus' (the MSc spelling at first perhaps obscuring the familiar *cushat*); 'Seuch, *furrow, gulph, ditch*'; 'Snell, *piercing, pungent, smarting, sharp, bitter*'. Others make a point of emphasising the culturally Scottish nature of their referents: 'Burdoun, *a big staff . . . also* the drone of a bag pipe, *in which sense it is commonly used in* Scotland'; 'Charlewan, *the constellation* Ursa major, called in *Scot.* the Plough or Charle wan, q. *Caroli. plaustrum*, in honour perhaps of *Charlemagne*, who first began the friendship and League, which continued so long between the *French* and *Scots*'; 'Gloy, *straw*. In the North of *Scotland* they stripe off the withered blades from the straw, and this they call *Gloy*, with which they thatch houses or make ropes of it.'

In some cases Ruddiman acknowledges an uncertainty, e.g. what colour *burnet* is; what kind of medicine *sewane* is; whether *ged* (pike) is related to *Jedburgh*; whether *neft* in Douglas is a word for 'beaten with hands' derived from *neif* (fist) or a misprint for *beft*; what could be the etymology of *tailzeve* – the last being a question which later scholarship has been no more successful in answering. In others he is demonstrably mistaken: for *bra, bray & brae* he proposes an Anglo-Saxon and two French etymologies, though the word's origin is in reality Norse; for *haar* he suggests German, Welsh, Irish, Greek, Spanish, French and Anglo-Saxon etymons but misses its actual source in Dutch; for *leman*, after rejecting two etymologies proposed by others he states his own preference for a derivation from *l'aimante*; for *slughorn* an interesting entry on its meaning is marred by a proposed Anglo-Saxon (instead of Gaelic) etymology. Errors of this kind are hardly deserving of censure: more serious are his mistaken definitions, but such cases are very rare, numbering, according to Aitken's count,[5] only twenty-eight; and all are excusable, especially given that Douglas' text includes several words used there for the first or even the only attested time. An example is *widdersynnis*: Ruddiman's article shows that he is familiar with the word; but since its first appearance in literature is in reference to the state of Aeneas' hair when he sees his wife's ghost, he can surely be forgiven for suggesting 'straight up, upright' for the meaning intended by Douglas. Overall, however, Ruddiman's Glossary is a monumental work, bringing the study of the Scots vocabulary at a stroke to the leading edge of contemporary intellectual endeavour.

Following on Ruddiman, the next substantial achievement in Scots lexicography was that of Allan Ramsay. A key figure – indeed, *the* key figure – in the Vernacular Revival, Ramsay had moved to Edinburgh from his native Lanarkshire in 1700, working first as a wig-maker, then as a bookseller, and participating actively from the start in the lively social and intellectual life of the capital. His first two volumes of poetry (published by Ruddiman, incidentally) appeared in 1721 and 1727; and in between them in 1724 came his anthology *The Ever Green*. Subtitled *A Collection of Scots Poems Wrote by the Ingenious Before 1600*, this is a selection principally taken from the Bannatyne Manuscript of 1560, including, as well as many anonymous poems, several by such outstanding figures as Henryson and Dunbar. *The Tea-Table Miscellany*, his five-volume collection of songs from his own time (some traditional, some by living poets, some wholly or partly his own) also appeared in 1724; and was reprinted in 1730 and several times thereafter.

Like Ruddiman, Ramsay was keenly interested in the linguistic aspect of writing in Scots and firmly committed to upholding its status; but his purpose went beyond enhancing the reading public's understanding of Scots literature of earlier periods: he was equally intent on proclaiming and proving that Scots poetry was not confined to the past. Past and present, indeed, are dynamically combined in his work: his 1721 volume includes the fifteenth-century *Christ's Kirk on the Green* as well as his extensions to it, while *The Ever Green* shows numerous signs of his individual editing (including, notoriously, his cheerfully impertinent 'Postscript' to what he entitles Dunbar's *Lament for the Loss of the Poets*) and contains his own poem 'The Vision', fictitiously attributed to 'Ar. Scot'. In this sense, his two-volume *Poems* collection, *The Tea Table Miscellany* and *The Ever Green*, though on the face of it anthologies of different kinds, may be seen as a composite set, collectively embodying his contribution, at this stage in his long and productive life, to furthering the development of Scottish poetry. In view of this, it is not surprising that the glossaries appended to the collections[6] not only show no difference of approach (they are of the simplest type, lists of words explained by single-word equivalents or short descriptive phrases, with none of the etymological notes and little of the detailed discussion of meanings found in Ruddiman) but overlap to a very large extent.

265

A GLOSSARY; OR, An EXPLANATION of the *Scots* Words.

A

A All.
Abaid Abade, Abode, ſtayed.
Abaiſit, abaſhed.
Abeit, albeit.
Abergown, Coat of Mail.
Ablens, perhaps.
Aboiſe, *abuſe*, above.
Abulziement, Habit.
Abune, above.
Adoun, downward.
Aff, off.
Aſt, *aſten*, oft, often.
Affeir, frighted.
Afrey, Fear.
Agit, aged.
Agaſt, afrighted.
Aidir, either.
Aik, Oak.

A R

Ain, own.
Aits, Oats.
Air, Time paſt.
Air, ſoon, early, *item* Heir.
Aith, Oath.
Akerbraid, breadth of an Acre.
Alaſt, aloft.
Allane, allone.
Almous, Alms.
Alkynd, all kind, or Sort of.
Als, as, and.
Amene, pleaſant.
Ane, one.
Anes, *anis*, once.
Antetewme, Example.
Apenit, opened.
Appleis, pleaſe.
Arles, earneſt.

Arti-

First page of the glossary of Allan Ramsay's *The Ever Green*.

The most cursory is that of *The Tea-Table Miscellany*, where only half a dozen entries (out of a total of little over 500) run to more than two or three words ('*Hagies*, a boiled pudding, made of a sheep's pluck, minced with sewet'; '*Leese me*, a phrase used when one loves, or is pleased with a person'; '*Mons-meg*, a very large iron cannon in the castle of *Edinburgh*, capable of holding two people'). The glossary for *The Ever Green* is more extensive and, by the nature of the collection, includes a number of words which are archaic in themselves or have specifically historical references. Several of these are from the familiar aureate register of Middle Scots poetry: *aureate* itself (glossed 'golden'), *celcitude* 'highness', *mellifluat* 'sweet flowing'. Others refer to characteristic medieval-culture items: *abergown* 'coat of mail' (this is of course *habergeon*, and the spelling of the last syllable suggests a misguided folk-etymology), *flane* 'an arrow', *menzie* 'company or retinue'. Of the many colourful insult words which appear in *The Flyting of Dunbar and Kennedie* (and other poems in the collection too), most are provided with ready definitions: *crawdon* 'faint hearted', *glunschoch* 'sour Fellow', *luschbald* 'a sluggard' (Ramsay is more confident here than the editors of the *DOST*, who leave the word undefined), *walydraig* 'a pitiful Creature, or the most worthless of a number'; though some (*carrybald, chitterlilling, heggirbald, mymmerkin, nagus*) he quietly omits from the glossary, and in the case of *pelour* 'a Pilgarlick' (i.e., bald-headed man) his definition, attractive though it is, is erroneous: the word means 'thief'.

This is far from the only error in the glossary; and it must be acknowledged that Ramsay on several occasions has resorted, to all appearances at least, to guesswork – though in most cases his guesses are at least sensible, and some are applied to rare or otherwise genuinely puzzling words. *Attercap* is glossed as 'wasp' instead of 'spider': in the collection its occurrence is in Kennedy's part in the *Flyting*, 'thou yrefull Attercap . . .', in which context it might be said that one noxious creature would do as well as another. Less reasonable is his glossing of *gruntill* as 'a Sow', which hardly makes sense in Dunbar's line from the *Flyting*: 'The Gallows gapes after thy graceless Gruntle.'[7] 'Wings' as a gloss for *fedderem* (*recte* 'plumage') is at least related to the context (Dunbar's *The Fenyeit Friar of Tungland*), but the line following that in which the word occurs, '. . . and slippit out of *it* full clene', should have suggested the error. His guess at 'court and enjoy' for *gimmer* as it occurs in the line 'In *May* gois Gentlewomen gymmer' from Alexander Scott's 'On May' is completely off the rails: this is the comparative form of a rare word *gym* meaning 'neat, spruce'. A surprising mistake is *merle* (*recte* 'blackbird') as 'the Merlin, a Bird', particularly as the word invariably occurs (in the collection) in its familiar collocation with *mavis*, which he defines correctly: a merlin is a kind of hawk. Other instances where the form of the archaic word has led him to mistaken guesses, but more credible ones, are *forwayit* 'gave Way' (*recte* 'wandered, got lost') and *knapska* (*recte* 'an iron skull-cap'), for which he suggests 'knapsack'. All these words have several attestations in medieval and some of them also in later literature: much rarer words, some with only single entries in the *DOST*, also occur in *The Ever Green*; and though his glosses for some of them are erroneous (*antetewme* 'example': *recte* 'text of a sermon'; *beswakit* 'blanched': *recte* 'drenched') his deduction of the meaning is correct in *dring* 'a Miser'; *empashed* 'hindered'; *eyndle* 'to be jealous'; *nek* 'a Term at Chess, when the King cannot be guarded from a Check'; and for the unique word (in the *Flyting*) *caprowsy*, for which *DOST* offers no definition, he makes the credible guess 'an upper Garment'. Ramsay shows nothing of the scholarship of Ruddiman in glossing his medieval texts; but, amateurish as his work is, it is far from negligible in either scope or quality.

The Glossary is not the only linguistic apparatus which Ramsay provides for *The Ever Green*: a series of rules, positioned as if the set were a footnote to the first poem in the collection, 'Chrysts-Kirk of [*sic*] the Grene', lists some regular correspondences in orthography between the old and the contemporary spelling – i.e. the contemporary *English* spelling; not any suggested spelling for Scots. In some such instances there is in any case no difference, beyond the orthographical one, between the two languages; but more often the pronunciation suggested by the historic Scots spellings was still current in Scotland and different from the English, Ramsay making no reference to the fact: '*Weil, Deid, Heid, Meid*, &c, Well, Dead, Head, Mead. The Diphthong *ei* us'd in many such Words as now require *e*, *ea* and *ea*'; and similarly *Shune, Mune, Sune*: Shoon (or Shoes), Moon, Soon; *Sae, Wae, Mae*: So, Wo, Mo; *Sang, Lang, Band*: Song, Long, Bond; and other examples. This list of rules is offered as explaining 'Words that have nothing else of the Antique, or difference from the *English*': the intended contrast is with Scots words which do not exist in English, for which the Glossary provides explanations. Accordingly, the Glossary includes relatively few words with English phonological cognates, though some admittedly have found their way in, for example: *A*, All; *Aik*, Oak; *Blaw*, Blow; *Bricht*, Bright; *Ee*, Eye; *Mak*, Make. As further aids to his readers' understanding, Ramsay provides footnotes explaining unfamiliar words or phrases: '*Haild the Dulis*, is a Phrase us'd at Foot Ball, or such Games, where the Party that gains the Dule or Goal is said to hail it, or win the Game'; 'Fudder, properly a Load, relating to Lead. It is 1600 Pound Weight: in our old Authors it often metaphorically means a *great many*.'

The glossaries of the two volumes of *Poems* contain more detail than either of the two collections. That of the 1728 volume differs from the 1721 in having somewhat more entries (a sampling of words glossed in the later book but not the earlier includes *Ambrie*, Cupboard; *Badrons*, A Cat; *Furlet*, Four Pecks; *Groff*, Gross, coarse; *Niffnafan*, Trifling; *Putt a Stane*, Throw a big Stone) but also in that some of the more extended definitions from the previous list are trimmed. The bracketed words are omitted from the later entries in, among others, the following examples: '*Branks*, Wherewith the Rusticks bridle their Horses. [A Halter fixt to two Pieces of Wood, which hang on either Side of the Nose.]'; '*Dreigh*, Slow, keeping at Distance. Hence an ill payer of his Debts, we call *Dreigh*. [Or when on Journey, if the Way prove longer than we expected, we say, *'Tis a dreigh Road*]'; '*Redd*, to rid, unravel. To separate folks that are fighting [, where one oft gets what we call the *Redding Strake*]. It also signifies clearing of any Passage'. In several such cases the omitted section includes a short proverb or aphorism: '*Dit*, to stop or close up a Hole. [*Dit ye'r Gab wi' ye'r Meat.*]'; '*Doited*, Dozed or crazy, as in old Age. [*Daft young, and doited auld*, the two Times of foolish Marriage]'; '*Kemp*, To strive who shall perform the most of the same Work in the same Time, [equal to that Proverb, (*Fool's Haste is no Speed*) is, *Kempers shear nae Corn*]'.

The first volume also contains a listing of Scots and English words showing phonological or orthographic correspondences. Ramsay's heading to this section, 'Some general Rules shewing wherein many *Southern* and *Northern* Words are originally the same, having only a Letter changed for another, or sometimes one taken away or added', of course shows the naiveté of his time regarding the relationship between spelling and pronunciation and that between closely related language forms; but his list is rather more systematic than Ruddiman's, and is in fact the most careful attempt that had yet been made to itemise the differences at this linguistic level between Scots and English. The Scots loss of *l* following a back vowel (*Ba, Ca, Fou; Bouk, Faut, Gowd*), the prevention of the usual fronting and raising of OE long *a* before *ld* (*Auld, Bauld, Cauld*), the fronting of an original *o* or *u* (*Anither, Fit, Hinny*) are illustrated with several examples. As with Ruddiman, his focusing on letters rather than sounds has led him to class correspondences of several different kinds under one heading: 'the *o, oe,* or *ow* is changed to *a, ae, aw* or *ai*' is made to apply to the rounding of OE long *a* in southern but not northern dialects, a distinction already operative by the ME period: *aith, alane, baith, hame, mair, saip, stane* for *oath, alone, both, home, more, soap, stone*; to the different developments of the OE sequence *aw*: *awn, blaw, craw, slaw, snaw* for *own, blow, crow, slow, snow*; and to the much later change by which short *o* was lowered to *a*: *aff, aften, amang, drap, saft, sang*. This section precedes the Glossary proper, which unlike that of *The Ever Green* contains very few phonological cognates.

Perhaps the most individual and certainly the most entertaining part of

Ramsay's annotations is the extensive sequence of footnotes to the Scots poems (and to a much lesser extent the English ones too) in the first volume (those of the second are not remotely comparable in either scope or interest). Many of these go beyond the scope of lexicography, such as the biographical notes on the disreputable Edinburgh characters who are the subjects of the 'Elegies'; but some provide definitions of words, in isolation or in short phrases, e.g. *Freiks*: Young Fellows; *Bougers*: Rafters (a rare word occurring in *Christ's Kirk on the Green*); *Cutty Stoup*: Little Pot, i.e. a Gill of Brandy; *Clokin Hen*: a hatching Hen; and several offer explanations of colloquial or cant expressions. 'Auld Reeky', a phrase which receives its first literary attestation in Ramsay, is explained as 'A Name the Country People give *Edinburgh* from the Cloud of Smoak or Reek that is always impending over it'; and other examples include 'Pike ye'r Bain. Is a Cant Phrase, when one leaves a little in the Cup, he is advised to pike his Bone, *i.e.* Drink it clean out'; 'Chandler Chafts. Lean or meagre Cheeked, when the Bones appear like the Sides or Corners of a Candlestick, which in Scots we call a *Chandler*.' In some cases a bawdy or vulgar expression is pointed out but not explained, or a euphemism is ironically provided with a literal gloss which fails to explain its real meaning: '*Coost a Legen-girth*. Like a Tub thet [*sic*] loses one of its Bottom Hoops.' Ramsay's highly diverting blend of knowledge, enthusiasm and boisterous humour makes in these notes for a memorable contribution to the expounding of Scots usages.

Though a landmark in its time, Ramsay's *The Ever Green* was no model of scholarly editing; and a more systematic approach to the task of presenting medieval texts was taken by David Dalrymple, Lord Hailes, in his *Ancient Scottish Poems Published from the MS. of George Bannatyne*, in 1770. Lord Hailes, by training and profession a lawyer, earns his place among the great Enlightenment figures principally by his work as a historian of both Scotland and the early Christian church: this collection is something of a sideline to the main achievements of his life; and indeed he as editor is not named in the book.[8] Nonetheless, not only is it in itself a better edition of the Bannatyne poems than Ramsay's in respect of both its greater fidelity to the text and the extent and quality of the scholarly apparatus provided, but the glossary that it contains is at least somewhat more systematic and more accurate than that of its predecessor. The book is, indeed, specifically offered as a corrective to Ramsay: Lord Hailes concedes that 'The editor of *the Evergreen* [who is never named in the introduction, though he is in the notes] was a person of singular native genius . . . But while I make this just acknowledgement to his merit, I must be allowed to observe, that he was not skilled in the ancient Scottish dialect. His skill indeed scarcely extended beyond the vulgar language spoken in the Lothians at this day.'

It must be conceded, nonetheless, that Lord Hailes' glossary is no more immune than Ramsay's to occasional errors. In Dunbar's 'to awppis and owlis', the first noun means 'bullfinches', not 'curlews' as its resemblance to *whaup* has misled the compiler into conjecturing.[9] Other mistaken definitions are *Cramp* 'to climb or ramp': *recte* 'swagger'; *Rawchtir* 'instrument of torture': *recte* 'beam, rafter'; *Schoir* 'scorn': *recte* 'threatening behaviour'; and the insult words *Bumbard* 'drunken': *recte* 'lazy person' and *Duddroun* 'spectre': *recte* 'slovenly person'.

In a gesture of scholarly integrity which marks a new stage in the development of lexicography, Lord Hailes gives a list of words and passages, with page and line references, for which no certain meaning could be found. Ramsay had suggested definitions for some of these, correct in the case of *braids* (is like, or takes after), *laits* (manners) and *plycht* (plighted), though wrong in that of *tarrow* ('to refuse': *recte* 'delay' or, in the context 'on twenty shilling now he tarrowis' in 'Johne Up-on-lands Complaint', 'waits expectantly'); but neither he nor Lord Hailes attempted to define them all. Of the words which both anthologies illustrate but which neither editor attempts to gloss, some are rare or nonce words (e.g. *derene* 'challenge', *padell* 'small leather pouch' and – again! – some opprobrious words, *brybour, custroun* and *tutivillar* which, if they have any specific meaning beyond being general insult terms, appear to connote 'vagabond', 'base-born fellow' and 'tell-tale') or textual errors (e.g. *ramukloch* as in '. . .gart all the bairnis sing / Ramukloch in thair bed' in 'Ane Ballat of evill Wyffis', probably a mistake for *bomulloch*). Lord Hailes and the 'several gentlemen' who worked with him, errors notwithstanding, have approached the task of presenting a selection of early poetry with a far greater degree of scholarship than Ramsay; yet the extent to which the result has surpassed *The Ever Green* as a work of lexicography (that it is far superior as an edition of the texts is not in doubt) is less than they would probably have hoped.

Following on Ramsay, other Scots writers now adopted as a regular procedure the practice of appending a glossary to their works. The North-East, with its highly distinctive dialects, soon began making its own contribution to the Vernacular Revival; and both the texts produced there and the glossaries accompanying them testify to the individuality of the local forms of Scots.[10] One of the first of these, published in Glasgow in 1755, is the 'key' to Robert Forbes' *Ajax his Speech to the Grecian Knabs*, a verse translation 'attempted in broad Buchans' from Book XIII of Ovid's *Metamorphoses*. Virtually nothing is known of Forbes' life except that he worked as a hosier in London, the evidence for this being his own advertisement (in Habbie stanzas) for the business, and what he tells us of one particular episode in his lively *Journal from London to Portsmouth*; yet this obscure writer has the distinction of bringing the North-East dialect in all its exuberant richness into the mainstream of Scottish literature: in one single short paragraph from his *Journal* no fewer than five words from the North-East dialect have their first attestation: *setterel,* glossed by him as 'thick-set, dwarfish'; *belly-flaught* 'skinn'd over head like a hare'; *confeirin* 'considering'; *connach'd* 'spoil'd'; and *feugh* 'whiff', i.e. puff away at a pipe.

His glossary contains no more than about 250 entries; but a surprising number are for words which receive their first attestation in his writings (and several of which have since become familiar from their use by later poets). Examples are *chuller* 'double chin', *brouden't* 'fond, enamour'd', *allagrugous* 'grim, ghastly', *clamehewit* 'stroke, a drubbing', *fittininment* 'concern, footing in', *forleithie* 'surfeit', *gillegapous* 'half-witted, crack-brain'd', *jouckry-pauckry* 'roguery, tricks', *misgrugled* 'rumpled, handled roughly', *ogertfu'* 'nice, squeamish', and *tarveal* 'ill-natured, fretful'; and others with a North-East ring are *freugh* 'frail, brittle', *gnidge* 'squeeze, press down', *kneefest* 'keenest, briskest', *knaggim* '*gout,* by-taste', *leithry* 'croud', *sleeth* 'sloven', and *staver'd* 'staggered'.

Of equal interest is the glossary to another landmark North-Eastern text published in 1778, the second edition of Alexander Ross's *Helenore, or the Fortunate Shepherdess.*[11] Ross's delightful pastoral epic was first published in 1768, after having already circulated in manuscript for several years among the Glenesk community of which he was an active and prominent member; but the glossary in the new edition, published through the agency of James Beattie, was one of the features which marked it as designed for presentation to the wider Scottish readership. The number of entries is slightly greater than in Forbes' glossary; and though the format is the familiar one of individual words followed by (for the most part) single-word definitions, explanations in the form of short phrases are more common than in the earlier list: a couple of examples are *cauts, summer cauts,* 'a tremulous appearance, near the surface of the earth, in warm sunshine'; *meethness,* 'extreme heat. In some parts of Scotland, it means soft weather'; *lucky,* 'adv. too much. As a subst. noun, it signifies an elderly woman, often the mistress of an alehouse'; and the only entry with a local geographical reference, *The Cairn, or Cairn-a-mount,* 'a high ridge of the Grampians, over which a public road passes'.[12] The phrase 'Broad Scotch Dialect', by contrast with Forbes' 'Broad Buchans', suggests that Ross was less concerned than his predecessor to emphasise a specific regional provenance for his literary idiolect; yet local words predominate to an even greater extent than in Forbes. Some that appear for the first time in Ross's book are *amshach* 'misfortune', *avrens* 'wild berries [specifically cloudberries]', *etnagh-berries* 'juniper berries', *curcuddoch* 'sitting close together', *new'd,* 'oppressed, kept at under', *ruther* 'noise, outcry', *scrabs* 'stumps of heath, or roots', *showd* 'to waddle in going', *swavered* 'walked wearily', *thram* 'to thrive'; and some for which his poems and the glossary provide virtually the only recorded attestation are *bob* 'taunt, reproach', *cranshachs* 'crooked, distorted persons', *dibberderry* 'confused debate', *hamstram* 'difficulty', *thout* 'a sob', and *wratacks* 'dwarfs'. Forbes and Ross in their glossaries give virtually no cognates, concentrating on distinctive vocabulary items; and both show a lively awareness of the highly individual word stock of the North-East.

The first edition of Robert Fergusson's collected poems, published by Ruddiman in 1773, contained no linguistic apparatus beyond a glossary of Spartan simplicity and the next two editions had not even this; the glossaries to the Kilmarnock Edition (1786) and the Edinburgh Edition (1789) of Robert Burns' *Poems, Chiefly in the Scottish Dialect,* by contrast, were among the most individual and informative yet produced. Though the mere fact of including a glossary was by now standard practice, the case of a glossary compiled for his own work by a poet of the first order is exceptional, and imparts a unique interest to the two collections. They differ in several respects. Most obvious is the scale: the glossary to the Kilmarnock Edition covers five pages; that of the Edinburgh Edition, no fewer than twenty-four. Certainly the later edition itself is more extensive, including several poems which the Kilmarnock volume had not contained; but the difference in size between the glossaries is not remotely proportional. The focus of Burns' brief introductory notes, too, is different. That of the 1786 text refers to the spelling of morphological endings; the second glossary is introduced by a short note on a few details of the relationship of spelling to pronunciation:

> The *ch* and *gh* have always the guttural sound. The sound of the English diphthong *oo,* is commonly spelled *ou.* The French *u,* a sound which often occurs in the Scotch language, is marked *oo,* or *ui.* The *a* in genuine Scotch words, except when forming a diphthong, or followed by an *e* mute after a single consonant, sounds generally like the broad English *a* in *wall.* The Scotch diphthongs, *ae,* always, and ea very often, sound like the French *é* masculine. The Scotch diphthong *ey,* sounds like the Latin *ei.*

This is clearly related to one major difference between the glossaries: the Kilmarnock contains scarcely any instances of Scots words which have direct phonological cognates in English and are glossed by these; the Edinburgh has dozens. *Ane* 'one, an', *Banie* 'bony', *Ca'* 'to call, to drive', *Fecht* 'to fight', *Fleesh* 'fleece', *Fow* 'full, drunk, a bushel, &c.', *Ower* 'over', and one or two other examples of the same correspondences are all that can be found in the Kilmarnock glossary; the Edinburgh has as its first entry *A'* 'all', and proceeds to numerous examples of such simple equivalents as *Aft,* 'oft', *Auld* 'old', *Brig* 'bridge', *Eneugh* 'enough', *Faut* 'fault', *Het* 'hot', *Mysel* 'myself', *O'* 'of', *Warl, or warld* 'world', and even *Dimpl't* 'dimpled', *Gracefu'* 'graceful', *Jumpin'* 'jumping', and many similar examples. There is no mystery about the reason for this: the Kilmarnock Edition was intended principally for Burns' fellow countrymen in Ayrshire, on whom he could rely to share his mother-tongue familiarity with the local speech; the Edinburgh Edition was for the metropolis and beyond, including England. This intention of appealing to English readers is also the reason, no doubt, for the inclusion of a few historical and geographical references in the Edinburgh glossary for which the readers of the Kilmarnock edition would require no explanation: *Benlomond* 'a noted mountain in Dunbartonshire'; *ENBRUGH* 'EDINBURGH' [small capitals *sic*: a distinction shared by only one other entry in the glossary: *GUDE* 'the SUPREME BEING; good']; *Mar's year* 'the rebellion A.D. 1715'; *Sherra-moor, Sherriff-moor* 'the famous battle fought in the Rebellion, A.D. 1715'; *COILA* [large capitals *sic*: a distinction shared only by *KYLE* 'a district of Ayrshire'] 'from Kyle, a district of Ayrshire, so called, saith tradition, from Coil or Coilus, a Pictish monarch'.

Not only does the Edinburgh glossary include a far larger selection of words than the Kilmarnock, but in some cases the definitions are more detailed or precise: as a few examples, *Croon* 'a hollow, continued moan [K]', 'a hollow, continued moan; to make a noise like the continued roar of a bull, to hum a tune' [E]; *Hecht* 'to forebode' [K], 'to foretell something that is to be got or given; foretold; the thing foretold' [E]; *Flichter* 'to flutter' [K], 'to flutter, as young nestlings when their dam approaches' [E]. The Edinburgh glossary is also distinguished by a substantial number of explanatory notes, following the precedents of Ruddiman and Ramsay: the Kilmarnock edition has very few of these (*Fittie-lan'* 'the near horse of the hindmost pair in the plough', *Muslin kail* 'broth made up simply of water, barley and greens', *Risk* 'to make a noise like the breaking of small roots with the plough'), but in the second book they are far more numerous and often take the form of historical or cultural notes rather than semantic explanations: a few examples are *Blue gown* 'one of those beggars who get annually, on the King's birthday, a blue cloke or gown with a badge', *Broose* 'a race at country weddings who shall first reach the bridegroom's house on returning from church', *Kelpies* 'a sort of mischeivous spirits, said to haunt fords and ferries at night, especially in storms', *Wraith* 'a spirit, a ghost, an apparition exactly like a living person, whose appearance is said to forebode the person's approaching death'. And a final difference, manifest only in a few details, between the two glossaries is that one or two of the Kilmarnock definitions have what appears to be a personal touch absent from the corresponding ones in the other glossary: *Blink* 'a glance, *an amorous leer*, a short space of time' [K], 'a little while, a smiling look, to look kindly, to shine by fits' [E]; *Houghmagandie* 'a species of gender composed of the masculine and feminine united' [K], 'fornication' [E]. Clearly Burns did not rely on his cheerfully notorious reputation in this area preceding him to Edinburgh!

Many of the words in Burns' glossaries are still common currency: in writing certainly, and to some extent in speech. Few Scots, at any rate, would be puzzled even today by *biggin, bield, eident, gawsie, leal, mense, mell, moop, nowte, nieve, ripp, shaw* or *thowless*. Some have been adopted into standard English: *collie, eerie, flunkies, forbears, grousome* (in the last two cases with a spelling change). Though Burns was much less concerned than Forbes or Ross to emphasise the characteristics of his local dialect in his poetry, a number of words are markedly South-Western or specifically Ayrshire:[13] *donsie* 'unlucky, dangerous', *drunt* 'pet, pettish humour', *ram-stam* 'thoughtless', *risk* 'to make a noise like the breaking of small roots with the plough', *squatter* 'to flutter in water [E: *as a wild duck*, &c.]'. Some words are notably rare: *histie* 'dry, chapt, barren', *icker* 'an ear of corn' – interestingly, those two appear to be North-Eastern in origin (could Burns have heard them in his father's speech?) – *ier-oe* 'a great grandchild', *melvie* 'to soil with meal', *winze* 'an oath'. Some have in Burns their first attestation, or first in the post-Union period: *daimen* 'now and then, seldom', *forjeskit* 'jaded [E: with fatigue]'; *grushie* 'of thick, stout growth'; *hog-shouther* 'to jostle with the shoulder'; *outler* 'lying in the fields, not housed at night'; *ramfeezle'd* 'overspent'; *snash* [K] 'abusive language', [E] 'abuse, Billingsgate [!]'; and one which was later to be memorably adopted by another great Scots poet, *penny-wheep* 'small beer'. Several words have glosses which appear to refer specifically to their use in certain poems (e.g., *breef* 'an invulnerable charm': the lines from 'Epistle to James Smith' 'Ye surely hae some warlock-breef Owre human hearts' form the only instance in the *SND* of the word in this sense; normally it means a legal writ); or they have more than one definition, each of which suggests a particular passage (e.g. *ferlie* 'a wonder, to wonder; also a term of contempt': the first sense has several possible illustrations, but the second surely refers to the opening line of 'To a Louse'). Both those glossaries, but especially that for the Edinburgh edition, illustrate not only Burns' keen interest in and intimate knowledge of the Scots tongue, but his deliberate artistry and status as a master manipulator of the expressive power of words.

One of the most elaborate glossaries to any eighteenth-century poet's work, and much the most elaborate to emanate from the North-East, is that provided by Andrew Shirrefs to his *Poems, Chiefly in the Scottish Dialect* (the title conspicuously echoing that of Burns' collections), published in 1790. Shirrefs, a bookseller and journalist who practised first in Aberdeen and latterly in Edinburgh, was a Marischal College graduate. One of his brothers achieved renown as a minister and the other as a lawyer, and it is likely that Shirrefs was prevented by physical infirmity from entering a learned profession: Burns, who met him in Aberdeen, described him as 'a little decrepid body with some abilities', and he refers to himself in his poems by his nickname 'Cripple Andy'. Whereas his *Jamie and Bess*, published separately in 1787, had a mere single-page glossary of forty-nine entries, that of the collected poems is forty pages long and ends with the confident statement that: 'A *complete* glossary . . . cannot be expected in a work of this kind, as our limits absolutely preclude the practicability of it; yet the Author is inclined to think that the above is more extensive than any thing of the kind that has yet appeared; at least, that he knows of.' Ruddiman excepted, that claim is certainly justified. A major reservation is that the alphabetical ordering of the entries is virtually non-existent beyond the initial letters, an obvious defect whose rectification might have removed several manifest lapses. Simple reduplications occur, the two entries placed on different pages or different places on the same page: *Linking*, walking smartly; *Linkan*, walking speedily. The same word may be defined twice: he has included Burns' *Moop* 'to nibble as a sheep' but also

Frontispiece and title page of Alexander Shirrefs' *Poems, Chiefly in the Scottish Dialect.*

supplied a more elaborate and colourful definition of his own as *Moup* 'to eat; generally used of children, or of old people, who have but few teeth, and and [*sic*] make their lips move fast though they eat but slow'. Etymological relationships may be unrecognised or mistaken: *Coodies*, or *quiddies*, 'wooden vessels used for chamber-pots' (p. 9), and *Cootie*, 'a wooden dish; also those fowls whose legs are clad with feathers, are said *to be cootie*' (p. 10) (*coodie* and *cootie* for a wooden vessel (irrespective of its purpose) are forms of the same word, but *cootie* in the other sense is apparently an unrelated term). Nonetheless, Shirrefs' glossary is one of the most interesting of the period, not only through being the biggest in scope but because of the evident care that has been taken to provide accurate and, in some cases, detailed definitions.

The introductory note is a verbatim repetition of that to Burns' Edinburgh Edition, with a significant, added sentence: 'The vowel *o*, and the diphthong *oo* are commonly sounded *ee*; as *do, dee, poor, peer,* &c.' This refers to a shibboleth of the North-Eastern dialect; and his retention of Burns' sentence on 'the French *u*', which immediately follows, is inaccurate with reference to his own medium: the historic front rounded vowel (which even in Burns' Ayrshire had almost certainly lost the rounding by his time) in the North-East was (and is) uniformly pronounced *ee*.[14] A set of 'general rules', in the manner of Ruddiman and Ramsay, refer to *l*-vocalisation and other familiar sound correspondences. The glossary, like that of Burns' Edinburgh Edition, includes many phonological cognates (*Aft* 'oft', *Fae* 'foe', *Sma'* 'small', etc.); and some of these show North-East dialect pronunciations such as *Forseeth* 'forsooth', *Fup* 'whip', *Mith* 'might', etc.

The glossary itself draws unabashedly on its predecessors, many definitions being identical to those in earlier works. Some North-Eastern words which had not appeared in either Forbes' or Ross's glossaries are *Cleidach* 'discourse of any kind, particularly applied to the Gaelic language', the same word as MacDiarmid's *clytach* here receiving its first attested usage; *Crany-wany* 'the little finger', a reduplicated and idiosyncratically spelt form of *crannie*, a familiar local word, but its first attestation in any form at all; and *Wishy-washies* 'bustling in discourse, a cant term for being slow in coming to the point'.

In several cases Shirrefs provides sets of alternative definitions, separated only by commas: *Cross, cross-grained* 'froward, cruel, unnatural, ungrateful, stubborn, dogmatical'; *Daft* 'merry, sprightly, foolish, mad, fond, anxious'. Many of his entries, as with Burns, are substantial notes: examples include *Cummer, caird* 'a term of reproach, similar in signification to the English word gypsie, or vagrant'; *Forspeak* 'to speak for; also a person is said to be forspoken when any sudden mischance happens on the back of a series of good fortune; or, when a child, formerly promising, suddenly decays, the child is said to be forspoken'; *Pirn* 'the spool or quill within the shuttle, which receives the yarn; *pirny cloth*, a web of unequal threads or colours, striped'. An interesting detail is the occurrence of several words or expressions for food: his definition of *haggis* is more precise and detailed than Burns', and a couple of his more unusual items are *Dawds and blads* 'broth with green colewort, boiled', and *Tartan purry* 'a sort of pudding made of red colewort chipped small, and mixed with oatmeal'. Though often, as noted, simply echoing his predecessors, he not infrequently elaborates on them: to Burns' four-part definition of *blink* he adds '*Blinket*, when applied to a liquid, signifies it is soured or spoiled; to a person, it imports disappointment'; to his precise explanation of *kelpies* he adds 'also an expression for a raw-boned youth'. The impression of slapdash carelessness which the chaotic alphabetisation is certain to convey masks the manifest pains that have been taken to ensure that this glossary is a compendious and accurate source of information regarding the language the poet used and the culture which he depicts.

Finally, as Ruddiman early in the eighteenth century initiated the scholarly study of the Scots vocabulary, another literary scholar at the dawn of the nineteenth brought this phase in the history of the subject to a conclusion. This was James Sibbald, like Shirrefs a bookseller and journalist: he was the founder of the *Edinburgh Magazine*, and the first review of Burns' Kilmarnock Edition, published there in November 1786, contributed substantially to establishing the poet's reputation. Sibbald's *Chronicle of Scottish Poetry from the Thirteenth Century to the Union of the Crowns* appeared in 1802, the year preceding his death; and the last of its four volumes, except for an introductory essay entitled 'Observations on the Origin of the Terms Picti, Caledonii and Scotti',[15] is devoted to a glossary: at over 400 pages, with each full page containing roughly twenty entries, this was by far the largest and most comprehensive glossary of Scots which had yet appeared. (Sibbald's own estimate for the size of the glossary is 6,000 words.)

The anthology is a work of imposing scale and quality, providing a compendious overview of the history of Scottish poetry. The change in the attitude to Scots held by the literati in the previous 100 years is made very clear, however: Ruddiman, as we have seen, clearly recognised the continuity between the language in which Gavin Douglas wrote and that of his own time, and showed no sign that he regarded the latter as in any way unworthy of its noble precedents; Sibbald, by contrast, writes: 'For the dialect which is now called *Scottish*, we are indebted to a few writers, of depraved taste, about the end of the seventeenth, and beginning of the eighteenth centuries; who, instead of contributing, like Drummond of Hawthornden, to the improvement of the written language of their country, chose to pen elegies on pipers, and dying speeches of hounds and horses, in the familiar dialects of the meanest vulgar'.[16] His glossary, which purportedly includes many words which do not appear in the poetry collection, 'has indeed some claim to be considered as a Dictionary of the antient language of Scotland':[17] the *ancient* language, be it noted. (It is probably not accidental that the last line of poetry in the collection is 'The Lion and the Leopard in one'.)

Though Sibbald's actual definitions are generally sound enough, it has to be acknowledged that his attempts to provide etymologies for the words are often no more than guesswork. Ruddiman, as previously noted, was not immune to etymological errors, but Sibbald's are more numerous and in many cases more outlandish; and as the study of languages had not stood still during the intervening century, his inaccuracies are to that extent less excusable. His limited knowledge of the Celtic languages and conviction of their lack of importance in the development of Scots is manifest: for *dawache of land* (i.e. *davoch,* a word for a measure of land derived from a Gaelic word for 'tub', referring to the amount of corn required for its sowing) he proposes a Germanic etymology; and of *ingill, ingle* 'fire, fire-place', a straightforward Gaelic borrowing, he states that 'the derivation of the word [is] unknown'. The origin of *Hogmanay* has always been, and still is, a notorious puzzle; but Sibbald's suggestions (whether original or relayed) 'the vulgar Teut. phrase, 'met *heuge ende meughe* eten,' cum voluptate & appetitu edere', 'perhaps a corruption of another well-known Teut. or rather Sax. phrase, viz. *hogen-hyne,* or *houlkenhyne,* signifying *own domestic servant*' and 'Greek *hagia-mene,* the holy moon' – carry about as much conviction as John Mactaggart's offer of 'hug me now'.[18]

To do Sibbald justice, by no means all the fanciful etymologies that he cites appear to be offered seriously. *Balow, Balelow* 'hush. An ingenious etymologist has fancied the later to be Fr. *bas! le loup,* hush! there's the wolf !' does not suggest that he accepts the suggestion; and the following note deserves to be quoted in full:

> Battie-bummel, Bommel-bautie, *simpleton, booby*. Here is a notable fund of etymological amusement. 1mo., it may be called an alliterative corruption or augmentation of the Teut. *bot-muyl,* homo stolidus, from *bot,* hebes, and *muyl,* mulus. 2do. it may be derived from the same Teut. *bot,* and *bommele,* sucus, q. *stupid drone*. 3tio. As *Blaitie-bum* occurs in the same sense, the derivation may be from Teut. *blait,* vaniloquus, bardus, gloriosus, and *bomme,* tympanum, q. *empty boster*. Lastly, from the Fr. *bat,* and Teut. *boom-woll,* cotton, q. *bag of cotton*.

Etymological amusement, intended or otherwise, is to be obtained in abundance from Sibbald's glossary; yet it would be an injustice to dismiss it as valueless.

Besides its exceptional size and scope, it includes many notably rare words, most of which are correctly defined. The suggestions offered for words of doubtful meaning or etymology are often far more credible than the ones that have been cited, and the fact that the errors are often patent and risible does not outweigh the fact that this substantial and detailed glossary, clearly the offcome of prolonged, sustained and painstaking effort, contains a wealth of reliable information. Flaws notwithstanding, it is a major work, and can be seen as the summation of the age in which the cutting edge of Scots lexicography was represented by lists compiled by poets and men of letters of the words in poetic collections.

Besides the glossaries to volumes of poetry, another source of information, of a different kind, on the Scots language of the eighteenth century is provided by the lists of 'Scotticisms' which several scholars compiled. This practice is often seen as symptomatic of the growing lack of respect for the Scots language that is such a prominent feature of eighteenth-century thought, and the compilers uniformly state that their 'Scotticisms' are better avoided; but in mitigation it can be argued that part of their intention was to make it easier for Scottish writers to reach audiences in England and its colonies as well as at home.[19] The first (and slightest) of these collections is David Hume's, originally included in his *Political Discourses* (1752) and reprinted on pages 686–7 of the *Scots Magazine*, vol. 22 (1760). A much more substantial list entitled *Scoticisms, Arranged in Alphabetical Order, Designed to Correct Improprieties of Speech and Writing* was published in 1779 by James Beattie, a philosopher, poet and classical scholar of renown whose derogatory attitude towards the Scots tongue expressed in this work is offset in part, at least, by his enthusiastic praise for the Scots poetry of Alexander Ross, and his part, already mentioned, in its publication. Sir John Sinclair of Ulbster, in addition to his achievements as politician, agricultural reformer and director of the monumental *Statistical Account of Scotland* (1791–8), found time to write a similar list of Scotticisms entitled *Observations on the Scottish Dialect* (1782), and a Glasgow schoolmaster named James Mitchell in 1799 produced a fourth, significantly entitled *Scotticisms, Vulgar Anglicisms and Grammatical Improprieties Corrected*, though his consists for the most part of repetitions from its predecessors.

Those lists are heterogeneous mélanges of vocabulary items, grammatical features, idioms and figurative expressions, and on occasion raise the suspicion that the authors are guilty of mere nitpicking (as when Hume informs us that *friends and acquaintances* and *paper, pen and ink* are Scotticisms to be shunned in favour of the English (and therefore correct) *friends and acquaintance* and *pen, ink and paper*. The assumption on which all the collections are based, too – namely, that Scottish usages are by their nature improper and to be avoided – has in many cases led the compilers to include, without discrimination, grammatical or other solecisms which are not particularly Scottish in their lists: Mitchell makes at least some attempt to distinguish the three categories of undesirable usages ('Scotticisms, Vulgar Anglicisms and Grammatical Improprieties') which he identifies in his title by marking specimens of each category, though they are all listed together in alphabetical order; and Sinclair concludes his treatise by warning his countrymen not to fall into the trap of adopting Cockney phrases such as *this here thing* and *that there thing, I knode, I heard on it, grass* for *asparagus* and *your'n* and *his'n*: 'It is a common observation, that bad habits are more easily, and indeed are more generally acquired, than good ones'; but Beattie and Sinclair include several examples of faults (as they regarded them) which were to be found as readily in English as in Scottish speech (e.g. the failure to distinguish *shall* and *will*) without consistently distinguishing those from genuine Scots usages. The 'Exercise' which Beattie provides at the end of his collection illustrates the variety of things that he lists as 'Scotticisms' (and indeed is most ingeniously composed to incorporate as many as possible of them in a short compass), as the first few lines show:

> When Paris was in his *twentieth and fourth* year, three goddesses are said to have *waited of* him as he was *laying* on the side of a mountain; each of whom promised him some good thing, if he would pronounce her the fairest. He gave judgment *in favours* of Venus. Soon after he went to Greece, where he *see'd* Helen the *prettiest* woman of *these* days, who was *married on* Menelaus King of Sparta. This Helen *has been* a very worthless woman; for, without *thinking shame*, she went off with Paris, taking with her *severals* of her attendants, and much wealth: and yet Menelaus was a good-natured man, and she could not pretend that he had ever *disabused* or *maltreated* her. Though *difficulted* how to act, he did not succumb under her misfortune: for he knew he could not be the *better of* that.

The use of compound ordinals (*twentieth and fourth* instead of *twenty-fourth*) appears to have been general Scots, at least in formal registers. *Wait of* (instead of *on* or *upon*) and *see'd* are specifically said by Beattie to be 'vulgar English' as well as Scottish (Sinclair, incidentally, includes in his list the still-current *wait on* in the sense of the English 'wait for'), and another faulty verb usage, *lay* instead of *lie*, has never been Scottish at all (on the contrary, *lie* used transitively can still be heard in Scotland). *Married on* and *better of* (*recte*, or at any rate *anglice*, 'to' and 'for') he apparently takes to be genuine Scotticisms; both, of course, are still to be heard. *In favours* and *severals* are presented as erroneous plural usages, though again both remained current long after Beattie's period. *Has been* for *must have been* gets no further discussion in his list; by contrast his remark 'the Scots often use *these* very improperly for *those*' comes at the outset of a long note on the demonstratives. The use of *difficult* as a transitive verb (*Difficulted ang.* 'puzzled, at a loss', according to Beattie's list) is again a genuine Scots usage with several eighteenth- and nineteenth-century attestations. Besides those assorted Scotticisms (or putative Scotticisms) of grammar, *think shame* (*ang.* 'be ashamed') is an idiomatic phrase; and the remaining three are lexical items with Scottish usages of which Beattie disapproves: *pretty* 'in Eng. is beautiful without dignity: but is often used in Scotland, when applied to persons, in the sense of *graceful*, or beautiful with dignity' (did he think the Scottish sense inapplicable to Helen of Troy?); *disabuse* 'is by many people in Scot. supposed to be the same with to *abuse*' (this usage is recorded in North-East Scots well beyond Beattie's time, illogical though it undoubtedly seems); and the entry for *maltreat* is simply 'to abuse — to treat ill', as if Beattie did not regard this as a word at all (though it has English as well as Scottish attestations).

Sinclair's *Observations* form the most systematically arranged of the various collections, and he is the most explicit in stating his aim: 'In garb, in manners, in government, we are the same; and if the same language were spoken on both sides of the Tweed, some small diversity in our laws and ecclesiastical establishments excepted, no striking mark of distinction would remain between the sons of England and Caledonia. The Author of this little performance, with pleasure contributes his mite to a purpose so truly desirable.' These are sentiments which cannot fail to provoke amusement after well over two centuries in which neither have they come one jot closer to reality, nor has the Scottish populace become any more convinced of their desirability. Sinclair divides his book into four sections: 'Phrases peculiar to Scotland' (for example, distinctive uses of prepositions: *to be reconciled with* [to] *a person, to be angry at* [with] *a man*, and differences in word ordering: *Anybody else's* 'anybody's else', *a pretty enough girl* 'a pretty girl enough'); 'Words peculiar to the Scots, or which they use in a sense different from the English'; 'Miscellaneous words and phrases'; and 'Legal and clerical words and phrases'. The last of these is of particular interest in illustrating the distinctive vocabulary of Scots law: *To homologate* [homologuer, Fr.] 'to ratify, or approve'; *A march* [marche, Fr.] 'a limit, or boundary'; *As effeirs* [affaire, Fr.] 'As is proper, or expedient'; *To assoilzie* [absolvere, Latin] 'to acquit'; *To excamb* [excambere, Law Latin] 'to exchange'; *The libel* [libellus, Latin] 'the writ, or inditement'; *To poind* [Saxon] 'to pound'; *Sorners* [sorehon, Irish] 'vagrants'; *Tinsel* (from *tyne*, Islandic, *to lose*) 'loss, damage'.

Sinclair's general Scots vocabulary list (the second chapter of his book) is a substantial collection, arranged in sections corresponding to parts of speech: he notes regretfully that many 'emphatical and significant' words have gone out of use, but 'what our language has lost in strength, it has gained in elegance and correctness'. He explicitly follows 'that excellent glossarist Ruddiman' in identifying (not always correctly) the languages from which the Scots words are derived (square brackets containing place of origin are Sinclair's): *To big* [Saxon and Islandic] 'to build'; *To cryn* [Belgick] 'to dry, or shrink in'; *To skail* [echeveler, Fr.] 'to scatter'; *To wale* [Gothic] 'to chuse, or pick out'; *A firth* [fretum, Latin] 'An æstuary, or arm of the sea'; *A tod* [German] 'A fox'; *Sough* [Erse] 'Whine'. Most of the entries are single-word equivalents, occasionally with comments such as '*Flit*, is still a provincial word in England' or '*Restrict*, is a word scarcely English, says Dr. Johnson [a frequently cited authority]'; occasionally a more detailed speculation on a word's etymology or usage is offered: '*Clever*, (erroneously made use of for) Quick, active or handy. *Clever*, is either derived from *cleave*, or, perhaps, it comes from the Scotch word *claver, to talk, or prattle*, which quick and active people are apt to do. The English, it may be observed, never use *cleverness* for *quickness*, nor *clever* for *quick*.'

His regular habit of referring to what the English say makes the premise of his collection almost painfully obvious. And in fact, it is not a collection of Scots words as such, for though undoubtedly it contains many of those (as a small sampling, *ding, fash, jouk, lowe; auldfarrant, caller, drumly, lyart; baubee, hansel, neb, quern*) it also contains numerous examples of words of which only certain usages are Scottish (e.g. *detract* meaning 'take away in general', *misgive* meaning 'to fail, or miscarry', *friend* meaning 'relation', *weary* as a verb) and many more of words which simply had gone out of use in metropolitan English speech (e.g. *trow, blyth, bygone*). Rather, it is a collection of usages which he judged would mark the speaker as unsophisticated or provincial, among which usages were Scots words; and for each entry, whether a genuine Scots word, an archaism or a word which Scots shared with some forms of dialectal English, the definition represents not what the word *means* but what you should replace it with in your speech. Sinclair's book, and the other compilations of 'Scotticisms', are of great linguistic and socio-historical interest; but their interest is not primarily as sources of information on the distinctive Scots vocabulary: only Sinclair, in fact, makes a point of including Scots words at all, Beattie arguing that, in a book listing usages which Scottish speakers should avoid, 'with respect to broad Scotch words I do not think any caution requisite, as they are easily known, and the necessity of avoiding them is obvious'.

The ground-breaking achievement of Ruddiman in the early years of the eighteenth century was never surpassed in the period under discussion. Though Ramsay, Lord Hailes, Burns, Shirrefs, Sibbald and others each made his own individual contribution, with its distinctive and in some cases very considerable interest and merit, to the study of the Scots vocabulary, and though collectively their efforts represent an imposing structure built on Ruddiman's foundation, they supplemented rather than superseded his achievement. It is also undeniable that the disappearance of the robust cultural patriotism associated with the use and study of Scots which had inspired the glossarists until well into the century, and its replacement by a sour disdain for 'the familiar dialects of the meanest vulgar', left its mark on the quality of their linguistic expositions. This is even more obviously true of the compilers of the various lists of Scotticisms: much can be gathered regarding Scots usages in grammar and idiom as well as vocabulary from the work of Hume, Beattie, Sinclair and Mitchell; but their basic motivation was precisely their conviction that Scots usages were by their nature undesirable. It was John Jamieson's realisation of the falsity of this conviction that prompted him to embark on his monumental *Etymological Dictionary of the Scottish Language*; and with Jamieson's work the next great advance in Scots linguistic scholarship was to begin.

THREE

Jamieson and the Nineteenth Century

SUSAN RENNIE

Frae Jamison's muckle buik the words tak wing.
Douglas Young [1]

At the start of the nineteenth century, a prospectus appeared for a new dictionary of the Scots language which would mark a watershed in Scottish lexicography. Compiled over twenty years by the Reverend Dr John Jamieson, the *Etymological Dictionary of the Scottish Language* was eventually published in two quarto volumes in 1808. The first complete dictionary of Scots, it was enormously influential on future lexicographers. A century later, George Watson acknowledged that Jamieson had 'laid the foundation of Scottish lexicography, and has been the basis of nearly all succeeding Dictionaries dealing with our language'.[2] The story of Scots-language lexicography in the nineteenth century is essentially the story of Jamieson's *Dictionary*. It began the century, was developed throughout it, and was still dominant by the end, having been revised and reissued in various forms after Jamieson's death. Even smaller, less scholarly dictionaries that appeared later in the century drew much, if not all, of their content from Jamieson.[3]

Jamieson was not the first to project a complete dictionary of Scots, although he was the first to see the idea through to publication. The previous century had seen a number of abortive attempts to compile a dictionary which would cover more than the existing literary glossaries. James Boswell conceived the idea of writing a Scots dictionary while studying in Utrecht in his twenties, and began to record the distinctive Scots words and usages which he knew were being eroded. 'The Scottish language is being lost every day,' he wrote, 'and in a short time will become quite unintelligible. . . . To me, who have the true patriotic soul of an old Scotsman, that would seem a pity. It is for that reason that I have undertaken to make a dictionary of our tongue, through which one will always have the means of learning it like any other dead language.'[4]

Although he never completed his scheme, enough of a manuscript survives to show that, had he completed it, Boswell's dictionary would have been a remarkable work. Even as it stands (with notes on around 800 words and phrases), it is a valuable record of eighteenth-century Scots, and includes the first recorded instances of words such as *bubbly-jock* and *chuckie-stanes*.[5] Later in the century, Boswell's friend and mentor, Lord Hailes, printed and circulated a draft specimen of a Scots dictionary, but he also abandoned the work before it progressed very far.[6] By the turn of the century, when Jamieson printed his prospectus, he was one of a number of antiquarians and literary scholars who had begun to compile a dictionary of Scots. Both John Pinkerton and James Sibbald had announced their plans for a Scots dictionary in their editions of early Scots poetry (for Sibbald, see Chapter 2) and George Chalmers also began his own dictionary project. One potential rival to Jamieson did reach publication, but only in part. In 1804, an Edinburgh surgeon, Robert Allan, published the first part of a projected dictionary based on his father's collection of Scots words, but no further parts appeared, possibly because the publication of Jamieson's *Dictionary* in 1808 made it no longer viable.[7] There were also plans furth of Scotland. The Rev. Jonathan Boucher from Epsom planned an 'archaeological and provincial' dictionary which would supplement Johnson by covering obsolete and dialect words which Johnson had omitted – including a sizeable amount of both Older and Modern Scots, which Boucher (in striking contrast to Jamieson) planned to treat as a dialect of English.[8] Jamieson at one point considered selling his materials to Boucher and abandoning his own work, but he was persuaded against this by his friends. Instead, the two projects became rivals and it was the publication of Boucher's prospectus in 1802 that spurred Jamieson into publishing his own dictionary proposal later the same year.

Jamieson and his *Dictionary*

Born in Glasgow in 1759, John Jamieson grew up in a family with strong dissenting belief, and followed his father into the ministry of the Secession Kirk.[9] At the age of twenty, he was appointed to serve as minister to the newly established Secession congregation in Forfar, and stayed there for the next eighteen years, during which time he married Charlotte Watson, the daughter of a local widower, and started a family. Over the ensuing years, the Jamiesons had seventeen children, ten of whom survived into adulthood, although only three were to outlive their father. In his professional life, Jamieson was a diligent minister, only retiring from the Secession Kirk at the age of seventy due to his failing health. Throughout his life, he published a number of theological works which were highly regarded in his day, and for one of which he was awarded a doctorate by the College of New Jersey (later Princeton University).[10] Jamieson's real interest and passion, however, lay in antiquarian pursuits. He was an enthusiastic

Portrait of John Jamieson by John Kay. The engraving is dated 1799, at a time when Jamieson was living in Edinburgh and compiling the *Dictionary*, and was first published in Kay's *Original Portraits* (1838), vol. 2, pp. 317–22. Willa Muir later described this portrait of Jamieson as showing 'a buirdly-looking man with a rather bland, rather brosy, clean-shaven face, a trifle heavy about the jowl, but with a smile lurking near the corners of the mouth' (Muir (1938) 'Dr John Jamieson', BBC radio script (broadcast 12 July), Scottish Theatre Archive, p. 2).

member (and later joint secretary) of the Society of Antiquaries of Scotland, and wrote numerous papers on Scottish history and antiquities. He had a particular passion for numismatics, and it was their mutual interest in coins which led to the first meeting between Jamieson and Walter Scott, in 1795, when Scott was only twenty-three and not yet a published author. Jamieson was also a keen angler, as the many entries relating to fishing terms in the *Dictionary* attest; and published occasional works of poetry, including a poem against the slave trade which was praised by abolitionists in its day.[11] Besides the *Dictionary*, Jamieson contributed to a number of major cultural publications. He wrote an article for the *First Statistical Account*, prepared extensive notes on the place-names of Angus for George Chalmers's *Caledonia*, and wrote a Scots poem ('The Water Kelpie') for the second edition of Walter Scott's *Minstrelsy of the Scottish Border*. It was through his antiquarian research that Jamieson developed his practice of tracing words (particularly place-names) to their earliest form and occurrence: a method which was to be the foundation of the historical approach he would use in the *Dictionary*.

Jamieson began his *Dictionary* at a time of fierce debate on the origins of the Picts and, by extension, of the Scots language, which some believed to be Pictish in origin. A group of antiquarians, foremost among them John Pinkerton, argued that Scots was a 'Gothic' language which had been brought to Scotland by Gothic-speaking Scandinavians.[12] Jamieson was intrigued by this theory, which seemed to posit a noble ancestry for the Scots language, in which it could no longer be regarded as a debased form of English. It was this belief in a separate, Norse origin for Scots that led Jamieson initially to seek connections between Scots and Scandinavian words, and between Scottish and Scandinavian customs, rather than exploring the shared history of Scots and Old English. In the 'Dissertation on the Origin of the Scottish Language', with which Jamieson

The former Secession manse in Forfar. Jamieson and his family lived here from 1780 until 1797, during which time he began work on the *Dictionary*.

prefaced the *Dictionary*, he elaborated his theory of the Scandinavian origins of the language, drawing evidence from early historical accounts and his own observations of place-names and Pictish archaeology. The 'Dissertation' was largely written in response to George Chalmers' exposition of the rival theory (that the Picts were a Celtic people) in the first part of *Caledonia*, published the previous year. (Chalmers was so incensed at Jamieson's 'Dissertation', which he took as a personal attack, that he broke off relations with his former friend, and published a bitter response in the second part of *Caledonia* two years later.)[13]

Creating the *Dictionary*

It has often been stated that Jamieson embarked on his *Dictionary* at the suggestion of the Icelandic scholar, Grímur Thorkelin, whom he met during the latter's visit to Scotland in the 1780s. Thorkelin had been commissioned by the Danish government to compile a list of the antiquities of Britain and Ireland, and was invited to stay at the house of Jamieson's friend, the MP and agricultural reformer George Dempster.[14] A memoir of Jamieson, published shortly after his death, gives the following account of what ensued:

> Before leaving Dunnichen Thorkelin requested the Doctor to note down for him all the singular words used in that part of the country, no matter how vulgar he might himself consider them; and to give the received meaning of each. . . . Jamieson, to oblige the learned stranger, forthwith purchased a two-penny paper book, and began to write down all the remarkable or uncouth words of the district. From such small beginnings, made more than twenty years before any part of the work was published, arose his four large quarto volumes, and that revolution of opinion as to the origin of the Scottish language . . . which he has maintained in the learned Dissertations which accompany the Dictionary.[15]

But although the celebrated meeting with Thorkelin did take place, Jamieson had in fact already begun to take an interest in Scots, and to consider the origins of the language, before his conversation with Thorkelin, having recently read Pinkerton's theory of the 'Gothic' origin of Scots. On the day after their meeting, in October 1787, he told Thorkelin that he considered it 'a most lucky circumstance that I have been in any degree honoured with your acquaintance. For ever since Mr Pinkerton's last Publication came to hand, my mind has been anxiously engaged in revolving his System, wishing, if possible, to put it to the test. For if it can be proved that a great part of what is called the Broad Scotch be really Gothic or Icelandic, it nearly amounts to a demonstration of his theory.'[16] Thorkelin gave Jamieson a practical way to test his theory, by suggesting that he conduct what would now be called fieldwork, collecting examples of Angus Scots for comparison with Scandinavian languages. In doing so, he set Jamieson on a course of research which would evolve over the next fifteen years into a plan for the first complete dictionary of Scots, leading Jamieson to later dub him 'the parent' of the *Dictionary*. But despite his early influence, Thorkelin played a relatively minor role in the subsequent progress of the *Dictionary*, partly because the outbreak of war in Europe meant that it would be several years before he and Jamieson were once again able to correspond.

As Jamieson's interest in Scots grew, he expanded his research to explore earlier forms of the language, and began to envisage a work which would encompass both Older and Modern Scots and thus show the continuity between the two. Although Ruddiman had included examples of modern, eighteenth-century Scots in his glossary of 1710, no one had before attempted a dictionary which would encompass both periods of the language. Jamieson's task was enormous, and as his compilation progressed, the *Dictionary* began to absorb an increasing amount of his time and resources. Unlike Johnson (and later in the century the Grimm brothers), Jamieson had no bookseller to back his scheme, and the *Dictionary* was entirely self-financed. Moreover, Jamieson was not a man of independent means, pursuing lexicography as a hobby. He was a working minister, with a dependent and growing young family. Where he could, he begged and borrowed books to supplement his own library. Fortunately, he was skilled at making friends, many of whom had better resources and connections, and became in effect patrons of the *Dictionary*. George Dempster, for example, supported Jamieson in the initial stages of his research by lending him books from his extensive library and providing intellectual stimulation and comradeship as Jamieson was planning his work. Jamieson later described how, 'if the weather was bad', he and Dempster 'found intellectual employment in the library, often in tracing the origin of our vernacular words in the continental languages.'[17] In later years, Walter Scott became another valuable supporter of Jamieson's work, not only lending him books, but introducing him to potential contributors, circulating prospectuses, and publicising the forthcoming *Dictionary* in his own literary works. After meeting Jamieson for the first time, in 1795, Scott memorably described their encounter in a letter to a friend:

> I have been introduced lately to a man whose acquaintance has given me a great deal of pleasure and whose character I think will entertain you. He is a Dr. Jamieson from Forfar, a man of Letters an author and a poet, an admirer of antiquities and a remarkably fortunate collector of coins of which he has a scarce and valuable selection.... He has been of late obliged to part with several of his coins in order to purchase Books to enable him to carry on a work upon the Scottish language on which he is at present engaged.[18]

In 1797, Jamieson received a call from the congregation of the Secession Kirk in Nicolson Street in Edinburgh to be their new minister. He accepted with enthusiasm, regarding the position as 'much more favourable to literary research and more advantageous to a rising family'.[19] By this date, he and Charlotte had ten children, ranging in age from a few months to fifteen years, and they would have a further seven children after their move to Edinburgh. Jamieson served the Nicolson Street congregation until his retirement from the ministry in 1829, during which time he was influential in healing the rift that had split the Secession Kirk into two rival synods (the Burghers and Anti-Burghers) for decades.[20] When they first moved to Edinburgh, Jamieson and his family stayed in the newly built Buccleuch Place, just south of the Old Town, but later (after publication of the *Dictionary*) they moved to larger premises at number 4 George Square, where Jamieson stayed until his death in 1838. As Jamieson had anticipated, the move to Edinburgh had a significant impact on his *Dictionary* research, in particular by giving him access to the rich resources of the Advocates' Library, many of whose early books and manuscripts he read, transcribed, and quoted in the *Dictionary* (see below).

Seeking Subscribers

Having no bookseller to back his plan, Jamieson decided to publish the *Dictionary* by subscription. In 1802 he printed and circulated his prospectus (*Proposals for Printing by Subscription, in Two Volumes, Quarto; an Etymological Dictionary of the Scottish Language; by John Jamieson, D.D.*), which he distributed through his network of friends and supporters; a shortened version was also published in the March issue of the *Edinburgh Magazine*. 'Within these few years,' Jamieson noted in his prospectus,

> a taste for Scotish literature has revived both in Scotland and England. Hence the want of an Etymological Dictionary has been felt more than ever; and it may well be supposed that all who possess a genuine taste for the literary productions of their country, would wish to encourage a work which is necessary, not merely for illustrating their beauties, but in many instances even for rendering them intelligible.

As well as emphasising the need for a Scots dictionary, the prospectus also whetted the appetite of potential subscribers by including five sample entries from the letter A. These already showed the historical and scholarly approach which Jamieson would use in the published *Dictionary*. Although the prospectus confidently claimed that the *Dictionary* was 'in a state of considerable forwardness', it would be a further six years before Jamieson was ready to publish his work. As he was covering the costs of printing himself, Jamieson had to procure enough subscriptions from potential buyers to be able to recoup his costs. He also continued to add new information to his text, right up to the time of publication. By the time the *Dictionary* was finished, it included approximately 15,000 entries.

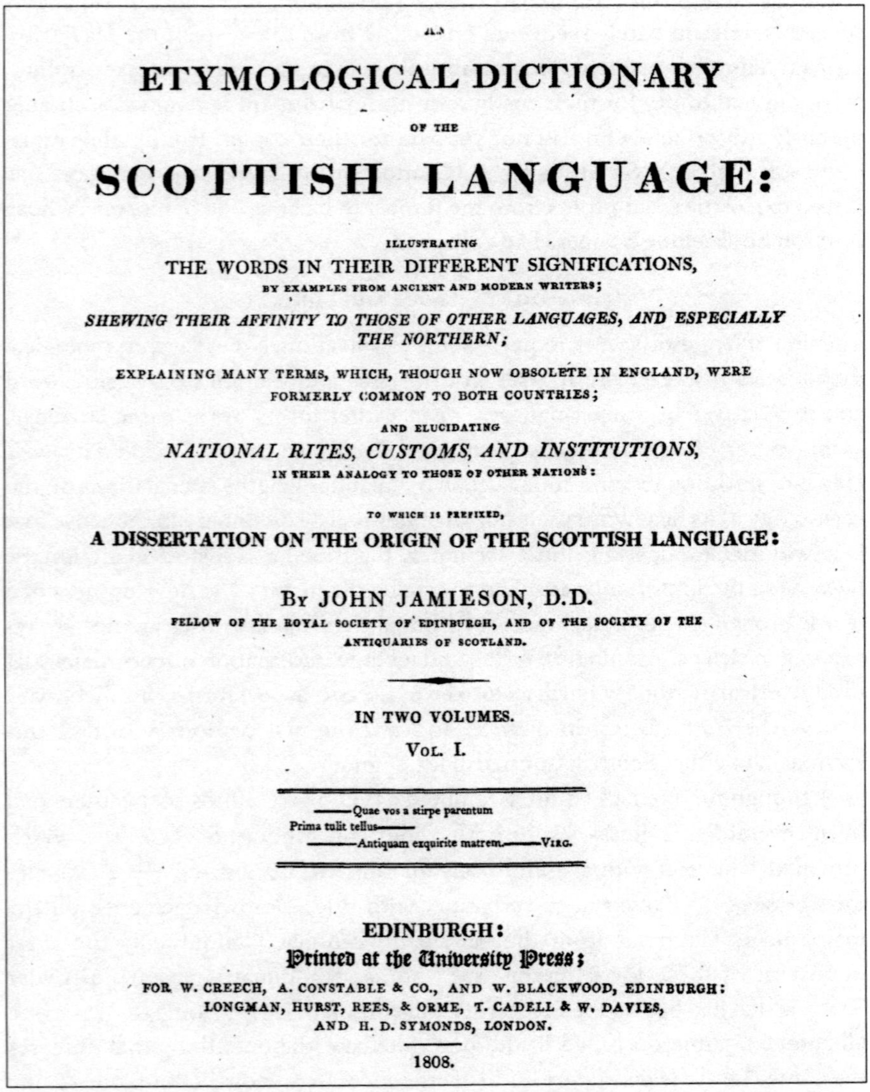

AN
ETYMOLOGICAL DICTIONARY
OF THE
SCOTTISH LANGUAGE:
ILLUSTRATING
THE WORDS IN THEIR DIFFERENT SIGNIFICATIONS,
BY EXAMPLES FROM ANCIENT AND MODERN WRITERS;
SHEWING THEIR AFFINITY TO THOSE OF OTHER LANGUAGES, AND ESPECIALLY THE NORTHERN;
EXPLAINING MANY TERMS, WHICH, THOUGH NOW OBSOLETE IN ENGLAND, WERE FORMERLY COMMON TO BOTH COUNTRIES;
AND ELUCIDATING
NATIONAL RITES, CUSTOMS, AND INSTITUTIONS,
IN THEIR ANALOGY TO THOSE OF OTHER NATIONS:
TO WHICH IS PREFIXED,
A DISSERTATION ON THE ORIGIN OF THE SCOTTISH LANGUAGE:
BY JOHN JAMIESON, D.D.
FELLOW OF THE ROYAL SOCIETY OF EDINBURGH, AND OF THE SOCIETY OF THE ANTIQUARIES OF SCOTLAND.
IN TWO VOLUMES.
VOL. I.
——Quae vos a stirpe parentum
Prima tulit tellus——
——Antiquam exquirite matrem.——VIRG.
EDINBURGH:
Printed at the University Press;
FOR W. CREECH, A. CONSTABLE & CO., AND W. BLACKWOOD, EDINBURGH:
LONGMAN, HURST, REES, & ORME, T. CADELL & W. DAVIES,
AND H. D. SYMONDS, LONDON.
1808.

Title page of the first edition of Jamieson's *Etymological Dictionary of the Scottish Language* (1808).

After twenty years of compilation, and fifteen months of production, the *Dictionary* was finally published in two quarto volumes in February 1808. The cost of paper had risen unexpectedly in the latter stages of production and Jamieson had been forced to increase the cost to his subscribers, from four to five guineas. One thousand copies of the *Dictionary* were printed, of which all but a hundred had been sold within two years of publication. Yet despite this apparent success, Jamieson barely recovered financially from the costs of the *Dictionary* project. A number of copies sent to subscribers in India were never taken up, and Jamieson had to pay for their costly return. He also spent several years chasing up tardy subscribers who had not yet paid for their copies. Family obligations also took their toll. Shortly after publication of the *Dictionary*, Jamieson was forced to use the scant profits from the project to bail out one of his sons, whose London bookselling business had collapsed.

Jamieson's Methods and Sources

The title of Jamieson's work requires some clarification. Nowadays, etymological dictionaries deal exclusively with word origins and the links between a word and its relatives in other languages, or in earlier forms of the same language, as in Walter Skeat's seminal *Etymological Dictionary of the English Language* (1879–92). Although Jamieson's *Dictionary* includes lengthy speculations on the etymology of its headwords, it is not an etymological dictionary in the sense that is now understood, and is more accurately described as a historical dictionary, because of the importance attached to tracing the history and development of a word through the historical record. Although Jamieson's entries are not always ordered in strict chronological order, and include information not normally part of a historical dictionary (such as spoken usage and dialect forms) his dictionary is nevertheless historical in method and was the first dictionary to take this approach, in either Scottish or English lexicography.

Although no one had before attempted a dictionary of this scope, there had been several Scots glossaries, to both Older and Modern Scots works, which provided Jamieson with a useful basis for some of his entries. His *Dictionary* incorporates, and often cites verbatim (with due acknowledgement), all the major Scots glossaries from the eighteenth century. Undoubtedly the most important of these for Jamieson was Thomas Ruddiman's glossary of Older Scots, which had been appended to his 1710 edition of Gavin Douglas' *Aeneis* (see Chapter 2). Jamieson called Ruddiman's glossary 'the only thing that deserves the name',[21] and the *Dictionary* is full of references to, and direct quotations from, Ruddiman's text. Jamieson looked to Ruddiman to help him define and illustrate Older Scots terms, but also (thanks to Ruddiman's notes on contemporary usage) as evidence of eighteenth-century Scots, as in the following example, where Ruddiman's definition is labelled 'S.B.' for 'Scotia Borealis' or 'Northern Scots':

> To WALLOP, WALOP, *v. n.* 1. "To move quickly, with much agitation of the body or cloaths," Rudd. S. B.

From an early stage, Jamieson had set himself to trace the earliest occurrence of every one of his headwords. It is for this reason that his *Dictionary* is seen as a landmark in the development of historical lexicography. Using the experience he had gained in antiquarian research, as well as his own fondness for literature, Jamieson painstakingly set about examining every source of Older Scots that was available to him. It is hard now to imagine the extent of this task. The scholarly dictionaries of Scots which followed Jamieson had access to modern editions of key Scottish texts. Even Johnson, half a century before Jamieson, was able to use contemporary editions of literary sources such as Spenser, Milton, and Shakespeare. At the end of the eighteenth century, when Jamieson began to compile the *Dictionary*, there were few reliable editions of Older Scots texts (Ruddiman's edition of Douglas being a notable exception) and, wherever possible, Jamieson preferred to consult the original manuscripts of his early sources. After his move to Edinburgh, he was able to consult the Bannatyne Manuscript in the Advocates' Library for citations from the Older Scots makars such as Dunbar and Henryson, and the manuscripts of Barbour's *Bruce* and Harry's *Wallace*, of which he later published his own scholarly editions, based on the work he had undertaken for the *Dictionary*.[22]

Jamieson pioneered the practice of providing full references for his illustrative quotations, so that his readers could judge for themselves 'whether the sense of the writers referred to had been rightly understood or not'.[23] Where evidence was available, he provided illustrative quotations for each sense of a word, drawing his citations from both literary and non-literary texts. For manuscripts, he even provided exact line references, and often variant readings or comparisons with printed editions of the texts. His entry for the Older Scots word AFFER ('condition, state'), for example, includes four fully referenced quotations from the manuscripts of *Bruce* and *Wallace*, and (in the sense shown below) also cites for comparison a printed edition of the latter from the seventeenth century:

> **2.** Warlike preparation, equipment for war.
> To Schortwode Schawe in haist thai maid thaim boun,
> Chesyt a strenth, quhar thai thar lugyng maid:
> In gud *affer* a quhill thar still he baid.
> *Wallace*, iv. 514. MS. *Effeir*, Edit. 1648.

Jamieson's selection of sources for his illustrative quotations was innovative for the time and contrasted sharply with the approach of Johnson, most of whose material was drawn from classic English authors. By contrast, Jamieson's sources are remarkably diverse and his approach engagingly modern. In the *Dictionary*, quotations from the Older Scots makars, like Dunbar and Henryson, and their modern descendants such as Burns and Ramsay, are interspersed with quotations from contemporary minor poets and examples drawn from newspapers, such as an advertisement from the *Edinburgh Evening Courant* for a lost dog, which Jamieson cites in his entry for COLLIE:

> COLLIE, COLLEY, *s.* 1. The vulgar name for the shepherd's dog, S.; *colley*, a cur dog. A. Bor. Gl. Grose.
> "There was lost in Prince's Street, on Saturday the 28th December last, a black and white rough *coley*, or shepherd's dog." Edin. Even. Courant, Jan. 20. 1806.

Unlike his rival, Jonathan Boucher, whose proposed dictionary was based purely on written evidence, Jamieson determined to give as much weight to spoken as to written Scots, being happy, as he put it, to base his evidence 'on the authority of the nation at large'.[24] For contemporary Scots, he drew on his own knowledge of the language of his native Clydesdale and that of his adopted county of Angus. But from the outset, he was also keen to recruit local informants: the first being his Forfar landlady, who supplied him with a list of some two hundred words. Unsurprisingly, the best represented dialect area in the *Dictionary* is that of Angus, closely followed by Lothian, for both of which areas Jamieson was able to draw on his own experience and on the contributions of nearby friends and colleagues. The entry for CLAMEHEWIT provides a typical example of how Jamieson relied equally on written and unwritten sources. Here, the first sense is based on literary evidence from eighteenth-century sources, with Jamieson quoting both Robert Fergusson and Robert Forbes, and the second on his own knowledge of Angus dialect:

> CLAMEHEWIT, CLAW-MY-HEWIT, *s.* 1. A stroke, a drubbing, S.
> –Frae a stark Lochaber-aix
> He gat a *clamehewit*
> Fu' sair that night.
> *Fergusson's Poems*, ii. 29.
> "Thinks I, an' I sou'd be sae gnib as middle wi' the thing that did nae brak my taes, some o' the chiels might lat a raught at me, an' gi' me *a clamiheuit* to snib me free comin that gate agen." Journal from London, p. 8.

2. A misfortune, Ang.

> Qu. *claw my heved* or *head*, scratch my head;
> an ironical expression.

Although Jamieson tried always to provide the earliest written evidence for each word, he did not always order his entries in strict chronological order: this would in any case have been impractical for a dictionary which based its evidence on both written and unwritten sources. In the example quoted above, the second quotation from Forbes predates the first one from Fergusson, as in this case Jamieson has ordered them alphabetically by the spelling of the headword form. Jamieson was also less interested in pronunciation than in other aspects of a word's history or usage, so that relatively few entries include any note on contemporary Scots pronunciation, although there are scattered comments, as in the entry for GOLDSPINK, which Jamieson notes is pronounced *goudspink*.

Jamieson's insistence on including Scots words 'on the authority of the nation at large' rather than relying on purely written evidence laid him open to error, and a number of entries in the *Dictionary* have been regarded by later editors as spurious or dubious. Yet by preserving so much spoken Scots at a time of increasing erosion of the language, his *Dictionary* became an invaluable source for later linguists as well as a rich resource for creative writers. The *Dictionary* and *Supplement* are cited in over 9,000 entries in the *SND*, and often Jamieson's text is the first evidence available of the existence of a Scots word or phrase. Examples of Scots words first found in Jamieson are *jab*, *pernicketie*, *plowter* and *wheech*, as well as words which later entered English usage, such as *nugget* and *slithery*.

Unlike most dictionaries of its day, Jamieson's *Dictionary* also includes a substantial amount of encyclopedic information relating to Scottish customs and folklore. The longest entry in the *Dictionary* is that for YULE, which runs to twelve columns of text and includes detailed descriptions of Scottish Yuletide customs, all referenced in Jamiesonian style by quotations from historical sources. The antiquarian style of this and similar entries may be seen from the following extract from the entry for LYK-WAIK ('the watching of a dead body during night'):

> This ancient custom most probably originated from a silly superstition, with respect to the danger of a corpse being carried off by some of the agents of the invisible world, or exposed to the ominous liberties of brute animals. But, in itself, it is certainly a decent and proper one; because of the possibility of the person, considered as dead, being only in a swoon. Whatever was the original design, the *lik-wake* seems to have very early degenerated into a scene of festivity extremely incongruous to the melancholy occasion.

Jamieson's views on the Norse origins of Scots coloured many of his etymologies. Although many of his speculations were overturned by later philological scholarship, his empirical methods, in seeking cognate forms across related languages, anticipated the methods of comparative linguists later in the nineteenth century. His scrupulous care in tracing and referencing sources, and his determination to include all available written sources, marked the beginning of what would come to be called lexicography on historical principles. In the mid-nineteenth century, before the advent of the *New English Dictionary*, Jamieson's methods were recognised as being so far in advance of current English dictionaries that a contemporary source lamented that 'the only good English Dictionary we possess is Dr Jamieson's Scottish one'.[25]

The *Abridgement* and *Supplement*

In the years immediately following the publication of the *Dictionary*, Jamieson began work on a supplementary volume. Initially, he planned this as a single volume which could be produced in a few years. In fact it took him eleven years and the *Supplement* eventually matched the original *Dictionary* in size, being published in a further two quarto volumes in 1825. During this period, Jamieson suffered a series of family tragedies. Two of his elder sons died in India in the space of a year, and he lost several of his younger children. In 1816, he wrote poignantly to a friend that he had 'now nine children in the grave'.[26] He was also suffering from increasing bouts of ill-health, which left him at times 'very little capable of literary labour'.[27]

Another reason for the delay was that Jamieson's energies were diverted into producing an abridged edition of the *Dictionary*, which was published in 1818. Partly, the *Abridgement* aimed to fulfil the demand for copies of the full *Dictionary*, which were now scarce and sold at a premium by booksellers; but it was also published in order to preserve Jamieson's intellectual property. Shortly after the *Dictionary* was published, Jamieson heard that an Edinburgh bookseller was planning to sell a pocket Scots dictionary which had been abridged from his work. Fearing the appearance of a pirated edition, Jamieson set about compiling his own *Abridgement*, basing his methodology on Johnson's similar scheme. He included most of the headwords from the main *Dictionary*, with shortened definitions and etymologies, but gave only authors' names as authorities, rather than full citations from literary works. The abridged entry for DOUCE, for example, condenses Jamieson's original definition of sense 1 ('Sober, sedate, not light or frivolous, applied both to persons and things') to a single word, and omits the original quotations from Ramsay and Burns, retaining only the references to both authors:

DOUCE, DOUSE, *adj*. 1. Sedate, S.
Ramsay
2. Modest, opposed to wantonness, S.B.
3. Of a respectable character, S. *Burns*.
Fr. *doux*, *douce*, mild, gentle.

Jamieson completed his *Abridgement* in just six months, from starting work in December 1817 to publication in June 1818. This time he was working to a tight schedule, having sold the publishing rights for £200 to a partnership of Edinburgh booksellers. Yet despite the speed of its production, the *Abridgement* was far more than a simple condensation of the *Dictionary*, and showed how Jamieson was keen to reflect the contemporary literary scene. The publication of *Waverley* in 1814 had encouraged a wave of new literary works, incorporating Scots in prose as well as poetry, especially in dialogue, and Jamieson took the opportunity to cite literary examples of Scots usage which had been published since the appearance of the *Dictionary*. For example, the *Abridgement* includes new senses of CALLAN, CANTRAIP and UNCO, which Jamieson had found in Scott's recent novels. There were also new references to the works of James Hogg, and to Elizabeth Hamilton's popular satire, *The Cottagers of Glenburnie*, which had been published in the same year as the *Dictionary*. More copies were printed of the *Abridgement* than of the original *Dictionary* (1,500 of the former, compared to 1,000 of the larger work) and priced at only 14 shillings, it sold well from the outset. It was the first of several abridged editions which did much to popularise Jamieson's work throughout the nineteenth and well into the twentieth century.

The 'pirate' dictionary which had prompted Jamieson to issue the *Abridgement* was published in the same year, and it was soon evident that it was an original work which bore little resemblance to Jamieson's text. *A Dictionary of the Scottish Language; Containing an Explanation of the Words Used by the Most Celebrated Ancient and Modern Scottish Authors* had been compiled by the Paisley-born poet, Ebenezer Picken, who had died in poverty in 1816. With around 5,000 headwords, it was based on the earlier glossary which Picken had appended to his own volume of Scots poetry, and was published posthumously by Picken's publisher, James Sawers. Far from pirating Jamieson, Picken included a gracious acknowledgement of the work of his fellow lexicographer, 'who, with steady ardour, and indefatigable industry, has brought to completion an undertaking, the utility of which can only be estimated by philological students—its labour by those who have engaged in similar pursuits',[28] and Jamieson found valuable material in Picken's work for his compilation of the *Supplement* a few years later.

Once the *Abridgement* was published, Jamieson resumed work on the planned supplementary volume to the full *Dictionary*. After the financial strains of the *Dictionary* project, he was loath to finance another lengthy publication and once again entered into an agreement with an Edinburgh bookseller. The *Supplement* was eventually published by William and Charles Tait, who paid Jamieson £700 for the rights to publish a 'third volume' to his *Dictionary*. Over the next six years, Jamieson substantially increased his reading programme to take account of the recent explosion in Scottish literary publishing. As he noted in the 1825 Preface:

> As the revival of a taste for the ancient language of our country has, since the appearance of the former volumes of this work, been remarkably displayed in many works of imagination, some of them of the highest character in this line of writing; I have availed myself of the vast variety of national or provincial words abounding in them, with which I was formerly unacquainted, and of many additional senses or illustrations of the words contained in the DICTIONARY. (p. vi)

Jamieson's reading list for the *Supplement* included nearly a hundred original works published between 1808 and 1825, and covered works by major nineteenth-century Scottish authors such as John Galt, James Hogg, Susan Ferrier, Christian Johnstone, and of course Scott, whose novels are still cited anonymously in the *Supplement*. As well as seeking new headwords, Jamieson used his reading programme to update and augment his original *Dictionary* entries. Keen to reflect current literary trends, he added many new illustrative quotations. The *Supplement* entry for BRANDER, for example, does not provide any new information or additional senses for the verb, but it does append two new quotations from Scott's recent fiction:

> To BRANDER, *v.a.* To broil on a gridiron.] *Add;*
> "But now, Janet, canna ye gie us something for supper?' 'Ou ay, sir, I'll *brander* the moor-fowl that John Heather-blutter brought in this morning." Waverley, iii. 236.
> It is also used as a neut. *v.*
> "Than for dinner—there's no muckle left on the spule-bane; it will *brander* though—it will *brander* very weel." Bride of Lammermoor, ii. 72.

Jamieson also continued the coverage of Scottish newspapers which had been such an innovative feature of the *Dictionary*, and increased his coverage of literary periodicals, such as the new *Blackwood's Edinburgh Magazine*, which had begun publication in 1817 and had serialised works such as Galt's *The Ayrshire Legatees*, which is cited in the *Supplement* from its publication in *Blackwood's*. As well as covering new Scottish literature, Jamieson took advantage of a number of reference sources which had been published, or made available to him, since publication of the *Dictionary*. The most important of these was John Mactaggart's *Scottish Gallovidian Encyclopedia* of 1824 (see Chapter 4). Although the *Supplement* was well into production by 1824, Jamieson found a considerable amount of new and valuable material in the *Encyclopedia*, and eventually managed to squeeze in over 800 citations from Mactaggart's work – although only from the letter G onwards, as the earlier letters of the *Supplement* had already been printed by this stage. Jamieson had already explored the available manuscript sources of Older Scots for the *Dictionary*; but there were occasional new manuscripts which came to his attention. In particular, the *Supplement* refers to a seventeenth-century glossary of 'Norish words' from the Northern Isles, which Jamieson saw in manuscript. In the hand of Sir Robert Sibbald, it is the original of the glossary which was published anonymously in James Wallace's *Description of the Isles of Orkney* in 1693, and is thus the earliest surviving example of a Scots dialect glossary.[29] Jamieson transcribed his information directly from the original manuscript, which was still in his possession on his death in 1838.

Several of the methods which Jamieson adopted now seem familiar, but they were far from standard practice for dictionary-makers at the time. One of these was the use he made of voluntary contributors. After the publication of the *Dictionary*, Jamieson became without competition a kind of National Lexicographer and was inundated with contributions from antiquaries, historians, and ballad collectors, who sent him Scots words and usages which had been omitted from the 1808 *Dictionary*. Although he did not have the resources to employ a network of assistants or fieldworkers, Jamieson still managed to recruit a remarkable team of specialist consultants. He was able, for example, to call on the expertise of those who were then editing the records of the old Scottish parliament, so that his citations and definitions were synchronised with that ongoing project. He asked Patrick Neill, the secretary to the Royal Caledonian Society, to vet his entries on Scottish flora and fauna; and asked contemporary authors such as Scott and Hogg about words that occurred in their poetry and fiction. He was also fortunate in attracting the help of an indefatigable team of voluntary collectors, who gathered Scots (and especially dialect) terms from the areas where they lived or had family connections. In the Borders, he recruited the entire Shortreed family (to whom he was most likely introduced by Scott), and sent them lists of terms he knew or suspected to be from that area. George Kinloch, a ballad collector whose family hailed from Aberdeenshire, provided him with citations from Scots ballads, as well as information on North-Eastern Scots. Indeed, Jamieson came to rely on Kinloch as a kind of assistant editor, as the printing schedule for the *Supplement* became increasingly urgent, and even delegated to him the task of compiling the *Supplement* bibliography. Other contributors, some of whom are acknowledged in the *Supplement* Preface, were Sir Alexander Boswell (the elder son of James Boswell), and the antiquary Charles Kirkpatrick Sharpe. However, the most prolific of Jamieson's collectors was Sir Robert Liston. Liston was a British diplomat who had grown up on a farm in Kirkliston, near Edinburgh. During his time in Constantinople, he whiled away his leisure hours by recollecting the Scots words of his youth and noting them down for Jamieson. His personal copy of the *Dictionary* survives and is annotated with notes on nineteenth-century Scots usage, over two hundred of which Jamieson used for the *Supplement*. Many of Liston's suggestions relate to agricultural terms, such as *aweband* ('a band for tying black cattle to the stake') and *cavings* ('the short broken straw from which the grain has been separated'), but he also provided Jamieson with lively usage examples, such as (for BUBBLE), 'There is a great *bubble* at your nose. Dight the *bubbles* frae your nose, wean.'

When a word was contributed by a trusted source, such as Kinloch, Liston, or Scott, Jamieson often used the original definition verbatim, so that the wording of some of the *Supplement* definitions is not originally Jamieson's, although he gave it his editorial approval. For example, the *Supplement* entry for WRATWEL is defined in words which were drafted by Robert Liston, and the definition of CONTIRMONT is in the words of Walter Scott:

> WRATWEL, VRATWELL, *s.* A small narrow slip of skin, that rises up on the side of the finger, near the nail, and becomes troublesome, sometimes inflaming, S. V. WARTWEIL.
> CONTIRMONT, *adv.* The contrary way.]
> *Give*, as definition, Against the hill, upwards.
> The term is metaphorically applied to any thing that is contrary to nature or the course of things.

Scott contributed substantially to the content of the *Supplement*. Jamieson warmly acknowledged his friend's assistance in the 1825 Preface, and he openly quotes a number of his comments in the text, as in the entry for GUMPTION below, although he also silently incorporated suggestions from Scott in other entries. Scott's personal copy of the 1808 *Dictionary* survives in his library at Abbotsford and includes numerous annotations in his hand, many of which were used by Jamieson in preparing the *Supplement*:[30]

> GUMPTION, *s.* Common sense, understanding, S.] *Add*;
> In a note on this article, Sir W. Scott remarks, that "painters call their art of preparing colours their *gumption*."

After the publication of the *Supplement*, Jamieson continued to gather material until his death in 1838, eventually filling three manuscript volumes of unpublished *Additions*. Although these were not published in any subsequent editions of the *Dictionary*, they were consulted by the editors of the *SND* and found to contain much valuable material. In particular, Jamieson had been gathering dialect terms from Shetland and Orkney, and his *Additions* include terms sent to him by new collectors, such as Thomas Barclay, a minister in Lerwick, who would later also act as a consultant for Thomas Edmondston (see Chapter 4). The *Additions* volumes also show how Jamieson continued to collect citations from recent Scottish literature, such as the later novels of Scott and Hogg. As in the *Supplement*, there is also a healthy representation of the works of Scottish women authors, such as Christian Johnstone and Susan Ferrier.

Jamieson's grave in St Cuthbert's, Edinburgh. The inscription reads: 'Here lie the mortal remains of the Rev. John Jamieson, D.D. who rendered invaluable service to his fellow men by his important labours not only as a faithful minister of Christ but also as a learned theologian, a profound philologist and lexicographer, and an assiduous investigator of the antiquities of his country. He was born at Glasgow on the 3d of March 1759, and died at Edinburgh on the 12th of July 1838, in the 79th year of his age.' The photograph was taken on the 250th anniversary of Jamieson's birth.

The Posthumous Jamiesons

Two new and complete editions of Jamieson's *Dictionary* and *Supplement* were produced before the end of the nineteenth century. The first of these was published by William Tait, who had previously published the 1825 *Supplement.* Tait had made a heavy loss on the *Supplement,* which had been published just before the financial crash of 1825–6. After Jamieson's death, he still had 350 copies (almost half the original print run) left in his warehouse, and he hoped to dispose of these by packaging them into a new, four-volume edition. For this, he enlisted the help of John Johstone (co-editor of *Tait's Magazine* with his wife, the novelist Christian Johnstone). Johnstone quickly put together a reissue of the original *Dictionary* text, interspersed with cross-references to the *Supplement,* which was issued as the first two volumes of the new edition; the third and fourth volumes were made up from leftover copies of the original *Supplement.* As Johnstone explained in his Preface:

> In this improved Edition of Jamieson's Dictionary, all the additional words in the Supplement are incorporated in alphabetical order, and the most popular meaning of each word is briefly given. The text has also been carefully revised and corrected, according to Dr. Jamieson's own directions, where the limited space would allow this to be done. Where it could not be done, the reader is referred to the Supplement, for the correction, or for additional information.[31]

For example, in the following entries in his new *Dictionary* text, Johnstone added the abbreviation 'S' to indicate that there was further infomation (including more detailed definitions and illustrative quotations) available in the corresponding entries in the *Supplement*:

> BROSIE, BROSY, *adj.* Semi-fluid; soft, inactive; bedaubed with *brose* or porridge. *S.*
> BROSY-FACED, *adv.* Having a fat and flaccid face. *S.*
> BROSILIE, *adv.* In an inactive manner. *S.*

This second edition of 'Jamieson' appeared in 1840–1. In fact, Tait had originally planned to include Jamieson's unpublished *Additions* as a fifth volume, but this scheme was never realised. As a preface to the second edition, Tait included a shortened version of the biography of Jamieson which appeared in *Tait's Magazine* in August 1841, and which was most likely written by Christian Johnstone, who wrote much of the literary content of the magazine.

A few years later, Tait again engaged Johnstone to produce a new edition of Jamieson's *Abridgement,* which had never been updated or reissued since its publication in 1818. This second edition of the *Abridgement* was published in

1846. It combined concise versions of Jamieson's *Supplement* entries with the text of the 1818 *Abridgement*, and was therefore far more integrated than Johnstone's earlier edition of the full *Dictionary*. In 1867, a third edition of the abridged Jamieson appeared, this time edited by Dr John Longmuir, a Free Kirk minister from Kincardineshire. Longmuir revised a few of Johnstone's entries from the previous edition, and also substantially increased the text by adding over 600 new words, gathered through his own research and from a few voluntary contributors. He also included an appendix of words from Shetland and Orkney, gleaned from the recently published *Etymological Glossary of the Shetland and Orkney Dialect* by Thomas Edmondston (see Chapter 4).

Following his work on the third *Abridgement*, Longmuir was asked by a Paisley publisher, Alexander Gardner, to prepare a new edition of the unabridged *Dictionary*, which this time would fully incorporate the text of the 1825 *Supplement*. This third edition of Jamieson's *Dictionary* was eventually published in four volumes between 1879 and 1882. Although it was begun by Longmuir, most of the text was edited by David Donaldson, who was engaged to assist Longmuir when failing health forced the latter to retire. Donaldson added so much new material (mainly drawn from Older Scots literary texts) that a supplementary volume was issued in 1887, making a fifth and final volume to the third edition.

Despite its inclusion of new material from recent publications of the Scottish Text Society, Donaldson's edition was viewed by some as behind the times. The third edition made some minor revisions to Jamieson, and corrected obvious errors, but did not substantially overhaul his original entries, some of which were now almost eighty years old. Jamieson's text, which had seemed so innovative and contemporary in 1808 and 1825, was beginning to look out of step with newer lexicographic projects such as Murray's *New English Dictionary* in Oxford (see Chapter 10). Soon there were calls for a Scots dictionary to supersede, rather than simply revamp, Jamieson. One abortive project was started by James Taylor, a former secretary to the Board of Education for Scotland, who advertised his plan for a 'new and complete Etymological Dictionary of the Scottish Language' in 1878. Taylor projected a three-volume work and enlisted the help of fellow philologists in his scheme, but his dictionary never got beyond the planning stage. It was not until the advent of the *SND* and *DOST* that any real alternative arose to Jamieson as a historical dictionary of Scots, although the *New English Dictionary* did include a substantial amount of Scots and incorporated and updated some of Jamieson's material.

Although linguists were frustrated by the lack of an alternative to Jamieson, the early twentieth century saw a new generation of writers in Scots who began to mine the *Dictionary* for creative inspiration. For the poets of the twentieth-century

Scottish Renaissance, such as Hugh MacDiarmid, who were writing as work was just beginning on the *SND* and *DOST*, Jamieson remained the standard reference source for Scots.[32] Douglas Young later encapsulated the richness of Jamieson as a creative source by describing the *Dictionary* as 'a kist o ferlies'.[33] The abridged editions of the *Dictionary* were especially useful in providing an affordable Scots dictionary that covered both modern and earlier forms of the language. At the turn of the century, Alexander Paisley commissioned William Metcalfe, a scholar of Older Scots, to produce a new edition of Jamieson's *Abridgement*. Metcalfe had previously published an edition of the *Legends of the Saints* for the Scottish Text Society, and he added substantial amounts of new material from his research on Older Scots.[34] This final edition of the abridged Jamieson was published in 1910, and appeared in a final reissue in 1927, just four years before the first part of the *SND* was published.

Besides these major revisions and abridgements to Jamieson, a number of authors published smaller lists intended to supplement Jamieson's text. One of these, compiled by J. Montgomery-Fleming, first appeared as a series of columns in the *Glasgow Herald*, which were later published together as *Desultory Notes on Jamieson's Dictionary* in 1899. Dr Andrew Crawfurd, a physician and ballad collector from Lochwinnoch, compiled an extensive 'Eik to Dr. Jamieson's Scottish Dictionary' in the 1820s, but his work was never printed, although the manuscript was bought by Blackie and considered for publication. His manuscript, now in the National Library of Scotland, was subsequently consulted by the editors of the *SND* and is cited in that work.

Other Nineteenth-Century Scots Dictionaries

Although there were no rivals to the full editions of Jamieson until the twentieth century, a few publishers saw a potential market for smaller, pocket Scots dictionaries to compete with the abridged editions of Jamieson. Picken's pocket dictionary, first published in 1818 (see above), continued to sell for several years, and came out in a final, fourth edition in 1827. In the same year, an Edinburgh bookseller published an anonymous *Dictionary of the Scottish Language; Founded upon that of John Jamieson*. The title is misleading, as this dictionary was not in fact based on Jamieson's work, but was a straight reprint of Picken. However, in the mid-nineteenth century, two works appeared which drew almost all of their content directly from Jamieson. Captain Thomas Brown's *Dictionary of the Scottish Language*, published in 1845, was aimed at markets outwith Scotland and promoted itself as a 'useful reference to persons who are perusing the writings of Burns, Ramsay, and Scott, together with other authors, both ancient and modern'. Brown, better known to posterity as a naturalist than a lexicographer, was originally from Perth but had settled in Manchester as Curator of the Natural History Museum. He had previously been commissioned by a Manchester publisher to compile a glossary for Wilson's *Tales of the Borders*. By this date, Jamieson's original *Abridgement* was out of print, and for a short while (until the publication of the second abridged Jamieson the following year), Brown's work was the only available concise dictionary of Scots. Almost all the entries in Brown's dictionary are lifted directly from Jamieson's 1818 *Abridgement* (as were those in his earlier glossary for Wilson's *Tales*), although some definitions have been condensed, and in some the wording is slightly altered. In defining the phrase *to gae backlins*, for example, Jamieson's original definition ('to go with the face turned opposite to the course one takes') becomes 'to walk backwards like a rope-maker'. There is also a scattering of original entries, as for example DEICH ('a precipitous cleft in a mountain'), which Brown had included in his glossary to Wilson's *Tales*. Brown's dictionary omits Jamieson's references to literary sources, as well as his regional labels, making it unclear which of his headwords were in widespread or current use. Compare, for example, his entry for DORTY with Jamieson's original, in which the regional distribution of the senses is specified:

> DORTY, *adj*. 1. Pettish, S. *Sir J. Sinclair*.
> 2. Saucy, malapert, S.
> 3. Applied to a female who is saucy to
> her suitors, S. *Ramsay*.
> 4. Applied to plants, when difficult to
> rear, S.B. Gael. *dorrda*, austere. (Jamieson 1818)

> DORTY, *adj*. 1. Pettish.
> 2. Saucy.
> 3. Applied to females who are saucy to their lovers.
> 4. When flowers or plants are difficult to rear they are
> said to be *Dorty*. (Brown 1845)

Shortly before Brown's dictionary was published, plans were begun for a new and original Scots dictionary to be compiled by the North-East poet and ballad collector Peter Buchan and published by Glasgow University Press. Buchan (who was then living in Glasgow) progressed far enough in his project to produce some sample entries, but his dictionary was never published. As was so often the case with Scots dictionaries, the appearance of a rival publication (either Brown's or the second abridged Jamieson) may well have dampened the publisher's enthusiasm.

As the century progressed, more Scots dictionaries were published to cater to the growing tourist market and interest in Scottish culture sparked by the works of Sir Walter Scott. The *Handbook of the Scottish Language*, published in 1858 under the pseudonym of 'Cleishbotham the Younger' (itself an allusion to one of Scott's fictional characters), was aimed at the non-Scottish reader and announced its intention to 'make familiar to the English scholar or the tourist the nervous force and clearness of the Scottish language'. Although the *Handbook* derived most of its headwords and definitions from Jamieson, it also drew a number of entries from Picken's pocket dictionary. The *Handbook* had an unexpectedly long life, as it was reissued as a pocket Scots dictionary, under the new title of *The Old Scots Tongue*, in 1975.

The growing European interest in Scottish culture, fanned by the popularity of Scott's work on the Continent, also led to the publication of the first 'European' Scots dictionary. In 1826, Robert Motherby, a Scotsman working as a language teacher in Königsberg, published his *Taschen-Wörterbuch des Schottischen Dialekts, or, Pocket Dictionary of the Scottish Idiom*, which claimed on its title page to be 'chiefly calculated to promote the understanding of the works of Sir Walter Scott, Rob. Burns, Allan Ramsay &c'. Motherby defined his headwords in English, but also provided equivalents in German, and his dictionary is therefore the first published work to gloss Scots words in a language other than English or Latin. His entry for *neb*, for example, gives as a definition: 'the nose, the bill of a bird, the point of any thing, *die Nase, der Schnabel, die Spike*'. Being mainly interested in modern, literary Scots, Motherby based most of his headwords and definitions on Picken, rather than on Jamieson's abridged edition, and also drew material from Ramsay's and Burns' poetic glossaries; he may also have been wary of basing his work too closely on Jamieson during the latter's lifetime. Motherby's dictionary also included a selection of proper nouns which feature in Scottish literature, such as *Arthur's Seat* and *Holyrood-house*, and an appendix on Scottish customs. It was successful enough to run to a second edition, which was published in 1828.

Towards the end of the century, Charles Mackay's *Dictionary of Lowland Scotch*, published in 1888, may be described as the first post-Jamieson dictionary of Scots. Although he makes frequent references to Jamieson's work, Mackay's entries are original, and he is careful to cite (and at times take issue with) Jamieson, rather than simply plagiarise or supplement his text. Like Brown and 'Cleishbotham', Mackay aimed his text at the English reader of Scottish literature. Published by Whittakers in London, his dictionary sought to be 'a guide to the better comprehension by English readers of the immortal works of Robert Burns and Walter Scott, and of the beautiful Scottish poetry to be found in the ancient and modern ballads and songs of the "North Countrie"'. A Gaelic scholar who had previously published *The Gaelic Etymology of the Languages of Western*

Europe, Mackay was also an enthusiast for Scots, and opened his dictionary with the following denunciation of current prejudices: 'The Scottish *language*? Yes, most decidedly a language! and not a dialect, as many English people believe.' Mackay's entry style is surprisingly discursive for a small dictionary, and in fact most of the content is taken from an earlier book, *The Poetry and Humour of the Scottish Language*, which Mackay had published in 1882. The headword count of his dictionary (just under 1,500 entries) is consequently quite modest; but several of his entries include etymological notes, and he also provides illustrative quotations from authors such as Burns and Ramsay, and from some more recent works such as *The Laird of Logan*. Mackay's work has the feel of a literary guide or compendium. He supplements his dictionary entries with a lengthy introduction on 'The Scottish Language and its Literary History', and provides an appendix of Scottish proverbs (based on the much earlier list compiled by Allan Ramsay), and a list of major Scottish writers, among whom he lists Jamieson.

Glossaries to literary texts continued to be produced throughout the nineteenth century, especially for new works whose content may not have been captured by either the full or abridged editions of Jamieson. An important example was the glossary published in the first edition of Walter Scott's *The Antiquary* in 1816.[35] Written by Scott himself, the glossary covered the Scots vocabulary of the first three Waverley novels – *Waverley*, *Guy Mannering* and *The Antiquary* – which had been published since 1814. Scott was careful to point out to his readers that his glossary was not intended as a dictionary, and to refer them to Jamieson for further information on particular Scots words, noting, for example, that 'the word CANNY, according to Dr Jamieson, is used in no fewer than eighteen different senses; but, in the following Glossary, we have only ascribed to it four'. His entries are refreshingly concise and accurate ('*Misguggled*. Injudiciously treated'), although occasionally he allowed himself a longer discussion, as in the entry for *Wear the jacket*, which describes an obsolete hunting custom, and many (including the latter) were quoted by Jamieson in his turn when he came to compile the 1825 *Supplement*. Scott also included some proverbial expressions in his glossary, such as *let that flee stick i' the wa'* and *He has nae the sense to ca' the cows out o' a kailyard*, defined as 'signifying that degree of incapacity which unfits a man for the easiest offices of life'. After 1818, of course, Scott's readers could find explanations of his Scots words in either Jamieson's *Abridgement* or later in the full *Supplement*.

Jamieson in the Twenty-First Century

Although Jamieson has now been superseded as the standard reference source for Scots, his *Dictionary* continues to be relevant. In 2008, for the bicentenary of its publication, the complete text of Jamieson's *Dictionary*, including his original 'Dissertation', was digitised and published online (at www.scotsdictionary.com), making his work freely available to a new generation of users. This new resource, combined with the ongoing digitisation of the 1825 *Supplement*, is providing new ways to access the information in Jamieson's text.[36] In particular, the frustrations of earlier users at Jamieson's lack of cross-references can now be set aside through the benefits of electronic searching. In the twenty-first century, lexicographers are still finding valuable information in this key nineteenth-century work.

FOUR

Specialised Word Lists

I. REGIONAL

ISEABAIL MACLEOD
with a section on Ulster by MICHAEL MONTGOMERY

Introduction

Scots speakers have long been aware of the dialect variation in the language and, especially over the last two centuries, many descriptions, comments and lists have brought these distinctions to wider notice. In 1792 Alexander Geddes, a Roman Catholic priest and Biblical scholar from Banffshire, a major but neglected figure of the later Scottish Enlightenment, published an article in the earliest publication of the newly formed Society of Antiquaries of Scotland.[1] Of three poems in the article, one is in English, one in Edinburgh dialect and one 'in the Buchan dialect (which may be called the Scottish Doric)', thus contrasting not only regional distinctions but also urban and rural Scots. The article outlines the need for a 'Scoto-Saxon Lexicon', all the more urgent as Scots loses ground to English, and he recommends that members of the Society of Antiquaries should 'collect the words and phrases that are peculiar to the people among whom they live'. Dialect variation is remarkably well covered in Jamieson's *Dictionary* given the resources at his disposal (see Chapter 3), and Thomas Ruddiman before him had noted at times the North-East Scots of his native Banffshire in his glossary to Douglas in 1710 (see Chapter 2). James Murray's *The Dialect of the Southern Counties of Scotland* (1873) is one of the key accounts of the Scots language and, before treating the southern dialects in detail, he outlined all the Scots dialects, contrasting north and south and grouping them into main and sub-categories; his dialect groups and north-to-south order were later used by the *Scottish National Dictionary* (*SND*) (see Chapter 6).

The north-to-south order is also used in this chapter, which concentrates mainly, but not exclusively, on lists published independently, though there are many unpublished lists and glossaries appended to other works. Since the early nineteenth century, regional dictionaries/glossaries have covered most of the Scots-speaking areas. They range in place from Shetland to Ulster, and in purpose and quality from the scholarly to the jokey. They were compiled for different reasons: some by very remarkable people working in adverse conditions; some to study the language before it disappeared; some to study the dialect's place in a wider sphere; some for specifically educational purposes; some mainly to entertain; many to make people more aware of the language around them; most of them with an element of local patriotism. The commonest aims were neatly encapsulated in the preface to J.S. Angus' *Glossary of the Shetland Dialect* (1914): 'The object which I have in view in publishing this Glossary is to help to preserve what yet remains among us of our old Norn language, and at the same time to give a fair sample of our dialect as it was spoken in the nineteenth century, and on to the present time.'

These lists are not of course all limited to local usage, but often contain words used throughout the Scots-speaking area, and occasionally some shared with English. The proportion of the narrowly local to the more generally used varies, and some compilers state their aims in this respect. George Watson in the *Roxburghshire Word Book* (1923) does not claim to produce 'a complete vocabulary of the Scottish vernacular of Roxburghshire, but rather a WORD-BOOK of its distinctive terms—past and present'. But all illustrate the language of the area at the time. Many of these lists were used as local sources for the *SND* and thus became part of a wider stream of knowledge about the language. Indeed word-collection schemes in the early stages of the *SND* included plans for a series of county word books (see Chapter 6). Only the *Roxburghshire Word Book* came to fruition, but the archive has the skeletons of others.

Shetland

The Northern Isles have produced some of the best in-depth studies of any of the dialects, and indeed the earliest known published regional glossary: a list of Shetland and Orkney words appended to James Wallace's *Description of the Isles of Orkney* of 1693 (see Chapter 3). Early, too, among the more formal publications is Thomas Edmondston's *An Etymological Glossary of the Shetland and Orkney Dialect, with Some Derivations of Names of Places in Shetland* (1866). Edmondston (1825–74) belonged to a landowning family at Buness in Unst.[2] Born in South Carolina, where his father had emigrated in 1799, he came to Shetland as a young man and for a time ran the estate. Owing to ill-health, however, he was unable to take a full part in the work of the estate and took up other interests, including study of the local dialect, of which his wife had the knowledge he lacked. This interest was partly aroused by Prince Louis Lucien Bonaparte when he paid a visit to Unst in 1858 on his dialect-hunting tour of Britain. Edmondston began collecting words and phrases from Shetland and Orkney[3] and the result was his *Glossary*, which was published by the Philological Society, and partly read at two of its meetings in London.

His preface includes a not uncommon gloomy forecast on the language: 'When the present old inhabitants have passed way, most of the old *Norn* will be buried with them.' This has fortunately not been totally fulfilled, but we owe a debt of gratitude to people like Edmondston who saw the dangers ahead and preserved what was still extant in their day, but of which much would disappear with the complexities of modern life. He acknowledges his debt to Jamieson's *Dictionary*, and words from his *Glossary* were in turn included in posthumous editions of Jamieson, first in the abridged version published only a year later.[4] He had contributions from Thomas Barclay (1702–1873), a Shetlander, also from Unst, a minister of the Kirk and Principal of Glasgow University, who had earlier provided Jamieson with Shetland material, especially in a manuscript list of Shetland words (see below and Chapter 3). The Preface has a warm acknowledgement to William Alexander Grant, an eccentric Shetlander who made a collection of Shetland words. He too met Bonaparte, who encouraged him to publish; nothing had appeared by the time of Grant's death in 1865, but in his papers Edmondston found a basic source for his *Glossary*.

The text contains a few phrases, some of them entered (not too helpfully) under the first word. For example, under I:

> I'LL BAKE THEE HAFFITS, I'll give you a box on the side of the head, S.

Where relevant the entries are marked S. for Shetland (as above) or O. for Orkney. He regretted the small number of Orkney words, which was due to a lack of response from possible Orkney correspondents. There are occasional indications of pronunciation, e.g. Skeil (pron. 'skeel'); for some words the vowels are marked with diacritics, but there is no clear indication of their significance. Etymologies are sporadic and predictably not always accurate, mainly making comparisons with Scandinavian languages. Edmondston thus made a useful amateur contribution to dialect studies at a time when there was very little available in the public domain.

James Stout Angus (1830–1927), whose *Glossary* is noted above, was a joiner to trade, and a poet of note in his native dialect. His collection *Echoes from Klingrahool. Poems: Mostly in the Shetland Dialect with a Glossary* appeared in 1898. In 1910 he published *An Etymological Glossary of Some Place-Names in Shetland*, and in 1914 *A Glossary of the Shetland Dialect*, a small book consisting mainly of words and their definitions, some of the latter using vernacular words, for example:

> SANGSTER, *n.* a bruni made of sillik livers and bere bursten.

This is surely far from helpful to many users, though *bruni, sillik* and *bursten* are explained in the text. Some definitions have period touches, as in:

> KOLLI, *n.* the old-fashioned open lamp, which has been superseded by the paraffin lamp.

There are some phrases, as in:

> HŪNS, *n.* the projection at the top of a mast which keeps the shrouds from slipping down: "Noo, Jimi, du man hize him ta da huns".

A few illustrate the concept rather than the word itself:

> SAIN, v.p. to save by invoking Divine protection: 'Gud be near dee, my bairn.'

The book ends with a seven-page list of 'Phrases and Maxims', listed, without explanations, in alphabetical order of the first word. Pronunciation is usually indicated by the use of a complex series of diacritics on the headwords, as in HŪNS, above, indicating an /ʌ/ vowel.

His preface expresses the hope that the book 'may be a means of entertainment to the old and of instruction to the young who may deign to peruse it'. A century after its publication it can still offer both pleasure and knowledge.

The most distinguished of the Northern Isles works is, however, the *Etymological Dictionary of the Norn Language in Shetland* by Jakob Jakobsen, which first appeared in Danish (1908–21). Jakobsen was born in the Faroes in 1864, the son of a bookseller whose shop still exists in Tórshavn. Partly educated in Denmark, he completed a doctorate on the Norn language in Shetland. His studies were influenced by anxiety about the future of his native Faroese: the virtual extinction of Norn in Shetland and Orkney seemed a dire warning as to what might befall Faroese if it did not receive the necessary support. He made an important contribution to its development, especially in written form, in efforts to meet the needs of the modern world.

His work on the *Dictionary* was carried out in the face of constant problems of ill-health and financial insecurity, and only his single-minded determination enabled him to achieve so much before his early death in 1918. We owe the English version of the *Dictionary* (1928–32) to his devoted sister, Anna Horsböl, which she undertook to produce after his death. This daunting task was made somewhat easier by the fact that his collection notes were in English. His work on Shetland place-names was published long after his death[5] and continues to be an invaluable resource for place-name scholars.[6]

AN
ETYMOLOGICAL
DICTIONARY
OF THE
NORN LANGUAGE
IN SHETLAND
BY
JAKOB JAKOBSEN

PART I

LONDON
DAVID NUTT (A. G. BERRY)
SHAFTESBURY AVENUE

COPENHAGEN
VILHELM PRIOR
KOBMAGERGADE

·:1928:·

Title page of *An Etymological Dictionary of the Norn Language in Shetland* by Jakob Jakobsen.

Jakob Jakobsen in Shetland.

Jakobsen's primary aim in his *Dictionary* was to study the limited survival of Norn in the Shetland dialects – part of his plan, never fully realised, to research the remains of Old Norse in the colonies of medieval Norway, comparing his native Faroese with the dialects of Shetland, Orkney, Caithness and the Western Isles. He collected widely throughout the Shetland Islands, noting differences in dialect and in the survival of Norn. Before his first visit to Shetland in 1893, his chief sources of information on the dialect came from Edmondston's *Glossary* and George Stewart's *Shetland Fireside Tales* (1877). He travelled to Shetland via Leith, spending three weeks in Edinburgh. With the help of the Shetland-born antiquarian Gilbert Goudie (who remained a helpful contact), he found in the library of the Museum of Antiquities an interleaved copy of Edmondston's *Glossary* with manuscript additions by Thomas Barclay. This proved a fruitful source.

He travelled on to Lerwick and then to other parts of Shetland, including Foula, Unst, Yell and various parts of the Shetland Mainland, on what proved to be his longest visit. He found younger people easier to question, though less knowledgeable than older members of the community; but the latter often did not understand what Jakobsen was trying to do and he sometimes used younger people to question older informants with their deeper knowledge. Many people helped him, as informants and as consultants, and he often spent considerable time with them, entering into their lives, which gave him the necessary knowledge for definitions which reveal details of Shetland life. His Introduction has warm acknowledgements to many of these people, not least Laurence Williamson of Mid Yell, William Ratter of North Roe and John Irvine, who was a shipbroker in Lerwick. He had considerable support from J.J. Haldane Burgess, a prominent Lerwick poet, novelist and antiquarian, who also helped Jakobsen's sister with the English edition of the *Dictionary*. He also made the acquaintance of James Stout Angus (see above).[7]

Jakobsen made further visits to the islands in 1905 and 1912. Of over 10,000 words he collected, he reckoned that only half were in general use, the rest having a patchy distribution[8] or being limited to one district, sometimes only known and occasionally used by old people. As well as ill-health and financial problem, he was further hampered by the First World War. In 1914 he was offered a post to teach Icelandic at the University of Aberdeen, and it was hoped that this would encourage the study of Scandinavian languages and history there and also help to secure financial support for Jakobsen's researches, possibly from the Carnegie Trust. Alas, the outbreak of the war prevented him from taking up the post, and he died before it ended.

His Introduction includes a detailed description of Shetland speech and its origins, and notes the survival of Norn in the modern dialect, especially in vocabulary. He notes survivals in particular areas of vocabulary, such as 'many old words and phrases relating to the state of the weather, the wind and the sea'. The substitutes which Shetland fisherman use for sea-tabu words are often Norse, as **gjongr** a steed, horse, from ON *gangari*. Changes in meaning from the Norn origin are noted: some words have a more general meaning and others a more restricted one, e.g. *kappi* or *kappisten* a stone used as a sinker for a fishing line, from ON *köppu-steinn* a boulder. There are also some grammatical survivals: the Norn system of inflections has gone, but a few remain in a fossilised form, e.g. *hoga* (pasture), from the accusative form of ON *hagi*.

The phonological complexity of Shetlandic, due to mixed Norn and Scots influences, is outlined in some detail in the Introduction, and pronunciation is given in the text in a fairly narrow form of the International Phonetic Alphabet, allowing for some indication of dialectal differences within Shetland. Geographical restrictions of use are indicated by abbreviations for island names or for parishes of Mainland, with a superscript marking smaller areas, e.g. 'U^{n}. . . . = the northern part of Unst', 'Nm^{g}. = Gunnister in the western part of Northmavine'. The text is enlivened by examples of usage, as in:

> **kav** . . . 4) *to eat greedily, taking large mouthfuls;* to **k.** in (U.; Conn.); de coo ['cow'] is kavin in.

There are also occasional notes on folklore, customs, festivals, as in **Kada** (name of a cow) in a fairy myth, the Kada of Taft. Place-name elements are occasionally given due prominence, as:

> **kamb** '. . . *a sharp-crested mountain ridge* . . . Now only a place-name'

with several examples, some of them now obsolete.

Etymology is, predictably, the core of the *Dictionary* text, wordy and wide-ranging, seeking semantic connections. It was natural to look for Norse origins, and Jakobsen attributed some words to this source which were in fact from Scots or Dutch; though he was aware of the difficulty of working out whether the source of a word was Norn or Norse-influenced Scots, and his careful presentation of the evidence makes his etymologies a good starting point for further research.

All this detail makes for a fairly dense text, and one can criticise the organisation and layout on grounds of clarity. Especially in historical works, it is very easy to lose sight of the needs of the user in the effort to fulfil the basic aim of recording detailed information. In particular, Jakobsen's system of cross-references is chaotic, e.g. **kablin-*tree*** is defined simply as 'see kavlin-tree', which appears as a third variant of **kavl-*tree***. All words beginning with C appear under K, without cross-reference; except for a note at the beginning of K: '(Under this are included some words, anglicised in form, beginning with *c*).' Various signs are used, in his own way, e.g. 'An asterisk (*) before a Shetlandic word denotes that it is obsolete; one before an Old Northern word denotes that it is not attested in the old literature.' The layout is, however, helped by a good bold type for headwords, italic for the basic words of the definitions, and roman for other information (the last two rather the opposite of the usual lexicographical convention for typeface patterns); he notes that 'heavy italics denote that the word is Lowland Scottish in form.'

A century after its first publication, Jakobsen's dictionary continues to be the major reference point for the study of Shetland dialect. Some aspects of it have of course been superseded: research has moved on, not least in etymology and in further collection of data. But it remains an astounding monument to one man's determination and dogged efforts in the face of so many difficulties.

Very different in scale and aim is John J. Graham's *The Shetland Dictionary*, published in several editions, the first in 1979. Graham (1921–2008) was a teacher of English and latterly headmaster of the Anderson High School in Lerwick. He had already published several books including *Grammar and Usage of the*

Shetland Dialect (1952, with T.A. Robertson). He was a lifelong supporter of Shetland language and culture, and indeed helped to arrange for a much-needed reprint of Jakobsen's dictionary in 1985. But he realised that it did not fulfil every need, and his little dictionary aimed to help to nurture the growing interest in the dialect and, in particular, its greater acceptance in schools. It is based on his own dialect, that of central Mainland. The bulk of the dictionary is the Shetland–English section but there is a shorter English–Shetland part, with a note advising checking of Shetland equivalents in the main section. Clear, simple definitions are enlivened by numerous illustrative phrases, some of them quotations. The Introduction begins with a short history of the dialect, the gloomy story ending on a note of optimism at the recent upsurge of interest, to which Graham contributed so staunchly. It ends with some sensible notes on spelling. As well as its print form, the dictionary is available electronically on the website www.shetlanddialect.org.uk.

The Shetlopedia website (http://shetlopedia.com) is another that supports an electronic dictionary,[9] which consists mainly a list of Shetland words with English equivalents. Some illustrative phrases are scattered about, probably stemming from its 'do-it-yourself' character as a wiki: as the dictionary's tagline says, it's 'the free, online, Shetland Dictionary that anyone can edit.'

A newcomer to Shetland lexicography is Alastair and Adaline Christie-Johnston's *Shetland Words: A Dictionary of the Shetland Dialect* (2010). Its copious word list is accompanied not only by definitions but also by some helpful examples of usage, and it ends with several classified lists, including a short English–Shetland list. It is regrettable that so many amateur dictionary-makers venture into etymology without the necessary scholarly knowledge or advice, leading, as in this case, to numerous errors and misconceptions. Northern Isles dialects are a particular minefield in this respect, given that some words of Norse origin may actually have come via Scots, with its many Scandinavian elements (from its Northern Middle English origins); it is indeed possible that some words come from both sources, the one reinforcing the other. It was an interesting idea in this book to distinguish, by blue type, words of Scandinavian origin, but this simply emphasises the problem of oversimplification. To give just one example, *kastik* a cabbage stem seems just as likely to come via Scots *castock* as straight from the ON source, especially since the pronunciation /ˈkastɪk/ is not confined to Shetland.

Orkney

The Orkney Norn by Hugh Marwick is in the same tradition as Jakobsen. Marwick (1881–1965) was born on the Orkney island of Rousay and, owing to family circumstances, he had an early struggle to gain university education. He became a schoolteacher, and from 1914 was headmaster of the Kirkwall Grammar School (then the Burgh School), and later Director of Education for Orkney. He was a founding and a very prominent member of the Orkney Antiquarian Society from its inception in 1922 and he contributed papers on archaeology, history and place-names to its proceedings until its closure in 1939. The origin of place-names was a particular interest and his *Orkney Farm-Names*, published in 1952, is one of the standard works on Orkney place-names.

Published in 1929 by Oxford University Press (at his own expense), his dictionary was based on research carried out earlier for an Edinburgh doctoral thesis. He acknowledged his debt to Jakobsen, whom he held in the deepest respect, though he did not always agree with him. He notes: 'Had he lived to carry out his purpose of a thorough treatment of the Orkney Norn, the present volume would have been largely superfluous.'[10] Like Jakobsen, he did not have the advantage of access to the *SND* and the *Dictionary of the Older Scottish Tongue* (*DOST*); his Scots sources are mainly Jamieson's *Etymological Dictionary of the Scottish Language* and the *English Dialect Dictionary*. He was, however, active in the early years of the preparation of the *SND*, as a member of the Scottish Dialects Committee which did the initial collecting (see Chapter 6). And his acknowledgements include Sir William Craigie, editor of the *DOST*, who read the final proofs. He admits that, in spite of twenty years of collecting, his book is only a start, and he hopes that this 'may quicken interest, and stir others to note down these old Orkney terms that are so swiftly and irrevocably passing out of use. In so doing they will not only advance scholarship but perform an act of patriotic piety as well.'[11]

His introduction has a detailed description of the language of Orkney past and present, the former based on the very limited evidence available. The diminution of Norn in the islands is outlined, but also its limited survival in the modern dialect: 'The speech of Orkney today must be termed Scots, but it is still richly stocked with words that were part and parcel of the Orkney Norn.'[12] As the title implies, the book concentrates on the Norn element and on the whole he omits Scots words, many of which have become current since 'English, or rather Scottish-English (if one may so term it) has been the medium of education in Orkney schools'. They are, however, included '(*a*) because there is good reason to believe they are genuine Norn words in Orkney – unborrowed from Scots, or (*b*) to indicate some peculiar local development of meaning, or (*c*) for the purpose of casting fresh light on their history'.[13] The grammar section of the introduction notes the disappearance of the Norn inflections and distinctions of gender, but also the survival, e.g. of Norse masculine nominative –r as in *chalder* (oyster-catcher), or of the feminine nominative –a as –o, as in *bikko* (bitch). Some Norn survivals are also pointed up in a section on 'Games, Proverbs, Riddles, etc', treated in more depth in an essay in volume 1 of the *Proceedings of the Orkney Antiquarian Society*.

Marwick's text is clearer and easier to follow than Jakobsen's; it is less dense and he makes even better use of clear contrasting typefaces. The punctuation clutter, with many unnecessary commas and colons, was standard in dictionaries at the time. Pronunciation is given in a broader form of the International Phonetic Alphabet than in Jakobsen. Here, too, cross-references are somewhat hit-or-miss: C- forms are under K without cross-reference; CH- words have their own list, with a note: '(Other words beginning with C will be found under K.)'. Etymologies, sometimes discursive, range widely and include place-name information, e.g. **wheel** ('to sit down to rest') from ON *hvíla,* no longer current in Orkney, but Marwick is aware of it in two place-names, one near a churchyard, the other once a resting place for coffins. The etymologies are not limited to Norse origins; e.g. **karr 2** compares northern OE and Gaelic. Some entries are encyclopedic, as **skat(t)** (land tax), which gives considerable detail of types of 'skatt' as well as the land measurements on which they were based. Many entries are enlivened by examples, as **gruggsy** . . . dirty, slatternly, in a mess . . . 'A -- ting o' a wife'. Some cover grammatical points, as **silt** (to hunger) . . . Used both act. and passively – 'I *silted* for . . . &c.', and 'Me mooth was just *silted* for a bit o' fish'. Some words or meanings are labelled geographically, with parish abbreviations, as [Ry.] for Rousay. Some indicate their source, notably Jak. for Jakobsen and E.D.D. for the *English Dialect Dictionary*.

The Orkney dialect has suffered more than its close relative in Shetland in reduction of use in various spheres, and it is therefore fortunate that Marwick was able to collect so much in the early twentieth century. More recently, however, Gregor Lamb has added to the record of Orkney dialect. Then a teacher in Stenness, Orkney Mainland, Lamb did a considerable amount of fieldwork in the 1980s. Appeals on Radio Orkney and in the local newspaper, the *Orcadian,* elicited data, including some considerable collections, and a series of lectures throughout the islands allowed him contact with many of the contributors. He used the information thus accrued to form the *Orkney Wordbook: A Dictionary of the Dialect of Orkney* (1988, 1995). It has an innovative method of indicating the time scale of words: the conventional dagger sign marks obsolete words and meanings, and an asterisk marks those known to be still in wide circulation in the islands; unmarked material is still known, but only in places. Later, with Margaret Flaws, another Orkney teacher, he produced the *Orkney Dictionary* (1996), a small dictionary aimed specifically at schools.

Northern Scots

The pockets of Scots language on the east coast north of the Moray Firth are represented by a few small books. The largest of these areas is of course Caithness with its mixed heritage, looking north to the Norse influences across the Pentland Firth and west to its Gaelic hinterland. Two modest word lists have appeared in recent years In 1992 Iain Sutherland, a prolific author of books on local topics, produced *The Caithness Dictionary*, which in his pessimistic Introduction he describes as 'more as an obituary than anything else'. Approximately fifty pages of the *Dictionary* consist of headwords and brief definitions, without phrases or examples; pronunciation is indicated by the spelling, based on that of 'his own native Wick accent', though there 'were about 50 different accents that I could detect'.

James Miller's *A Caithness Word Book* (2001) has more detail. The introduction includes a history of the dialect and an outline of local pronunciation. Otherwise indication of pronunciation is in the choice of spelling, e.g. a ch-spelling for words where initial /dʒ/ is unvoiced, as **chink** for Scots *jink*. There are some phrases, some clearly quotations; the source of some of these and of many definitions is indicated by initials, whether of books or of people. Etymologies, as often in this type of publication, are not reliable. With the ready availability of the *Dictionary of the Scots Language* (*DSL*) online (see Chapter 7), it will be easier in future to improve these, and also to distinguish between what is narrowly local and what is more widely used.

Easter Ross has pockets of Scots in a formerly Gaelic-speaking area, brought by incomers from various parts of the Lowlands over the centuries. In particular there are (or were) distinctive dialects in the fishing villages of Cromarty and Avoch on the shores of the Black Isle. In the early stages of the *SND*'s word-collecting around 1910, a small printed booklet of Avoch and Cromarty words was used as a questionnaire for the area, understandably concentrating on sea terms.[14] More recently, in 2009, Am Baile, Highland Council's bilingual website on Highland history and culture (www.ambaile.org.uk), produced a booklet, *The Cromarty Fisherfolk Dialect, Dualchainnt Iasgairean Chrombaidh*, using written and oral sources, the latter including the few remaining speakers of the dialect.

North-East

In 1866 Rev. Walter Gregor published *The Dialect of Banffshire with a Glossary of Words not in Jamieson's Scottish Dictionary*. Gregor was a minister of the Kirk, from 1863 to 1895 in Pitsligo, Aberdeenshire, but alongside his pastoral duties he was a man of very wide interests: folklore, archaeology, natural history, literature, language(s) and history. He helped to found the Scottish Text Society and edited three Older Scots texts for it. He was also a founding member of the Folklore Society. His knowledge of languages was wide and, as well as his numerous contributions to *Folklore Journal* and *Folklore*, he wrote articles in French for the publications of the Societé des Traditions Populaires, of which he was a member. He was one of the Scottish contributors to the *EDD*. (One wonders how much time was left for his parish work.)

His glossary should thus be seen as part of a very rich cultural life. Its primary aim is stated in the title: Jamieson's coverage of the North-East was known to be sparser than that of most central areas, and Gregor set out to fill the some of the gaps. He frequently notes where he differs from Jamieson. Given the date of publication, he probably used the 1840–1 edition of Jamieson, and there is

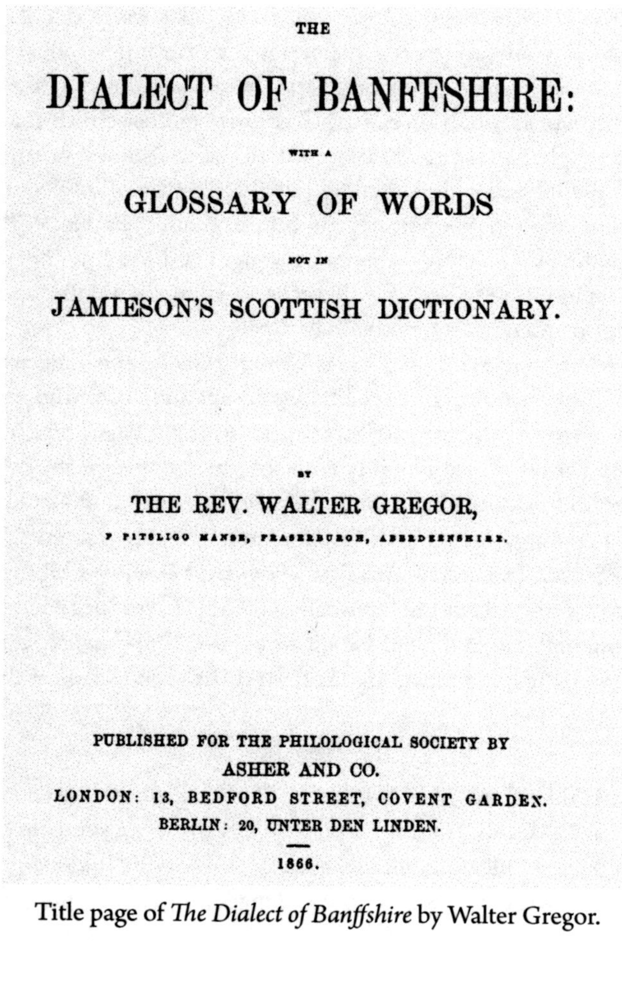
THE

DIALECT OF BANFFSHIRE:

WITH A

GLOSSARY OF WORDS

NOT IN

JAMIESON'S SCOTTISH DICTIONARY.

BY

THE REV. WALTER GREGOR,

F PITSLIGO MANSE, FRASERBURGH, ABERDEENSHIRE.

PUBLISHED FOR THE PHILOLOGICAL SOCIETY BY

ASHER AND CO.

LONDON: 13, BEDFORD STREET, COVENT GARDEN.

BERLIN: 20, UNTER DEN LINDEN.

1866.

Title page of *The Dialect of Banffshire* by Walter Gregor.

evidence that some of his data was included in the much expanded 1880s edition of Jamieson. For example, under *ranter*, Gregor has:

> RANTER, *v.a.*, to do any kind of work in a hurried, careless manner. (See Jamieson under *ranter*).

Jamieson (1880) has:

> To RANTER, *v.a.* ... [3. To do any kind of work in a hurried, careless manner, Banffs.]

The square brackets indicate new material added to this edition.

Like Jamieson, he makes good use of quotations, but his are much less literary, and they give the impression of having been noted down from the current language of the area rather than having been concocted for the purpose, for example:

> LUNNER . . . (4) To labour at an argument; as, "He tried t' prove predesteenation, an' for mair nor twa oors he *lunnert at* it, an' he eynet jist fahr he begood.".

Some are overlong for their purpose:

> FLAP . . . "Fin wee wir gain' i' the feedle (field), we cam upon a liverock's nest, an' *flappit* 'ir sittin' on't"

SND (volume IV) used the latter quotation but shortened it (by omitting the first clause):

> FLAP . . . **II.** *v.* . . . **2.** *tr.* To come upon (a wild animal) by surprise, *sc.* so as to cause it to *flap*.
> Bnff. 1866 Gregor *D. Banff* 48:
> We cam upon a liverock's nest, an' flappit 'ir sittin' on't.

Pronunciation is mainly indicated by the use of a somewhat phonetic spelling. There is an occasional note on pronunciation and the Introduction gives a detailed account of the variations in the four districts into which he divides the county: fishing, lower, middle and upper.

A considerable contribution to North-East Scots (now known as 'the Doric'; see Chapter 6, note 52) has been made by Douglas Kynoch, an Aberdonian who worked in television and radio both in his native city and in Glasgow. His publications include *A Doric Dictionary: Doric–English, English–-Doric* (1996, 2004), a lively and clear presentation of the present-day language of the area. Some words have been culled from literary sources, and these are indicated by a key; for instance, G refers to the Aberdeenshire poet Flora Garry. While mainly a list of words with their equivalents in the other language, it does contain the occasional idiom, for example (under **hotter**):

> **gie a vrang hotter** make a wrong move.

Pronunciation is occasionally indicated, either by the spelling, or by a little note, for example:

> **hunger** *n.* (*ng* pronounced as in singer) hunger; a mean or avaricious person.

A few personal and place-names are included, especially nicknames or local forms of North-East place-names, for example:

> **Gaimrie** *pr.n.* local name for the village of Gardenstown.

Two other recent books, *Buchan Claik* by Peter Buchan and David Toulmin (1989) and *Spikkin Doric* by Norman Harper (2009),[15] both tend toward entertainment rather than instruction, but they have illustrative phrases that reflect their language. William Morrice Wilson's *Speak o' the North-East* (1993) is another reference book on North-East Scots, but of an idiosyncratic kind. It contains neither definitions nor English translations of its contents but consists simply of lists of North-East words and phrases displayed in numerous, quite fine subject categories, such as:

> SPICK ABOOT GABBIE FOWK
> At weemen fowk's aye claikin / gabbin.
> They were knackin awa thegither.

followed by many more examples. It ends with lists of 'BAIRNS' RHYMES', 'PROVERBS', etc. Its purpose is made clear in the Introduction: based on Wilson's own collections and that of members of his family, going back to the nineteenth century, it aims to awaken the memories of speakers of the dialect and to arouse interest in others.

Dundee

The Scots of Dundee has some features particular to itself, not used even in the surrounding Angus countryside, not least in the pronunciation of the vowel in English 'I' or 'try', usually represented by '-eh-', as in 'drehv' for drive, or 'Eh'll treh', as on page 14 of *Dundonian for Beginners* (1990, 2005). This book takes the jokey approach to word lists to considerable lengths but, within its limits, it does give an accurate impression of this unique dialect, especially by indicating pronunciation in a fairly crude phonetic spelling. The author Mick McCluskey is a writer and film-maker and has published other entertaining books about the city. A website (www.dundonianforbeginners.co.uk) gives the text in electronic form, along with other features.

Fife

Two booklets give glimpses of Fife dialect. Mary Murray's *In my Ain Words: An East Neuk Vocabulary* (1982) portrays in some detail the language of this corner of Fife, and in particular that of her native Cellardyke. There is a long section on fishing vocabulary and, predictably, fishing pervades some of the other sections. Pleasantly illustrated, it contains cultural as well as linguistic information, not least on festivals, weddings and funerals. *Fine Ham an' Haddie* (1996), produced by Fife Council Central Area Libraries, has a short list of words and meanings followed by phrases and brief subject sections. The aim is 'to record our local use of words and phrases before they are lost', but they quote James Boswell writing in a similar vein in 1764 (see Chapter 3).

West Lothian

Another little book which deals with a limited area is *Scots Words and their Meanings as Used in West Lothian* (1996, 2008), compiled by the Broadly Scots Group, an informal group of older speakers of the dialect anxious to pass it on to a younger generation. While written in a soberer vein than the Dundee book, it endeavours to present the language in an accessible way, helped by illustrations contributed by local schoolchildren.

Argyll

Traditionally, Argyll is associated with Gaelic rather than Scots, though most of it is Scots-speaking now; the speech of many areas would merit further study for their mixture of Gaelic and Scots influences. One district, South Kintyre, is of particular interest because of the shifting populations of native Highlanders, Lowlanders and Irish who have lived there. As early as the mid-seventeenth century, groups of Lowlanders, from Ayrshire and Renfrewshire, were settled there. The dialect still retains Gaelic elements, although there are few Gaelic speakers left there now. One of the local contributors to the *SND* was Latimer McInnes,[16] who came to Campbeltown as a boy and was immediately struck by the peculiarities of local speech; this led to a lasting enthusiasm for the dialect, and he collected from both oral and the few written sources he could find that were 'strictly faithful to the dialect'. He used the information he collected in articles for the *Campbeltown Courier*, and in 1936 they were reprinted in a booklet, *The Dialect of South Kintyre*, an eccentric mixture of description of the language and its history and a number of rather oddly grouped lists, as well as rare texts in the dialect, including 'Flory Loynachan', a yearning love poem reproduced with a much-needed glossary.

Glasgow

Glossaries of Glasgow speech have been both entertaining and informative, counteracting – though sometimes emphasising – negative attitudes to urban Scots. Among the best is *The Patter* by Michael Munro (1985 and still in print). It was first published at a time when awareness of Glasgow Scots was increasing, due in part to its use in novels such as those of James Kelman and in popular television shows such as *Rab C. Nesbitt* and *Chewin' the Fat*. It was followed by two later versions, *The Patter: Another Blast* (1988) and *The Complete Patter* (1996), where the light-hearted aim is aided by cartoons by John Byrne, well known for his entertaining plays on Glasgow life. Munro seeks 'to reflect the language that I hear and see around me' and he makes no apology for the humour he uses: 'I know from reader reaction that this would be of limited interest without my attempts to amuse in my treatment of the material.' His main tool is his lively illustrative phrases, all reflecting current language, such as:

> **skelf** (a splinter): 'Ah telt ye ye wid get skelfs in yer bum if ye sat on that fence.'; also used figuratively meaning a thin person: 'Imagine Gus bein married tae a wee skelf like her.'

He does however have a section headed 'Yer Auld Patter'; with words referring to outdated concepts, such as **caur** meaning tramcar. There is also a section on rhyming slang, much commoner in urban Scots than generally realised. One example is **paraffin (ile)** meaning style: 'Ye never see Wee Jack gaun oot without a bit a paraffin aboot him.' (The word appears in the *SND* (1968), but its rhyming slang origin was not recognised at the time.) Munro is a commercial lexicographer, working mainly with Collins, and was one of the editors of the *Collins Gem Scots Dictionary* (see Chapter 7).

The Illustrated Glasgow Glossary: Awra Words Awragirra by Albert Mackie (1984) tends more towards entertainment than instruction, using Stanley-Baxter type pronunciation spellings, for instance: '**Assymetry** A burial place such as the Necropolis.'[17]

South-West

The earliest of the regional word lists (of any length) is John Mactaggart's *The Scottish Gallovidian Encyclopedia* (1824) and it is in many ways the most remarkable, in its idiosyncrasy and in its coverage not only of the language of the area, but also of the land, its people and its customs. A native of Kirkcudbrightshire, Mactaggart (1791–1830) was himself an idiosyncratic character. Rejecting school, where he showed early promise in mathematics, he worked on his father's farm for some years, educating himself, especially by reading a copy of the *Encyclopaedia Britannica* which he borrowed from a neighbour. He briefly studied his 'favourite natural classes' at Edinburgh University but, like school education, he found these useless. For some years he moved around Scotland and England, spending some time in London in teaching and journalism. He managed to acquire experience in engineering, for a time with a gas company, and with John Rennie on the Plymouth Breakwater. In 1826 the younger John Rennie recommended him for a post of clerk of works in Canada, on the construction of the Rideau Canal, which connects the Ottawa River with Lake Ontario. He did well but had to return to England because of ill-health. On his return in 1828 he published an insightful account of his time there in *Three Years in Canada*. When he died in 1830, he left several ambitious projects unfulfilled, including a Scottish and a Canadian encyclopedia.

The *Encyclopedia* was published in 1824, but it had a short life as it was withdrawn from publication after complaints from the father of the beautiful 'Miss H—', whose lowlife tastes and loose ways were described in the entry **The Star of Dungyle**. Only a few copies survived, and a reprint of 1876 comprised only 250 copies. Thus this rich mixture of words, people and places has only become widely available in recent reprints.[18] His somewhat rambling and self-deprecating introduction reveals a clear love of Scotland, its people and the Scots language. He is proud to be a '*Scotch peasant* . . . they are not only an honour to the land they live in, but a credit to the whole world, though I, for one, add little to their glory'.

Definitions vary in eccentricity; there is no grammatical information or indication of pronunciation; we do not know how he chose his spellings and there are few variant forms. When they occur, as in KIRSENING OR CRISENING, there is no cross-reference. Etymologies are few and unreliable, e.g.:

> GARDY-VINE . . . It is from the German, "a gin bottle".

The introduction notes that etymologies may be found in Jamieson's dictionary: 'For if he pleases, he may give, if he can, the derivations of my words, caught as flying from the *Peasant's mouth*.' The book should not be judged as a conventional dictionary, but rather as a one-off outpouring of an extraordinary mind. Some entries have considerable detail of all sorts of aspects, and poems abound, used for varied purposes, some of which are probably his, while others may be from traditional sources.

Some of the word entries are simple enough, e.g.:

> **wat**—Not dry.

Others however are embellished:

> **abee**--Alone. *Let me abee* . . . much used by children, and wanton maidens.

His idiosyncratic definitions, however, include a few which are surprisingly modern, using full-sentence definitions:

> **souter'd**– We say a card-player is *souter'd* when he loses all.

Some words are illustrated by literary quotations, but not by a line or two, as in more conventional works. For example:

> **string o' wullgeese**—a string of wild geese; these birds come to us from the Norlan nations in strings.

It is accompanied by eleven stanzas of Standard Habbie (his own?), with 'string' in stanza five, and 'wild geese' in stanza eight.

He includes specifically Scots words in definitions, usually italicised, but sometimes he is unaware that he is using Scots (as we often are even now):

> **sturnill** – An ill turn; a back-set.

It is however the encyclopedic entries (and notes in other entries) which are the most noteworthy aspect of the book; for example, **adder-beads** has four pages of description, a folk tale of its origin, and a long poem: 'This is a very silly Poem, but given here merely because it treats of that mystic subject of the adder-bead.' **Gallowa'** has a description of the land and its people. Local customs are described, as in KIRNS describing 'Harvest sports', an important feature of the agricultural year; in the above-noted KIRSENING, where 'large parties are invited and feasting and fun are the result', a long poem exuberantly describes in particular the gastronomic delights of one such occasion. And there are several vivid accounts of local worthies, such as: '**Geordie Wushart**—An eminent rustic bard', with three pages of description and poems: 'The above poem is tolerable, but had it been more *Scotchified*, I would have liked it better.' Perhaps the most astonishing is the entry for '**Mactaggart**—This is no less a personage than myself'. Its 8½ pages are a useful source of biographical information and include a 24-stanza poem.[19]

In 1988 the Association for Scottish Literary Studies published a very different book, *A Galloway Glossary* by Alastair Riach. In 1942 his interest in the local dialect had been kindled when he spent a short time as a minister in the area. Thirty years later, after many years in the academic world, mainly in Newfoundland, he returned to this interest. With advice from the Linguistic Survey of Scotland and enormous help from his wife Dorothy, he collected data over many years, using a questionnaire and numerous interviews with older speakers. The result was 'a glossary of traditional Galloway dialect words either still in use or remembered as having been used in the life-time of the informants'. Riach has described the project in detail in issues of *Scottish Language* and its predecessor.[20] It is basically a simple word list with definitions, but no pronunciation, etymology or examples of usage; the entries do however have a numbered key to the parishes where the word was recorded, and a letter code for Mactaggart (whose life and book he outlines in the introduction) and S.R. Crockett (1859–1914), a prolific popular novelist from Kirkcudbrightshire. It thus provides a broad picture of the dialect of Galloway in the mid-twentieth century.

A snapshot of a South-West dialect appeared in 1998, though written in the 1920s, in *A Mid-Nithsdale Glossary: Dumfriesshire Dialect Seventy Years ago* by William Scott. First published in the *Transactions of the Dumfriesshire and Galloway Natural History and Antiquarian Society*,[21] Scott's brief list contains numerous examples of usage, some accompanied by proverbs, rhymes or anecdotes. Although highly selective and rather amateurish, it does give glimpses of a particular dialect, not least in the examples, collected over many years. He was partly motivated by the revival of interest in Scots language at the time, feeling that it came too much from 'men of culture who make a study of our language'. To him it was better to record the language of the countryside, not least that of the remote glen where he spent his retirement as an acting postman.

Roxburghshire

George Watson played a role in several of the major dictionary projects of the early twentieth-century (see Chapters 5, 6 and 10), and he used his considerable lexicographic experience to portray his home dialect, long left behind but well remembered, in *The Roxburghshire Word-Book: Being a Record of the Special Vernacular Vocabulary of the County of Roxburgh, with an Appendix of Specimens* (1923). Watson was a dedicated worker, and this book was produced in what time he could spare from his work on the *OED*:

> The vernacular of Roxburghshire is my native speech, which I used in Jedburgh until twenty-six years of age. Being repeatedly struck, in the course of my work on the *Oxford English Dictionary* (since 1907), with the historic value and philological interest of Roxburghshire words, I began some years ago to compile evidence with a view to promote the aims of the Scottish Dialects Committee. But the present

> store of wordlore would have been far from complete, had I not enlisted the sympathies of zealous helpers in each district, to whom I sent innumerable lists of vernacular words methodically extracted from our county's voluminous literature. (Convulsed as the country was by the Great War, this work was carried on with no little difficulty; and the garnering was still prosecuted under much greater disadvantages during two years 'on active service' on the Western Front, 1917–8.)[22]

It may thus be seen as part of the *SND* plan (already mentioned) to create regional word lists, and Watson's role in the early stages of the *SND* was considerable.

He based the text on any local writing he could lay his hands on, as well as on his own knowledge and that of his informants in the different districts, to whom he sent lists of words culled from the literary sources. His introduction notes three main divisions: Tweedside, Teviotdale and Liddesdale. It includes a detailed analysis of pronunciation, using the International Phonetic Alphabet, and the text has the occasional guide to any word that might cause a problem. The entries include etymologies, illustrative phrases and referenced quotations. All this creates a dense and complex text, further complicated by the fact that the references are listed chronologically rather than alphabetically. 'John Halliday', for instance, takes a little time to find, as his date of 1847 places him more or less in the middle of the three-page list of sources. The appended specimens of the dialect noted in the sub-title include extracts from seventeenth-century burgh records and later quotations from literature, in both prose and verse. There is also an appendix of gipsy terms, of particular interest in Roxburghshire, as the main Scottish gipsy settlement was at Kirk Yetholm, in the east of the county near the border. Watson notes the wider use outside the gipsy community of some of these words, such as *barrie, chore* and *deek*; indeed, they are now used much more widely in South-East Scotland.

The book is a very professional and detailed description of the Scots of the county, all the more remarkable for having been compiled at such a distance and alongside demanding professional duties. It is to be regretted that other counties did not receive similar treatment at the time.

Conclusion

I have tried to indicate not only the geographical range of these lists but also the variety of their content and sources. As well as having different aims and purposes, the compilers wrote from very different standpoints. Locals recorded their own dialects, sometimes partly from a distance, often realising the fragility of these forms of speech in the face of a widening modern world with its new methods of communication. Outsiders from their different perspective sometimes saw a value in the dialect that was not obvious to their local informants. While few had lexicographic training, some had scholarly skills in other fields and spent years of study on the dialect. But many were amateurs, often simply noting down the language as they heard it over a period of years, some more for entertainment than for information.

Extant contemporary writing reveals very little of the regional variation of the Older Scots period. After Scots ceased to be the 'language of court and castle', in the anglicising trends of later times it remained strongest among ordinary folk, in their own varieties. From these springs more writing appeared in various dialects, continuing to the present time. In many ways Scots still survives best in its dialects and in the loyalty to them of their speakers.

The Lexicographical Record of Scots in Ulster

(by Michael Montgomery)

To those living in North-East Ireland or South-West Scotland who can see the other side at any of three narrowing points, or to those any farther along the coast aware of sea-bridges of modern or ancient times, the ties between Ulster[23] and the Scottish mainland have for ages been too instinctive for demonstration. And the double helix of Gaelic and Scots that has historically bound the two shores reminds us all of the cultural and linguistic sharing that has gone both ways. So it was that slightly more than four centuries ago, small groups of Scots-speaking Ayrshire folk came to North-East County Down and South-East County Antrim – two bastions of Scots speech in Ulster today.[24] During the seventeenth century the Scots language, Presbyterianism and a range of Scottish traditions were firmly planted in the province, as perhaps 100,000 Lowlanders arrived, mainly from the south-west. Besides Down and Antrim, Scots settled in counties Donegal and (London)Derry, and then spread inland to much of the rest of the province.

The Ulster Plantation (1610–25) also brought many Londoners and English Midlanders to Ulster, a fact with lexicographical implications ever since, as varieties of Scots, English, and Irish came to co-exist, compete with, influence and penetrate one another in one of the most complex linguistic landscapes in the British Isles. Most important, this complexity has meant that, with their local geographical coverages and the mixed nature of material included in them, dictionaries and glossaries have not usually separated Ulster Scots from Ulster English, nor indeed did the *Scottish National Dictionary* entirely do so. Robert Gregg (1963, 1985)[25] used pronunciation to outline a core Ulster Scots territory in four counties, but Scottish lexical elements are both more widely dispersed and often more difficult to isolate than on the mainland of Scotland. In practice, lexicography in Ulster has until quite recently subsumed 'Scots' and 'Scotch' material under 'English', just as linguists in or from Ireland continue to subsume 'Ulster Scots' under 'Irish English'.[26]

For a century and a half, constant collection by amateurs has, unevenly and intermittently, produced a series of glossaries and dictionaries with Ulster Scots material. Without such dedicated individuals, the lexicographical record would be next to non-existent, as institutions have only occasionally provided support toward publication. Unquestionably, the foundational work on Scots in Ulster is William Hugh Patterson's 1880 *A Glossary of Words in Use in the Counties of Antrim and Down*, whose publication in London by the English Dialect Society ensured its wide notice. It became the principal written source from Ireland used by Joseph Wright for his *English Dialect Dictionary*, and far and away the most frequent one for Ulster used by the *SND*, which drew 839 citations from it.[27] About his methodology and sources Patterson says virtually nothing, but his statement that 'in many places it was a difficulty how to spell the words, because I only had them as sounded'[28] implies that he probably did most collecting himself. He provides parts of speech, definitions, and illustrative examples, but no cross-references or etymologies. About currency, he acknowledges that 'some of the words in the accompanying Glossary are now obsolete, and doubtless in a few years a much greater number will have become so'.[29] However, like other pioneering compilations, especially in a region as awash with self-interested antiquarians as was Ulster, Patterson's prediction was not entirely borne out. Many of his entries or examples were incorporated without note into private collections, gaining artificial currency there.

Whether prompted by the notice given to Patterson's work from rural Antrim and Down or otherwise, three other collectors were soon at work in Ulster (in addition to P.W. Joyce in Dublin, who began soliciting word lists from throughout the island in 1892). In a five-instalment 'Glossary of Words in the Ulster Dialect, chiefly used in the Midland and North-Western Counties' (1904–6), John J. Marshall expressed chagrin that 'the great majority of persons writing on this subject seem to think that by Ulster Dialect is meant that form of speech present in Antrim and the Ards district of Down'[30] and presented a compilation fully half as large as Patterson's, mainly from County Tyrone. By 1901 John W. Byers, a Professor of Midwifery at Queen's University, had begun contributing word lists to the Belfast newspaper *The Northern Whig* and earning a reputation as a collector of dialect. In his lifetime his most substantial publication was *Sayings, Proverbs, and Humour of Ulster* (1903), but in time his estate donated to the Ulster Folk and Transport Museum a great wealth of his raw material, including a 1,200-page typescript draft dictionary (*c.*1910). It became the principal and the largest private collection on which the *Concise Ulster Dictionary*[31] was based.

Actually preceding Marshall and Byers was a third collector, Henry Hart in Donegal, the largest county in Ulster and the most linguistically complex because of its sizeable Gaeltacht in the north and west and concentrations of Ulster Scots speakers in the east. A botanist by training, Hart began collecting around 1880 and read a paper on Donegal dialect before the Philological Society in London in 1899, but he died in 1908, with any plans for publication now unknown. Thirty years later under the auspices of Jeremiah Hogan of University College Dublin and the Royal Irish Academy, Michael Traynor assumed editorship of Hart's material, augmenting it greatly by several years of fieldwork, circulating check-lists, and reading all available works by Donegal writers from 1800 to the 1930s. The resulting volume, *The English Dialect of Donegal: A Glossary Incorporating the Collections of H.C. Hart, etc.* (1953), was a work of 350-plus pages that is closer to a historical dictionary than any other volume produced on the English of Ireland to date. This magnificent, little-known work of scholarship dates citations taken from published sources, provides frequent etymologies, and cross-references terms to Dinneen's *Irish–English Dictionary* (1927), the *OED* and the *EDD*. In using the last of these, Traynor became the first person working on Ulster speech to specify when terms had been documented for Scotland. In giving pronunciations in broad phonetics and in dividing senses, its treatment forms an exacting basis for comparison, as the Ulster Dictionary Project was to discover forty years later.

In the 1950s, movement was underway to create an Ulster Folk Museum (later the Ulster Folk and Transport Museum) in County Down. In the early 1950s Angus McIntosh of Edinburgh University had approached G. Brendan Adams to distribute the Scots section of the Linguistic Survey of Scotland lexical questionnaire in parts of Ulster, a task coordinated through the Belfast Naturalists' Field Club for 131 speakers, more than half of whom were in Antrim or Down. Under the auspices of the BNFC and the Ulster Folklife Society, fieldwork continued, as did the gathering of private collections (such as that of Byers), and by 1960 Adams was appointed Dialect Archivist at the museum. When Adams' post became full-time in 1964, a vision to compile a province-wide dialect dictionary began to grow at the museum. Much progress was made quickly, with John Braidwood of Queen's University assuming editorship of the *Ulster Dialect Dictionary* project and being seconded on sabbatical to the museum in 1965 to prepare and organise citation slips.[32] Drawing on this material in a series of five articles on bird names[33] showed the potential for lexicographic treatment of a single semantic field, recording the local and standard English names and the habitats of hundreds of species. Momentum on the *UDD* was short-lived, however, as Braidwood returned to university life and administration, and according to academic lore, even had his only copy of a monograph-length work on bird names go missing at the publisher's. Adams continued to collect folklife material and to prepare citation slips, but the dictionary was to incubate for two decades. Adams died in 1981 and Braidwood in 1988, the latter having remained nominal editor but making little apparent progress even after retiring in the mid-1980s. Even so, the ground was soon to produce a near embarrassment of riches in the province's lexicography,[34] in part growing from the intense interest in local history, folklife, and dialect throughout Ireland (at one point in the mid-1990s the six counties of Northern Ireland had 100 local historical societies or clubs, many of which produced periodicals). In 1990 a school teacher, Rae McIntyre, edited a small volume from the Ulster Scots heartland (*Some Handlin': The Dialect Heritage of North Ulster, Collected by Pupils and Friends of Ballyrashane Primary School*), and in 1991 William O'Kane produced *You Don't Say?: The Tyrone Crystal Book of Ulster Dialect*, covering all of the province and containing many terms of Scottish ancestry. Of much greater scope and significance were two other projects that brought to print decades-long investments of work, both of them through the initiative of a single individual, Philip Robinson, a geographer at the Ulster Folk and Transport Museum who had assumed responsibility for the Ulster Dialect Archive in the mid-1980s. Following consultations with A.J. Aitken in 1988, Robinson laid the groundwork for the Ulster Dictionary Project headquartered at the museum, which secured four years of funding from the Northern Ireland Department of Education to produce the *Concise Ulster Dictionary* (*CUD*). Caroline I. Macafee (see Chapter 7) was appointed editor for the volume, which was to be primarily a dictionary for secondary schools that would meet the objectives of the department's revised 1989 curriculum. Among its objectives were to 'know about some regional differences in accent and dialect and understand that these have been influenced by other parts of Ireland, the UK, and the world' and to 'explore a wide range of colloquial words and expressions which occur in everyday speech in Northern Ireland'.[35] A fifth year of funding enabled the *CUD* to include etymologies (to enhance awareness of historical linguistic diversity) and line illustrations of many animals, implements and other objects. With its timeframe, editorial work was limited to existing collections, with no reading programme for new citations possible or fieldwork to confirm older materials. Early on, it became clear that the Byers and Traynor works alone could furnish the bulk of material, given their comprehensiveness and the lack of overlap between them; other sources, though numerous, could contribute far less. The principal tasks lay in such things as lemmatising spoken forms (including many borrowings from Irish) for which there was no accepted standard English spelling, and crafting scholarly entries accessible to schoolchildren and their teachers. Many editorial issues Macafee faced were precedent-setting, because no comprehensive dialect dictionary for secondary school students was known. *CUD* was published in 1996.

Following publicity about the inception of the Ulster Dictionary Project, a retired secondary schoolmaster from North Belfast, a native of rural north Antrim, ventured to the Folk and Transport Museum to introduce himself and seek advice. This was James Fenton, who for thirty years had been collecting material for what would become the definitive lexicographical work on traditional Ulster Scots, *The Hamely Tongue: A Personal Record of Ulster-Scots in County Antrim* (1995, 2000, 2006). As with so many others who have sought to capture passing traditional speech, Fenton's effort had a modest, serendipitous start:

> About 1960, I think it was, when [my wife] and I were down the country visiting my parents in Ballinaloob, it occurred to me that I was hearing words that I had almost forgotten, words which I realised, because of the way things were changing in the countryside, might be lost. I simply began to write words down as I heard them and as they occurred to me myself.[36]

After showing an early list to a friend and being invited to talk to a folklore group in Larne, Fenton developed an expanding network of contacts which he pursued until he believed that he had gathered all the Ulster Scots material of his native county. Among the dictionary's numerous innovations were an original system of orthography for representing the pronunciation of Ulster Scots words, exhaustive compilations of idioms and collocations, and documentation of currency of nearly every term in the volume for a core group of thirteen older informants dispersed around the county. Fenton circumscribed his area for collection based on pronunciation markers, e.g. whether local speakers said 'toon' and 'braid' rather than 'town' and 'broad'. Within these bounds he pursued leads relentlessly. He began to consider publishing his material only when, on a visit to the museum in 1992, he was invited by Philip Robinson to offer it to the nascent Ulster-Scots Language Society's Ullans Press. After its publication in 1995, the work proved so popular and was scrutinised so thoroughly that it brought a tide of additions, postponing Fenton's quest for exhaustiveness until at least an enlarged second edition could be prepared. This was published in 2000, with 20 per cent more material, and was reissued in 2006.

Fenton's dictionary will remain the point of reference for the Ulster Scots spoken in the first half of the twentieth century, and even somewhat before, for his informants often supplied items known as children from kin of earlier generations. The primary record still to be completed is that of Ulster Scots of the eighteenth and early nineteenth century, when it was the medium of numerous poets and a scattering of other writers, none of which were cited by the *SND*. For some time the Ulster-Scots Language Society has pursued plans for a historical work, and it is to be hoped that the work will be completed in due course and contribute toward completing the lexicographical record of Scots.

II. LEGAL AND TECHNICAL

ISEABAIL MACLEOD

Along with the Church and education, Scots law was one of the three areas of Scottish public life that remained separate at the Treaty of Union in 1707. Its terminology differs considerably from that of the rest of the United Kingdom, based as it is on Roman/civil law rather than on common law, and thus with more Latin terms. It is therefore perhaps surprising that the first general Scots law dictionary on any scale appeared as late as the early nineteenth century. Earlier works, from the sixteenth to the eighteenth century, tended to be circulated in manuscript form to the small number of members of the Scottish legal profession, thus extending the medieval practice of hand-copying longer than in most other fields.[37] One of the exceptions is Sir John Skene's *De Verborum Significatione*, a glossary to a body of medieval laws published in the 1590s; it is discussed in Chapter 1, as one of the earliest examples of Scots lexicography. The glossary in the third (1694) and subsequent editions of Sir George Mackenzie's *The Institutions of the Law of Scotland* is also dealt with in some detail in Chapter 1. A manuscript 'Scots Law-Lexicon' by John Spotswood, dates from the early eighteenth century. Spotswood (or Spottiswoode) was an Edinburgh lawyer, teacher of Scots law and Keeper of the Advocates' Library.

In the nineteenth century the field was dominated by what is familiarly known as *Bell's Dictionary*. The first edition, by Robert Bell, an advocate and lecturer in conveyancing, was published in 1807, its title, *A Dictionary of the Law of Scotland Intended for the Use of the Public at Large, as well as of the Profession*, giving a clear idea of its purpose. It 'goes little into the history, and in no shape into the antiquities of the law',[38] but Skene's *De Verborum Significatione* is added as an appendix. The third edition (1826) was revised and partially expanded by Bell's son William, who continued the expansion in the fourth edition (1838), *Dictionary and Digest of the Law of Scotland*; this was virtually a new work, adding many sources, such as quotations from institutional writers and references to authorities. It formed the basis for editions later in the century entitled *Bell's Dictionary and Digest of the Law of Scotland / Adapted to the Present State of the*

Law and in Great Part Re-written by George Watson. Watson, an advocate, made considerable additions, added in square brackets, as had been done in later editions of Jamieson's *Dictionary* (see Chapter 3).

In 1946 a small book appeared, the *Students' Glossary of Scottish Legal Terms*, by Andrew Dewar Gibb, Regius Professor of Law in the University of Glasgow and a founder member and leader of the Scottish National Party. This fairly basic list was updated in 1982 by A.G.M. Duncan, who taught Scots Law in the University of Edinburgh. The latest edition, *Glossary of Legal Terms* (5th edn, 2009) by Stephen R. O'Rourke, an advocate, is part of the 'Law Basics' series from W. Green, the Scottish legal publisher, now part of Thomson Reuters but still based in Edinburgh. The new title would surely send its original, Scottish Nationalist, author birling in his grave! The omission of *Students'* indicates a widening of the intended market to 'anyone with a general interest or need to be familiar with Scottish legal terms of art'.[39] A list of acronyms and abbreviations is appended. Another small book also provided quick reference, J.A. Beaton's *Scots Law Terms and Expressions* (1982). A selection of current terms, many of which are treated at some length, it is aimed at students and the general public, and it answers some of their queries in non-technical language, but using a rather dull layout.

With the rising importance of European law in all member states, a glossary was included in the *Stair Memorial Encyclopaedia*[40] in 1988, entitled *Glossary: Scottish Legal Terms and Latin Maxims and European Community Legal Terms*. The Scottish section has a generous number of Latin maxims, deemed all the more necessary with the decline in classical studies. While it concentrates on modern terms, it includes a few historical terms that may be encountered in documents, such as *liege poustie* (soundness in mind and body) and *udal tenure* (a landholding system in Orkney and Shetland); and some may have lasted longer than might have been supposed, for example, *stouthrief* (theft with violence) which appeared in an Act as late as 1975. A useful feature is a simple pronunciation key for words such as *multures* (pronounced 'mooters'; grain due to a miller for grinding one's corn) and *spulyie* (pronounced 'spool(y)i'; to remove someone's possessions against his or her will). The (shorter) European section is adapted from an English publication. It was reissued as a separate book in 1992, and a new edition, *Glossary of Scottish and European Union Legal Terms and Latin Phrases* appeared in 2003, with the Scottish and European terms united in one list.

The wealth of Latin terms in Scots law was brought out in John Trayner's *Latin Maxims and Phrases Collected from the Institutional and Other Writers on Scotch Law with Translations and Illustrations* (1861); it aimed to help 'students of law to acquire a knowledge . . . of the Latin law maxims and phrases in common use, a knowledge which in many cases could not be acquired by a mere acquaintance with classical Latin.'[41] (The modern student is unlikely to have even this 'mere acquaintance'.) It went into several editions and was reprinted in 1986, and again in 1993 and 1998, as *Trayner's Latin Maxims*. A shorter book with the same purpose, *Select Scots Law Maxims* by T.J.D. Connolly and J.C. Brown, appeared in 1934. H.L. MacQueen added a useful short list of Latin phrases to his general work for Scots Law students.[42]

Other publications serve as reference books in different ways. The *Digest of the Law of Scotland, with Special Reference to the Office and Duties of a Justice of the Peace*, by Hugh Barclay, Sheriff-Substitute at Perth, first appeared in 1851. A practical handbook in alphabetical order, it covers legal terms, some in considerable detail, and has long entries on various topics, as well as on Acts of Parliament (where relevant to JPs, in full text). It treats at some length subjects such as game, thought to be of practical use to country gentlemen.

Some publications with 'dictionary' in the title are not law dictionaries in the conventional sense. For example *The Decisions of the Court of Session* (1811), generally known as *Morison's Dictionary of Decisions*, is a compilation in forty volumes of reports of cases decided in the Court of Session arranged under alphabetically ordered subject headings. The *Scottish Contemporary Judicial Dictionary of Words and Phrases* (1995) is described by its author W.J. Stewart, a Glasgow solicitor and academic with a strong interest in language and dictionaries, as 'a selected dictionary of the English language (including words and phrases) so far as these words have been interpreted in the Scottish courts',[43] as opposed to a law dictionary dealing specifically with legal terms. He quotes its predecessor, *Dictionary of Words and Phrases Judicially Defined, and Commented on, by the Scottish Supreme Courts*, by A.W. Dalrymple and Andrew Dewar Gibb. Stewart was also the author of *Collins Dictionary of Law*, now available online. It covers European law and that of Commonwealth countries, and thus includes Scots law terms. Other short glossaries of Scottish legal terms will be found on the websites of the Scottish courts (www.scotcourts.gov.uk) and of HM Revenue & Customs (www.hmrc.gov.uk).

Technical Word Lists of Scots

Scots technical and specialist word lists are few and far between; in recent times, technical works have tended to deal with the formal vocabulary shared with English, rather than the local words and expressions used by many practitioners. But there have been several interesting books over the centuries, covering a wide range of subjects and appearing from unexpected sources.

Mining

The mining industry in Scotland has produced two very different glossaries. The *Glossary of Scotch Mining Terms* (1886)[44] by James Barrowman is a fairly conventional list of terms with their definitions and the occasional illustrative phrase. Barrowman (*c.*1849–1933) was a mining engineer, mineral factor on the estate of the duke of Hamilton and later secretary of the Mining Institute of Scotland. He thus had wide experience of Scottish mining. The book contains a few terms limited to one or more areas, and also some obsolete terms – but these have not been marked, as the author considered it would be impossible to do this accurately in all cases. He realised that words might be obsolete in some areas but still be in use elsewhere.

In the 1970s the Manpower Services Commission set up schemes to provide temporary work for the unemployed as a means of helping them back to work. By one such scheme, under the auspices of Fife Colleges, six fieldworkers/editors were employed to collect data on Fife mining, resulting in 1980 in the very professional *Glossary of Mining Terms Used in Fife*, edited by R.D. Kerr. Definitions are backed up by initials of sources, whether of informants or of published sources, the latter notably the *SND* and Barrowman's little book (see above), from which a preliminary list was compiled; this list was then checked and amplified by means of recorded interviews with about eighty miners and ex-miners. The participants were probably not aware that they were documenting an industry that would all but disappear in a very short time, and it is a great pity that similar exercises were not carried out in other mining areas.

Building

Building is an area where some technical terms are used in formal as well as informal registers, with Scots thus extending beyond the vernacular and the narrowly local, for example *rone* (roof gutter) and *astragal* (glazing bar) are used in formal documents as well as in casual conversation. In 1975 appeared a little *Glossary of Scottish Building* by Glen L. Pride, a St Andrews architect, and in the 1990s he updated and expanded it with help from the Scottish National Dictionary Association. With support from the Rutland Press and Historic Scotland, the new book was published in 1996 as the *Dictionary of Scottish Building.* As well as an alphabetical list of terms, some illustrated by the author's own line drawings, it has a classified list, and an essay on Scottish measures by A.C. Simpson and R.D. Connor, authors of *Weights and Measures in Scotland* (2004), the definitive work on the subject.

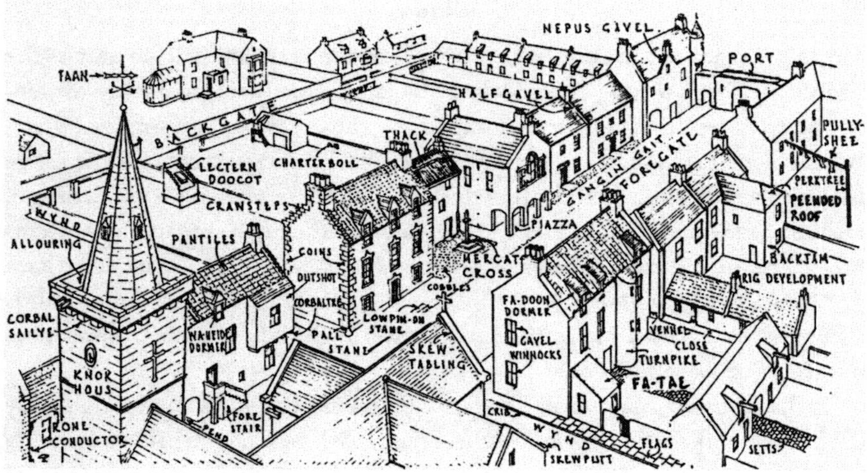

Illustration from the *Dictionary of Scottish Building* by Glen L. Pride.

Agriculture

In the late eighteenth and early nineteenth centuries, the Board of Agriculture published surveys of the agriculture of counties throughout the British Isles, and two of the Scottish volumes have glossaries appended. William Leslie's *General View of the Agriculture in the Counties of Nairn and Moray* (1811) includes a 22-page glossary, with general vocabulary as well as strictly agricultural terms such as *gimmer* (a young ewe), *thets* (horse traces) and *thraw-crook* (an implement for twisting straw into rope). It also contains a few terms from other (related) fields, such as brewing, coopering and textiles. The volume for Ayrshire, William Ayton's *General View of the Agriculture of the County of Ayr* (1811), has a much shorter glossary, with mainly general Scots vocabulary.

More recently, Adam Gray's *Scots Agricultural Glossary* (1997) was compiled partly in response to queries from people researching family history, and it thus includes a considerable amount of historical material, with many legal and administrative terms connected with land ownership and tenure, such as *baron court* and *thirlage* (though not *thirled to the mill* (of tenants, obliged to have corn ground at the landowner's mill)). As well as strictly agricultural terms such as *byre-end* (gable end of a cowshed), *shear* (reap with sickle), it has a rather odd selection of general vocabulary such as *callet* (wench, trollop) and *stumpie* (worn quill pen). Presumably these must have cropped up in documents somewhere or other.

Though not specifically concerned with agriculture, Lawrence R. Burness' *A Scottish Historian's Glossary* (1997) again covers the vocabulary of land and its management, as well as that of legal documents and of trades.

Fishing

Fish, especially the commonest species, tend to have varied vernacular names, some of them indicating different stages of development. Robert Watt of the Marine Laboratory Aberdeen collected a large number of Scottish names, published in 1989 in an interesting booklet, *A Glossary of Scottish Dialect Fish and Trade Names*.[45] It has three sections, the first of which is a classified list grouped by family, with the Scots name, English explanation, and an indication of where these words are used. This reveals the variety of names; for example, twenty-four names for cod, many for different stages, such as:

poullach	half grown fish MF. [= Moray Firth]
Scots Willie	small codling Sh. [= Shetland]

The second section is an alphabetical list of Scots names with English equivalents, and the third lists terms in fish processing, e.g.:

Crail capon	Haddock dried but not split	Fif. [= Fife]

and in fishing methods:

Herring tack	A shoal of Herring	Scot. [= Scotland]

FIVE

Dictionary of the Older Scottish Tongue

MARGARET G. DAREAU

> For all our working lives we have looked on the *Dictionary of the Older Scottish Tongue* as one of the great continuing enterprises of literary and linguistic scholarship.[1]

The *Dictionary of the Older Scottish Tongue* (*DOST*) is a great store of treasures for the researcher or the merely curious. Its twelve volumes offer a unique point of entry into Scottish medieval and Renaissance society, a tangible link with Scotland the nation as it was when it enjoyed full independence. The *DOST* can, in the light of the development throughout the twentieth century of the ideas that underpin it, fairly lay claim to being a building block of modern Scotland; yet its history reveals precarious moments. This account of that history[2] seeks to record these moments, along with the powerful sense of purpose and endeavour that informed the production of the *Dictionary*, and was expressed in the dedication chosen for Volume XII: 'To Scots everywhere, lovers and students of the Scots language and all those who have given freely of their time and knowledge to help achieve the completion of this work.' This dedication expressed the feelings of the staff who were present at the last stage of this momentous endeavour; an attitude that, like so many other things in so long a project, developed over time – although, even at the very beginning, the seed was already there. Four main periods of substantial innovation affecting the text of the published dictionary can be discerned. They have their counterparts in events in the 'external history': the history of funding, publication and academic support. This chapter is an account of how the editors responsible for the dictionary text during these different periods perceived their lexicographical task, the changes they introduced, and how they dealt with external events.

1916–1948

From at least as early as 1916, William Craigie had begun planning a dictionary of Older Scots, to be edited on historical principles, with quotations used to support the definitions, in the style of the *Oxford English Dictionary* (*OED*) (see

Chapter 10). Sir William Alexander Craigie (1867–1957)[3] grew up in Dundee. He studied at St Andrews University and at Oriel College, Oxford. Appointed to the staff of the *OED* in 1897, he became its third editor after Sir James Murray, a fellow Scot, and Henry Bradley in 1901. Having lectured in Scandinavian languages from 1904, he was appointed Rawlinson and Bosworth Professor of Old English at Oxford in 1916. Craigie was an exceptional linguist: a Scots speaker, he also learned some Gaelic from members of his family, and from an early age he studied other languages. He had a particular interest in old and modern Icelandic, which became a lifelong interest. He gave support to the early twentieth-century revival of Frisian, including the setting up of the Frisian Academy in 1938. His scholarly work was not confined to his huge contribution to lexicography; his Icelandic studies included three volumes of specimens of Icelandic rimur (metrical romances, 1952). He wrote widely on English and on Scots, especially Older Scots, and supported many learned societies, not least the Anglo-Norman Text society, which he helped to found in 1938. He was knighted on the completion of the first edition of the *OED* in 1928 and other honours included many honorary degrees and a knight-commandership of the order of the Icelandic Falcon.

In 1919, Craigie read a paper entitled 'New Dictionary Schemes' to the Philological Society in London.[4] He suggested that, following the completion of

Sir William Craigie.

the *OED*, a number of supplementary dictionary projects should be undertaken. These 'period dictionaries' would each be concerned with a discrete chronological period in the history of English. He considered such a series of dictionaries necessary to allow comparisons to be made relating to the changing character of English over the centuries. Specifically mentioned were dictionaries of Old English (OE), Middle English (ME), Early Modern English (EME), and 'the older Scottish'.

He went on to describe the distinctive character of the Scots element in the *OED*:

> But while the older Scottish tongue has thus received very generous treatment in the Dictionary, the appearances it makes there are necessarily scattered and to a great extent subject to accident. At the best, it is submerged in a great mass of earlier, contemporary, and later English with which it has little in common. Considered by itself it is a very definite thing, beginning with the fourteenth century, flourishing as a literary medium from about 1375 to 1600, and maintaining a precarious existence in writing till towards the close of the seventeenth century, when a new period definitely sets in and continues unbroken down to the present day.[5]

Craigie chose to edit the dictionary of Older Scots himself, an indication of his attachment to his Scottish roots, though he spent most of his life furth of Scotland. The *DOST* in its origins was part of his programme for the history of English, as were the dictionaries proposed in his original talk and those added in the published version, the *Dictionary of American English* (*DAE*) and the *SND* (see Chapter 6). He believed that his dictionary of Scots must be restricted to the period up to 1700 but expressed the hope that the editing of the *DOST* and the *SND* would be cooperative and such that comparisons between the earlier and later periods would be facilitated. His plan for the coverage of the *DOST* was to take in the whole word-stock to 1600:

> and to continue the history of the language down to 1700, so far as it does not coincide with the ordinary English usage of that century. Words not found before 1600 are also included when they are not current, or are not used in the same sense, in English of the period, or when they have some special bearing on Scottish history or life. The closing of the record with 1700 rests on the practical ground that after that date few traces of the older literary language remain, and Scottish survives only as a dialect, differing so much both in form and vocabulary from the earlier standard that the two periods can be fully and consistently treated only in separate dictionaries.
>
> The full vocabulary of the language throughout this older period is included, because any attempt to limit it to words or senses entirely or specially Scottish would (in the lack of complete dictionaries of Middle and Early Modern English)

> constantly render selection difficult or arbitrary, and would also fail to exhibit fully the relationship between the languages of Scotland and England during the period when they were most distinct from each other.[6]

This question of the status of Scots post-1700 is central to the question of how to record the word-stock of Scots. Craigie was in no doubt that Scots remained a language only until around 1700, but it was a language to that date even if it had been incorporated into the *OED* as if it were merely a dialect of English. Thereafter, having for the most part no formal function in what was now British society, it remained in existence as a collection of dialects. Later, a different way of seeing this developed. This took into account the fact that, although Scots fell into disuse for formal functions, it was used informally by many sections of society, retaining the character of and recognition as a language, to some extent at least, throughout its dialect areas. This is indicated by the use of the label 'Gen. Sc.' in the *Scottish National Dictionary* (*SND*). It is thus true to say that Scots has never become merely a collection of dialects. Craigie's eventual successor, A.J. Aitken, in the Introduction to the *Concise Scots Dictionary* (*CSD*), expresses the position of all the editors from his time on: 'All of these are attributes of a language rather than a dialect. Manifestly Scots is to be seen as much more than simply another dialect of English.'[7] But Craigie had set the pattern, though the cut-off date of 1600 was less rigorously applied by Aitken. If a word was included as an entry at all, its whole history up to 1700 was covered, and all words originating prior to 1600 were included. Thus only words appearing in the record after 1600 and in every way coinciding with English usage would be considered for exclusion. Later editors included all words evidenced in the *Dictionary*'s citation slips. However, excerpting of seventeenth-century sources was much less full than for earlier centuries and few texts were excerpted after the 1970s, so from Aitken on there is little variation in coverage. Recent research, however, suggests that much more Scots continued to be used in seventeenth-century private materials (letters, etc) than had been realised or was available to the *DOST*. The seventeenth and eighteenth centuries – the centuries of overlap between the Older Scots (OSc) and Modern Scots (ModSc) periods – have been under-researched, although more recently the Corpus of Scottish Correspondence has been compiled by Dr Anneli Meurman-Solin of the University of Helsinki. This corpus of early Scottish epistolary prose texts comprises '500,000 words of running text representing royal, official, and family letters, based on original manuscripts dating from the period 1500–1730 and originating from the various areas of Scotland'.[8]

The basis of the *DOST* corpus lies in the used and unused citation slips belonging to the *OED*. In 1921 Craigie set about expanding this collection. He had the assistance of Isabella Hutchen, his sister-in-law, as a volunteer reader. She continued in this work for twenty-four years until 1945, over which period she excerpted some 300 volumes of printed and manuscript material, as well as organising the excerpting of other volunteers. She also helped with the sub-editing of letters A to F. His wife Jessie, too, was of great assistance in the early stages of the project, and his sister Mary Craigie copied out several major texts, including Andrew of Wyntoun's *Chronicle* and Gilbert Hay's *The Buke of the Law of Armys*, adding many thousands of quotations to the corpus.

In 1925 Craigie became Professor of English at the University of Chicago in order to edit the proposed *DAE*; and although still working on the *OED*, he also made a start on editing the *DOST*. George Watson (1876–1950),[9] a self-educated printer from Jedburgh in the Borders, was appointed in 1907 as assistant to Craigie on the *OED*. At an early age Watson had taken a keen interest in the history and language of his native area, as well as in other subjects, such as astronomy and music. He became a member of the Hawick Archaeological Society, of which James Murray was a founder member. It may thus have been through Murray that his experience was brought to Craigie's attention.[10] He made numerous contributions to the society's *Transactions*, including, in 1916, one of the earliest outlines of Scottish lexicography.[11] He also contributed to the early research for the *Scottish National Dictionary*, not least in his study of his own dialect, the *Roxburghshire Word Book* (see Chapters 4 and 6). Watson worked on the *OED* for many years, continuing to read proofs during active service at the front in the First World War, 'even, on one occasion, in a captured German dugout'.[12] When Craigie left for Chicago, Watson played an increasing role in the later stages of the *OED*, some of which was felt to be beyond his capacities, but his commitment and prodigious hard work were beyond doubt. When he joined Craigie in Chicago in 1927, as well as working on the *DOST*, he continued to work on the *OED* (see Chapter 10) and made a major contribution to the *DAE*. He was given little credit for his prodigious efforts, especially on the last of these projects.[13]

In 1929 the University of Chicago Press made an agreement with Craigie, as a member of the university staff, to publish 'A Dictionary of the Older Scottish Tongue' in 25 parts of 120 pages each, Chicago meeting the cost of publication. This quite limited scale forced Craigie to devise techniques to limit output: 'For reasons of space as well as to indicate the relative importance of the words, those having only a limited currency are printed in smaller type. For the same reason, two methods of presenting the illustrative quotations have been adopted, the briefer form being employed for words which are not of historical importance, or do not differ materially in form or sense from the modern English equivalents.'[14] For instance:

Abak, Aback, *adv.* . . .
Troy-bk. ii. 2835 (sche eschewede sumquhat abak). WYNT. viii. 6771 (gais abak) . . .
HENR. *Fab.* 429 (to fle abak); 1034 (abak he socht).

and for words of greater importance:

Abbasy, Abbacy, *n.* . . . Off byschaprykis, or abbasyis, Or ony kyrkis benyfyis; WYNT. VII. 723. The Abbasys and priourys within the said diocij of Saintandrois; **1469** *Acts* II. 98/1. Mony of al the abbasyis . . . of Scotland war in Inglismennis handis; BELL. *Boece* II. 369.

Craigie's view of the nature of the dictionary differs somewhat from that expressed in the introduction to the dictionary he had spent his life compiling, the *OED*: 'The dictionary, it will be obvious, is not merely a linguistic record. A large number of the words it contains are of historical or legal interest, are intimately connected with the older life of the Scottish nation or are descriptive of the special features of the country. The history of many of these has hitherto been imperfectly traced, and much light is thrown upon them by the fuller evidence here provided.' The Preface to Volume I of the *OED*, however, says: 'The Dictionary of the English Language is not a Cyclopaedia: the Cyclopaedia describes things; the Dictionary explains words, and deals with the description of things only so far as is necessary in order to fix the exact significations and uses of words.' Craigie's proposal for the dictionary of Middle English likewise expresses his wider view of what a historical dictionary might provide: 'A complete dictionary of Middle English would be a work of marvellous richness and interest, not merely in respect of the language but for the light it would throw upon the manners and customs of the time.' Indeed it became clear to the editors of the *DOST* that the only way to understand the meaning of a word in its medieval/Renaissance context is to allow the source materials to convey as full a picture as might be of the use of the word; this is as true of a word still common in the modern language as of some long-obsolete term. The type of short quotation illustrated above is often much less informative than it might have been if a little more context had been included.

Craigie's background in comparative philology may have been the source of another characteristic of his style of editing, his separation of 'words' into a number of separate entries. For instance, there are five separate entries associated with the various phonemic strands of **Gif** *v.* 'to give':

Gef, Geff, *v* [Var, of *geif*, GEFE *v* . . .], **Gefe, Geif, Geyf,** *v.* [Var. of GEVE *v.* with normal Sc. use of *f* for *v.*], **Geve, Gewe,** *v.* [ME. *geve* (14th c.), ON. *gefa* . . .], **Gif, Gyf,** *v.* [ME. *gyf*. . ., OSw. *giva* . . ., varying in vowel from ON. *gefa*] and **Give, Gyve,** *v.,* [ME. *give, gyve,* var. of GEVE *v.,* GIF *v.* In later use prob. adopted from English.].

and

Firlot, *n.* . . . [Var. of FERLOT. See also FORLOT and FURLOT.] 1. The fourth part of a boll . . .; **Ferlot,** *n.* . . . [Reduced from *ferthelot,* 'fourth part'. Cf. FIRLOT and FURLOT.] 1. The fourth part of a boll.; **Furlot(t, Furlet(t,** *n.* . . . [Var. of FIRLOT. Cf. FORLOT, FOURLOT.] 1. A firlot or bushel.; **Fourlet, -lit,** *n.* . . . [Var. of FIRLOT, FORLOT.] A firlot.; **Forlot,** *n.* . . . [Var. of FIRLOT. See also FOURLET, FURLOT.] A firlot.

The foregrounding of these aspects of the word to the extent of numerous separate entries for the 'same word' was, it now seems, given undue importance in the early volumes. It offers a repetitive text that is difficult to negotiate; and, perhaps more importantly, it ignores the distinction between the spelling as such (the written language), how the spelling may be interpreted in terms of pronunciation (the spoken language)[15] and how either of these relates to the etymology. Many of the distinctions thus given prominence may well be no more than the vagaries of spelling (perhaps indicating different pronunciations, perhaps not) rather than suggestive of different etymological sources. To illustrate how this material would have been dealt with at a later date (c.1985), this word was taken as the subject of an essay 'A Re-editing of Gif', compiled by the *DOST* staff and contributed to the volume of essays *The Nuttis Schell,* [16] presented to A.J. Aitken. The re-editing also illustrates the change in scale brought about by Aitken, with much more material available to edit, and a change in attitude whereby assumptions were no longer made about which words were of historical interest, or whether they differed materially from English.

The Craigie entries are not highly detailed, though sufficiently so, considering the scale on which he was expected to work. Ancillary information might be added in small print:

Boll, Bow, *n.*[1] . . . A measure of capacity for grain, . . .
Bolla occurs freq. in Latin documents and acts from 1240 onwards.

From Aitken onwards Latinised examples are illustrated by quotations in square brackets:

Pit(t, . . . *n.*[1] . . . **4.** In *pit and gallows* . . .
[In ferro in fossa et in omnibus aliis libertatibus ad curiam pertinentibus; 1124 *Early Chart.* 43 . . .] Al barounis the quhilkis hes galowys and pyt of thyft alsua sal haf galowys of slachter of men; *Acts* I. 7/2.

Craigie's etymologies, depending on the date of the first Scots example, supply comparative examples from ME or from EME, and occasionally from both; and then from any anterior source or cross-reference as appropriate:

> **Futeball** . . . [Late ME. *fotebal* (1486).] a. The game of football . . . that na man play at the fut ball vnder the payne of iiij^{d}; 1424 *Acts* II. 5/2.

> **Fraction** . . . [e.m.E. and F. *fraction*, L. *fractio*. The sense appears to be peculiar to Scottish.] **a.** A proportional payment . . . for the fraction of three trowps horse . . .; 1658 *Melrose Reg. Rec.* I. 191.

Headword structure has perhaps altered less than any other element. Craigie chose the 'more etymological'[17] of two or more forms as the first headword, thus **Abade** not **Abaid**. This approach continued throughout, so **Stur(e**, **Stuir**, despite the fact that '*stuir*' is the uniquely Scots form. In the final volumes this rule was applied less rigorously; on some particular occasions other criteria were taken into account and the more typically Scottish form comes first, as in **Thirl(l**, **Thrill**, **Thral(l**, or in **Tym(e**, **Tim(e**, the one much more frequently found. Other common and/or phonologically distinct forms are given as secondary headwords. Thereafter, all attested forms are listed. Sometimes unattested forms are used, for instance (**Andeing**,), (**Pultryman**,), (**Weltir**,) to locate related entries together in the strictly alphabetical listing. Brackets are used freely to indicate multiple spellings as economically as possible: for example, **Prof(f)it(t)abil(l**; the final set of brackets is not closed. To the same end, part-words are allowed, even, in some volumes, used as the first headword, e.g. **Proced-**, **Proceiding**, . . . **procead-**, **procid-** . . . **proseding**, **-ynge**.

It would be true to say that Craigie's volumes provided the editorial basis developed and refined by his successors.

1948–1981

In 1948 Adam Jack Aitken was appointed assistant editor. Jack Aitken (1921–1998) grew up in Bonnyrigg, Midlothian. He graduated from the University of Edinburgh with honours in English language and literature in 1947, after serving in the Royal Artillery during the Second World War. Until 1979 he combined work on the *DOST* with teaching Scots language in the Department of English Language of the University of Edinburgh. Along with David Murison (see Chapter 6) he played a key role in establishing the teaching of Scots language and literature in Scottish universities. In their search for solutions to the dictionaries' staffing problems, they recommended the setting up of small separate departments, hoping that these might share staff with the dictionaries.[18] Except for a Department of Scottish Literature in the University of Glasgow, this hope has not yet been realised; but Scottish literature is now more widely taught in the Scottish universities, and Scots language is accepted as an academic subject.

Aitken was a very active consultant to the *Concise Scots Dictionary* (see Chapter 7) and, as well as on lexicography, he wrote numerous articles on Older and Modern Scots, many springing from the need to provide material for teaching purposes. Several were incorporated into the introduction to the *DOST*.[19] He played a key role in many language bodies, notably the Association for Scottish Literary Studies and the Forum for Research in the Languages of Scotland.[20] Aitken was central to the upsurge of interest in Scots from the 1960s; his former students are among the many Scots scholars in the field today, and his influence in Scots language studies continues worldwide more than a decade after his death.

The beginning of this second phase in some ways might more appropriately be dated from 1952, when the organisational structure of the *DOST* changed radically and Aitken was beginning to find his feet as an editor and to prepare for the changes he would make over succeeding years. 1948–52, however, saw the beginnings of these changes, with the appointment of Aitken very definitely moving the *DOST* from being the last lexicographical preoccupation of one remarkable individual to its position, gradually achieved from that point on, as part of the Scottish academic establishment.

A.J. (Jack) Aitken.

Craigie, now living in retirement at Watlington, Oxfordshire, continued to influence the *DOST*. He had, by virtue of his position as Professor of English at the University of Chicago, arranged for the publication of the *DOST* by Chicago University Press on very advantageous terms. However, a number of factors contributed to his finding it impossible to stick to the terms agreed: there was the fact of his working (largely) alone and the difficulty of the material, but principally, the scale to which Craigie was contracted was inadequate. As a consequence, although the *DOST* continued to be published by the University of Chicago Press until as late as 1981, there were a number of crises, the first in 1950. In 1949 Craigie had written to Rollin Hemens, assistant director of the Press, to inform him that it had become clear that the Dictionary could not be completed in twenty-five parts but was likely to run to ten or twelve more. Though Chicago remained fully committed to completion of the *DOST*, Hemens continued to press for a reduction in scale. Craigie could not see this as a viable solution: 'This could not be done by a simple reduction in the scale; it would involve a real change of method which would greatly reduce the value of the Dictionary as a record of the language, while it would not materially lessen the work of preparation.'[21] Hemen's response is extraordinary, in its revelation of the true grimness of the situation, but more importantly in his reaction to it:

> Based on completion of the first approximately ten parts, it then looked as though the total would not be twenty parts, but twice that number, or more. That completely upset the financial arrangements which we had made . . . At times it becomes discouraging and somewhat disheartening to fight for the funds necessary to keep this production and publishing program for the Dictionary going. At one time, only a few years ago, I was instructed to have production stopped . . . I wilfully disregarded those instructions. I believe we should do all that we can to complete publication of the Dictionary . . . I continue to hope that by working together each of us possibly a little more carefully, the production of your Scottish Dictionary can continue.

Ironically, the excessive scale Hemens complained of is itself, in the light of later production, inadequate, and the first two volumes of the *DOST* are badly in need of revision. Nonetheless, Chicago was being pushed well beyond the bounds of what might be expected of a publisher, even one whose primary function was to serve the academic community; particularly since the work in question was one with no immediately apparent connection with American linguistics: the importance of the contribution of Scots to American English, as yet unknown at that date, could not be a factor. (**Wow!** is an irresistible example: it has attained its worldwide popularity through its frequency in contemporary American English; but it is actually of Scottish origin, with attestations from as early as the fifteenth century.) It was, however, the actions of Hemens over this period that assured the survival of the project which, in the hands of a lesser man, would undoubtedly have been terminated by Chicago.

In 1949 Sir William Craigie set down his thoughts on the future of the *DOST*. The situation was summarised in a letter from Professor Angus McIntosh[22] to the Secretary of Edinburgh University, Charles Stewart:

> (1) Sir William Craigie who is now 82 has completed about 2/5ths of the great Dictionary of the Older Scottish Tongue.
>
> (2) Having found that A.J. Aitken (of this University) is proving an excellent Assistant, he seems to be inclined to hand on the task to him. He believes that two or three others will be needed to help him.
>
> (3) He thinks strongly that Edinburgh (where Aitken is at present working) is the ideal place to operate the project. To encourage this, he has bequeathed all his books connected with it to the University if they will make them available to the Dictionary staff.
>
> I should like to make the following comments:–
>
> There are probably numerous technical problems, housing of material, financing, etc. which will need to be solved, but I believe that this is a magnificent opportunity for us to build still further on the linguistic side, and that Craigie is right in thinking Edinburgh is the proper place.[23]

McIntosh was eager to secure the management of the project within the Scottish universities. His perception of the value of the project both to Scotland and to Edinburgh is clear.[24] He worked tirelessly, using all his skills of persuasion and his contacts within the academic world to bring his vision about. In November 1951 the matter was brought before the Scottish Universities' Conference by Edinburgh University. The outcome was that the Scottish universities agreed to give what help they could with accommodation and a modicum of financial support, hoping to raise most of the new funding required to create a viable project from wealthy American foundations. They would take responsibility for the production side if Chicago continued with publication, which, if all went well with fundraising, would no longer be a financial burden. The *DOST* became for external management purposes a department within the University of Edinburgh, under the direction of a committee, the Joint Council for the Scottish Dictionaries (*DOST* and *SND*). This committee from the first included representatives of the old universities of St Andrews, Glasgow, Aberdeen and Edinburgh; and these were joined in 1968 by the new University of Dundee and in 1973 by Stirling. The dictionaries from then on were funded in part by the universities, as a joint project, and in part by a variety of charitable foundations. The

Carnegie Trust for the Universities of Scotland was the principal one, supporting the *DOST* from this date until its completion in 2001. Hopes of major support from other American sources, such as the Ford Foundation, were not realised. A full list of all funders can be found in the preliminary material to Volume XII.[25]

When Craigie died in 1952 at the age of ninety he had succeeded in securing the future of the *DOST* both in terms of his own successor and external academic support. He was a notable scholar in many fields, besides being one of a line of extraordinary Scottish lexicographers; equally extraordinarily, Craigie's editorship of the *DOST* took place in the last part of his life, largely during his retirement. In 1955, when Aitken took over as editor, Hemens consulted C.L. Wrenn, Fellow of Pembroke College and Rawlinson and Bosworth Professor of Anglo-Saxon at Oxford, as to the value of the *DOST*. Chicago was at this time underwriting a small publishing loss. It is perhaps worth quoting some of the points that Professor Wrenn made in his extremely full reply. After expressing approval of the relatively recent integration of the organisation of the *DOST* into the Scottish university system, and praising the staff, including the two newly appointed assistant editors Betty Hill and Hans Meier, he went on to make some general points:

> To some extent the value of the Dictionary will ultimately depend on its association with the Scottish National Dictionary which is also being directed by the same Joint Dictionaries Council and there is an obvious advantage in the two Dictionaries being thus intimately related . . . The Dictionary of the Older Scottish Tongue is a vital companion piece to the Ann Arbor Middle English Dictionary which relies on the existence of the former and has specifically excluded all Scottish material. Here again the importance of either Dictionary depends in some measure on the completion of the other . . . The importance and worth of the Dictionary of the Older Scottish Tongue will continually increase with the fuller development of Scottish studies which is being pursued, for example, by the University of Edinburgh School of Scottish Studies. As these studies come more and more to take their proper place in the picture of N.W. European culture in the Mediaeval and Renaissance periods, it will more fully come to be realised how absolutely indispensable and admirable the Dictionary of the Older Scottish Tongue really is as a working tool.[26]

Aitken began his regime by expanding the Dictionary's corpus. He added many sources to the collection and had others, already excerpted, re-read. His readers included Mary R. Taylor, who read over 160 substantial volumes; A. McKerral, Mrs Janet Pottinger and Dr M.P. Ramsay, who each read between 80 and 100 volumes; A.H. May and his daughter, who were together responsible for excerpting over 70 volumes; and Professor M.L. Anderson, who supplied transcripts of some 50 manuscript volumes and many other smaller pieces, and excerpted several rare sixteenth-century printed grammars. There were many other substantial contributors, and others too who read fewer volumes, contributed quotation material or allowed access to archives.[27] By the time of the publication of Volume III, Aitken had more than doubled the list of sources, adding a further c.700 titles to the c.600 listed in Volumes I and II. His expressed intention was to produce a dictionary that was as complete a record of the language as was within his power. He had transcripts made of a great many inaccessible works, which in some cases remain unique. New material continued to be excerpted throughout, but the period of substantial excerpting ended in 1963. The corpus eventually covered every available printed source and most manuscript sources: cartularies, rentals and tax rolls of religious institutions; parliamentary, treasury, burgh, trade and church records; collections of laws and legal writings; testaments, family papers, account books, inventories; literary prose, history, polemic and poetry; and a miscellany of other material from heraldic tracts to grammars, traditional lore and proverbs[28] – in total, around two million citation slips.

In 1953 Aitken calculated the likely number of parts in the finished Dictionary by a comparison with the size of the *OED*. He reckoned that for **A–Indentit** each of the *DOST*'s parts of 120 pages corresponded to 376 pages of the *OED*. This equation allowed him to calculate that, corresponding to the total of 15,487 pages in the *OED*, the *DOST*, when completed, would have 4,920 pages or 41 parts, as against Craigie's agreement for 25. In fact the *DOST* was completed in 62 parts, amounting to some 8,000 pages, around half the page length of the *OED*.

In the early 1960s Aitken, with Paul Bratley of the Edinburgh University Computing Unit, created the Older Scottish Textual Archive of computer-readable texts, consisting of a number of fifteenth- and sixteenth-century literary texts. Its programmes produced not only concordances, but also alphabetic indexes with word counts and dictionary slips for selected word forms. The programmes were further developed by Neil Hamilton-Smith of the Edinburgh Regional Computing Centre. The results were available for searching on paper and made use of by the editors. The project was early in the history of the use of computers in lexicography and a stepping stone in the developments leading to the electronic age in the late twentieth and early twenty-first centuries.[29]

Aitken also widened the scope of the editing: sense analysis was refined and the illustration of usage came more and more to be considered an important part of an entry. His attitude is outlined in a handwritten note:

> Since many readers consult the dictionary for precise definitions of archaic and Scots words and technical terms, the present editor, commencing with the letter **J**, has departed from Sir William Craigie's cautious and conservative practice in this respect of providing brief, generalised, often portmanteau definitions, and

has aimed at a more elaborate subdivision by usage, with fuller, more precise and more detailed definitions, sometimes accompanied by brief notes of an encyclopaedic nature when the material for this lay to hand. Further, it has been a principle to supply as far as possible those quotations which are most helpful in this direction.[30]

Whereas Craigie limited the scale of entries where Scots seemed to differ little from English and was apparently already fully covered by the *OED*, Aitken widened the scope of the editing. For instance, **Ga** *v.* and **Go** *v.* 'to go', edited by Craigie, cover barely four columns in the *DOST*, in comparison to thirty-five columns of **Go** *v.* in the *OED* (the *DOST* having two columns to the page where the *OED* has three); whereas **Lay** *v.* and **Ly** *v.*, under Aitken, cover fourteen and nine and a half columns respectively, to the *OED*'s twenty-four and thirteen and a half. The refinement of analysis of senses and the fuller illustration of usage both increased the number of citations, and encyclopedic information too added to the length of entries. From this time on the cultural information available in the dictionary entries has been regarded as truly important, indeed as one of the *DOST*'s great glories. **Lord** *n.* (edited by Aitken), for example, runs to thirty-two columns (**Lord** *n.* in the *OED* occupies just short of eight), with thirty-four main senses illustrating Scottish usage of the word in immense detail (it is, in a medieval society, an immensely important word):

> **Lord**, *n.* . . .
> **I.** . . . **7.** *plur.* The nobles or lay magnates of a kingdom (commonly, the Scottish kingdom) . . .
> Also **b**. applied to specific sections or factions of the nobles, *Lordis of (the) Congregatioun*, . . .
> **8.** *spec.* A 'lord of Parliament'.
> **a.** A member of the class of great landowners, as dukes, earls . . .
> **b.** Further *spec.* An important baron below the rank of earl (and thus originally entitled only 'lord' as in sense 21) who was among those whose attendance at Parliament . . . Such 'lords' thus constituted a new rank of the titled nobility of Scotland, below the earls but above the lesser barons or 'lairds' . . .
> **II.** . . . Applied . . . to members of Parliament or General Council or of the sovereign's Council . . .
> In these senses frequently embracing persons who were not 'lords' in many of the other senses, such as commissioners for the burghs in Parliament, or Ordinary Lords of Session as well as members of the Privy Council who were not noblemen.

Aitken was equally keen to illustrate linguistic aspects, phonological and dialectal relationships, for example:

> **Lippie, Lepy, Leipie,** *n.* . . . [Origin doubtful.
> Appar. confined to the northern and eastern half of the country, from Caithness to the Forth. Also in the mod. dial. of the same region, in the form *lippie* (occas. *leppie*) only. (Cf. also LEIP.)
> Perh. a dimin. of ME. *lepe, leep,* (north.) *leippe* (1495–6), e.m.E. *leap,* OE. *léap,* a (large) basket, a basket for catching or keeping fish, and (in Sussex) a measure, given as two-thirds or as half of a bushel. There appears however to be no certain trace of the simple *lepe* (= basket) in Scots, though it was appar. in common use in north. ME. On this theory the form *lepy, leipie* would be the orig. one and the surviving *lippie* would represent a variant of this with late vowel-shortening.]

or etymological relationships:

> **Loch, Louch(e,** *n.* . . . [Gael. (Sc. and Irish) *loch.* Cf. also LOW n. (and LOWIS n. pl.).
> ONorthumb. (Lindisf. Gosp.) has *luh,* perh. of Welsh rather than Irish origin, rendering L. *fretum* and *stagnum,* but on phonological grounds this can hardly be the source of the Scottish word. On the other hand it is possible that the history of the latter partly coincides with north midl. and north. ME. *louh, lough* (Manning), *lowgh, logh* (north., c 1400), and e.m.E. and mod. Eng. and mod. north. Eng. dial. and place-names *lough(e* (also *lowf*), which also seems difficult to derive from the recorded ONorthumb. form and is perh. more likely to be from the Irish. If so, the Scottish word was doubtless re-inforced, if not re-introduced, from the local Gaelic. Similarly Anglo-Irish has *logh, lough,* reinforced from Irish Gaelic, from 1512.]

And in terms of layout, Aitken systematised the presentation of material, supplying comparative examples from both ME and EModE, where they were available, and organised information intricately according to its closeness in location and dating to the Scots:

> **Mister,** *n.* . . . [North. and midl. ME. *mister(e* (Cursor M.), *myster, -re, mester* (14th c.), *-ire, maistur* (*c.* 1400), need, necessity, but after the fifteenth c. appar. only Sc., ME. and e.m.E. *mister, mystere,* mestier, early ME. *mester* (Ancr. R.), craft, employment, art, OF. *mestier, mester* (F. *métier*), (1) service, office, occupation, (2) instrument, made-up article, (3) need, necessity.] . . .

The density of detail, given the complexity of the etymology, is typical.

The development of the infrastructure for funding and academic support from 1952 led to an expansion of the project as a whole. At all times after the appointment of Aitken, there was a staff of assistant editors and clerical or editorial assistants, varying in numbers from a minimum of one (Aitken) and a part-time clerical assistant in the 1950s to a maximum of three or four assistant or junior assistant editors and two clerical or editorial assistants in the early 1970s. Aitken remained sole editor until 1973, when he was joined by Dr James A.C. Stevenson. Stevenson (1917–1992) grew up in Edinburgh and graduated from Edinburgh University, with honours in English language and literature. He served in North Africa in the 8th Army during the Second World War. He taught English in schools in Scotland and in universities in Egypt and Pakistan before joining the *DOST* in 1966 as assistant editor; he became associate editor in 1970 and editor jointly with Aitken in 1973.[31] He succeeded Aitken as editor-in-chief in 1983. Throughout the 1960s and 1970s, under their leadership, the pressure to produce copy that Craigie had suffered became less intense, and the project became much more a matter simply of scholarship.

Stevenson's description of the scope of the Dictionary took a step beyond that of Aitken: 'But the aim of the *DOST* is not simply or even chiefly the definition of unfamiliar or obsolete terms. It could rather be described without undue pretension as an attempt to provide a key to the whole range of Scottish culture from 1200–1700. There is an abundance of useful and curious information, much of it not available elsewhere, on every aspect of life in these five centuries.'[32]

Stevenson's definitions remained similar in level of information to Aitken's, but he divided the text into copious paragraphs (indicated by (1), (2) etc) illustrating syntactic or semantic features. For example:

> **Pint, Pynt**(**e**, *n*. . . . A pint, in the usual senses and
> collocations.
> **a**. The measure of capacity for, chiefly, liquids; this
> amount (of) the liquid, or other substance, specified. . . .
> (1) Et j pynt vini; . . . Foure pynts tar . . . For 17 pynts acavite . . .
> (2) . . . For a pynt now mon [we] pay . . . Ande ilk pynt . . .
> For ij s. the pynt . . .
> (3) That euerie salmond barrel . . . sall contene twelf gallounis
> of the Striuiling pynt; . . . The pynt of Stirling . . .
> The Scottish pinte . . .

These paragraphs are not, generally speaking, individually defined; but the analysis allowed scope for many more quotations, as each paragraph was allowed a maximum of twelve quotations but there was no limit on the number of paragraphs. The fineness of the grammatical analysis contrasts sharply with the semantic information offered. Some further information is offered in small print as the definitions of the sub-senses, but nowhere are we told the capacity of a pint, that it is equal to one eighth of a gallon, for instance. Knowledge of the modern word is assumed to be sufficient. Contrast this with Dareau's entry for **Stane,** *n.*:

> **Stan(e n.** . . . **III. 26** A unit of weight for goods in bulk, considered as comprising a set number of pounds (latterly 16), the multiplier depending to some extent on the period and the type of produce weighed, which also determined the appropriate pound unit. First defined in the Assize attributed to David I as 15 pounds, where the pound is 15 Cologne ounces, with the stone of wax at 8 pounds. . . . The stone of the 1426 Assize is of 16 merchant or 'Scots' pounds . . . for an interpretation of the legislation see R. D. Connor & A. D. C. Simpson, The Weights and Measures of Scotland (forthcoming, 1998). The trone stone, or Lanark stone, of 16 trone pounds, was the weight unit of internal trade, equivalent to 20 Scots pounds to 1563 and subsequently 20 trois pounds.

The Joint Council had hoped that both dictionaries would be finished in the 1970s, but only the *SND* came to completion in that decade. In 1980 the academic funders threatened withdrawal of support if a firm end date was not established. The Conference of the Scottish Universities' Courts said that it would be unlikely that the universities would continue to support the Dictionary after 1988, a year after the Carnegie Trust had said it would terminate its financial support. Without target dates and time restrictions editing was taking too long. The calculations of Aitken and Stevenson proved that this date could not be met following the traditional method. Lexicographers will recognise the scenario: engaged in the compilation of a massive work such as the *DOST*, the *Middle English Dictionary* (*MED*) or the *OED*, the editor has only a limited number of chances to get each entry right.[33] Aitken was a perfectionist and had over many years imbued the dictionary enterprise with his own need to go the extra mile for perfection, impossible though it might be. It is that which, in large part, has made the *DOST* the monument to scholarship that it is: that, and Aitken's own intellectual abilities and his success in relaying his credo to his successors. Any criticism of his methodology or any other aspect of his work pales into insignificance in comparison with what he achieved not only for the *DOST* but for Scots scholarship in his long and productive life. Above all, he set Scots scholarship on its feet; *nous autres* merely follow in his footsteps.

Aitken and Stevenson devised a plan to finish the *DOST* by means of what they called the '*OED*-Dependent Method'. This consisted of basing dictionary entries solely on the equivalent entry in the *OED*:

> We accept OED's sense-analysis and definitions as given and simply assign our quotations as best we can to their places in the OED scheme, providing our own definitions only for those additional words and applications which we cannot fit into the OED scheme . . . And we propose to offer no etymological note and to undertake no research to ensure the precision of definitions or to provide encyclopaedic notes and comments beyond those already in OED. But we would continue to provide exemplification at least as copious as now of all words, senses (according to OED's analysis), forms and collocations, with all their distributions.[34]

At this point, Chicago withdrew as publisher: the scale of the Dictionary had doubled, at least, compared with the 1929 agreement, and adequate funding had never materialised. The Joint Council met in emergency session to address the question of the future of the *DOST*. A panel of lexicographers and scholars of Older Scots, asked to recommend a way forward, reported that the *OED*-Dependent method of editing was very much second best.

The proposal was also aired (brilliantly) by Aitken at the Third International Conference on Scottish Language and Literature (Medieval and Renaissance), held in Stirling in July 1981. The conference delegates were the scholars most reliant on the *DOST* and therefore most aware of the losses they would sustain were it to be completed according to the *OED*-Dependent method. The report on the front page of the *Scotsman* the following Saturday read:

> Sixty experts from all over the world have signed an open letter condemning the possibility of cuts in the project which, they say, would amount to 'an appalling blot on Scottish scholarship'. The letter states: 'For all our working lives we have looked on the *Dictionary of the Older Scottish Tongue* as one of the great continuing enterprises of literary and linguistic scholarship and have looked forward to its completion according to its present plan and format as a major contribution to the cultural life of Scotland and the world.'[35]

The outcry thus unleashed, as Aitken had fully expected,[36] was sufficient to ensure a return to autonomous editing but with no guarantee that funding would continue beyond the working lives of the current staff. These consisted of two senior editors (Aitken and Stevenson) of similar age and nearing retirement, a recently appointed assistant editor (Harry Watson), and an editorial assistant (Eileen Finlayson) in post since 1975. All new (or returning) staff from this time on were employed on annually renewable contracts. In 1984 the Friends of the

Dictionary of the Older Scottish Tongue was set up to assist with fundraising.[37]

By February 1983, Aberdeen University Press (AUP), by then part of Robert Maxwell's empire, had taken over publication. AUP installed a microcomputer in the *DOST* offices, and from then until 1994 edited copy with a minimal level of tagging was prepared for printing in house, and recorded for the first time in electronic form. That, however, was the sum of the editorial changes introduced as a result of the crisis. In the light of experience since 1994, perhaps Aitken won too easy a victory. There was no incentive to consider the sorts of new management structures that might have accelerated output without loss of quality.

1981–1994

After the retirement of Stevenson and Aitken, in 1985 and 1986 respectively, Harry Watson became editor-in-chief. Watson (1946–) grew up in Cellardyke, Fife and graduated from the University of Edinburgh, with honours in English language and literature. He spent some years teaching English in Sweden and Germany before joining the *DOST* as junior assistant editor in 1979. He became assistant editor in 1982 and editor in 1983. From 1988 he was designated senior editor and director, and administrative director in 1997. Marace Dareau rejoined the editorial team in 1984 after four years' absence working on the *Concise Scots Dictionary* (*CSD*) (see Chapter 7). Margaret Grace Dareau (1944–) grew up

DOST office, 27 George Square, Edinburgh, 1980s.

in Dumfriesshire, right on the dialect boundary between the Borders and the South-West. She graduated from Edinburgh University, with honours in English language and literature. She joined the *DOST* as junior assistant editor in 1968 and became assistant editor in 1970. Her career was interrupted in 1973 and again in 1979 by the arrival of her children. She became editor in 1984, senior editor in 1988 and editorial director in 1997. After 1988, Watson dealt with day-to-day administration and Dareau took over responsibility for editorial policy.

Editorial methodology was influenced by Dareau's experience of the *CSD*. Its senior editor, Iseabail Macleod, experienced in the publication of modern dictionaries, had introduced the concept of the user to the mainly academic editors of *CSD*. It was Macleod's strongly held view that the ultimate test of a dictionary is that it satisfy the needs of its user group. Dareau took this very much to heart in the editing of *DOST* that came after her return in 1984. Aitken had seen the Dictionary, essentially, as a record of the language, but Dareau took the view that it might be more useful to all its users if the centrality of the language in society was treated as one of the fundamentally important elements of the editing process. Craigie valued what the language might reveal of the workings of an earlier society; specifically Scots material is thoroughly covered in the first two volumes of *DOST*, but his overall coverage is inadequate. Aitken, with much more material to work with, included much more detail but tended to stick rather closely to the analysis offered in the *OED*. Comparison with English has always (rightly) been seen as important; however, if the process of constructing an entry relies too heavily at the outset on the parameters laid down in the *OED* entry for English, the opportunity to reveal the natural development of the word by a consideration of the Scots material on its own may be lost and with it, in the process, many subtleties of Scots usage. So it was not just a question of what was clearly and obviously Scots. Craigie said the same, that Scots was 'scattered' throughout English senses in the *OED* or 'submerged in a great mass of earlier, contemporary, and later English with which it has little in common.'[38] Along with this structural element goes the question of the amount of information (apparently) not strictly needed to make clear the meaning of the word – the 'encyclopedic' element. It is a matter both of what is organised into senses and definitions, and how it is arranged. From around the beginning of **S**, while not neglecting the essentials of etymology and linguistic history, the functioning of the word in society was given as much importance as its purely linguistic nature. Dr Hans Meier, himself formerly a member of the *DOST* editorial staff, had said in the 1960s: 'Under Aitken, *DOST* has become more fully than ever an encyclopaedia of older Scottish culture and a first class reference book for Scottish historiography.'[39]

Aitken, however, still described what he was doing in terms primarily of linguistic analysis:

> These more or less linguistic considerations are our main business as editors of the *DOST*. But since they are achieved by a display of quotations from the original texts we cannot but also provide incidentally, though the quotations, information about the things or concepts denoted by the words treated . . . From the letter H we have tried to make our definitions of precise terms of whatever specialty as accurate as possible and have added a large number of descriptive notes to technical terms of this sort. Naturally this often requires research in secondary literature . . . Much of the results of this is, among dictionaries, unique to *DOST*.[40]

The change Dareau made was to foreground the view that the aim of historical lexicography is to provide the most useful tool possible for all those likely to be users of the *Dictionary*, historians as much as linguists. For example, **Service** *n.* is defined firstly in its relation to the social order whereby land is held in return for service to a superior, unlike the *OED* where the first two main definitions are '**I.** The condition of being a servant; the fact of serving a master' and '**II.** The work or duty of a servant; the action of serving a master', a purely linguistic distinction. This was the style followed by Aitken in his original editing in the early 1980s; in his entry all the references to the feudal aspects of the word were scattered throughout the entry (as Craigie had described). During her revision of the microprocessed copy, Dareau recast this entry giving the first senses as: '**1.** The condition of serving a superior in a feudal relationship . . . **2.** The duty in return for which land might be held of a superior, chiefly military service . . . **3.** The condition of serving another or being in his employment . . . **4.** The action of serving another . . .', focusing on the culture of fifteenth- and sixteenth-century Scotland rather than on that of nineteenth- and early twentieth-century Britain.

The 1980s and 1990s also saw the elimination of Craigie's style of separating entries on the basis of spelling differences. This style was time-consuming to produce, with all the material being edited together as a single entry then split into the desired number of variant entries, each sense being cross-referred to the main entry. Not only does it take longer to edit but, because there are more divisions, more quotations tend to be included than is strictly necessary, so more checking, keying and proofreading has to be done, and such entries are difficult to consult.[41] Above all, such divisions are liable to obscure the subtler levels of semantic variation, wherein much that is characteristic of Scots is to be found. Dareau and Watson agreed that all spelling forms that could be designated as variants would be included in one entry: '**sall**' and '**schall**'; '**speche**' and '**speke**'; '**ta**' and '**tak**'; '**to**' and '**till**'; '**tresaurar**', '**thresaurar**' and '**thessaurar**'; and '**waw**', '**wall**' and '**waiff**'. The etymologies of these entries all contain a full explanation of the likely route of derivation and any further influences on that derivation.

For instance the '*speke*' variant in the entry **Spech(e** *n.* may be taken to derive from the northern English form, but influence from the verb is also likely. This produced entries where all relevant information for each semantically defined unit is found at a single site, allowing easy comparison of how the forms relate to each other; different spellings are located in separate paragraphs rather than in separate entries. An interesting example occurs in the *DOST* entry **Sir(e** *n.*, where all of the Scots material equivalent to that to be found in the *OED* entries **sire** and **sir** is included, encompassing all of the forms '*sire*', '*sir*' and '*schir*'. This allows the user to see both the development of the meaning and how the spelling forms are distributed in terms of the meanings. On the other hand, since '*sir*' and '*sire*' occur as separate words, differently spelled (since spelling is now fixed, in English at least) and differently pronounced, in modern English, it makes sense for the *OED* to determine the word division by this shortening of the vowel before a name.

It may seem strange to determine the entry divisions like this and, especially, in an example like **To, Till** where 'to' and 'till' are not etymologically related, but function in Older Scots as if they were the same 'word'. The *DOST* is a historical dictionary, not an etymological one, and since it deals only with medieval and Renaissance material it does not have to take the modern language into account; indeed it should not be influenced by the modern language – that would be anachronistic. Each dictionary orders its material in terms of its own criteria and to satisfy the needs of its user group; so in a sense there is no fixed dictionary entity called a 'word', there is an entry of which the structure depends on the nature of the dictionary. The new edition of *CSD*, for instance, will have an entry for **tae** 'to' and one for **till** 'to' not only because their senses and usage has changed since 1700 but because the user group of a modern, concise dictionary specifically aimed at the general public would expect such a differentiation. It is also true to say that from **T** on the *DOST* was produced under a highly circumscribed regime. The time taken for decisions about how to arrange the entries for the citation slips of '*tresaurar*', '*thresaurar*' and '*thessaurar*,' for example, was time taken from more essential editing. Taking the route that etymology is the determining factor suggests two entries containing those deriving from Latin *thesaurarius* and those from Old French *tresor(i)er*. But do the *thr-* forms go in the entry derived from Latin or the one derived from French? This seemed a trivial use of time when no difference in meaning is detectable in OSc. A single entry seemed much more satisfactory:

> **Thesaurar(e, -er(e, Tresaurar, Thresaurar,** *n.* [ME and e.m.E. *tresurer* (c1290), *thresorer* (1292), . . . *thesuerer* (1544), . . . *treasurer* (a1586), OF *tresor(i)er,* late L. *thesaurarius.*] **1.** A treasurer. . . . **a.** Thesaurare; WYNT. VIII 2103 (W) (see (*b*) below). . . . (*b*) . . . Hw of Karsyngame That that tyme wes trezorare [*C.* tressourare, *W.* thesaurare] . . . WYNT VIII 2145. . . . (*d*) Thresaurar; 1519 *Montgomery Mem.* 90.

The etymological section was also simplified into a chronological record of the material in related languages that might be of relevance to the source or development of the word and ordered in a (more or less) standard fashion:[42] ME, EModE, OE, ON, MDu., MLG, or F., L., or other anterior source, e.g.: '**Tabil(l, Table, Taffel(l,** . . . [ME and e.m.E. *table* (1175), . . . OF *table,* L. *tabula,* MDu., MLG *tafele* . . .]'. If there was reason to think that the Scots word had come directly from a language other than English, the evidence from that language would come first, e.g.: '**Tartan(e,** . . . [OF *tiretaine* (1247) a sort of cloth half wool, half some other yarn (Godefroy Comp.), stuff of which the weft is wool and the warp linen or cotton (Wartburg), *tridaine* (?14th c., toile de fil et de coton bleu et rouge), *tyretenne, tirtaine* (1449–1501), . . . Cf. also ME *tartaryn* (1343), *tartryn* (1339), *tartyn* (1454, E.E. Wills 133/2 "thė testour & canape ther-to palid tartyn white and rede": MED suggests ?read *tartaryn*), . . . Cf. TARTAR n.].'

1994–2001

The outcome of a review of the structure and working practices of the *DOST,* initiated by Dareau and brought about by Professor Alexander Fenton, honorary secretary and treasurer of the Friends of the *Dictionary of the Older Scottish Tongue,* and Dr Victor Skretkowicz, the chairman of the Joint Council, was that funding might be easier to obtain if a completion date of 2000 were to be guaranteed. The editors, Dareau, Watson and Lorna Pike, agreed to investigate whether completion according to this timescale was feasible; with the proviso, agreed by staff, review board, and project manager alike, that the volumes of the *DOST* published thereafter would maintain the quality of those already published. Dareau and Watson had been joined by Kathryn Lorna Pike (1956–) who grew up in Fort William. She graduated from Edinburgh University with honours in English language and linguistics. She was an editor of *CSD* (1979–84), and was appointed editorial assistant on the *DOST* in 1984, assistant editor in 1987 and editor in 1990. Pike is now project coordinator of *Faclair na Gàidhlig,* the historical dictionary of Scottish Gaelic (see Chapter 9).

The task facing the staff of the *DOST* in 1994 was to complete the editing and proofreading of a quarter of the dictionary, T–Z, as well as the pre-keying, tidying

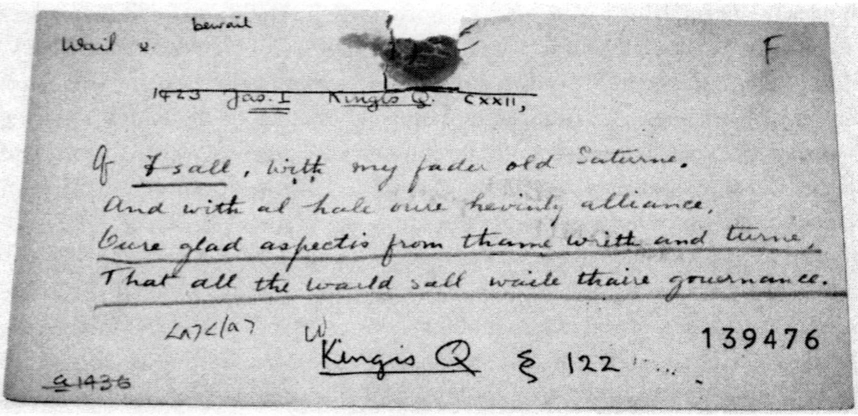

OED slip reused for DOST.

up and subsequent proofreading of the **S** material **Schot–Syze**, amounting to one and a half volumes, already edited when the review took place. The completion of T–Z by 2000 necessitated the production of two parts per year. It was up to the editorial team to devise procedures to meet this deadline. The review had suggested the use of computer technology in the editing as well as in post-editing processes, where a great time saving was made by the employment of a data-entry agency[43] to key the edited copy from slips. Experience on the *MED* and the *Dictionary of American Regional English* (*DARE*), dictionaries of a similar scale, consulted by Watson at this time, suggested that working on-screen was difficult, even starting from a point where the slip collection was held in electronic form. The *DOST*'s slips were largely handwritten, some still original *OED* slips. The production of an electronic corpus of all the as-yet untouched slips to allow on-screen editing would have meant keying at least twice the number of slips finally published, and the start of editing would have to wait till this was done. The six and a half years available until the end of 2000 was already an incredibly short time for the editing of three volumes. If the task were to be completed, faster methods of working must be found and editing must start as soon as possible.

By October 1994 the editors had verified that if they each edited half a drawer of the eighty-two drawers of citation slips remaining (200,000 slips) in eighteen days they would meet the finish date. Working at this rate – about twice the speed previously regarded as reasonable – required a different sort of editing, but given the changes in methodology outlined below, and an unprecedented level of teamwork and commitment, this was what was done. Edited copy (bundles of citation slips) was sent to Manila for keying, so only the slips actually published were keyed. Shortening the traditional editing process without loss of quality was achieved by rethinking every process with a view to simplifying choices and speeding up the time required for thought. Sub-sense divisions were restricted to those immediately obvious to the editor, allowing speedy sorting of sub-senses with a minimum of worrying over the rights and wrongs of a particular case. This applied, especially, to minor grammatical or semantic divisions displayed under the sub-section labels (1), (2), etc. The illustration of the detail of the grammar shared with English and thus of no special interest in terms of Scots had grown substantially over the letters P–S. In the case of **Restor(e** *v.*, for instance, the divisions (1), (2), (3) and (4) might have been reduced to a single sub-sense with only the constructions evidenced in (5) and (6) treated separately. This could reduce the number of quotations in the entry to twenty instead of thirty-six, making a saving of sixteen quotations in the cost of keying and printing, and time spent proofreading, without any real loss in quality, as the quotations that would have been eliminated are all covered, in terms of sense, distribution, etc, by quotations retained. This technique saved time and effort, and further time was saved by freely permitting exceptions in the case of difficult decisions. Although many more stringent rules of working were introduced at this time, they confirmed a style of editing that was developing in many of its essentials long before 1994, as can be seen above in the description of the structure of an entry and the etymology. The outcome was in most elements desirable in its own right rather than a less than ideal solution imposed by circumstances.

On the other hand, one procedure tested had only partial success. In the process of editing, about half the slips for any word became copy, the other half were rejected. According to the previous method of editing, all the material was processed, what was not required for publication only being rejected after the editing was completed. Indeed, the reject was kept in the same format as the copy to be rechecked at a later date. A system was now tried by which a 'first reject' was made straight away, leaving less material to edit thereafter and saving a good deal of time. This technique had always been used in the case of very large entries where, on a first read through of the material, the editor would remove not only duplicate copies of citations but also others that were repetitive. However, it turned out to be only partially successful when applied more generally. There were a number of straightforward words, such as **Tran(e** *n.* where this technique could be used to good effect, but most words were too complex to risk eliminating a lot of material early in the process. Nonetheless, the general injunction to reject repetitive material as early as possible was found to be effective.

Further time-saving procedures were used, such as the approach to problem-solving. Instead of spending time searching in secondary sources, staff corresponded by email with a network of experts all over the world, from Professor Jonathan Glenn at the University of Central Arkansas, who was working on Volume II of the prose works of Sir Gilbert Hay, to Brian Smith, archivist, in Zetland (OSc for Shetland): our 'A–Z' of problem-solving. The completion of the *DOST* was something to which many scholars gave time and expertise during this period, solving difficulties, for instance with manuscripts, that would previously have been unresolvable: for instance, Dr Keith Williamson of the Institute for Historical Dialectology, Edinburgh University, was always willing to check a quotation from the manuscripts he was working with, and the staff of the National Archives of Scotland on quite a few occasions supplied photocopies of pages of *Edinburgh Testaments*.[44] The whole user community, centred on the Scottish Medievalists and the Scottish Text Society, was eager to see the completion of the *DOST* and willing to speed it along. Their support and encouragement were of inestimable value.

Some benefits that had not previously been available were instigated by the review. Professor William Gillies of the Department of Celtic at the University of Edinburgh was appointed project manager, and William Aitken, secretary of the Joint Council, formerly director of Management Information Services at the University of Edinburgh, undertook the task of monitoring and refining the production schedule drawn up by the staff in the months subsequent to the review. Previously the editorial staff had been responsible for day-to-day management, as well as drawing up reports and organising some of the fund-raising effort. After the appointment of Gillies and Aitken, that burden was very largely taken on by them.

The quality and size of the team were also critical. It consisted of the three full-time editors and one full-time and two part-time editorial assistants, rising to five editorial assistants from 1997. The team combined size and experience to a greater degree than at any time in the past. This point relating to the importance of experience had been made by Aitken in 1980:

> Some remarks [were made] . . . that one could buy three or more junior editors for the price of two seniors and that younger people worked faster than older. The implication of the former and the fact of the latter are untrue in the context of *DOST* (or any other similar dictionary, such as *MED*), at least if any regard at all is given to quality. More experienced persons in fact produce acceptable results much faster, because they already know much the junior has to find out *ad hoc* because they are more skilled at analysis and at the devising of definitions and because they have confidence in their findings where a junior hesitates and vacillates.[45]

The solution of replacing more experienced, more expensive staff by cheaper juniors was also suggested in 1994. However, over the succeeding six years, Aitken's analysis proved correct. Over the period, the team of editors remained unchanged, and their commitment and experience was vital.

The job of the editorial assistants[46] changed dramatically, becoming a question of meticulously proofreading the dictionary entries, checking not only the actual text but the layout and structure – an enormous task, quite different from anything clerical or editorial assistants had undertaken in the past. Keying the material at a relatively early stage meant that quotations could be sorted electronically. The extensive verification of the quotation material required prior to publication was greatly accelerated by this ability to check all the quotations from a text in a single pass.

The Register of Titles was revised by Dr Christine Robinson of the English Language Department at the University of Edinburgh, with the specialist help of Mr Ian Cunningham, former director of Special Collections in the National Library of Scotland, and Dr Athol Murray, former Keeper of the Records of Scotland. The *DOST* was extremely fortunate in securing the services of such distinguished scholars for what is a key element in the tools offered by the *Dictionary*.

The editing of the *DOST* was completed in December 2000, and the proofreading by the end of June 2001.

Conclusion

The sorts of changes outlined above are an inevitable part of a long-term project such as the *DOST*. Scotland has changed enormously since 1919 when Sir William Craigie first set out his plan for a series of 'period dictionaries'. It is inevitable that the perceptions of the editors of the *DOST* should reflect these changes and that these changing views of what Scotland is and has been, and how its language has related to its society over the centuries, should be reflected in the editing of the *Dictionary*. The project changed from the work of a single scholar into an enterprise supported and funded by six of Scotland's universities and a good number of charitable foundations, and latterly by the Scottish Office and the Scottish Arts Council. Now lexicography has moved into the twenty-first century with the digitisation of the two major Scottish dictionaries, the *DOST* and the *SND*. The outcome of this project, the *Dictionary of the Scots Language* (*Dictionar o the Scots Leid*) (*DSL*) (www.dsl.ac.uk) is now in the care of Scottish Language Dictionaries (SLD), a company set up in 2002 to bring the organisations together, reuniting the two parts of the language, formerly severed at 1700 (see Chapter 7). This division at 1700 was a reflection of the scholarly views of the time, as well as the practical problems of constructing a single dictionary for the whole of Scots; possibly the only way forward in the 1920s, it now need no longer be so. Craigie had hoped that the *DOST* and the *SND*, although dealing with the language in different ways, might be organised so as to allow the connections between the older language and the modern to be apparent. This is not always the case with the 'big dictionaries', given that they were edited independently along very different lines but, as far as is possible, such connections are being made in the editing of the new edition of *CSD* (see Chapter 7). Whether this will ever result in a 'seamless' *Dictionary of the Scots Language* is open to doubt: the structures of the *DOST* and *SND* are too different for an easy transition; and it is not clear that it is necessary or desirable. The *DOST* as an intensive look at the language of the early period, in tandem with *SND*, which is in effect a dialect dictionary as well as dictionary of the historical period from 1700, both searchable electronically, together offer enormous potential for investigating any particular aspect of the language at any date.

SIX

Scottish National Dictionary

ISEABAIL MACLEOD

> The *Scottish National Dictionary* presents a kaleidoscope of dissolving views of Scottish life and character, and thus makes a direct appeal to all Scots or folk of Scottish descent who take a pride in the language and history of their country.[1]

Introduction

At the beginning of the twentieth century there were gloomy views about the future of the Scots language, and indeed forecasts of its imminent demise. Such head-shaking was nothing new, with evidence of it as far back as the eighteenth century (see Chapter 3). In the introduction to his poems in Scots, R.L. Stevenson observes: 'The day draws near when this illustrious and malleable tongue shall be quite forgotten.'[2] In 1938 a letter to the *Scotsman* expressed the opinion that Scots was 'vanishing slowly. Perhaps it would not be too much to say that a Scottish language is now non-existent, and only local dialects survive to remind us of a language which once produced an epic such as Barbour's the Bruce.'[3] And Professor John Orr felt the need for a linguistic survey of Scotland (and Britain) before the dialects disappeared: 'The "Linguistic Atlas of Scotland" would be not only a treasure house of words, but also a magnificent monument to a rapidly receding past.'[4] There were also gloomy views about the internal state of the Scots language. In a lecture in 1932, the novelist Eric Linklater emphasised the inadequacies of Scots for the modern world. Scottish literature should be preserved, 'taught in schools as Greek and Latin were taught', but new Scottish literature should be in English. The lecture aroused a storm of protest.[5] In 1956, in a public lecture in Queen's College, Dundee, David Murison expressed further gloom: 'Already we see the rot in the gutter speech of our cities, and ugly rot it is.' It seemed that the 'alternative to good Scots' was not good English but 'forces' slang, Americanese and gangster talk.[6]

It is gratifying to see, now in the twenty-first century, that these dire predictions have not been totally fulfilled. The language has certainly diminished alarmingly over the past century, not least in the use of fewer distinctive Scots words by most of its speakers. On the other hand, with more enlightened attitudes to minority languages and some official support (though not enough), its outlook is not as grim as it was half a century ago. There is more writing in Scots, in prose as well as poetry, and more use of Scots words in a wider sphere. The *Scottish National Dictionary* is itself evidence of the strength of the language, covering as it does a wide range of language, a great deal of which is still in use, at least in some part of Scotland or sphere of activity. It includes:

- Formal and legal language: *culpable homicide* (manslaughter), *furth of* (out of), *outwith* (out of, beyond);
- Scottish Standard English: *ashet* (oval serving plate), *gigot* (leg of mutton), *short leet* (short list);
- Words with no good English equivalent: *dreich* (dreary, dismal), *dwam* (daydream), *swither* (hesitate, dither);
- Scots meanings of English words: *messages* (purchases, one's shopping), *sort* (fix, mend), *uplift* (collect, pick up);
- Regional words and expressions: *gweed* (good), *fit like?* (how are you?) – both North-East.

It also includes the specialist and sometimes narrowly regional words, which are indeed disappearing along with the way of life they represent, notably agricultural terms, such as parts of the plough and other implements.

History

It was, however, partly a desire to capture a dying language before it disappeared that encouraged research a century ago. A comprehensive dictionary was naturally seen as a vital part of any such enterprise, and William Craigie played an important role in the creation of a sister project to the *DOST* for the modern period. In December 1907, after a decade editing the *OED*, he gave a lecture in his native Dundee to the Scottish branch of the English Association on the subject 'What steps should be taken to secure the co-operation of members in collecting Scots words, ballads, legends, and traditions still current?'.[7] In the audience that evening was William Grant, who was inspired to think further as to how this might be done. This may be regarded as the spring from which the *Scottish National Dictionary* eventually flowed, and Grant became the prime mover in these early developments.

At the time of the meeting, he was a lecturer in English and Modern Languages in the Free Church Normal College in Aberdeen. A native of the North-East, where Scots remains strong to this day, he was born in Elgin in 1863. He had an MA in classics from Aberdeen University and studied in France, Belgium and Germany. His varied teaching career ranged between English, classics and modern languages in schools as far apart as Elgin, Glasgow and Arbroath. From 1908 to 1928 he taught phonetics at the Aberdeen Training Centre (teachers' training college). His *Pronunciation of English in Scotland* (1913) (following the general plan of 'Mr Daniel Jones's *Pronunciation of English*') gives a detailed description of the pronunciation of Scottish Standard English, with transcriptions in the International Phonetic Alphabet.[8]

Immediately after the meeting in December 1907, the branch set up a Dialect Sub-Committee, which became the Scottish Dialects Committee (SDC), with Grant as convener, 'to arrange for the collecting of materials in the Scottish Dialect'.[9] It had thirteen members, including William Craigie and five lecturers in phonetics at Scottish Training Centres for teachers. In March 1909 Grant reported to one of their meetings in Edinburgh (chaired by Professor H.J.C. Grierson, of King's College, Aberdeen) on 'What still remains to be done for our Scottish dialects',[10] summarising the reports of two meetings of the SDC in 1908. The committee were of the opinion that there was still room for an 'investigation into the present condition of the Scottish dialects', and determined that they 'would seek to make the record of our language as complete as possible'.[11] Grant put forward ideas for ways of collecting information on current Scots, all the more urgent because the dialects were 'undoubtedly giving way before the influence of general education and modern means of communication'.[12] It was considered that Jamieson's *Dictionary* (see Chapter 3), for all its merits, had inadequate coverage, especially in that it concentrated mainly on the dialects of central Scotland. The other main sources of information on Scots at the time were the *OED* and the *English Dialect Dictionary*, both of which had a considerable amount of Scots material (see Chapters 10 and 7). There remained a need for better coverage of all the Scots dialects. 'A New Scottish Dictionary' should contain: '(1) All the words used in the language from the present time as far back as our literary records go; (2) the meanings and usages of these words, defined by phrase or quotation; (3) their pronunciation; (4) their etymology.'[13] Lack of pronunciation guides was considered the main deficiency in Jamieson, all the more important because of the phonological variations between the dialects, especially in vowel phonology. The gap was ably filled in the new dictionary from the experience in phonetics of Grant and his colleagues in other training centres.

The work of the SDC was clearly hampered by the First World War, but it managed to continue collection and to maintain a programme of publication of its Transactions, appearing in 1913, 1916, 1919 and 1921. As well as a statement of aims and lists of contributors and sources (especially newspapers), they consist of selective word lists with pronunciation, definitions, quotations and some etymology. Although it was many years before work began officially, one can already see the beginnings of a new dictionary of modern Scots. The committee also published the still authoritative *Manual of Modern Scots* (1921) by Grant and J.M. Dixon, and the *Roxburghshire Word-Book* (1923) by George Watson (see below and Chapter 4). There were plans for a series of such county word books, but no others came to fruition. The SDC produced various pamphlets, including one on 'The Scotch Dialect of Avoch and Cromarty' in Easter Ross; its peculiarities had been pointed out by the Celtic scholar W.J. Watson, a native of Tain.[14]

In the 1920s there were further moves towards a new dictionary. Craigie continued to add his weight to the project, giving a series of lectures in 1924 in Edinburgh 'and five other Scottish centres' on 'The Study of the Scottish Tongue', trying 'to enlist volunteers for the preparation of a new Scottish Dictionary.' It was to be based on the historical principles of speech sound and the careful examination of quotations 'illustrating the first and last appearance, and every notable point in the life-history of every word.'[15] He stressed the need for oral as well as written quotations. He arranged for the Scottish material in the *OED* files to be made available to both dictionaries. While he emphasised the necessity for a dictionary of the older tongue, he recognised the need for one of the modern language as 'recorded in literature and preserved in speech from the latter part of the seventeenth century to the present day'. In the published version of his 1919 lecture (see Chapter 5), he noted progress: 'The Scottish Dialects Committee has also within the past year [1925] definitely undertaken to deal in a similar way with the modern period (from about 1700.).'

A considerable contribution to the planning of the dictionary was also made by George Watson (see also Chapters 4, 5 and 10). In fact, in 1916 Craigie had suggested to Grant that Watson could help with 'the Modern Scottish dictionary' and that he could be a link between the Older Scots and the modern dictionary: 'He not only expressed his willingness to do so, but has actually begun to prepare for the task . . . It would be excellent if the two Dictionaries could be produced concurrently, so that the one could link up with the other and the continuity (or otherwise) of the words be clearly shown. In that case Watson might be a kind of connecting medium for both.'[16] Unfortunately, this level of cooperation was not achieved, but Watson did correspond with Grant on detailed points of style and content, as well as on more general policy, including the scope and length of the *Dictionary*, and he continued to comment on it, often in great detail, even after he moved to Chicago in 1927. He gave advice on 'Methods for garnering Materials for the "Scottish National Dictionary" . . . These might be widely cast (e.g. in the leading dailies or weeklies or even the local weeklies) for general guidance of the sporadic or occasional helper.' In the same letter he recommends that 'the district feature should be combined with the historical feature' and that some works 'should be left alone as not representing or based upon the actual spoken vernacular. Special care, in fact, might be exercised in leaving unread works which are conglomerate, archaic, pseudo-archaic, spurious, or otherwise unreal or scarcely real in respect of the vernacular.'[17] Watson was also noted in the minutes of a meeting in 1931 as a 'liaison officer between the two dictionaries',[18] but there is no record of his participation after that date.

By the late 1920s it was considered that, after twenty years of voluntary activity, the time was now approaching when editing and publication should be set as more definite goals. Grant got the use of a large room in the Aberdeen Training Centre in St Andrew Street and, with the help of a typist, began classifying slips. By 1928, he was working with two assistants, supported by donations, subscriptions and modest grants from the Carnegie Trust, while still maintaining a system of voluntary readers and supervisors. It was now clear that more secure funding was required, and moves were made to set up a new body 'to undertake the actual production and publication of the new dictionary, and to procure the necessary financial assistance'.[19] Grant had approached the Burns Federation, and its president Sir Joseph Dobbie, an Edinburgh lawyer, proved to be an enormous support in the setting-up process and over the years to come, especially in the initiation of a subscription scheme and in gathering donations.

The Scottish National Dictionary Association Ltd (SNDA) was set up as a company limited by guarantee and incorporated in 1929, with Grant, now retired from teaching, as literary director and editor, assisted by a Representative Executive Council and a Dialect Advisory Committee. It took over all the collections and functions of the Scottish Dialects Committee, which was to be represented on the Executive Council of the new body. Sir Joseph Dobbie[20] became its first president and his Edinburgh office in Melville Street became the headquarters of the new association. The council included several of the main supporters of the SDC's word collection; for prestige purposes, there was a list of honorary vice-presidents, with some distinguished (and often surprising) names among them, including Ramsay MacDonald, Stanley Baldwin, the Duchess of Atholl, John Buchan, Professor H.J.C. Grierson (now Regius Professor of Rhetoric and English Literature at the University of Edinburgh), Charles Murray (the North-East poet, billed as 'Author of *Hamewith*') and the Sultana of Johore (a Glasgow woman who had recently married the Sultan).

There was considerable controversy about the title of the dictionary; Craigie was shocked by the word 'National' in the title and he complained to Grant that the 'use of "Language" and "National" without any qualification would naturally suggest that the work would treat of the language as a whole, and certainly of that period during which it has most claim to be called a "language".' Thus it 'would only be appropriate as a general title for the two works, – a combination which unfortunately is not possible on account of the differences in the material.'[21] He tried unsuccessfully to persuade Grant to alter the title, and he later wrote that he did not want to be included among the supporters of the new dictionary: this title 'would naturally suggest that this work takes precedence of any other in the same field. To subscribe to this would look like subordinating my own work (which I am not inclined to do).'[22] He did however resume his support after Grant's death in 1946 (see below). Certainly, in later years the use of the word 'National' proved to be a problem in appeals for funds as it sometimes gave the impression that the SNDA was a publicly funded body like the National Library or the National Museums, and to others it suggested a connection with the Scottish National Party.

Grant was very anxious to begin publication as soon as possible after the setting up of the SNDA, though he realised this would be impossible 'unless I get more relief from the incubus of propaganda and financial worry'.[23] The first part appeared in 1931 and Volume I in 1933. In spite of the financial stringencies of the 1930s depression, Volume II came out in 1941, but Second World War shortages soon held up publication. Further delays resulted from Grant's last illness and his death in 1946. He was succeeded by a young classics graduate whose life work was to become the completion of the *SND*.

David Donald Murison was born in 1913 in Fraserburgh, son of a joiner, and moved to Aberdeen at the age of seven. A lad o pairts, he did brilliantly at

David Murison.

Aberdeen Grammar School (where a teacher said to him 'Laddie, ye'll burst yer brains'), and at the universities of Aberdeen and Cambridge; for two years he taught Greek at Aberdeen University, alongside the poet Douglas Young, who became a close friend. Like Young a conscientious objector, he worked as a forester and a market gardener near Stirling during the Second World War. Like A.J. Aitken on the *DOST*, he held university posts as editor of the *SND*, being lecturer and later senior lecturer in the universities of St Andrews and Aberdeen, teaching Scots language in the English department of the latter during the 1960s.

After his retiral he also taught Scots at the University of Glasgow (1975–8). Indeed, along with A.J. Aitken, he was one of the main supporters of the move to have Scots accepted as an academic subject (see Chapter 5). The language's debt to him is incalculable. Along with ceaseless lexicography, he supported Scots with numerous articles, talks and other publicity throughout the country, including speeches at Burns Suppers, where he was a popular deliverer of the Immortal Memory. In 1977 he published *The Guid Scots Tongue*, a lively and readable as well as an authoritative short history of Scots, and his other publications include *Scots Saws* (1981), proverbs and sayings, ancient and modern. Though he was a keen peruser of railway timetables, the publicity tours were his only journeys: holidays were to him an unwarrantable luxury and, after his return from Cambridge, he scarcely left Scotland. His concentration was on 'getting to Z'.[24] Some years after retiral, he moved back to his native Fraserburgh, where his deep attachment to the place was reflected in his studies in local history. Sociable and witty, often in an ironic vein, he could also be thrawn and dour, refusing all public honours, even absenting himself from the dinner to celebrate the completion of the *SND* in 1976; he was described by a friend as 'aggressively modest'.

He made huge improvements to the *Dictionary*, both in its content and in its methodology, many of them advised by Craigie, and he also had advice from J.M. Wyllie, editor of the *Oxford Latin Dictionary* (see Chapter 10). Wyllie became a member of the Executive Council in 1946 and continued to help in an advisory capacity for some years. As well as considerable correspondence with Craigie and Wyllie, Murison had discussions with them in Oxford in the spring of 1947.[25] Above all he widened the source base, organising an increased reading scheme and expanding the sources of oral information. He did an enormous amount of the additional reading himself in his 'spare' time, and also tracked down and sometimes purchased for the *SND* rare or solitary copies of local works for excerption. He edited Volumes III–X, as well as organising the Supplement and other end matter in Volume X, most of which he compiled himself. Another innovative contribution was the long informative article for each letter of the alphabet. He is thus, justifiably, seen as the principal creator of the *SND*.

Grant's part, however, should not be underestimated, and it should not be forgotten that he spent over twenty years in planning and collection before the editing began, and many more struggling to continue the work under adverse circumstances. His introduction in Volume I has stood the test of time, and his account of the phonetic and other characteristics of the different dialects remains one of the best detailed descriptions of Scots. The preface to Volume III notes the death of the *SND*'s first editor, 'to whose scholarship, patriotism, energy and undaunted optimism the work owes its very existence and indeed its survival through great difficulties and discouragements. To those who continue his work he left two mottoes, *Nil desperandum* and *Never deval*, which were his own inspiration in the many vicissitudes of the monumental task he had set himself and which will remain the watchword of the Dictionary to the end.'

The project remained in Aberdeen for a few more years, moving from St Andrew Street to King's College in 1947; but in 1954 the SNDA joined the *DOST* at 27–29 George Square, Edinburgh (where they remained until 2009), alongside the (then quite new) School of Scottish Studies and the Linguistic Survey of Scotland. The Survey collected data on Scots and Gaelic from all the dialect areas, and the Scots section was published as *The Linguistic Atlas of Scotland* in three volumes.[26] Office accommodation was provided free by the University of Edinburgh, as it had been in Aberdeen by the Provincial Committee for teacher training and by the university. As we have seen, the early work of collection and publication was carried out almost entirely on a voluntary basis, but by 1928 Grant already had two assistants, and a small salaried staff was maintained throughout.

Fundraising and Publicity

The funding problem was neatly encapsulated by George Watson in 1929: 'The financing of the dictionaries is a very difficult task. People who have money (and there are many) are not "dictionary-minded". Those who work on dictionaries, on the other hand, do not get or have the money.'[27] Grant in his early report to the Scottish Branch of the English Association[28] noted the 'NEED OF FUNDS AND HOW THEY MAY BE OBTAINED', a question that was to dog the project to its end and beyond. When editors were employed, the need for funding greatly increased, and by the 1930s the problem was acute. In 1939 it was decided that production should be suspended until debt was cleared, and the position became so precarious that Grant proposed drawing only £10 per month of his salary until the crisis was over.[29]

One of the main sources of funding from the early days of the SNDA was the subscription scheme whereby, for a modest outlay, subscribers could receive the parts of the dictionary as they were published. It could be paid as a lump sum or in instalments, and enormous efforts were made to raise new subscriptions and to get payments from those who had already signed up. The price ranged from £15 in 1929 to £30 in 1958 and to a cost of £100 in 1974, near completion. The sum of £30 in the 1950s might now seem like the bargain of the twentieth century, but people who took out these subscriptions say that at the time there was no guarantee that the *Dictionary* would ever be finished. Subscribers, many of them institutional, are listed in the volumes, as are patrons.

There were constant appeals to various sources, most of them falling on stony ground. Appeals to Parliament for government support in 1929, 1938–9 and 1946 were particularly fruitless. An editorial in the *Scotsman* in 1938 stated: 'It is not creditable to Scotland that the great undertaking of the Scottish National Dictionary should be held up owing to lack of funds.'[30] The reason given for lack of government support was that there were no suitable sources for funds for such a project. It was, however, pointed out that in 1896 Lord Balfour had secured a grant from the Royal Bounty fund to ensure completion of the *English Dialect Dictionary*.

A note of 16 December 1946 states:

> The question of financial help from Treasury sources was raised in Parliament during the Conservative administration by Mr. Tom Johnston in questions to Mr. Walter Elliot and Mr. J Colville, Secretaries of State . . .: the answers were briefly to the effect that there were no public funds available for such a purpose.
>
> Practically the same answer was given by Mr. Johnston when himself Secretary of State to Mr. Elliot's question'[31]

It was noted that many other countries support their dictionaries much better, for example, 'Holland, Denmark, Norway and even Iceland'.

The Education Department was similarly unresponsive, and local authorities were thus discouraged from helping. Some did, however, many county councils contributing by means of subscriptions for their libraries and schools. Lanark County Council's recommendation was that: 'We consider that this new Dictionary will be a notable contribution to Scottish literature for all time. It is the duty of every local authority and organisation in the country to give financial assistance to the promoters.'[32] In particular, the 'Four Cities'[33] eventually gave substantial grants over a period of years; Volume VIII of the *SND* is dedicated to them in appreciation.

As with central government, appeals had been made to the universities from the beginning, largely without success, apart from a few small donations and the funding of Murison's salary from the 1940s in the form of lectureships at the universities of Aberdeen and St Andrews. In 1939, at a meeting of the Scottish Text

Society, Sir William Craigie proposed a plan for support for both dictionaries by the universities, even though he realised it was an inauspicious time. In 1952, however, a memorandum was sent by Professor Angus McIntosh to the principals of the Scottish universities, then four in number, proposing the setting up of a system whereby both the *DOST* and the *SND* were funded and worked more closely together. The Joint Council for the Scottish Dictionaries was set up, with representatives of the four universities, both dictionaries and the Carnegie Trust for the Universities of Scotland. Edinburgh University took over the administration of the Joint Council and provided the dictionaries with accommodation (see Chapter 5). The Joint Council secured salaries for Murison, two editors and an editorial typist. As well as contributing their own funding, it helped to raise further money by means of various appeals; subscribers to the appeals are listed in subsequent volumes of the *SND*. More editors were provided for in the 1960s to ensure that the completion target was reached by 1974; this was very nearly achieved.

The Carnegie Trust for the Universities of Scotland, with two representatives on the Joint Council, was a major player in this process, and in fact it was a constant supporter of the *SND* from the beginning. Most of the meagre funding in the early stages came from this source, the earliest application being made as early as 1908. The Trust supported, for example, the production of the *Transactions of the Scottish Dialects Committee* as well as the printing of word lists and leaflets. It also gave help with payments to Grant's assistants in the late 1920s, and provided scholarships for editors from the 1930s to the 1950s. Other bodies contributed, including the British Academy, and many appeals were made to trusts. The most fruitful of these was to the Pilgrim Trust; after unsuccessful applications in 1930 and 1936, it gave a grant of £7,500, which funded the publication of Volume VII in 1968.

Clubs and societies both at home and abroad were approached, and the Burns Federation gave stalwart support, encouraged by Sir Joseph Dobbie, its president 1927–30 and the first president of the SNDA. In 1939 the Federation's honorary secretary, John McVie,[34] helped to set up a 'League of Donors' which, from 1940, brought in contributions from many sources and places. As well as Burns Clubs worldwide, other societies, including the Saltire Society, were encouraged to contribute. Appeals were also made to local associations of the Educational Institute of Scotland, and this scheme helped the SNDA through one of its most difficult crises. McVie helped in numerous other ways to see the SNDA through wartime and later financial crises; he was president from 1946 to 1966.

From a very early stage, efforts were made to get contributions from Scots abroad, with limited success. In 1939 a letter from 'an American Scot' to the

Aberdeen Press & Journal and other newspapers 'made a stirring appeal . . . offering to contribute £100 and inviting other patriotic Scots to do likewise'.[35] He was David Grey, of the St Louis Burns Club, who had been a subscriber since 1937; he supported the League of Donors scheme, did a great deal of lobbying on the *Dictionary*'s behalf and, in spite of the difficulties of wartime conditions, several hundred pounds were raised, a considerable amount of which was donated by himself. The League of Donors scheme also approached possible donors in North America, such as the Scottish Clans Association of the United States of America.

Legacies occasionally provided a welcome windfall. Towards the end there were legacies from the poet Helen B. Cruickshank and from Robert Paterson, a Burns enthusiast, the latter funding the publishing of Volume X. A very large anonymous legacy arrived rather too late for the *SND* but helped greatly with future developments (see Chapter 7).

All of this required publicity and the editors themselves played a major role, giving talks to numerous clubs and societies throughout the country, as well as broadcasts and articles in newspapers and journals. Leaflets were distributed both at home and abroad. Although publicity was closely linked to fundraising, a vital necessity throughout, it also appealed for contributions to the word collection; volunteers responded, and without them the work could not have been carried out. Press coverage was considerable from the beginning, not least in the *Scotsman*, the *Glasgow Herald* and the *Aberdeen Press & Journal*, but it extended widely, to Scottish local newspapers, some English, and from time to time a few abroad, such as the *Montreal Star* and the *Statesman*, Calcutta.

Method

There were many changes in working method from the early days of voluntary effort to the struggling team of salaried staff at the end. Voluntary contributions, especially to the word collection, continued to play an important role throughout, but the processing of the quotations and oral references collected, the raw material of the dictionary, required trained editors. Careful examination of a large body of quotations and selection of a small number for inclusion is the core of the editorial work on a historical dictionary. The *SND*'s quotations were excerpted by volunteer readers from about 6,000 texts (listed in the bibliography in Volume X). The quotations were written out on slips with details of region, date, author, title and page number, giving half a million slips, now stored in the National Library of Scotland.[36] The slips also contain oral quotations, the result of several methods of collection. Their eventual presentation in the *Dictionary* gives a picture not only of the history of the word, but of Scottish life and culture over two and a half centuries.

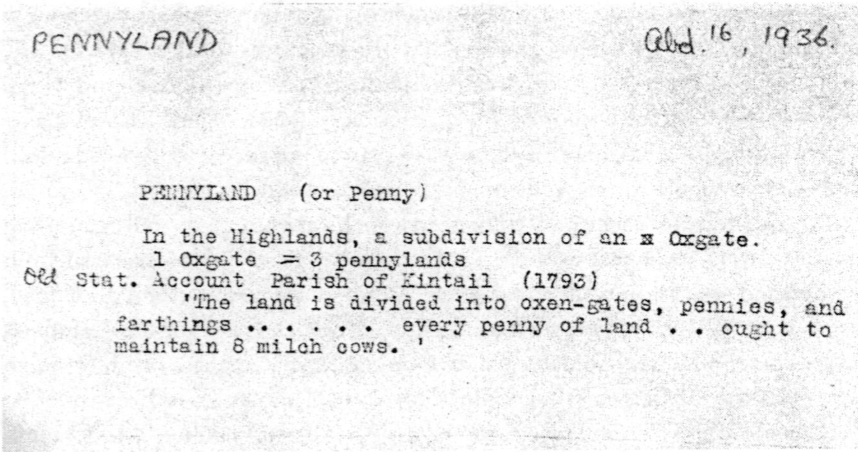
PENNYLAND Abd.[16], 1936.

PENNYLAND (or Penny)

In the Highlands, a subdivision of an x Oxgate.
1 Oxgate = 3 pennylands
Old Stat. Account Parish of Kintail (1793)
'The land is divided into oxen-gates, pennies, and farthings . . . . . . every penny of land . . ought to maintain 8 milch cows.'

SND slip.

Volume I contains a list of the original contributors to both written and oral collections, and there are additions in later volumes. There is a complete list in Volume X, but the earlier lists give a clearer picture of where the oral information came from, as the contributors are listed in alphabetical order of county, etc. The complete list, on the other hand, simply gives names and place of residence, not always an indication of the dialect described, which was often that of the person's early life rather than their current abode: for example, Rxb.[5] (W.A. Munro) is listed in Volume X simply with an Edinburgh address (see below, for an explanation of area abbreviations and superscript numbers). In the earlier years the collectors were organised by a supervisor in each area; the early lists also designate the other role or roles of the contributors: 'E. = Excerptor; O. = Organiser of District Excerptors; R. = Reviser of Typescript'; S. = Sub-Editor', i.e., has been 'helping in the preliminary preparation of articles for the Dictionary'.[37]

In the preface to Volume I, three of the contributors were given special mention: George Wilson, Banff, (E.O.R.) was the main collector in the North-East in the early stages; J.D. Westwood, principal English teacher at George Heriot's School, Edinburgh (E.O.R.), helped to compile the bibliography in addition to his other roles; and George Soutar (E.O.R.), Professor of English Language and Literature, University College, Dundee, was the main collector for Angus and also a vice-president of the SNDA. A native of Montrose, he gathered considerable amounts of data, both oral and written, on the dialect of Angus and the Mearns. His intention to publish a book on the subject came to nothing, but his papers were later given by his family to the *Dictionary*, on condition that they were kept together 'for anyone who might continue their father's researches in Angus Speech'.[38]

This is one of the regional studies, published and unpublished, noted on p. 147 and in Chapter 4, which provided important sources for the *SND*. George Watson's *Roxburghshire Word Book* has already been mentioned, and Hugh Marwick (Ork.[2]), the author of *The Orkney Norn* (see Chapter 4), was also a staunch supporter. In the 1920s there was a plan to produce county word books covering the whole country; the intention was to produce a 'popular account of the local dialect,' for each county, financed from local sources. As well as arousing interest among local people, these were to have provided the raw material, both written and oral, for the different dialects. Although this plan was not developed, other regional studies contributed. Latimer McInnes (Arg.[1]), from Campbeltown, contributed very valuable material on the Kintyre dialect, much of which he published in *The Dialect of South Kintyre* (1936), interesting because of its Scots and Gaelic features (see Chapter 4). An able successor to Mr McInnes from the 1970s on is Angus Martin, a Campbeltown postman, also a poet and historian of note, who draws on his work on the Argyll fishing industry in the 1970s, as well as on later observation.[39]

Sir James Wilson[40] (Bwk.[1] and Fif.[1]) wrote three important studies of Scots dialects, carried out in the hope that they would play a part in the Scots dictionary that was already being planned when the first was published in 1915. He wanted to give a clear indication of pronunciation, especially for words that differ from English only in pronunciation, and for this he developed his own innovative respelling system. *Lowland Scotch as Spoken in the Lower Strathearn District* (1915) compares the pronunciation of the Scots of his native parish of Dunning with that of Standard English. It was followed by *The Dialect of Robert Burns as Spoken in Central Ayrshire* (1923) and *The Dialects of Central Scotland* (1926), dealing with Fife and Lothian. Although his respelling system drew considerable criticism, not least from Craigie, his method did give a clear picture of the dialects as spoken by native speakers.

Ulster Scots (see also Chapter 4) was not as well represented as most other parts of the Scots-speaking area, but use was made of Ulster dialect dictionaries, notably William H. Patterson's *Glossary of Words in Use in the Counties of Antrim and Down* (1880) and Michael Traynor's *English Dialect of Donegal* (1953). A small number of local experts, including two who had made their own collections of Ulster words, made contributions in the early stages: Rev. W.F. Marshall[41] and J.J. Marshall,[42] who also suggested other possible sources of information. In the 1960s, Professor John Braidwood made numerous suggestions and recommended the use of data from the collections of the Folklore and Dialect Section of the Belfast Naturalists' Field Club.[43]

Among later prominent contributors (1940s–60s) was W.L. Lorimer,

William Grant and assistants in the *SND* office, Aberdeen.

Professor of Greek at the University of St Andrews and translator of *The New Testament in Scots*. His work on the latter and on the *Dictionary* enriched each other, and he helped the SNDA in many other ways, becoming chairman of the Executive Council from 1953 till his death in 1967.[44] It will be noted that, among the *SND* quotations from local newspapers, there are many from the *St Andrews Citizen*, excerpted by him.

As the work progressed, the need for salaried staff increased, but it was always a struggle to find funding even for a modest number. One of the longest-serving editors was Marjorie Stewart, from 1932 until 1954, when the SNDA moved to Edinburgh. During the Second World War, she took over the day-to-day running of the SNDA when Grant's health was failing, and in 1946 she was officially appointed as assistant editor and secretary. Some editors worked with Carnegie Research Scholarships (for research, 'the subject matter of which is a definite part of the Scottish National Dictionary'): they included Marie Mathieson (1935–7), Dorothy Gordon (1937–44) and Dr Joyce Collie (1954–66), who later became a minister of the Congregational Church in Aberdeenshire (and subsequently of the Church of Scotland). Already a contributor to the *Dictionary*, Alexander Fenton was senior assistant editor 1955–9. He subsequently had a distinguished career in what is now the National Museums of Scotland, during which he kept in touch with the project and used its methods in his work on Scottish ethnology, in 'a move from words to things'. Mairi Robinson (née Macnicol) was one of the editors during the later years of the project and went on to become editor-in-chief of the *Concise Scots Dictionary* (see Chapter 7).

Among the shorter-term appointments was F. Marian McNeill, well known as the author of *The Scots Kitchen* (1929); in 1929 she very briefly assisted Grant. A subsequent editor for a slightly longer period was Angus Macdonald, whose PhD thesis was later published as *The Place-Names of West Lothian* (1941). Many young graduates spent a year or two on the *SND* before moving on to other fields. Sheila Martin from Aberdeen worked on the dictionary for a year in the late 1930s; she soon married the Rev. David Steel, and became the mother of David Steel, leader of the Liberal party and first Presiding Officer of the new Scottish Parliament.

Collection

As noted above, the data collection was begun by the Scottish Dialects Committee and its aims were set out in Grant's lecture in March 1909.[45] With Craigie, the committee believed that 'the field of "ballad" and "legend" has been pretty well gleaned', and that they should 'make the record of our language as complete as possible, (1) by gathering in words, meanings, and usages which have not yet been recorded in any dictionary; (2) by an exact description of the pronunciation of existing Scottish words; (3) by dividing the country into dialect areas corresponding to differences in pronunciation'.[46]

From the beginning, both written and oral sources were used. Books, newspapers and other written material were sifted and the results produced not only raw material for the eventual dictionary but, more immediately, lists of words which could be sent to possible informants and thus used for collection of oral material. The committee's aim was to find correspondents in the different dialect areas and to provide them with such lists, along with printed slips for new words or meanings and detailed instructions on how to proceed. For the phonetic survey, Grant compiled lists of words which revealed the differences between the dialects.

In the early stages correspondents were asked to concentrate on new words and meanings, using Jamieson and the *English Dialect Dictionary*, if available, as guides. There was a proposal to start a fund to provide railway fares for contributors who 'have to go to remote districts to investigate sounds'.[47] There was a need for three classes of correspondent: (1) those who would simply indicate the words still in the dialect and words not hitherto recorded; (2) those who were not expert but willing to indicate pronunciation using 'normalised' Scottish spelling; and (3) 'those who have some phonetic training'. With Grant's professional expertise, detailed recording of pronunciation became a major part of the survey; for the third level he hoped to get help from some of his own students in Aberdeen and from those in two other phonetics departments, in the Edinburgh and Dundee Training Centres. He himself travelled the country recording Scots with a Dictaphone. He and his wife spent their entire summer holidays eliciting words, especially from older speakers, at first cycling round the country, later travelling in a small car.

In the search for correspondents, it was suggested that 'much assistance might be got from country literary societies, Burns Clubs, country ministers and schoolmasters, who might, at least, forward to the Committee the names of people with special local knowledge. The columns of the country newspaper might also be utilized to draw forth information about local words, phrases, and place-names.'[48] This is indicative of the strong rural bias in *SND*, right from the beginning, with scant attention paid to the urban Scots of the large cities, following the attitudes of the day, which regarded the rural dialects as 'good Scots' and urban as slang or debased English. Grant also noted that those 'whose knowledge of Scotch is too scanty to enable them to fill up our lists, might hand their copies to those interested in dialect study . . . or recommend the objects of the inquiry to patriotic and literary societies and to county clubs in our large towns'.[49]

Local newspapers did indeed prove a good source of information. The *Northern Scot and Moray & Nairn Express*, for instance, published the SDC's lists for their area around 1920, with spellings representing local pronunciation, such as 'Cweet, a coat' or 'Skeel or Skweel, a school'; these elicited useful responses, some of which were published in subsequent issues of the paper, as 'Beezom, heather brush—Also used and so pronounced as a term of reproach to a female'. The *John o' Groat Journal* also published lists of Scots words in 1911–12, used for Caithness in the *Transactions of the Scottish Dialects Committee*, and in the 1920s they sent slips culled from their columns in Scots.

Scotland was divided, as planned, into dialect areas according to pronunciation, and these are clearly indicated in the two-tone map in Volume I of the *SND*. The areas are further divided by pre-1975 county, listing roughly north to south. Of course the counties do not provide precise boundaries, and we find Angus divided between the northern and central areas; likewise Ayrshire and Dumfriesshire straddle two main areas. And the areas themselves are not, as Grant points out, 'like watertight compartments, entirely separate from each other'.[50] The lines on the map along the coastline from Caithness to Dundee indicate certain key words – for example, 'fa' for 'who' and 'meen' for 'moon' – marking dialect features of the adjoining areas.

Map of *SND* dialect areas.

The mainland has three main dialect areas, northern (n.Sc.), mid (m.Sc.), and southern (s.Sc.) Scots, of which mid is the most widespread, and 'the importance of which is enhanced by the fact that it is the home of our conventional literary language'.[51] Mid is subdivided into east mid Scots (em.Sc.), centred on Edinburgh; west mid Scots (wm.Sc.), centred on Glasgow; and south mid Scots (sm.Sc.), the South-West – the last is often argued to be a separate dialect area.

Division	*Abbr.*	*Subdivision*	*Abbr.*	*County, etc.*	*Abbr.*
INSULAR SCOTS	I.Sc.			Shetland	Sh.
				Orkney	Ork.
NORTHERN SCOTS	n.Sc.	north northern Scots (b)	nn.Sc.(b)	Caithness	Cai.
				(Sutherland)	(Sth.)
		north northern Scots (a)	nn.Sc.(a)	Cromarty	Crm.
				Easter Ross	e.Rs.
				Black Isle	Bl.I.
		mid northern Scots (b)	mn.Sc.(b)	Inverness	Inv.
				Nairn	Nai.
				Moray (or Elgin)	Mry. (Elg.)
				Upper Banff	U.Bnff.
		mid northern Scots (a)	mn.Sc.(a)	Lower Banff	L.Bnff
				Aberdeen	Abd.
				Buchan	Bch.
				Deeside	
	Nai., Mry., Bnff., Abd., Bch. and Deeside = north-east Scots (ne.Sc.)				
		south northern Scots	sn.Sc.	Mearns (Kincardine)	Mearns (Kcd.)
				east Angus (west Forfar)	w.Ags.. (w.Fif.)
MID SCOTS	m.Sc.	east mid Scots (a)	e.m.Sc(a)	east and south-east Perthshire	e. and se. Per
				Stirling	Slg.
				Fife	Fif.
				Kinross	Knr.
				Clackmannan	Ccl.
		east mid Scots (b)	em.Sc.(b)	Linlithgow (west Lothian)	Lnl. (w.Lth.)
				Edinburgh (mid Lothian)	Edb. (m.Lth.)
				Haddington (east Lothian)	Hdg. (e.Lth.)
				Berwick	Bwk.
				Peebles	Peb.
		west mid Scots	wm.Sc.	east and west Dumbarton	e. and w. Dmb.
				south Argyll	s.Arg.
				Bute	Bte.
				Renfrew	Rnf.
				Glasgow	Gsw.
				Lanark	Lnk.
				north Ayr	n.Ayr.
		south mid Scots	sm.Sc.	south Ayr	s.Ayr
				Wigtown } Galloway	Wgt. } Gall.
				Kirkcudbright } Galloway	Kcb. } Gall.
				west Dumfries	w.Dmf.
SOUTHERN SCOTS	s.Sc.			Roxburgh	Rxb.
				Selkirk	Slk.
				east and mid Dumfries	e. and m. Dmf.
ULSTER SCOTS	Uls.			Antrim	Ant.
				Down	Dwn.
				Londonderry	Ldd.
				Donegal	Don.
				Tyrone	Tyr.

List of Scots dialect areas and counties as used in the *SND*.

East mid Scots is further divided into east mid Scots (a) (to the north and east of the Firth of Forth), and east mid Scots (b) (to the south of it). Southern is the smallest area geographically, consisting of the counties of Roxburgh, Selkirk and part of Dumfries, but its vowel system is markedly different from that of its neighbours (and has some similarities to northern English dialects). The northern area has three main sub-divisions: north, mid (ne.Sc.) and south. The mid dialect, stretching from Nairn, near Inverness, to Stonehaven, just south of Aberdeen, is the North-Eastern Scots known today as 'the Doric'; though the term was until recently used to refer to Scots from any area.[52] Outside these mainland areas are Insular Scots (I.Sc.) (Shetland and Orkney), with their strong Norse elements, and Ulster Scots (Uls.), rooted in the considerable migration of Scots there in the seventeenth century and maintained by constant comings and goings across the Sheuch over the centuries. Although the Highlands and Islands were not considered to be Scots-speaking areas, their speech does of course include Scots elements, as well as features from Gaelic influence.

As far as possible, quotations from written sources are attributed to these divisions. Oral sources are designated by a county or area abbreviation, especially in the early volumes with a superscript number referring to a particular correspondent. Thus Mry.[2] and Abd.[27] refer to the two editors, Grant and Murison, the former also noted as Kcb.[5] (his father was a surveyor in Kirkcudbright); Sir William Craigie is Ags.[6] These indications of currency are given in geographical order from north to south, according with the list on pages xlvii–xlviii of Volume I. A county abbreviation without a number may indicate general use of the word or meaning in that county, for example:

> 'LUMMER, *v.* Of a dark sky or fog: to clear up, to become brighter and lighter (Cai. 1956)'.

When editing began, collection of oral material was extended by sending draft typescripts to the collectors in the various dialect areas for checking with local informants. In the 1940s, under Murison, plans were made to increase the oral collection. There was a suggestion to set up a dialect society for this purpose, but Craigie felt that a more efficient method would be to use a questionnaire. He wrote to Murison:

> I am not sure that the necessary additions could not as quickly be made by an appeal to subscribers as by the formation of a Dialect Society. If a clear explanation of what is wanted, and the reasons for getting it without delay, were issued with the next part of the Dictionary, together with a list of words collected from the type-scripts, there might be a sufficient response to make it less important to

> get the Dialect Society going immediately, although there might still remain good work for it to do.[53]

Beginning with letter D in 1948, such a list was sent out to subscribers with each part of the *Dictionary*, and also to local collectors, local newspapers and others. It consisted of a list of material already collected for the next part, in brief form, but showing existing distributional evidence. Informants were asked to add and emend from their own areas and, if possible, note alternative words for concepts, where relevant. For some words it also asked for pronunciation using 'whatever spelling best reproduces the sound in your dialect'. The typescript subsequently became a second round of consultation.

The reading scheme, greatly expanded under Murison, continued almost to the end of the project. Thus both written and oral collection brought in much more data, enabling increases in the content in later letters of the alphabet, as outlined in the introduction to Volume V (see below).

Content

The content of the *Dictionary* has two major differences from that of the *DOST*. First, while the *DOST* covers the whole language, including what is shared with English, the *SND* concentrates on what is distinctively Scots: in the words of its sub-title, 'all the Scottish words known to be in use, or to have been in use since c.1700'. Given the centuries of anglicisation of formal language, it would otherwise have reached unmanageable proportions. Second, although it lacked many of the genres of administrative papers available to the *DOST*, it had other written material, such as modern newspapers, at its disposal, but above all it was able to use spoken as well as written sources. Another, less tangible, difference is the aim of the *SND* to inform the general public as well as to record the language for scholars. Grant stated, in a letter to George Watson in 1930: 'You must remember that our Dictionary is for popular perusal. The Dictionary of Older Scots appeals mostly to scholars. I have my mind made up that ours must be as readable as possible.'[54]

The *SND* thus has an anomalous position between a historical dictionary of the Scots language and a dialect dictionary, reflecting varied attitudes to Scots in the modern period. In its aim to present 'a kaleidoscope of dissolving views of Scottish life and character',[55] the *SND* does not shun encyclopedic information, for example:

> PUIR. . .II. *n*. . . . Special combs : . . . (5) *puirshouse, peers-* (ne.Sc.), a poorhouse, workhouse. Gen.Sc. Poorhouses were uncommon in Scot. till the passing of the Poor Law Act of 1845; . . .

> PSALM, *n., v.* . . . **I.** *n.* As in Eng., but in Scot. referring esp. to the metrical version of the Psalms adopted from French Protestant usage in the 16th c. and now regularly employed in congregational praise in the Presbyterian Churches.

The last volume adds further valuable encyclopedic information with supplementary lists of 'miscellanea', such as personal and place names, fairs and markets. It also contains a 'list of scientific terms with Scottish connections', found to be particularly frequent in botany and geology, for example *forsythia, gardenia, strontium.* These were compiled by Murison at the end of the project; his colleague A.J. Aitken wrote: 'I do not believe there is any other person, living or dead, who could have executed so well these fascinating cameos of lexicography.'[56] Volume X also contains the Supplement, a bibliography of the works quoted, a list of abbreviations used and a table of weights and measures.

Many changes will be seen in the work throughout its ten volumes, not least in the density of information. When one considers that several decades of collection separate the publication of the first and last parts, it is no surprise to find that the material in the *Dictionary* text acquires new breadth and depth, while the Supplement shrinks in later letters. About halfway through, the Introduction to Volume V states that 'the material to be edited has been constantly augmented during the progress of the work, new words and additional usages have been found and the treatment of individual articles has become more generous in respect of definition and illustration, as can readily be seen in the increasing size of the Volumes'.

The increase in content is actually greater than numbers of pages might suggest, since the layout of the early pages is much more generous than in the later sections, with much greater use of run-on entries in later letters. Typefaces are of quite large size throughout, which made it possible to produce a Compact Edition in 1987, supplied with a small magnifier but capable of being read without one by anyone with normal eyesight.

Headwords

Layout of entries varies with the type of entry and length of the treatment. The first headword is usually the main vernacular form, although sometimes a separate entry is given for the English form, where there are several Scots meanings; for example:

> LAIF, *n.* Also *laiff, lafe* . . . Sc. forms of Eng *loaf*. . .

> LOAF, n. Also *lof* (Sh.). For hist. Sc. forms see LAIF. Gen.Sc. usage: bread, esp. flour bread. Now only dial. in Eng.

A.J. Aitken and David Murison

Other headword forms follow; in some entries these are numerous, as Scots has never had a standardised spelling system (see also Chapter 7). Style of presentation varies throughout the work. In the early letters the main forms are in capitals, followed by others in small capitals:

> CARB, CARBLE, CARB'L, CARBUL, CERB *v.* and *n.*[1]

Later, subordinate forms are in italic:

> HIRST, *n., v.* Also *herst; hurst; hist.*

Some have source references:

> HEEST *n., v.* Also *heest* (Ayr. 1912 G. Cunningham *Verse* 157), *heist* (Mry. 1897 J. Mackinnon *Braefoot Sk.*xiii.); . . .

In some longer entries the forms are given in a special section, as in:

> **TAK**, *v., n.* . . . **I.** *v.* **A.** Forms: Pr.t. *tak;* †*tack* (Sc. *a.*1714 *Earls Crm.* (Fraser 1876) II. 484), *takk, tauk* (Sc. 1819 *Blackwood's Mag.* (Dec.) 320); *tuk* (Wgt. 1880 G. Fraser *Lowland Lore* 109). . . . Pa.t *teuk* . . .

Where available, place and date are added (as above) to forms, building up a picture of their distribution. Indication of timescale is also given by marking the headword (or part of an entry) with a dagger meaning obsolete, or with a double-ended dagger, meaning obsolescent. As well as verb forms, plurals of nouns, comparatives and superlatives of adjectives and adverbs are included where relevant.

Pronunciation

The *SND* is the first dictionary of Scots to give systematic detailed information on pronunciation. As noted above, lack of pronunciation guides was considered the main deficiency of Jamieson's *Dictionary*, and although the *EDD* did give some indication of pronunciation, it rarely gave account of dialect variation. Except where the pronunciation can be deduced by the normal rules of Scottish Standard English, transcriptions are given, in the International Phonetic Alphabet, for headwords and occasionally for sub-entries. The scheme was devised by Grant, along with the other lecturers in phonetics who formed part of the early SDC, based on careful analysis of the sounds of the different dialects. The details of the vowel and consonant systems of the various dialects are clearly set out in the Introduction in Volume I, along with the principles on which the scheme is based. (See also Chapter 7 on pronunciation in the *Concise Scots Dictionary.*)

Regional pronunciations are given due prominence:

> THOCHT . . . [θoxt; Ork., s.Sc. θʌu(xʍ)t; I.Sc. toxt, tʌut]

> HEID . . . [Sc. hid, but em.Sc.(a), mn.Sc.(b) hed, Cai., Rs. (h)eid]

A plus sign indicates that the regional pronunciation is used in that area in addition to, rather than instead of, the more general one:

> LANG SYNE . . . [laŋsin, ne.Sc. + sin]

Other variations, such as grammatical functions, are indicated:

> TAE . . . [*prep.* tɪ, unstressed t(ə); *adv.* te:, tø, sm.Sc. ty; ne.Sc. ti:]

The long articles on each letter of the alphabet contain a great deal of detail on its pronunciation in various positions in a word and in different dialects.

Definitions

The definitions, backed up where possible by quotations and/or indication of oral usage, inevitably vary in the amount of detail they give. Some give simple equivalents, e.g.

> MOG . . . **II.** *n.* A botch, mess, muddle . . .

Others have detailed explanations, e.g.

> MOGGAN . . . **I.** *n.* **1.** The leg of a stocking, esp. a coarse woollen stocking without a foot, worn as a gaiter . . .

Some contain encyclopedic information, as noted above, and some simply state the word's relation to its English cognate, as described under 'Etymologies' below.

Organisation of Entry

Where relevant, the entry is divided first into word classes, by roman numerals in bold caps. Divisions of meanings can have several layers in a long entry, using bold Arabic figures; Arabic figures; lower case roman numerals; and then lower case letters (the last three all in parentheses): **1.** (1) (i) (a). Longer entries may be divided in other ways, with sections for derivatives, combined forms and phrases, in various arrangements. In the early part of the alphabet, some derivative and combined forms were in separate entries, for example BLACK in Volume II is followed by eighty-three combined forms (from BLACK-AIRN (malleable iron) to BLACK WRACK (a kind of seaweed) and seven derivative forms, including three uses of BLACKIE in separate entries (bird, bee and dirty appearance). By contrast REID in Volume VII, in the later style of the *Dictionary*, has eighty in one long listing, followed by a separate listing of their quotations. BLACK occupies almost six pages and REID almost four. This is a considerable saving of space, but REID is much more difficult to consult (not helped by inadequate differentiation of typefaces).

In some entries, categories of combined forms and phrases are given their own division, for example:

> **mak,** . . . **I.** *v.* . . . **A.** Vbl. Forms . . . **B.** Usages: **1.** in combs. and phrs. with *advs.* or *preps.*; (1) *to mak aboot* . . . **2.** Other combs. and phrs.: (1) *mak-a-dü, mak'kadu* . . . **3.** Combs. with ppl.adj. *made*: (1) *made diet* . . .

In other entries, such as **march** *n.*[1], different meaning divisions each have their list of compounds and/or phrases, in this case those connected with **1.** the border of a country (for example *march treason*) and **2.** the boundary of a property, farm or community (for example *march baulk*). Occasionally, combined forms appear with the relevant meaning, even although there is a separate combined forms category. For example, **mouse,** which begins with a list of Combs.: (1)–(14), from *mouse-catcher* (a variety of weasel) to *moosey-whiy-beard* (the whitethroat). But two other combined forms, *mouse-end* and *mouse-piece* (both meaning a lump of tissue at the end of a leg of mutton), appear under section **3.**

Etymologies

The formal etymology, at the end of the entry, traces the history of the word back to the main sources of Scots in Old English, Old Norse, Old French, Latin, Gaelic/Old Irish or Middle Dutch. Especially in later letters, dated Older Scots forms are included, painstakingly extracted by Murison from the *DOST* files for as-yet unpublished volumes, as in:

> NIEVE *n.* . . . [O.Sc. *newe, nave,* fist(s), 1375, *neful,* a handful, *a.*1400, . . .].

The relationship of the Scots word to English is stated; indeed in some cases the only etymological information is in the note: 'As in Eng.' or 'Sc. forms of Eng. . . .' or 'Sc. forms and usages of Eng. . . .' – in effect, a first definition at the beginning of the entry, as in:

> HEY, n.[1] Also *hei, h'y.* Sc. forms and usages of Eng. *hay.*

The etymology at the end of such entries contains only Older Scots forms:

> [O.Sc. has *hay* as in Eng. from 1375, *hey* not appearing until 1644.]

Quotations

In the documentation of the language the most important element in the *Dictionary* is the presentation of the quotations. They give body to the definitions, widen knowledge of the language and its breadth and scope, and cover a wide range of sources and genres. The quotations are preceded by an abbreviation for the dialect area, or Sc. for literary Scots; this label embraces the works of writers such as Ramsay, Scott and Stevenson, e.g. (under MENSE *n.*[1] **5.**)

> Sc. 1721 Ramsay *Poems* (S.T.S.) I. 25:
> I slade awa' wi' little Din, And muckle Mense.

as well as examples of legal or other formal writing, e.g. (under IMPIGNORATE)

> Sc. 1769 Erskine *Principles* II. viii. § 1:
> A wadset . . . is a right, by which lands, or other heritable subjects, are impignorated by the proprietor to his creditor, in security of his debt.

Grant's Preface complains of writers who 'borrow obsolete words from Middle Sc., some with discretion, and others ignorantly and indiscriminately, obscuring the meaning to the ordinary reader'.[57] He feels however that they cannot be totally neglected, but quotations from their works are marked (E) for 'eclectic', which he considers to be 'a word which carries no reproach, and is, therefore, preferable to 'synthetic',[58] e.g. (under CRAMASIE **1.**)

Sc.(E) 1879 P. H. Waddell *Isaiah* 8:
Tho' yer fauts be like scarlet-bluid . . . aye, tho' they war cramosie-red, like woo they'se be wushen white.

Date, author and title (with page number, etc) also precede the quotation; a date after the title indicates a later edition used for excerption, e.g. (under HAND *n.* **2.** (10)

Slk. 1822 Hogg *Siege of Rxb.* (1874) xi.:
He has sitten at his supper hand and neive wi' the deil

As noted above, newspapers and magazines, including local publications, provided useful citations; the full date is given (sometimes with page number), e.g. (under RUCH *adj.* **3.**)

Sc. 1937 *St. Andrews Citizen* (30 Jan.) 3:
Even in the poorest farm-house is to be found what we in Scotland call "a rough table" . . .

Some illustrate local usage, e.g. (under HEEZE *v.* **1.** (3))

ne.Sc. 1957 *Mearns Leader* (18 Jan.):
The yells o' the loons hyzin' them on their road.

Proverbs, ballads, etc are quoted with the date of the collection from which they were excerpted. In the case of proverbs, many come from the early eighteenth-century collection of James Kelly, *A Complete Collection of Scottish Proverbs*, e.g. (under PUTT *v.* **2.** (1))

Sc. 1721 J Kelly *Proverbs* 371:
You putt at the Cart that's ay ganging

Good use was made of existing reference books, notably Jamieson's *Dictionary*, e.g. (under HAND *n.* **9.** (28) (b))

Rxb. 1825 Jam.:
He's as hand-rackle a fallow as is in a' the parish.

and also of regional glossaries, e.g. (under TAK *v.* **B. 1.** (1) (i))

Bnff. 1866 Gregor *D. Bnff.* 188:
The servan' took aboot the aul' man wee a' care.

Quotations from manuscript or oral sources are accompanied by the county abbreviation and date, e.g. (under NIEVE *n.* **4.** and NIP *v.* **3.**)

> Sh. 1934:
> Dey wir at da nevs.
>
> Edb. 1957:
> I tried to be nice to her, but she was gey nippit in her answers.

Most of the quotations are ordered historically, from the earliest to the most recent, but in the early parts (up to the end of letter D) they are first ordered geographically according to the dialect area, following the order of the *SND*'s north-to-south listing.

Conclusion

In 1975 the editing was brought to completion, in a remarkably short time for a major historical dictionary: forty-five years from publication of the first part to that of the last volume. This was due in large measure to the almost superhuman efforts of David Murison, and the equally superhuman patience of his long-suffering wife, Hilda, who also helped with the excerpting of texts. The role of Jessie Grant should also be noted: she helped her husband enormously in the early stages of the work. When Grant was awarded an LLD by the University of Aberdeen in 1933, she was given a special presentation for her help in the enterprise. Most press reports of the occasion described her part in providing a happy home and loving encouragement, but one newspaper interviewed her, relating how she had been involved in the word collection from the beginning, and how she helped on the business side and made great efforts to raise subscriptions.[59] Clearly women were expected to help with fundraising,[60] and indeed the role of women in the project was considerable, especially behind the scenes: most of the assistant editors were women. In the past most lexicographers and their assistants were men, but as changes in society in the twentieth century brought more women onto the labour market, the profession attracted women; especially from the mid century on, it was found to be compatible with family life, as there were possibilities for flexibility. In the twenty-first century, many of the leaders of lexicographic projects are women.

The final volume was published in 1976, at a time when attitudes to Scots were changing in a positive direction, and various new initiatives contributed to a forward momentum. The Scots Language Society was founded in 1972, its magazine *Lallans* providing a platform for writing in prose as well as verse. The Association for Scottish Literary Studies (founded 1970), as well as its role in supporting literature, provided help for the increasing role of Scots in education. The teaching of Scots in schools faces many difficulties, but some measures to increase it have been successful (see Chapter 7). Scots is now taught in some of the Scottish universities, and this is due in no small measure to the efforts of two of the Scots dictionaries' editors, Aitken and Murison. This has extended to overseas departments, especially in North America and Europe. The two historical dictionaries have played a major role, not least in that their very presence has helped to counter the view of Scots as a mere dialect. The provision of reliable information has contributed to the success of all these enterprises.

As the *SND* approached completion, the SNDA found itself at the crossroads. Some thought that, its goal now achieved, it could wind up its affairs. Others, however, saw that, especially in the prevailing climate, further research and documentation of Scots was needed. As will be shown in Chapter 7, the *Dictionary* furthered and enabled more developments in the lexicography of Scots that bring the riches of both the *SND* and the *DOST* into a wider sphere. The appearance of the historical dictionaries on the Internet in 2004 has given them a worldwide platform undreamt of by their early creators.

SEVEN

Other Twentieth and Twenty-first Century Scots Dictionaries

ISEABAIL MACLEOD

Concise Scots Dictionary and After

In the early 1970s, as noted at the end of Chapter 6, the SNDA faced major decisions about its future. Plans were unexpectedly focused by a large anonymous legacy left to the SNDA rather too late to be of any help in the production of the *SND*. There was considerable discussion as to how the money should be used: some members of the Executive Council thought that, as soon as the *SND* was published, the SNDA, having fulfilled its function, should close down and donate residual funds to its sister project, the *DOST*. Others, however, felt that there was more to be done for the Scots language as it rose to greater prominence, both in education and in other spheres.

In the meantime a suggestion had arisen for an abridged version of the two historical dictionaries; in 1970 Professor Angus McIntosh raised the idea at a meeting of the Joint Council for the Scottish Dictionaries, where it was well received, and in 1971 he proposed the plan to the SNDA Council, on which he represented the Joint Council (see Chapter 5). It was agreed that a plan should be set in motion for a one-volume dictionary, distilling the information in both the *DOST* and the *SND* and thus covering in compact form the whole history of Scots from its earliest medieval records to the late twentieth century. A sub-committee was set up, and in 1972 a report, including projected timing and cost, was produced by A.J. Aitken. A detailed pilot study, trying out different possible levels of detail and ways of laying out the information, was carried out between 1973 and 1975 by Aitken and Mairi Robinson who, as a young graduate, had made a distinguished contribution to the later stages of the *SND*, as assistant editor and later senior assistant editor. With the legacy and other residual funding, the association found that, for the only time in the seventy-plus years of its existence, it had money to spare, considered sufficient to fund a small editorial staff for a few years to carry out the project, and this was set in motion in 1975. The dictionary became known as the *Concise Scots Dictionary* (*CSD*), the first of a series of smaller dictionaries designed to bring some of the riches of the two major works to a wider public. It aimed both to inform the general public – and thus to raise interest in the Scots language – and also to provide a quick reference source for scholars in various academic disciplines.

By 1980 it was clear that, with galloping inflation, the available funding would certainly not be sufficient for the *CSD*, and a fundraising campaign was launched, with appeals to public bodies, including local authorities, trusts and companies, and to the general public. This struggle continued for many years on a hand-to-mouth basis, well beyond the end of the *CSD* project, with minimal funding supporting an inadequately small staff. Grants from the National Lottery, from the European Communities and from the Carnegie Trust helped certain later projects. A few of the local authorities did contribute (one or two on an annual basis) and, from 1990, there was some core funding from the Scottish Office, and later from the Scottish Arts Council, which had earlier made considerable intermittent contributions. But it was not until 2009 that viable core funding was provided by the Scottish government for the continuation of the dictionary work, with an enlarged staff much more able to cope with the demands of their projects, which are so important in twenty-first century Scotland.

The work of the SNDA could not have continued throughout these difficult years without very generous voluntary help on various aspects: with word collection, with fundraising and with management; a great debt is owed to the Executive Council, in particular its convenors at that time. And the SNDA was particularly grateful to its indefatigable treasurers, who were so generous with their time.

In the early years of the twenty-first century the *DOST* was about to reach completion, and at this stage it was decided that a new organisation was needed to manage the future of both historical dictionaries and their successors. In 2002 Scottish Language Dictionaries (SLD) was formed to take on this role; the SNDA was absorbed into the new organisation and the Joint Council ceased to act for the *DOST*, although the member universities retained representation on the SLD board. Its first convenor was Professor Christian Kay of the Department of English Language, University of Glasgow, and co-editor of the *Historical Thesaurus of the Oxford English Dictionary* (see Chapter 10). Margaret Dareau, editorial director of the *DOST*, became SLD's first director and she was followed by Dr Christine Robinson, a Scots scholar, with wide experience in academic and public life, who was already SLD's outreach officer.

Concise Scots Dictionary

In 1975 compilation of the *CSD* began at 27 George Square, Edinburgh under the direction of Mairi Robinson, with A.J. Aitken as consultant. Two other editors were appointed: Ruth Martin, a young graduate, full-time; and for a short time

Patricia Wilson, a teacher of English in Edinburgh, part-time. After some years on Collins and Chambers dictionaries, the present author joined the team on a part-time basis in 1979, on various aspects of the SNDA's work, from 1986 as editorial director. What was initially a three-year appointment on the *CSD* in fact continued until her retiral in 2005. Also in 1979 the team was joined by Lorna Pike, later a *DOST* editor and now project manager of *Faclair na Gàidhlig* (see Chapter 9). Margaret Dareau was also involved, in the earlier and later stages of the project, in gaps in her long career on the *DOST*. At the proof stage Pauline Cairns joined the staff; she too has had a much longer career with the Scots dictionaries than she expected, and is now senior editor with SLD.

The editors' task was to reduce the ten volumes of the *SND* and the even longer (though unfinished) *DOST* into a compact single volume. How was this done? The main reduction had to be in the almost total omission of the quotations, though a very few were retained, without attribution, where they were considered helpful in clarifying a meaning or a usage. For instance, under **grannie** . . . **5.** as a contemptuous response . . . *'We might have improvised. . .' 'Improvised yer grannie'.*

Rare material was omitted, and the editing rule was that, to qualify for inclusion, the word, meaning or form normally had to have at least three pieces of evidence (quotations or references – see Chapter 6) in the two parent dictionaries. More controversial was the omission of words, forms and usages that were limited, in their entire known history, to Shetland, Orkney and Caithness, on the grounds that such material is Norn, not Scots, in origin and would thus be better treated in a separate dictionary.[1] Words shared with other Scots areas are however included, and thus the *CSD* is by no means lacking in Northern Isles words. The senses of a word shared with English are omitted, but indicated by the inclusion of a sense linking it to the English word (see **stane** below). This technique allowed a very great quantity of material to be subsumed in a simple, (hopefully) readily understood form.

One of the major editorial problems was how to deal with the latter part of the alphabet where the *DOST* was not yet complete. It was only available up to letter O, with some proofs of P appearing towards the end of the project. It was possible to do some checking of other letters which were at a sufficiently advanced stage of editing, but for the rest of the alphabet the main source was the Scots material in the *OED*. The editors went through the *OED* text (not yet in electronic form), marking the Scots items column by column, also noting where the word coincided with English usage at the time. If shared with English, the word, form or usage was included only if its first evidence was a century earlier than English, or its last evidence a century later. The last group is numerous,

stane &c, stone &c *la16-*; **steen &c** *la16-, now Ork N* [sten; *Ork N* stin] *n* **1** = stone *la14-* **2** (1) a measure of weight, varying according to time, district, and the commodity *la15-* (2) a piece of metal used as a standard stone-weight *la16, Pbls, only Sc.* **3** *curling* = *curling stone* (CURL) *18-* **4** a testicle *20-*,
vti **1** = stone *la16-* **2** *vt, freq proverb* press (a cheese) by putting a large box of stones on top of the cheese vat *19-, now Abd Ayr.*
stonack &c = *ston(e)der*, la19–e20, Inv.
stoned &c 1 = stoned *16–*. **2** *of fruit* having a stone or stones *16-*. **3** *of a horse* not castrated, entire *16-, now Sh Ork Rox.*
ston(e)der *la20, NE,* **stondie &c** *20-, Abd,* **stoner** *la19-, NE Stlg* a large brown earthenware marble. **stonie** *adj* = stony *16-*. *n.* a small coloured marble *la19-, NE Fif WC, SW.* **stonie** (**tig**) name for varieties of the game of tig *19-, now Kcb Dmf.*
~ **bing** a heap or pile of stones *la19-, Fif WC Kcb.* ~ **blind** *lit and fig* completely blind *la14-*. ~ **cast** a stone's throw *la14, la18-, now local Sh-Fif.* ~**chack &c**, ~**chacker &c**, ~**chack-art 1** the stonechat *18-, now local Ags-S.* **2** the wheatear *19-, now Sh NE.* ~ **chipper** the wheatear *20-, Lnk SW.* ~**crase &c**, ~ **graze** ? a boil or abscess in the foot *el9, SW.* ~**dumb** completely silent *19-, now Sh.* ~ **dyke** a (*usu*) *dry-stane* (DRY) wall *la15-*. ~ **dyker** a person who builds (*dry-stane*) walls *20-*. ~ **fish** the gunnel *16-e19*. ~ **horse** *etc* an uncastrated horse *18-e20.* ~(**k**)**napper** a person who breaks stones *la19-, NE-S.*
~ **knot** a very tight knot *la18-19.* ~**mine** *mining* a road from underground workings which cuts across the strata *20-, Fif Lnk Ayr.*
~ **raw** the lichen *Parmelia saxatilis*, used for dyeing *la18-, now SW.*
~ **tired** very tired; lazy, bone idle *20-, S.* ~ **-wring** ? colic attributed to the presence of a stone in the kidney *e16, only Sc.*
~ **and lime** masonry, masoned stone *18-*.

Entry for **stane** from *CSD*

with many survivals in Scots from earlier periods of shared vocabulary. Interestingly quite a number of words, such as *gloaming*, twilight, (originating in Old English) later came back into Standard English, along with others such as *slogan*, which had been Scots from the beginning. The novels of Sir Walter Scott were a rich source of such transfers. The Older Scots data in the *SND*'s etymologies (see Chapter 6) were useful, and other sources were selected glossaries to Older Scots texts, chosen to give as wide a range as possible of types of writing and of the timescale. These included glossaries to the following: Klaus Bitterling's 'Der Wortschatz von Barbours "Bruce"' (1970);[2] Robert Lindsay of Pitscottie's *The History and Cronicles of Scotland*;[3] and three Edinburgh PhD theses on Older

Scots: Jane Slater's 'An Edition of Early Scots Texts from the Beginnings to 1410' (1952), Margaret Robertson's 'The Auld Laws' (1952) and, where relevant, Sarah Caldwell's 'The Relative Pronoun in Early Scots' (1967).

For certain major authors – Robert Henryson, William Dunbar, Gavin Douglas, Allan Ramsay, Robert Fergusson and Robert Burns – it was agreed that even a single occurrence would qualify for inclusion, and glossaries to their works were checked for that purpose. On the other hand words found only in other reference works were omitted, even if there were three or more occurrences, on the grounds that such information may simply be copied from one book to another.

Editors were more or less forbidden to do any new research, as it was considered that, if they started, like their predecessors they could take decades rather than years to complete the work. A minimum of new information was, however, added for fields such as law, mining (using a new glossary; see Chapter 4) and Scottish churches (for which a chart is included as an appendix). Some modern urban Scots was added: for instance, common nicknames for football clubs, such as Hibs and Hi-bees for Hibernian, as these are now a prominent part of vernacular vocabulary.

Given that the spelling of Scots, in spite of the efforts of various groups in the later twentieth century, remains almost as variable as it was in the medieval period, the choice of suitable headwords for *CSD* entries was difficult. It was decided to include all the main headwords in the *SND* and the *DOST*, partly to help readers to find the entries in the parent dictionaries if more detail was needed; these were sometimes followed, after a semi-colon, by one or more subsidiary headwords (see **stane** above). Generally speaking, the subsidiary list avoided what were termed 'predictable variants', i.e. those which regularly interchange with one another, such as -ou- and -oo-, -ch- and -gh-. Such variant forms are listed in the Introduction – though how many users make use of such introductory material is open to question.

Though most of the data in the *CSD* was drawn directly from the main sources, the information on pronunciation was given a thorough overhaul by A.J. Aitken,[4] and recast in a more strictly phonemic framework. He included transcriptions for obsolete words (preceded by an asterisk), transcribed 'with the pronunciations they would have had if they had survived to the present day'. He did not, however, try to indicate where earlier stress patterns differed from those of today. The transcriptions are based on spelling and rhyme evidence and on scholarly knowledge of earlier patterns. Although the *SND* is the main source for the modern Scots pronunciation, information was added from others, such as the *Linguistic Atlas of Scotland* (volume 3), the *English Dialect Dictionary*, and studies on Scots such as those of Sir James Wilson, George Watson, Jakob Jakobsen and others. Aitken also used indications from spellings and rhymes, as well as his own knowledge and that of colleagues and others. As in the *SND*, pronunciation is only given for words that do not follow the normal rules of Scottish Standard English pronunciation. The transcriptions are intentionally broad, the symbols sometimes covering different local realisations of the same phoneme, in particular:

> [ɑ] as in *saut* (salt), *cause, saw* ranges from the sound of the vowel in Northern English *hat*, through that of the first vowel in south-east English *father*, to that of the vowel in *bought* in most varieties of British Standard English. The Northern and Southern Scots dialects favour one or other of the first two of these sounds, the Central Scots dialects the last. *CSD* [ɑ] represents all three.[5]

Vowel length is marked only occasionally as it can normally be deduced from the Scottish Vowel-Length Rule.[6] The principles behind the phonetic transcriptions are set out in detail in the *CSD* Introduction, and that section can also serve as an excellent general guide to the pronunciation of Scots and Scottish Standard English.

In the *SND* and the *DOST*, timescale is shown by the range of quotations and, for the modern period, references (see Chapter 6). This information was telescoped in the *CSD* by means of a dating system to the nearest half century. Thus *la14-* means that the first evidence is in the late fourteenth century, i.e. between 1350 and 1399; the open dash means it is still current. *16-19* means there is evidence from the early sixteenth to the late nineteenth century; *la15-e18* between 1450 and 1749, and so on. If there is a long gap in the evidence, the date ranges are separated by a comma: *e16, 19-* means some evidence in early sixteenth century, nothing more till the early nineteenth, but pretty well continuous evidence from then until the present. These dates may refer to whole entries, to sections or to forms. If a form is undated, that means it covers the whole range of the entry or section to which it belongs.

Likewise, geographical distribution is given in an abbreviated form, using the *SND*'s list of areas and counties, but in a slightly simplified form. Both lists are given in the *CSD* Introduction. Some of the abbreviations have been altered for clarity, and the main difference is the use of C (Central) instead of m.Sc. (Mid Scots), so that em.Sc. (b) (the area south of the Firth of Forth) becomes sEC. Groups of areas are joined together, in the listed order north to south, so that *Sh-EC* indicates usage virtually anywhere down the east coast. '*Local*' means used sporadically throughout the Scots-speaking area, and it can be used to indicate

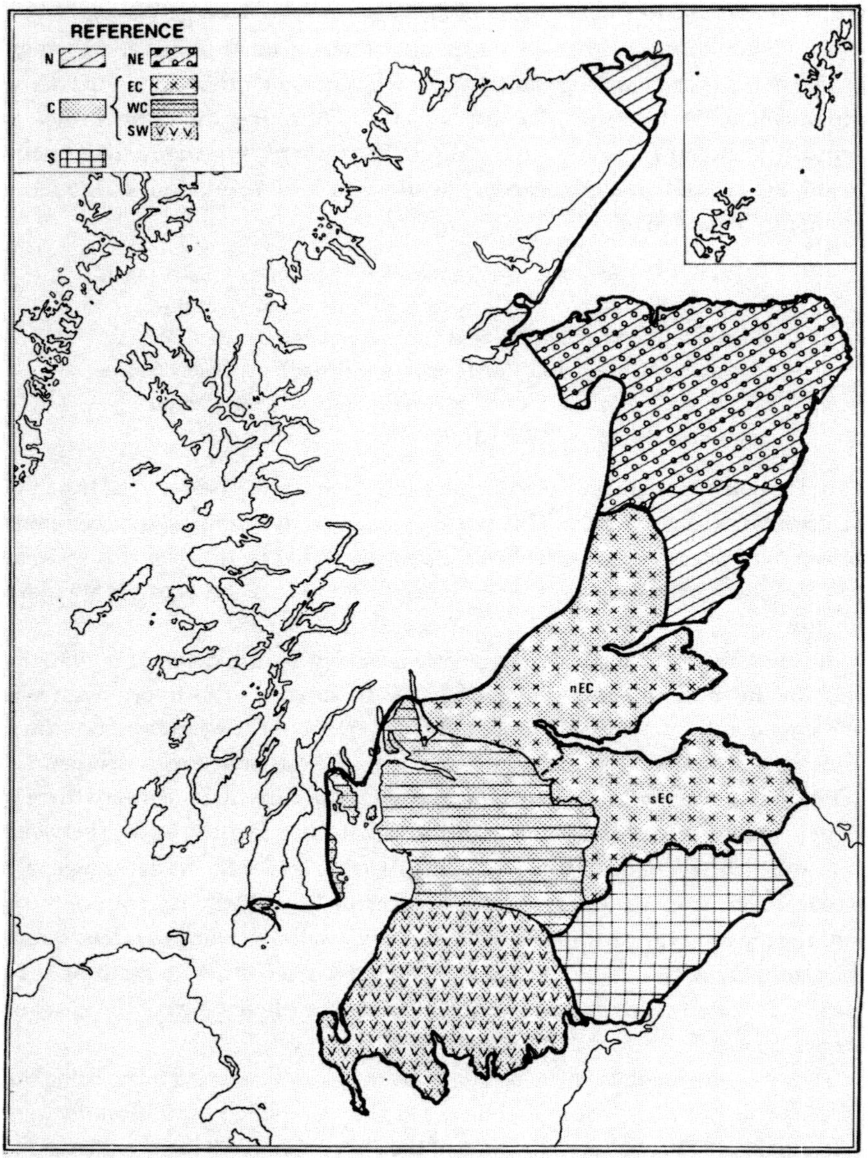

Map of the main dialect divisions of Scots, as used in the *CSD*: N (Northern Scots), NE (north-east Scots), C (mid Scots), EC (east mid Scots), WC (west mid Scots), SW (south mid Scots), S (southern Scots)

a smaller area; thus *local NE-Fif* means used sporadically from the North-East down to the Forth, and so on; and '*chf*' (for chiefly) means used mainly but not exclusively in that area. Quite often these labels are used with '*now*', indicating its present distribution, which was considered the most important aspect for most users (see **stane** above, *vti* 2).

Where possible, related words are 'nested' together (see **stane** above), i.e. different word classes are treated under one headword, and derivative and compound forms are included in the entry for the main form, listed in separate lists and followed by phrases and idioms using the main form or one of its variants. Grammatical information, such as past forms of verbs and plurals of nouns, are included, usually at the beginning of the entry or of the appropriate word-class section, for example:

> **pit**[1] . . . *v, pt also* **put, pat &c** *la16-, now local,* **pit** *la19-, local Cai-WC* . . .
> **ee**[1], *n, pl* **een &c, ene** *la14-e17,* **eyne &c** *la14-19,* **ewine &c***la14,* **eyes** *16-,*
> **ees &c** *la16-* . . .

Collocational information is expressed in various ways, e.g. with typical noun complements of adjectives:

> **thrang** . . . **5** *of persons or animals* busy, fully occupied . . .
> or with typical objects of verbs:
>
> **mask** . . . **2** (1) make or infuse (tea) . . .

Etymologies, at the ends of entries, are in as simple a form as possible. As in the *SND* the word's origin is sometimes given at the beginning of the entry by means of the first definition which indicates its relation to English (see Chapter 6 and **stane** above, *n* **1** and *vti* **1**). Where etymologies would of necessity be of some complexity, the user is simply referred to the parent dictionaries, as in [see *SND*] or [see *DOST*].

In addition to its main text of over 800 pages, the *CSD* has a long introduction, consisting mainly of detailed notes on the use of the *Dictionary*, but beginning with an eight-page 'History of Scots' by A.J. Aitken, which remains one of the best accounts of the language currently available. Tables of Scottish measures and a chart of the complex history of Scottish churches (as noted above) are added as appendices.

It became possible to have the *CSD* computer-typeset, and the success of this exercise was due in no small measure to its editorial secretary Liz Glass, who skilfully converted slips to the rather rudimentary typesetting coding system available at the time. The fundraising campaign was successful enough to allow completion by 1985, and the dictionary was published by Aberdeen University

Press to great acclaim. So successful was it that the first printing of 11,000 copies was sold before publication day and an immediate reprint had to be set in motion. Following as it did the publication of W.L. Lorimer's *New Testament in Scots* in 1983, the *CSD* is reckoned to have played a significant role in the resurgence of Scots at the end of the twentieth century. Not only does it aid the comprehension of Scots of all periods, it also helps in writing and speaking by providing in accessible form a wealth of information on all aspects of the language, thus allowing people to check the appropriateness of what they say or write.

The original plan was to produce a new edition after a decade or so but, as described below, other pressures intervened and it was not until the early years of the twenty-first century that work began on *CSD2*. Considerable additions are being made, not least with updates from the National Word Collection (see below). Another important aspect is the addition of material from the latter part of the *DOST* that was not available for the first edition in the 1980s. Further, the material exclusive to Shetland, Orkney and Caithness which was omitted from the first edition is being included. Considerable changes are being made to the structure and style of the entries. Rather than following the historical order of the parent dictionaries and *CSD1*, the new edition will give the most prominent current meaning first. All headwords, in the commonest current form, will be defined in full, rather than being simply related to their English cognates as in *CSD1*. There will be less 'nesting', and different word classes – noun, verb, etc – will have their own entries, each including relevant derivative forms, compounds and phrases. Pronunciation in the International Phonetic Alphabet (IPA) will be given for all current headwords and variants, and every entry will have an etymology. Obsolete forms, derivatives, compounds and phrases will be marked †; and forms will no longer be dated – they will be either current or obsolete. The aim is to provide more information than in *CSD1* in as accessible a form as possible.

Pocket Scots Dictionary

At the completion of the *CSD* in 1985, the SNDA found itself once more at the crossroads. Should it simply close down, or was there more to be done? At this later stage there were, fortunately, fewer council members who took a negative view than at the end of the *SND*, and it was decided that the work should continue on two broad fronts. The first was continuation of its publication programme, aiming to reach an even wider public. The second was the initiation of a new programme of word collection, without which it was clear that new publications would rapidly lose any claim to represent the Scots of the present day. For a few years, publication continued to take priority; this was in some measure due to the (quite mistaken) view that the new books would bring in money that would help to fund the research. A more important factor was the need to provide resources for the Scots language in education, clearly the most vital area in any attempt to encourage and preserve the language. Although Scots was now encouraged rather than punished in schools, there was little practical work done in the field, except by some inspired teachers in certain schools. It was hoped that published material would help.

For this reason the *CSD* was followed in 1988 by the *Pocket Scots Dictionary* (*PSD*), published partly with the schools market in mind. Therefore the *CSD* text was not only shortened but simplified for clarity, aims that are not always compatible: a small number of definitions are actually longer than the *CSD*'s. A limited number of the commonest and most confusing variant spellings are given, with further information in the Introduction. For pronunciation, it was considered that IPA was not suitable for this market, but some information is given for words that might cause a problem, either by using a respelling, such as **fleech** [fleetch], or by hints of various kinds, for example **douce** [rhymes with 'goose'] or **droich** [-ch as in 'dreich']. Again, there is further information in the Introduction. Some indication of geographic spread is given, with simpler labels than in the *CSD*, for example *Shetland E Central*, rather than *Sh EC*. Most of these labels indicate broad areas, as above, and only occasionally counties and cities, as in the *CSD*; where included, these are given in unabbreviated form: *Argyll*, *Edinburgh*.

Concise English–Scots Dictionary

For some time there had been pressure from certain quarters to produce an English–Scots dictionary, both from writers trying to widen their Scots vocabulary and from teachers. Many Scots have Scots words and phrases deep in their memories that don't readily surface when needed, and this seemed a useful means of retrieving them. It was decided that the *PSD* should be followed by another modest work, again with schools in mind. Teachers reported the need for English–Scots material to help children to write in Scots, especially in areas – alas, the majority – where the language has already receded to a large extent. But there was also consideration of the more general market: writers looking for the *mot juste* and the more casual user seeking, for instance, a Scottish greeting for a Christmas card. Owing to the exigencies of the publishing world, only one modest volume could be produced at that time.

A generous offer had come from William Graham, an Ayrshire schoolteacher who had spent a lifetime encouraging the use of Scots, not least in his *Scots Word Book* (1977). His work came in for a lot of criticism for its lack of rigour and, above all, lack of documentation. But his not unreasonable response to this was that the holders of these opinions were doing nothing to create better versions and were thus in no strong position to complain. Over several decades he had built up a large collection of English–Scots material and, as the prospect of publishing it in its original form was now remote, he very kindly offered it to the SNDA. The text was deficient, especially in indications of timescale and geographical distribution, and above all of sources: was this or that word known to the author, read in literature, limited to other dictionaries? It was however possible to use selected material from it as a base to which more was added from various other sources, and an SNDA style was applied. Other sources included the SNDA's new Word Collection and the English–Scots index of the *Scots Thesaurus* (see below), useful for the areas of vocabulary which it covered. Various computerised schemes for manipulating the data were considered but, given the time and resources available and the computer technology of the time, they would not have been cost-effective. In order to ensure that no important concepts had been omitted, relevant English words and their Scots equivalents were extracted from the *PSD* and listed alphabetically as a back-stop check. By these somewhat desperate means the *Concise English–Scots Dictionary* (*CESD*) was published in 1993.

Like the *PSD* it concentrates on modern words, but a few obsolete words are included (marked with the conventional dagger) for writing about older periods or in their style. Also as in the *PSD*, regional words are treated with clear labelling. Register labels, such as *informal, literary, gipsy,* are particularly useful in the *CESD*, given the need for help in selecting which Scots word to use, for example:

> **if** gin, an, in, gif *mainly literary.*

There was of course no space for the numerous spelling variants in the *CSD*, and the *CESD* normally has only one, at most two, and very occasionally a regional variant, for example under **higgledy-piggledy** . . . throuither, throwder *NE*, . . . Even the *PSD* has a few variant spellings, but with the *CESD* a definite choice had to be made and the SNDA found it necessary to give more attention to the vexed question of Scots spelling. In the choice of which spellings to use for the Scots equivalents of English headwords, various criteria were used and consideration was given to a number of factors, the main one being usage. As noted above there had been various moves to standardise spelling, largely unsuccessful, and indeed opposed by some who regard the variety and flexibility of Scots as one of its great joys. This works well enough for poetry, but for teaching Scots in schools a need is felt for some standardisation.

Many language activists would favour really radical reform, revoking the anglicising trend which began at least as early as the sixteenth century and was given a large boost by Allan Ramsay and his contemporaries in the early eighteenth. In 1947, some of the Lallans poets got together in an Edinburgh pub and produced the 'Scots Style Sheet',[7] a list of spelling forms designed to bring some uniformity into their work. Above all it did away with the apostrophe, as in o', wi', which had given the impression that these words were corruptions of English. The use of the apostrophe is still found, as in *Hallowe'en* rather than *Halloween,* but less so now. Its use of -aa- for [ɑ], as in 'avaa', has been used, especially by some North-East writers. Otherwise the style sheet had limited influence, though it led others to debate the question of orthography over the following decades. In 1985 the Scots Language Society (SLS) produced their 'Recommendations for Writers in Scots', again setting out rules, though not rigid ones, for spelling reform, basing them on the whole on existing evidence, but from any period and including Older Scots forms. These were examined very carefully by the SNDA in forming policies for the *CESD,* but some of the recommendations were found to be backward-looking and did not seem helpful in the aim to spread the use of Scots more widely in the community. In particular, some of the historical forms did not seem helpful to learners of Scots. In addition to unfamiliarity, one of the problems is that, paradoxically, the historically preferable spelling does not always elicit the modern Scots pronunciation. This is particularly the case with the -ou- (Scots) / -oo- (English) digraphs representing [u]: 'house' will be pronounced [hʌus] rather than [hus], whatever is said in the Introduction; it seems that 'hoose' is now the established Scots spelling, whatever its origins. The SLS rules recommend the spelling 'houss' to represent the Scots pronunciation, an ingenious suggestion, but this spelling is last recorded (in the *DOST*) in the sixteenth century

Other discussions have taken place over the years, but to little effect, and the SNDA's policy in the *CESD* was to follow usage, with information from the growing body of data in the new Word Collection. In the modern age the lexicographer's role is seen as a describing rather than a prescribing one, aiming to record the language rather than to guide its progress. Nevertheless, dictionary makers have to accept that, whether they like it or not, dictionaries will be used to some extent and by some people as a standard. It was known that the headwords of the *CSD* were already used by some in this way. The policy of following usage, as far as available information permitted, has been continued and refined in later dictionaries, including *CSD*2, and the resulting spelling is offered as guidance rather than as a rigid rule. In 1998, the SNDA produced the first Scots spellchecker, called (punningly) 'CannieSpell', which was designed to integrate with common word-processing programs such as Microsoft Word. The spellings used were based on those in SNDA dictionaries, and again followed usage rather than prescriptive rules.

Scots School Dictionary

Another demand from the market was for a two-way dictionary and the result was the *Scots School Dictionary*: *Scots–English/English–Scots* (*SSD*), a further shortening and simplifying of the *PSD* and *CESD* in order to produce a dictionary specially geared to the needs of schools. After centuries of neglect or opposition, official attitudes to both Scots and Gaelic have become more positive in recent decades. The inclusion of supportive statements in the Scottish Office Education Department's curriculum guidelines in the early 1980s encouraged respect for 'the language children bring to school'.[8] As well as encouraging greater awareness of the languages and their dialects, the 2009 Curriculum for Excellence also contained supportive statements about Scots. There are, however, still great difficulties in the path to real progress in education. Lack of capacity (and willingness) on the part of many teachers is not helped by a very full curriculum or by a lack of resources. Some gaps in the latter were filled in recent years, notably in 1996 with *The Kist*, an anthology of Scots and Gaelic (the latter with translation), along with teaching materials to fit in with the 5–14 curriculum policies; it was produced by the Scottish Council for Consultation on the Curriculum[9] and was a landmark in the teaching of Scots in schools. (The teaching materials are, alas, no longer available.) Another important initiative is Itchy Coo, an imprint founded in 2002 with funding from the Scottish Arts Council to produce publications in Scots for children of all ages, from nursery schools to senior classes. It also did a great deal to promote Scots in schools, including hundreds of school visits and teacher training sessions (until its Education and Outreach Programme closed in 2011).[10] When the *SSD* was published in 1996 it thus became part of a forward movement in the encouragement of Scots in schools. But as well as its primary educational purposes, with its compact format it was found to be a useful small reference book for Scots language, and it was later renamed the *Essential Scots Dictionary*.

As with the *CESD* it was possible to add a certain amount from the new Word Collection, and there were further additions of regional material from consultants in various areas, thus using oral as well as written sources. This exercise was made possible by a fortunate coincidence of grants specifically for the project both from the Scottish Office and from the European Communities.[11]

The SNDA produced other teaching material for Scots in schools, including a book of activities. But the most obvious need was for electronic resources, and the SNDA's contribution in 1998 was the *Electronic Scots School Dictionary*, a CD-ROM funded mainly by a grant from the Scottish Arts Council National Lottery Fund and creatively organised by Susan Rennie, who had considerable lexicographic experience with the Oxford dictionaries and with Chambers.

Technical aspects of the project were overseen by the Scottish Council for Educational Technology (now part of Learning and Teaching Scotland). The entire dictionary text was recast with sentence-type definitions, and accompanied by games and activities, and other features, notably 'Scotstoun', illustrating various aspects of a virtual Scots-speaking community, and the 'Grammar Broonie', a lively guide to Scots grammar, its title by analogy with the grammar wizards of English electronic publications of the time; an expanded version in paper form was published in 1999. The main aim of the CD-ROM was to reveal Scots to children as a language of the present, and indeed the future, rather than an old-fashioned way of speaking used mainly by their grandparents. Soon after this, as Internet usage became more widespread in schools, the SNDA created a section on its website, the Scuilwab (www.scuilwab.org.uk), which now provides material for both teachers and children, as well as for other learners of Scots, with lively activities and texts, and a useful list of further resources. SLD's outreach policy also helps by concentrating on schools.

Scots Thesaurus

The innovative *Scots Thesaurus* (1990) gives a different view of the Scots language, displaying it in fairly detailed subject categories in order to make people more aware of its richness and diversity. Although it also has obvious potential for educational uses, it is aimed mainly at a more general market and may be seen as a companion volume to the *CSD*, on which it was based. The book was produced when computer technology was at a much less advanced stage, but there was a typesetting file of the *CSD* available. This text was tagged with codes for subject fields and it was considered that this would provide not only a useful editorial tool but also a source for new reference books. One plan was for books or booklets on various subjects: several were proposed at various times, including sports and games, food and drink, legal terms, and building and architecture. Only the last of these actually appeared, as the *Dictionary of Scottish Building* (1996) (see Chapter 4).

In the late 1980s, however, it was decided to produce a composite volume, covering as much of the *CSD* as was feasible in one manageable book. It was not possible to include the whole range of subject areas, and so certain categories were chosen, mainly of traditional areas of life in Scotland. These are listed in full at the beginning, and there is further guidance to the detail of the contents in an index in English, which can also be used as a partial English–Scots dictionary. In some cases, especially where there is no exact Scots equivalent of the word, the index simply indicates the relevant category, as in **sewing** 13.1.7, which consists of a page of sewing terms. The entries use the *CSD*'s definitions and indications of regional variation, and a dagger sign for obsolete words (for example †**margolene** marjoram), but omit pronunciation and etymology, as well as most grammatical information and spelling variants. The SNDA was aided in this project by part-time help from Dr Caroline Macafee, later editor of the *Concise Ulster Dictionary* (1996) (see Chapter 4).

2 FARM ANIMALS

2.1	Cattle
2.2	Sheep, goats
2.3	Pigs
2.4	Horses, donkeys
2.5	Dogs
2.6	Cats
2.7	Domestic fowl
2.8	Description
2.8.1	General
2.8.2	Parts of the body
2.8.3	Behaviour, reproduction
2.9	Calls, noises

'Farm animals', from the list of sub-categories in the *Scots Thesaurus.*

horse *specific breeds, types, colours, ages* 2.4; cuddy; gry; horse-beast, †horse-fete; naig, †runsy; †steid 2.4
horse-collar brecham 7.9.1
horse diseases 2.4
horsefly *see* GADFLY
horse-hoe *specific types* 7.7.1; shim 7.7.1
horses *farming* 7.9.1
horsetail *specific types* 4.4

'Horses', from *Scots Thesaurus* index

The *Thesaurus* can be viewed as a form of signposting into some of the vast store of information in the dictionaries from which it derives: the *CSD*, the *SND* and the *DOST*. The content concentrates to a great extent on the natural world and material culture, with areas such as farming and fishing that have strong regional vocabularies, but it also includes fields like law, religion and education, where Scottish life has maintained its terminology at a more formal level. The longest section is 'character, emotions, social behaviour', which in some ways reveals aspects of the Scottish character – for example, in the fact that the section on terms of criticism is twice as long as that on terms of praise. Does the long section on thrift, miserliness, avarice, with numerous terms for 'miserly, mean', confirm the national stereotype? Probably not, but there is certainly a preponderance of negative over positive terms. Some sections, especially farming, go quite deeply into the various aspects of traditional country life and thus help to preserve the terminology of a lifestyle which is now all but gone; this is emphasised in the Introduction by Alexander Fenton.

Like the *CSD* and the *PSD*, the *Scots Thesaurus* was published by Aberdeen University Press, then owned by Robert Maxwell. After the collapse of the Maxwell empire in 1992, another publisher had to be found for the SNDA dictionaries. For a few years they were published by Chambers and, from 1999, by Edinburgh University Press.

Word Collection

During the years of editing the *CSD*, there had been little time for the first of SNDA's aims: research on the language. By the mid 1980s it was clear that it was essential to resume the research alongside the continuing publishing programme. Data collection had been the main activity of the early pioneers of the *SND* and had continued in full force alongside the editing until the early 1960s. Of necessity it had been much reduced during the last years of the *SND* editing, and thereafter more or less put on hold to concentrate on the *CSD*. But publications could not be starved of new information indefinitely; even later data was by now twenty or more years old. In 1985 a modest word-collection scheme was set up alongside the continuing demands of the publishing programme, using both written and oral sources. Its setting-up was helped by a subvention from the European Communities.

The main search was for new data, of which there was more than might be expected in a language often regarded as being on the point of extinction. An amusing example of new usage is rhyming slang; as noted in Chapter 4 it has long been known to be more than a Cockney phenomenon. Expressions such as *corn beef* for 'deef' or *Mick Jagger* for 'lager' can be useful to the lexicographer in that the rhymes would not work in English and they are thus confirmed as Scots rather than more widely used slang. The search also aimed to fill gaps in the record, in particular to find confirmation of continued use of what was already recorded, and it is encouraging to find so much still used somewhere, even if not as widely as in the past. Occasionally words thought to be long obsolete were found to be still in use; for example **blind nail**, meaning a headless nail, previously only recorded in the Older Scots period, was found to be still in current use in Edinburgh.

Given the very meagre resources at the time, the editors had to depend to a large extent on voluntary help with the Word Collection. On a low budget, gathering from written sources is slightly more manageable than oral collection, and a modest reading scheme was set up; it is still running. Publishers have been generous in donating books which readers can mark up for later processing rather than copying the information onto slips. The aim is to cover recent writing as well as some earlier texts. Newspapers and magazines are a useful source of language information and change, and it is gratifying to see that Scottish media are more receptive to Scots material than they used to be, both in occasional articles in Scots and in sporadic inclusion of Scots words and usages.

With no resources for formal fieldwork, collection of oral material had to rely at that time on more casual means, such as the observations of the staff and colleagues, and contributions from the general public (sometimes in response to publicity) and a number of correspondents. In the 1990s these included a prisoner in Saughton Prison in Edinburgh who, as he said himself, had ample opportunity to hear Scots from many different dialect areas. A potentially rich source of oral material is to be found in the transcripts of the numerous oral history schemes up and down the country, especially since the interviews were not carried out for linguistic purposes, and responses may thus in many cases be more natural. (With specifically linguistic surveys, there is always the danger that informants give the researcher what they think is the desired response.) Excerption of such scripts is, however, very time-consuming and only small quantities of the data have been gleaned.

The first project to use this new material on any scale was a New Supplement to the *SND*. By the 1990s, as noted above, even its later information was decades old and it was decided to create an electronic body of new data to bring the record up to date and to fill gaps, as far as was possible with the meagre resources available. This was achieved in 2005 with the help of a grant from the Heritage Lottery Fund.

Collection continues into the twenty-first century, along the same broad lines, but with the advantages of increased resources and of improved methods of storage and retrieval. A Reading Scheme and an Oral Collection Scheme form the National Word Collection, still dependent on voluntary help to bring in data to be processed by experienced editors. These are explained and elaborated on the SLD website (www.scotsdictionaries.org.uk), which is an invaluable means of eliciting help from the public

Electronic Methods

While A.J. Aitken investigated the use of electronic aids for the *DOST* at an early stage (see Chapter 5), David Murison's aim was to complete the *SND* as soon as possible and, to him, bringing in radical new methods at a late stage would have been too great a distraction. The SNDA's first foray into the electronic world was with the computer-typesetting of the *CSD* in the early 1980s, and the typesetting file thus produced was used in later projects, not least, as noted above, the *Scots Thesaurus*. When the Word Collection was resumed, it was clear that an electronic scheme for storage and retrieval was essential. Several were tried over the decades, some more successful than others. Negotiations were begun with Pergamon Press, like Aberdeen University Press part of Robert Maxwell's empire. After the debacle of 1992, the SNDA worked for some years with Compulexis, an independent organisation based in Oxfordshire, and later with other computer consultants. By 2008 a Microsoft Access database system had been set up for the Word Collection and a new database is currently (2012) under development to improve the functionality of the online DSL.

An important goal for the SNDA was the creation of an electronic version of the *SND*. It had been typeset in hot metal and when the first part was printed in the early 1930s, computer-typesetting was still decades away in the future; even when the last volume came out in 1976, it was still a relatively new technique. In the 1990s special funding was sought for an electronic system and various methods were investigated. Eventually, after years of exploration (and fruitless attempts at fundraising), a pilot project, the eSND, was set up with a grant from the Carnegie Trust, with the aim of digitising a sample of the *SND*.[12] The digitisation methods used for the *SND* formed the basis for a successful funding bid to the Arts and Humanities Research Board (now the Arts and Humanities Research Council), under their Resource Enhancement Scheme. A three-year project was set up at the University of Dundee; it covered the conversion of both the historical works, the *SND* and the *DOST*, and was managed by Susan Rennie with Dr Victor Skretkowicz, chairman of the Joint Council, as its academic host in Dundee.

When the *SND* digitisation project was first discussed in the early 1990s, it was hoped that the initial conversion could be done by OCR (optical character recognition) methods, especially as the type is generously large and very clear. At that time, however, the technology was not sufficiently advanced to cope with the complexity of the *SND*'s structure, and re-keying seemed to be the only option. Some years later, however, the OCR option became possible after all and the text was scanned at the Centre for Data Digitisation and Analysis at Queen's University, Belfast; apart from the latter part of the *DOST*, which had been computer-typeset and was thus already in electronic form. The resulting text was proofread to pick up any residual errors and then parsed automatically to add structural markup, in the form of XML (eXtensible Mark-up Language), which allows refined searches to be run on the underlying data.[13] Searches can be carried out on the Dictionaries' main texts and their supplements, either together or separately, and they can be searched either by headword or by a full-text search. The DSL website (www.dsl.ac.uk) also contains the introductory material from both dictionaries, their bibliographies (which can also be searched) and the *SND*'s maps.

The two dictionaries were published on the web in 2004, for the first time together in their full form, under the title of the *Dictionary of the Scots Language/ Dictionar o the Scots Leid* (DSL), thus providing detailed information on Scots from its earliest medieval records to 1976, when the *SND* was completed. In 2005 the New Supplement (see above) was added, giving the *SND* a modicum of much-needed updating, and a history of Scots to 1700 (specially written by Caroline Macafee) was added in 2007. Owing to the conditions of the grant the website is 'free at point of access', which has been a great boon not only to those concerned with Scots language at all levels, but to the wider scholarly community and to the general public (although less so to the then cash-starved SLD). It was not possible to make alterations to the texts within the limited scope of the initial three-year project. An application for a further three years' funding in Dundee was unsuccessful but, with improved resources, SLD's plans are now underway for the development of the material as well as its updating.

Other Scots Dictionaries of the Period

Chambers Scots Dictionary

At the beginning of the twentieth century there were three main sources of information on the Scots language: Jamieson's *Etymological Dictionary of the Scottish Language*, still in print in a condensed version (see Chapter 3); the *Oxford English Dictionary*, which had only reached letter J by 1900 (see Chapter 10); and the *English Dialect Dictionary* (*EDD*), published by Oxford University Press in six volumes from 1898 to 1905.[14] The *EDD* was compiled by Joseph Wright partly from the collections of the English Dialect Society, along with other works (listed by W.W. Skeat) and the research of A.J. Ellis. Wright also collected data from numerous informants by means of a lengthy questionnaire. While the *EDD* concentrates on the dialects of England, it does cover the other parts of the British Isles, and Scotland is reasonably well represented. Wright had about twenty voluntary readers from various parts of Scotland, including quite a few from the south-west.

One of these was Alexander Warrack, and after the completion of the *EDD* he had the idea of using the material collected to produce a Scots dictionary. Encouraged by W.A. Craigie, he set about the task, with considerable help from

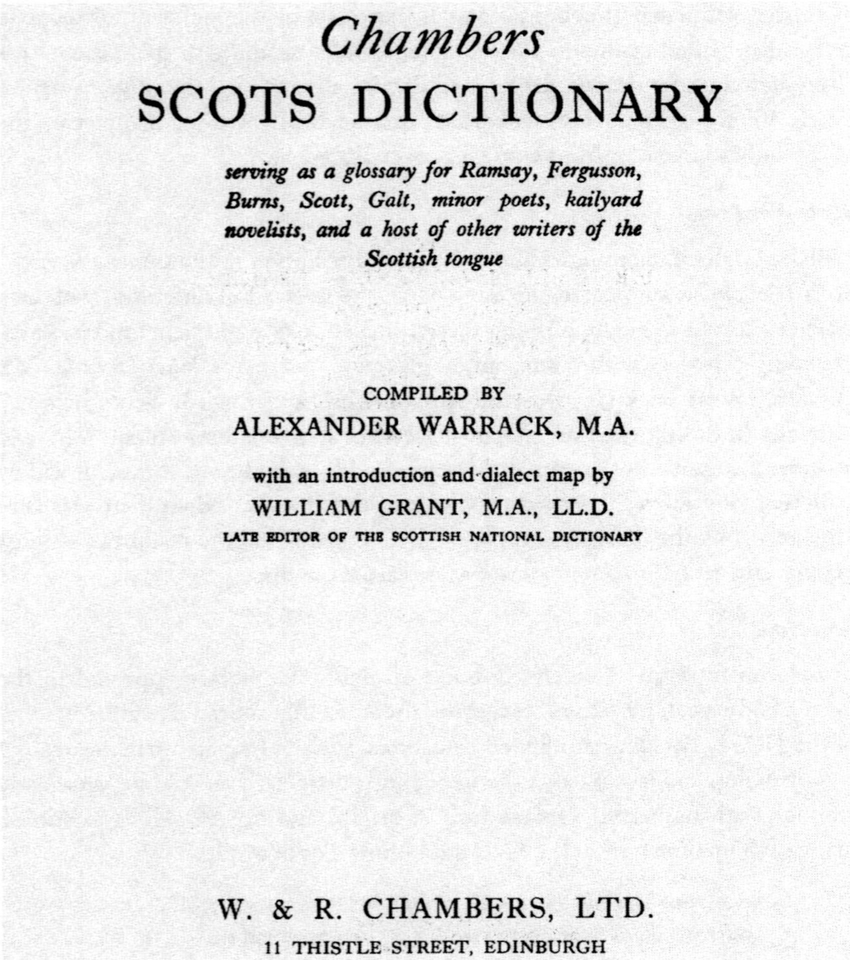

Chambers

SCOTS DICTIONARY

serving as a glossary for Ramsay, Fergusson, Burns, Scott, Galt, minor poets, kailyard novelists, and a host of other writers of the Scottish tongue

COMPILED BY

ALEXANDER WARRACK, M.A.

with an introduction and dialect map by

WILLIAM GRANT, M.A., LL.D.

LATE EDITOR OF THE SCOTTISH NATIONAL DICTIONARY

W. & R. CHAMBERS, LTD.

11 THISTLE STREET, EDINBURGH

Title page of *Chambers Scots Dictionary*.

Craigie, as is clear from his original Preface and Dedication.[15] Finding a closed door at Oxford University Press, he offered his work to Chambers in Edinburgh, then growing in importance as publishers of English dictionaries (see Chapter 10). In 1911 it was duly published as the *Scots Dialect Dictionary*, later renamed *Chambers Scots Dictionary*, the title under which it continued to be published, in unaltered reprints, until the early 1990s. It gained in prestige from an introduction by William Grant, which provided an outline of Scots dialects. The *Dictionary* is a useful basic list of words and their meanings, but with no hint as to their provenance or their position in time or geographical distribution. The number of entries, estimated at about 60,000, is increased by the inclusion of separate entries for variant spellings: for example, **drouk** (meaning to soak, drench) is also entered under **drawk**, **droke**, and **drook**, all with slightly different definitions. When Jamieson reprints became unavailable, it was for many years the only handy source of information on Scots vocabulary.

Scots Word Book

William Graham, mentioned above for his contribution to the *Concise English–Scots Dictionary*, supported the Scots language over a long lifetime, both as a teacher and as a writer, publishing several small books about Scots and in Scots, including a novel (with a substantial glossary), *Scorn my Inheritance* (1996). His *Scots Word Book* (1977), with Scots–English and English–Scots sections, provides basic information in an unsophisticated but convenient way, and includes a summary of grammatical points and lists of idioms. Although widely criticised (see above) it served a useful purpose at a time when there was very little available: the recently completed *SND* was beyond the resources of most people, and even the *Chambers* was a less casual purchase.

Scoor-oot

In 1989 an innovative and lively book on Scots vocabulary appeared in the form of *Scoor-oot*, by James Stevenson, then recently retired as editor-in-chief of the *DOST*. Divided into fifteen categories, such as human attributes; eating and drinking; and law, it treats the words and particularly the phrases in a lively manner, with numerous explanations of origins and use as well as examples, many of them drawn from the *SND* quotations. For example:

> **scoor-oot** The custom, now less observed than formerly, of scattering coins at or after a wedding to be scrambled for by children. . . . In 1964 a mother commented ruefully, 'It'll no be the first time he'll have lost the knees oot 'is BREEKS at a *scoor-out*.' [the quotation is from Fife][16] . . . In other parts of Scotland *scatter*, *scramble* and *poor-oot* may be used in the same sense.

Small capitals indicate that the word has its own entry elsewhere.

English–Scots lists

James Nicol Jarvie's *Lallans*, an interesting if slight work, appeared in 1947.[17] This title in the 1940s might suggest a Scots–English list to help to read the works of the Scottish Renaissance poets but the sub-title, *A Selection of Scots Words Arranged as an English-Scots Dictionary with Pronunciation and Examples*, reveals

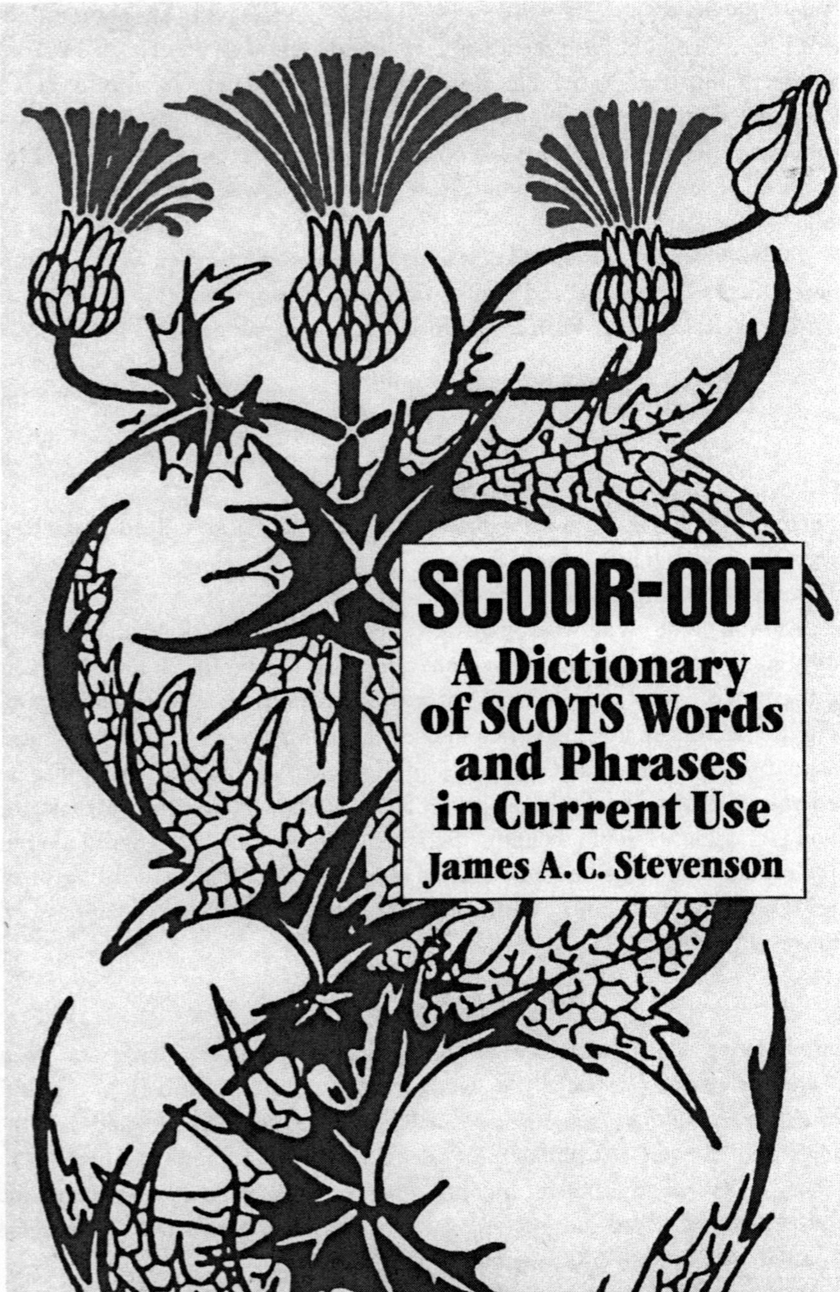

Cover of *Scoor-oot* by James Stevenson.

a very different purpose, and the list occupies the greater part of the book, along with a short Scots–English section and some supplementary material. A preface in Scots mainly laments the diminishing of the Scots language; a second preface in English also states that the book makes no claim to be a 'learned work' and 'pretends more to entertain than to educate . . . for deeper study the *Scottish National Dictionary* will soon be available'. In 1947, this was something of a pious hope.

The arrangement of the entries is unusual, containing English word, pronunciation, Scots equivalent, and a quotation with its pronunciation and English translation; it must have been a nightmare for the typesetter. Thus:

> SHORT. *Spoken,* ***cuttay.*** *Spelt,* **cutty.**
> Weel dune, cutty sark! – Burns.
> WEEL DUIN, CUTTAY SAARK !
> *Well done, short shift!*

This may have been the first English–Scots dictionary and, indeed, there have been very few such lists, of any length.

Though not indicated in its title, the *Lowland Scots Glossary* by Iain MacKinnon (1966) is another English–Scots dictionary, on a very small scale. It is an English–Scots listing, divided into quite small categories. It has some very odd Scots words and some strange features. MacKinnon uses abbreviations such as (neo.) neologism invented or composed (as **ironmonger** airnster.), or (adp.) adapted form or word (as **General** Lead-maister, wyse-maister). Are these his neologisms, and did he do the adapting? Some Scots equivalents are archaic, but there is no indication of this in the dictionary; for example, **Dowager** Dowrier. ('Quene-dowriar' was frequently used of Mary of Guise in the sixteenth century; see *DOST*.) A list of idioms 'translates' rather stilted English into genuine Scots phrases and proverbs.

Scots Language in Europe

Scots has long aroused interest in Europe; in the nineteenth century, it was largely for literary reasons, especially in Germany (for example, Robert Motherby's *Taschen-Wörterbuch des Schottischen Dialekts* (1826) is noted in Chapter 3). In the 1960s David Stevenson's booklet, *En Liten Scotsk-Norsk Ordliste: A Short Scots–Norwegian Wordlist,* aimed to highlight the resemblances between Scots and Norwegian. It lists an idiosyncratic selection of Scots words with Norwegian (Bokmål) and English equivalents.

Another little German book, *Scots: Die Sprache der Schotten* (2005), is aimed at the tourist market, but a professional attitude underlies its light-hearted approach. The author, Manfred Malzahn, has a degree in Scottish literature and he provides German visitors with a useful introduction to Scotland. Part of a German travel series, the book has guidebook as well as phrase-book features. Visitors are also provided with linguistic, and some cultural, information in *The Scots Travelmate* (2005) from Lexus Ltd in Glasgow, again part of a series.

Other Small Scots Dictionaries

Collins has a long tradition of producing dictionaries for a popular market (see Chapter 10), and they added to this in 1995 with the *Collins Gem Scots Dictionary*,[18] describing it as 'a dictionary of living Scots', covering 'everyday language, official and technical language and literary language'. The Collins editors include Michael Munro, author of *The Patter* (see Chapter 4). It has sentence-type definitions, good example sentences and phrases. Pronunciation guides were necessary; for example:

> **pech** (pronounced **pe**CH) To **pech** is to pant for breath, especially because of effort or exertion: *We were all peching by the time we reached the top*. To be **peched out** is to be exhausted and out of breath.

It gives origins of some words and includes encyclopedic information, such as geographical areas and historical events. The book has no pretensions to be an academic study, but for its own purpose, and as far as it goes, it might be described by the Scots expression 'guid gear gangs in sma buik'. It was followed in 2009 by a shorter book, *Scottish Words*.

The Concise Dictionary of Scottish Words and Phrases (2006) by Betty Kirkpatrick has a short word list, which leaves space, even in a small book, for explanations of various kinds. Some of these are etymological, e.g. **keelie** . . . [from Gaelic **gille** a young man]; while some are on customs, e.g. under **guising**, there is a note on how American customs are influencing the Scottish Halloween. It also has numerous helpful example sentences, many of them illustrating the word in Scottish Standard English rather than in vernacular Scots, e.g. (under **deave**) *The kids were deaving us for ice cream*. The *Scots–English, English–Scots Dictionary*, edited by David Ross and Gavin D. Smith, has a much longer word list but merely gives headwords and their equivalents, without any attempt at discrimination.

Online Dictionaries

More and more dictionaries are appearing online[19] – often only online – and, in addition to the magnificent resource of *Dictionary of the Scots Language*, several less sophisticated sites have appeared for Scots. They include the *Scots Dictionary*

Online, part of *Scots-Online: Pittin the Mither Tongue on the Wab* (www.scots-online.org), a wide-ranging site covering many aspects of Scots language. Though mainly a list of words and their meanings, it does give pronunciation in the International Phonetic Alphabet. It advises users that it is 'a rough guide' and points them in the direction of the SLD dictionaries. An English–Scots section is admitted to be 'more like a thesaurus than a dictionary', as a search simply calls up all the entries which contain the desired word. With an emphasis on slang usage in Scots, the *Scottish Vernacular Dictionary* (www.firstfoot.com) claims to be a 'Scottish local dictionary', although most of the words on its (rather short) word list and their illustrative phrases are widely used.

These are just two examples of the numerous casual, do-it-yourself lists appearing online. They are a long way from the carefully researched historical dictionaries, though they do serve their own purpose, not least in raising interest in the language. All major dictionaries will of necessity be online in the future, with the great advantage of a greater ability to keep pace with ever-changing language in a changing world.

PART II

Gaelic Lexicography

Introduction

WILLIAM GILLIES AND LORNA PIKE

From its beginnings down to the present time Gaelic lexicography has mostly been conducted by devoted individuals without institutional backing or funding. It was said of the late seventeenth-century Celtic scholar and lexicographer Edward Lhuyd that he 'despised the Fatigue of learning [the Gaelic] Language, and travelling wherever it was spoke, that he might attain its different Dialects . . . He bore patiently the Denial of promised Helps, and was basely deserted by his mean-spirited Subscribers to the Dictionary.'[1] These words would have struck a chord with Edward Dwelly at the beginning of the twentieth century, and with not a few other Gaelic scholars in the interim.

Another recurrent motif in the history of Gaelic dictionary-making is that of association with the Word of God. By comparison, scientific and philological aims, although strongly represented at the genesis of the tradition, did not resurface until the later nineteenth-century emergence of Celtic or Gaelic Studies as an academic subject. By that time a gradually increasing range of Gaelic publications, together with the equally gradual development of Gaelic itself as a written medium, had given rise to a series of substantial dictionaries designed to reflect the language as a whole and service the emergent poetic canon as well as the prose literature of biblical texts, sermons and (eventually) secular prose-writing. The high-water mark of this early phase of activity was Edward Dwelly's *The Illustrated Gaelic Dictionary* (first published between 1901 and 1911), which held sway until late twentieth-century social and political developments increased pressure for handbooks that were more relevant, less austere and, above all, more user-friendly (including learner-friendly).

In the medieval Gaelic literary tradition, we can point to gatherings of difficult vocabulary, glossaries and other aids to understanding from the seventh century to the seventeenth; and the afterglow of this learned activity had at least a marginal impact on the modern lexicographical works described below. The 'language of the people' was another matter; dialect studies and similar had to wait longer for such attention, and belong more to the age of 'folk' studies, linguistic fieldwork and Gaelic language revival, bolstered by the confidence and nostalgia of émigré Gaels during the last century and a half.

For most of the twentieth century, including the Gaelic Literary Renaissance, Gaelic speakers got by with Dwelly's *Dictionary* and revisions or reprints of a few of its predecessors. Towards the end of the century, however, the needs of language revitalisation and the belated institutionalisation of Gaelic led to a fresh wave of dictionary-making activity, to answer the needs of learners of Gaelic and those who sought to use the language in new contexts. Beside these efforts, Glasgow University's Historical Dictionary of Scottish Gaelic project from the late 1960s onwards aspired to bring Gaelic firmly within the ambit of professional, corpus-based lexicography, as opposed to the labours of compilation and introspection undertaken by individuals, however scholarly and perceptive. Although the Glasgow venture did not bear fruit as originally conceived, advances in computer technology now allow it to facilitate the ongoing Faclair na Gàidhlig project, of which more anon.

EIGHT

From Medieval Beginnings to 1911

WILLIAM GILLIES AND LORNA PIKE

We owe the existence of the earliest Gaelic literature to the glossarial and exegetical activities of monks and biblical scholars, who established a bridgehead for the vernacular Gaelic language to enter the world of literacy in the seventh century or even earlier. The *Thesaurus Palaeohibernicus*, which contains the surviving specimens of contemporary writing from the Old Irish period, consists mostly of this Christian scholastic material, in which explanatory glosses figure very largely.[1] As the native literature of law, verse-craft and poetry gradually attained written status, these categories likewise attracted scholarly annotation in the form of glossing and commentary, as can be seen in the case of law tracts like the *Senchus Már* or the elegy for St Columba known as *Amra Coluimb Cille*.[2] As time went by and the practices of writing, adapting and creating written literature developed, the need was felt to provide formal glossaries of, for example, early legal or poetic texts, whose meaning was becoming obscure but which were still felt worthy of attention. In the pre-Norman period, the Glossary of Cormac, King-Bishop of Cashel, compiled c.900, is the best-known example; the practice of studying these early texts was maintained in the post-Norman period by such learned families as the O'Davorens and O'Clerys.[3]

The scribal tradition of late medieval Scotland contains examples of this aspect of Gaelic manuscript culture. The National Library of Scotland manuscript NLS MS 72.1.7 contains a short list of *Dubfocail* (literally 'Dark words', i.e. obscure or difficult words), and NLS MS 72.1.38 contains a more substantial list of such old literary words under the heading *Cóir anmanna* ('The propriety of names').[4]

This glossarial tradition crossed seamlessly over into print in the eighteenth century in the form of glossaries or glossarial footnotes supplied with early broadsheets and collections of poetry. The transition from manuscript to print clearly created new audiences and new ways of exploiting older literature, just as the transition from oral to written literature had done centuries earlier, and with these came the need for explanatory prompts and assistance.[5] Indeed, the same policy of collecting difficult words commended itself to the Scottish Gaelic Texts

Society (SGTS), founded in 1934; it can perhaps be regarded as the price the Gaels seem willing to pay in order to indulge an abiding passion for continuity in literature.[6]

Quite distinct from this functional, exegetical mainspring of the Gaelic lexicographical tradition, one can identify a philological impulse towards the classification and study of languages and cultures in the context of late seventeenth-century scientific thought in Britain, with implications for Gaelic and the other Celtic languages. The Rev. Robert Kirk, who in 1690 oversaw a printing of Bedell's Irish Bible for Scottish Gaelic speakers, in roman letters and with a glossary of Irish words which did not transpose easily into Scottish Gaelic, also compiled a *Vocabulary*, which was published in 1702 after Kirk's death by W. Nicolson for 'the curious reader . . . desirous to make himself a little acquainted with [Scottish Gaelic].'[7] We note here the classificatory principle implicit in Kirk's thematic arrangement of his subject matter, which is arranged in such sections as 'Of Heaven', 'Of God', 'Of Created Spirits', together with several sections relating to the natural world and a couple relating to the human world. This thematic arrangement was based on that found in John Ray's Latin–Greek–English *Dictionariolum Trilingue* (1675), and it is reminiscent also of the questionnaires regarding rites and customs which figured in ethnological enquiries sponsored by a group of Oxford and London scientists and antiquarians including Robert Boyle, Robert Sibbald, John Aubrey and Edward Lhuyd.[8] Of these scholars, Edward Lhuyd was especially important for Gaelic lexicography because his taxonomic interests were so well founded and so resolutely pursued. He had a firm grasp of the Celtic and Goidelic levels of linguistic relatedness and how these were reflected in synchronic dialectal and register distinctions within Irish and Scottish Gaelic. He coped efficiently both with manuscript sources for the earlier language and, in the field, with illiterate Gaelic-speaking informants. Although he died before his ambitious scheme for the study of the languages of the British Isles could be realised, he was the father of Gaelic dialectology and a major contributor to Gaelic lexicography, as can be seen from his manuscripts and papers, and from what he managed to publish in *Archæologia Brittanica* (1707).[9]

The next work to be mentioned, Alexander MacDonald's *A Galick and English Vocabulary* (1741), was the product of yet another distinct impulse: the intertwined aims of moral–spiritual and linguistic–political initiatives designed to tie the Highlands more securely into a bilingual and ultimately anglophone British world. Nevertheless, the antiquarian and scientific instincts whose roots go back further than the eighteenth century continued to make themselves felt. Repositories such as the National Library of Scotland and the older universities' libraries contain various collections of Gaelic dialect vocabulary or technical terminology, plus some more ambitious lexicographical compilations, made by Highlands and Islands ministers and priests, schoolmasters, tacksmen, soldiers and others, from the later eighteenth century to the earlier twentieth. Others remain in private hands, and doubtless many have been lost. Some were utilised in printed dictionaries, which will be noticed below; others found their way into journals like *Transactions of the Gaelic Society of Inverness*, or were published separately with scholarly annotation (e.g. Father Allan McDonald's *Words and Expressions from South Uist*). All bear testimony to aspects of a devotion to their language which Gaelic speakers seem to have carried with them at all times.

The Birth of Gaelic Lexicography

The first dictionary of Gaelic, and indeed the first printed secular book in the language, was published in 1741 under the auspices of the Society in Scotland for Propagating Christian Knowledge (SSPCK). The Scottish wing of the Society had been formed in 1709 to spread the Protestant religion. It focused on the Highlands and Islands as hotbeds of religious superstition and sought to educate all children to grow up to be useful citizens. In 1716, following the failure of the 1715 Jacobite Rising, the Society outlined its policy in a memorial, as follows: 'Nothing can be more effectuall for reducing those countries [i.e., the Highlands and Islands] to order and making them usefull to the Commonwealth than teaching them their duty to God, their King and Countrey, and rooting out their Irish [i.e., Gaelic] language, and this has been the care of the Society so far as they could for all the schollars are taught in English, and none are allowed to be masters of the Societie's Charitie Schools, but such as produce sufficient certificats of their piety knowledge and loyalty.'[10]

Accordingly, the use of Gaelic was prohibited in SSPCK schools. The result of this policy was that children learned to read and write in English but understood very little. In 1722, a sub-committee was appointed to examine this situation and propose a solution. This group reported that Gaelic should be used in the classroom to facilitate understanding of English. Their report asked, amongst other things, 'whither an English and Irish vocables [i.e., a dictionary] may not be of use in this matter, and Schollars obliged to Learn so many words weeklie.'[11] It was to be a further three years before the Society finally decided on the structure and methodology of such a dictionary. The sub-committee proposed that

> The Schoolmaster should oblige their [*sic*] Schollars every Saturnday to get by turn a certain number of Irish words into English, and for their help in this, that there be written an English and Irish vocabulary, and sent to these schools where

> Irish is spoke, and the Committee having had diverse English and Latine vocabularies laid before them, they make choice of that Entituled the new vocabularie for the use of Schools, to which is added a Collection of the most Comon Adjectives to Verbs, the fifth edition printed by Mr James M'Ewing anno one thousand seven hundred and twenty, and appointed that a letter be written to the Presbytery of Lorn, entreating they may nominate one of their number to compose the said Irish vocabularie, by puting Irish in place of Latine in that above-mentioned . . .[12]

Thus, Gaelic was to be used to help bring about its own extinction. Nineteen years after its first recorded mention, the dictionary was published. The chosen compiler was the renowned Gaelic poet Alexander MacDonald, Alasdair Mac Mhaighstir Alasdair.[13] Born at Dalilea in Moidart, probably between 1690 and 1700, he was employed by 1729 as a teacher and catechist at the SSPCK school at St Finnan's Isle in Ardnamurchan. Unusually for his day, he was literate and learned in both Gaelic and English. It is believed that he studied at Glasgow University (though he does not seem to have graduated), and his poetry shows that he was acquainted with the classics and with Scots and English literature.[14] As an ardent champion of the Gaelic language, he is hardly likely to have sympathised with the SSPCK's reasons for producing the dictionary.

Leabhar a Theagasc Ainminnin (literally 'A Book to Teach [the] Names [of things]') closely followed the structure of MacEwing's *A New Vocabulary for the Use of Schools* (1720),[15] but Gaelic replaced Latin. The vocabulary itself is grouped under ninety-seven thematic headings and consists chiefly of lists of nouns. Headings cover a wide variety of topics, including religion, food and drink, household furniture, weights and measures, etc. MacDonald must have had considerable difficulty in compiling a Gaelic–English vocabulary using English as the starting point. Many words are necessarily contrived: for example, words are included for 'camel' and 'pelican'. There are over 4,000 entries.[16] Most contain one word in Gaelic corresponding to one word in English, though multiple definitions can occasionally occur in either language. It is interesting to note that the dictionary also includes some Scots words. Although it has not been possible to access the 1720 edition of *A New Vocabulary for the Use of Schools*, the eighth edition (1749) contains the following statement in relation to Scots: '*But because several* English *Words are not understood by Children, and the Generality of our People, it was judged necessary to join the* Scottish *Names to such of them as seemed to need Explanation*.'[17] Obviously, problems in understanding English were also prevalent among Scots-speaking children.[18] Following *A New Vocabulary* MacDonald gives 'a collection of the most common adjectives, together with their most usual abstracts and adverbs'. To this is added the specifically Gaelic category of adjectives of the third declension; and examples of the most usual Gaelic verbs. Interestingly, there is a criticism of MacDonald's treatment of verbs in the advertisement at the end of the book: 'And here we cannot also but acquaint the Reader, that all or most of the Verbs in this Vocabulary, from Page 143 to Page 162, are expressed, in the Galic, by single Words; tho' our Author, generally, expresses them by a needless Circumlocution.' This comment is not completely justified, since *A New Vocabulary* gives English infinitives ('to say', etc.), whose literal equivalent in Gaelic is expressed by the preposition *a* 'to, for' plus the verbal noun. Additionally, Gaelic standardly expresses many verbal notions periphrastically by the verbal noun plus one of a small number of very common verbs (*dèan* 'do', *thoir* 'give', *cuir* 'put' and *gabh* 'take' are the commonest), so that the responsible lexicographer needs to let the reader know which of these common verbs is used to express the verbal notion in question.

MacDonald has added an appendix containing words and terms used in divinity, much of it relating to the terminology of sin in Roman Catholic, Episcopalian and Jewish usage, and in the Old Testament. There is also a table of offices, etc, of weights and measures, degrees of consanguinity, and names and order of books of the Bible with the number of chapters. He claims that this section contains frequently used words and terms that were omitted from *A New Vocabulary*. He identifies his sources as the Irish Confession of Faith, Catechism, Book of Common-Prayer in Irish, and whatever additional sources he could find.

Even the briefest examination shows what an ambitious undertaking this dictionary was. MacDonald rose to the challenge of his task, approaching it as a scholar. Although his work doubtless had shortcomings as a learning aid for children, it is a fascinating compilation which contains much of interest to present-day Gaelic scholars. Many words appear in Scottish Gaelic form (as opposed to Classical Gaelic or Irish Gaelic) for the first time. In his Preface, MacDonald regrets being absent at the final stages of publication and invites users to submit any errors or misprints for inclusion in a future edition. There was no future edition, but MacDonald's *Leabhar a Theagasc Ainminnin* was influential in determining the style and tone of subsequent Gaelic dictionary-making. Many of his definitions, and even some eccentricities and printer's errors, were copied or imitated by succeeding dictionaries, including those of William Shaw (1780), Robert Mac Farlan (1795), the Highland Society (1828) and the *Irish–English Dictionary* (1817) of Edward O'Reilly.

As a footnote to the SSPCK's involvement in lexicography in the years leading up to the publication of Alexander MacDonald's *Leabhar a Theagasc Ainminnin*, we may note that the teacher, catechist and Gaelic spiritual bard Dugald Buchanan, who was in Edinburgh in 1767 supervising the printing of the Gaelic New Testament, was approached by the society and invited to prepare 'a small Dictionary for the use of their schools' based on the lexicon of the New Testament. Buchanan responded that a Gaelic dictionary would have to have a much wider basis than that to be of any real use, and the project was apparently shelved. But it is still interesting to see the SSPCK associating Gaelic lexicography with the battle to save the souls of young Highlanders at this time.[19]

Laying the Foundations

Almost forty years later, the Rev. William Shaw (1749–1831) published his *Galic and English Dictionary* (1780). A native of Clachaig in Arran, Shaw was educated in Ayr and at the University of Glasgow. In 1774 he made the acquaintance of the English lexicographer Dr Samuel Johnson, who was to be a great source of encouragement in his work. In the Preface Shaw explains that the reception of his *Analysis of the Galic Language* (1778)[20] encouraged him to turn his thoughts towards the compilation of a dictionary. Friends had suggested this might be accomplished by public subscription, since fieldwork would be necessary in both Scotland and Ireland. There had been financial problems, and Shaw had doubted at times whether his work would ever be published. Eventually, however, the subscription funds proved sufficient to support publication.

Shaw saw his task as one of preservation, and expressed great regret at the reluctance of others to do anything on behalf of their dying language. In the spring of 1778, he travelled from London to the Highlands with the aim of collecting from oral and written sources in as many areas as possible. Orally gathered material formed the major part of his collection. Of the written evidence, most came from the collections of Sir James Foulis of Colinton, who had learned Gaelic and amassed a considerable library of Celtic antiquities. Shaw then proceeded to Ireland, where he seems to have depended more on written sources. There Lieutenant-Colonel Charles Vallancey, another student of the Gaelic language, made his manuscript collection available, and Shaw had free access to books and manuscripts in Trinity College Library in Dublin. By the time he returned to London in 1779, he had collected nearly 30,000 articles for his dictionary.

Shaw claimed that his *Dictionary* contained nearly every word in both Scottish and Irish Gaelic – a bold claim, considering that the whole work was completed in under two years. It is probable that, like lexicographers before and since, Shaw made use of word lists and dictionaries already available in order to expedite his work.

The dictionary was published in two volumes: the first Gaelic–English and the second English–Gaelic. The Gaelic–English section is slightly larger, listing around 15,000 headwords. Shaw's analysis of the language is weak, and his aim was clearly to record rather than to explain or analyse. A positive result of this lack of ambition is that he gives words exactly as they were written in his sources without even orthographic alteration. As with Alexander MacDonald's *Vocabulary,* the entry structure is very simple. There is no etymology and very little grammatical information. Some entries show an engaging candour, for example:

> Muca-meala. Something vegetative, which I do not know; the words I met with in a descriptive poem of the island of Arran.

He occasionally permits himself a personal comment:

> Mailis. Malice. I doubt this to be Galic.

The English–Gaelic section contains around 12,000 headwords; here too, analysis of the language is almost non-existent, though Shaw states that he has ranked the Gaelic equivalents to the English headwords, giving the commonest first and the most ancient or obsolete last. As to his coverage, it seems possible that Samuel Johnson's *A Dictionary of the English Language* (1755) has been used as the basis for the English–Gaelic section, since there are strong similarities in typography and content. For example, Johnson's entry for 'muff' is:

> MUFF. A soft cover for the hands in winter.

Shaw gives:

> MUFF. Folach croicuin do na lamhan anns a' gheamhradh. ['A hide covering for the hands in the winter.']

Lexicographically, then, Shaw's work is pretty basic, comprising little more than a word list. However, its alphabetical presentation, in contrast to the use of subject headings, made it more readily and widely useable than MacDonald's work and it would fulfil a need until more rigorously compiled Gaelic dictionaries were produced. We must recall that early English–Gaelic dictionaries were clearly used by Gaelic speakers to provide prompts for the meaning of unfamiliar English words, at least as much as by English-speaking learners of Gaelic.

The last Gaelic dictionary of the eighteenth century was that compiled by Robert Mac Farlan. Mac Farlan was the first and only 'Professor of Gaelic' appointed by the Highland Society. When it was published, in 1795, he dedicated his *Nuadh Fhoclair Gaidhlig agus Beurla* to the Society's members in recognition of their support.

In his Preface, which was printed both in Gaelic and in English, Mac Farlan remarks that Gaelic has 'for ages past' been gradually declining,[21] and expresses deep regret at how little it is valued. His main concern was the lack of a standard Gaelic orthography. He believed that the publication of religious texts, vernacular verse and proverbs had occasioned some progress in the standardisation of spelling, and expressed the hope that his dictionary would also be of value in this respect. He hoped that his work would be of interest to antiquaries and to members of the clergy, and that it might facilitate the learning of English in Highland schools. He tells us nothing of how he compiled the dictionary, or what sources he used.[22]

Before the word list, Mac Farlan gives his 'Rules for Reading the Gailic Language'. While this is a thorough and well-structured account, it uses examples from Gaelic in a way that would only be informative to those already familiar with the language, e.g., '*Eu* sounds long in *feur*, grass, *eudach*, cloths, *feusag*, the beard'.[23]

The vocabulary is presented in a style similar to that of Shaw's dictionary. It contains over 11,000 headwords in the form of a basic word list. Definitions are chiefly given as one-word equivalents with each sense division given on a new line. For example:

Cairt. { rind, bark of trees.
a cart.
the compass. }

The range of vocabulary is fairly wide, covering everyday items, geographical features, agricultural terms, military terms, personal names and place-names. Biblical words and names are also included, although coverage is not comprehensive. Mac Farlan's contribution to Gaelic lexicography was basic, but his dictionary would have fulfilled his stated aim of enabling users to read the published texts of the period and facilitating the learning of English in schools. By comparison with Shaw's work, it lacks the problematic admixture of Irish forms.

In the early part of the nineteenth century, significantly more material was being published in Gaelic. The Gaelic Bible was now available in its entirety, and there was a significant increase in the availability of secular texts, including the first journals and James MacPherson's *Ossian*, the Gaelic version of which was published, soon after MacPherson's death, in 1807.[24] Dictionaries were increasingly needed to support the developing written language. Peter MacFarlane's[25] *Focalair Ùr Gaelig agus Beurla*, published in 1815, responded to this need. MacFarlane (1753–1832) was a schoolmaster in Appin and a translator of religious works into Gaelic, such as Blair's *Sermons* (*Aireamh thaghta de shearmoinibh E. Blair*) and Bunyan's *Pilgrim's Progress* (*Cuairt an oilthirich: no turus a Chriosduidh*) (both 1812). He had also been involved in the reprinting of the 1796 edition of the Gaelic New Testament. He was the first Gaelic lexicographer to explicitly consider the needs of learners when compiling his dictionary, as we can see from the following prefatory note, which also gives us some indication of the needs of early nineteenth-century users:

> The want of an ENGLISH and GAELIC VOCABULARY has long been a desideratum with those who wish to be acquainted with the language in which OSSIAN, the son of FINGAL, composed and sung. The compiler of the Vocabulary now presented, has appeared as the Translator of some Practical Books of Divinity, and the sale they have met with, evinces a favourable reception from the public. He has frequently been importuned to publish a Vocabulary, such as he now presents, beginning with the English, and giving the corresponding explanation in Gaelic, marking the different parts of speech; which is the first attempt of the kind, so far as he knows, ever presented to the public.[26]

The dictionary is in English–Gaelic and Gaelic–English format. The main dialectal bias is towards mainland Argyllshire Gaelic. In the English–Gaelic section, there are roughly 14,000 headwords. Like its predecessors, MacFarlane's dictionary baldly lists Gaelic equivalents for the English headwords. Where more than one equivalent is offered, there is no indication of which equivalent to choose in a particular context. Sometimes definition by explanation is offered, where Gaelic has no direct equivalent, for example:

> February, *s.* Dara mìos na bliadhna; mìos an dubh-chabhuidh
> ['The second month of the year; the month of the dark (snow-) drifting.']

Some entries clearly show that he was fitting Gaelic into the framework of an existing English dictionary, for example:

> Billingsgate, *s.* Cainnt shalach, trod
> ['Foul language, scolding.']

The headwords in question suggest that MacFarlane may have used Johnson (1755), perhaps mediated through Shaw (1780). Some other entries (e.g., 'Dùn') suggest that he has drawn on Robert Mac Farlan's dictionary (1795).

The Gaelic–English section contains roughly 9,000 headwords. Some basic grammatical information is usually given, for example:

> A', sometimes for *ag*, the sign of the present participle
> Do, *pron.* Thy. *It is the sign of the dative*
> Leabhar, *s.* A book

MacFarlane occasionally cites sources:

> Aingealtachd, *s.* Frowardness,
> Prov. ii. 14.
> Sgèith, *v.* Shape, cut out. *Perthshire dialect*
> Ursa, *s.* A bear *Lhuyd*

and occasionally gives examples:

> Saod, *s.* State, condition; trimmed. "Ciod an saod a th'ort?"
> *How are you*
> Saoil, *v.* Think—An saoil thu?
> *Do you think?*

These innovations presumably indicate an awareness of developments in English and Scots lexicography, such as the works of Samuel Johnson and John Jamieson.[27] MacFarlane also includes a short section entitled 'General Rules for Reading the Gaelic Language', with a footnote indicating that these are chiefly taken from those prefixed to the Gaelic Bible. He gives the Gaelic alphabet and some explanation of the sounds of the language, using both English and Gaelic examples. He also draws on his own knowledge of other languages, which shows a genuine concern to give accurate instructions, though it may on occasion assume too much knowledge on the part of his users, for example: '*Ch* has the sound of the Greek χ, or of *gh* in *lough* as the Irish pronounce it; or as *sought* is pronounced in the broad Scotch dialect.'[28] His dictionary is typographically clearer and more obviously structured than its predecessors. He has chosen a vocabulary of everyday Gaelic, well suited to the published works of the time. In terms of the history of Gaelic lexicography, the most significant aspect of this work is the fact that MacFarlane saw his remit as explaining the language, where his predecessors aimed merely to record and preserve it.

Gaelic lexicography continued to evolve with the work of Robert Armstrong (1788–1867), who produced arguably the first major dictionary of Gaelic, *A Gaelic Dictionary*, published in 1825. The son of a schoolmaster in Dull and Kenmore in Perthshire, Armstrong was educated at St Andrews University. Although he trained for the ministry, he followed a career as a schoolmaster in London. The dictionary has a dedication to King George IV in which Armstrong says he believes that the status of his book will be enhanced if Gaels can see that it has been issued *fuidh fhasgadh d' Ainm mhòir* ('under the shelter of Thy great name').[29] The king later made him Gaelic Lexicographer in Ordinary, an unsalaried post which nevertheless conveyed a measure of recognition and approbation. Armstrong doubtless benefited from the pro-Scottish mood that was in vogue at the time of the king's famous visit to Edinburgh in 1822.

Armstrong appears to have been *au fait* with developments in lexicography in the British Isles as a whole. Adopting the now firmly established descriptive approach to dictionary-making, he aimed to provide a resource which would serve both those who knew no Gaelic and scholars of the language. This, of course, remains one of the great challenges of lexicography down to the present day. Equally importantly, and with an admirable degree of vision, he sought to do all he could to facilitate the work of future lexicographers.

Armstrong's dictionary has Gaelic–English and English–Gaelic sections, each containing roughly 34,000 headwords. The high number is partly due to Armstrong's desire to improve accessibility for the learner by listing prepositional pronouns in separate entries, e.g. LEAM ('with me'), LEAT ('with you'), LEIS ('with him'), etc, in addition to LE ('with'). He made every effort to link derivatives with their sources and compounds to their components. For the first time, the genitive singular of nouns is given in the entry. Oblique cases of nouns and tenses of verbs are given as separate entries when they involve an unpredictable departure from the normal citation forms. Wherever possible, each sense has a referenced quotation of usage accompanied by a literal translation. Armstrong was aware of the challenges presented by the differing phraseology of Gaelic and English idiom and of the need to provide coverage of different registers of Gaelic. Typically for the period in which he was compiling his dictionary, Armstrong gave unquestioning pride of place to the recently published Gaelic *Ossian*.

Armstrong also broke new ground by providing etymological information. He did so with the aim of establishing the antiquity of the Celtic languages. His work pre-dated the heyday of comparative philology, which assigned Celtic a sure place within the Indo-European language family, and it contains some misconceptions on that account. Thus, although he admits he has been unable to prove it, he subscribes to the erroneous view that the Gaelic of Scotland is more ancient than that of Ireland. Some of his entries have detailed etymological notes, that of DÙN occupying half a column. Here Armstrong postulates in a pre-scientific, almost medieval way that DÙN could be the root of *duine* 'man', in the sense that man is the highest of the terrestrial creatures.

Armstrong's English–Gaelic section makes some effort to disambiguate senses in the source language, for example:

> LEAF, *s.* Duille, duilleag; bileag. Leaves (*of trees*), *duilleagan, duilleach*; (of a book), *duilleagan.*

He still works with equivalents rather than explanatory definitions, but the semantic analysis has clearly developed beyond that of Shaw. Armstrong was very concerned about the variability of Gaelic spelling, and his dictionary is claimed to follow the orthography of two writers considered to be unimpeachable authorities: the Rev. John Stuart of Luss, translator of the Holy Scriptures, and the Rev. Dr John Smith of Campbeltown, author of a Gaelic metrical version of the Psalms. Sources are acknowledged for lexicography, philology, and matters of antiquity. Named Gaelic lexicographical sources include MacDonald (1741), MacFarlane (1815), Shaw (1780) and the Irish dictionaries of O'Brien (1768)[30] and O'Reilly (1817).[31] On the English side, 'Perry's Dictionary' is named.[32] Etymological authorities listed include Edward Lhuyd (1707). Armstrong's *Gaelic Dictionary* also includes 'A Grammar of the Gaelic Language', with regard to which he acknowledges the work of Shaw,[33] O'Reilly and 'O'Connor'.[34] His dictionary is deservedly esteemed; it might have been more influential had it not been eclipsed by the publication, only three years later, of the Highland Society's dictionary.

The Highland Society, founded in 1784 to promote the interests and culture of the Highlands and Islands of Scotland, published its *Dictionarium Scoto-Celticum* in 1828. The Royal Highland and Agricultural Society of Scotland now has an entirely agricultural remit; but from 1784 until 1844 it functioned as a kind of Gaelic academy, amassing an archive of manuscripts, papers and printed work.[35] It appointed its own bard and piper and, as its 'Professor of Gaelic', Robert Mac Farlan. In 1806, a committee of the Society was set up to organise the production of a large-scale dictionary.

The title page indicates the ambitiousness of the project: 'A Dictionary of the Gaelic Language; comprising an ample vocabulary of Gaelic words, as preserved in the vernacular speech, manuscripts, or printed works, with their signification and various meanings in English and Latin, illustrated by suitable examples and phrases, and with etymological remarks, and vocabularies of Latin and English words, with their translation into Gaelic. To which are prefixed, an introduction explaining the nature, objects and sources of the work, and a compendium of Gaelic grammar.'

The work was dedicated to the king. This was not only the first dictionary to be overseen by a committee but also the first to be compiled by a team: the Rev. Dr John Macleod, minister of Dundonald, assisted by Ewen MacLachlan (Gaelic scholar par excellence and librarian of King's College, Aberdeen), the Rev. Dr Alexander Irvine of Little Dunkeld, and the Rev. Alexander Macdonald at Crieff. Progress through the press was overseen by the Rev. Mackintosh Mackay, minister of Laggan.

The Introduction seeks to place Scottish Gaelic in context with the other Celtic languages: Armoric (i.e., Breton), Welsh and Irish already had substantial and serviceable vocabularies and dictionaries, while Scottish Gaelic remained

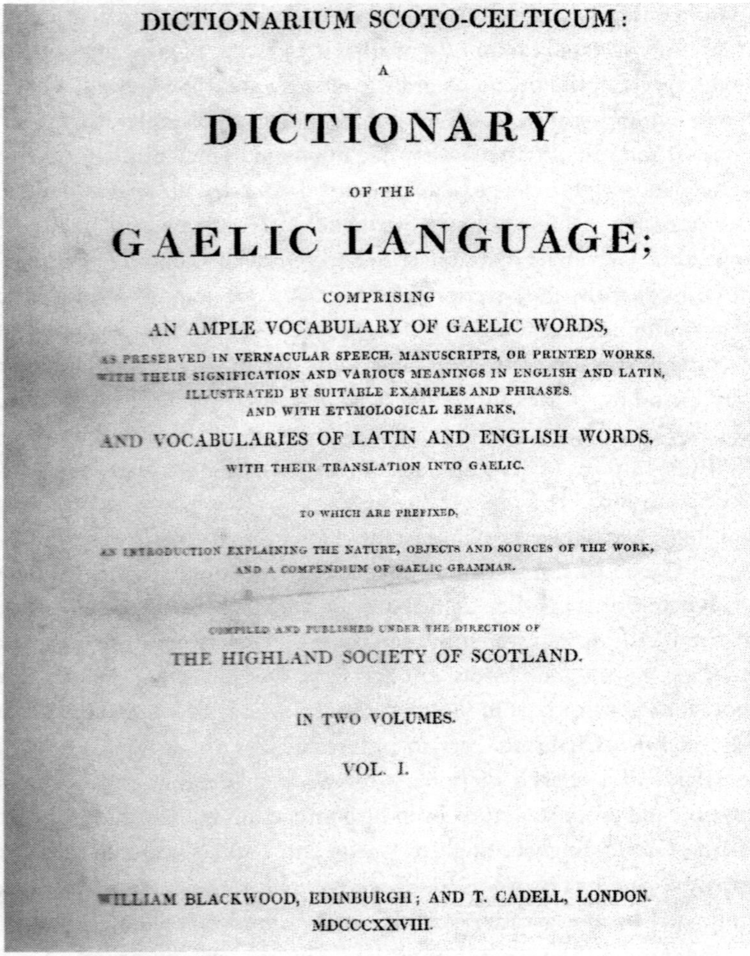

DICTIONARIUM SCOTO-CELTICUM:

A

DICTIONARY

OF THE

GAELIC LANGUAGE;

COMPRISING

AN AMPLE VOCABULARY OF GAELIC WORDS,

AS PRESERVED IN VERNACULAR SPEECH, MANUSCRIPTS, OR PRINTED WORKS,
WITH THEIR SIGNIFICATION AND VARIOUS MEANINGS IN ENGLISH AND LATIN,
ILLUSTRATED BY SUITABLE EXAMPLES AND PHRASES,
AND WITH ETYMOLOGICAL REMARKS,

AND VOCABULARIES OF LATIN AND ENGLISH WORDS,

WITH THEIR TRANSLATION INTO GAELIC.

TO WHICH ARE PREFIXED,

AN INTRODUCTION EXPLAINING THE NATURE, OBJECTS AND SOURCES OF THE WORK,
AND A COMPENDIUM OF GAELIC GRAMMAR.

COMPILED AND PUBLISHED UNDER THE DIRECTION OF

THE HIGHLAND SOCIETY OF SCOTLAND.

IN TWO VOLUMES.

VOL. I.

WILLIAM BLACKWOOD, EDINBURGH; AND T. CADELL, LONDON.

MDCCCXXVIII.

Title page of the *Dictionarium Scoto-Celticum: A Dictionary of the Gaelic Language; . . . Compiled and Published under the Direction of the Highland Society of Scotland* (1828).

comparatively neglected and unknown. The Society therefore set itself the aim of remedying this gap by producing a major dictionary of Scottish Gaelic for both the British public and students of philology in Europe at large. Their objective was to produce a dictionary of all that could be collected of 'the Scoto-Celtic language' from written or oral sources. The dictionary was to focus primarily on words which were in use at the time of compilation. Obsolete words would be included where they helped to explain etymologies of current words or to provide information on culture-specific items. Senses would be listed on the basis of frequency of occurrence, with the most common coming first. The provision of carefully selected examples was considered to be of great importance: 'In every light in which the purposes of lexicography are to be viewed, whether of a dead or a living language, it is the exhibition of such examples, that gives to it confirmation and value.'[36] The Society had intended to include citations from all the Gaelic manuscripts in its possession in the dictionary, but Ewen MacLachlan had only transcribed a few of these by the time of his premature death in 1822. Moreover, those which he had transcribed were not considered to be of general appeal; consequently, they were rarely used. All quotations were to be given exactly as in the original sources; but many of these had been written down in idiosyncratic ways. The dictionary deals with this mostly orthographic uncertainty by including entries for variant spellings and linking these to the main headword by cross-references. Its own spelling system was based on that used in the SSPCK editions of Scriptures, as developed by the scholarly editors of the most recent editions.

Etymology was viewed as important. However, the lack of etymological research in Gaelic by the 1820s meant that only the most obvious etyma were given. Cognate words in other Celtic languages are included at the end of entries – apart from Irish, which was supposed to be so closely connected to Scottish Gaelic as to make comparison unnecessary. On the other hand, cognates were noted, as appropriate, in German, Anglo-Saxon, Scots, Swedish, Danish, Icelandic, Hebrew, Chaldean, Persian and Arabic.

The Highland Society's dictionary reveals considerable improvements in presentation and entry structure, even by comparison with Armstrong's. It is in three parts: Gaelic–English, English–Gaelic and Latin–Gaelic. In Part I, there are roughly 10,000 headwords. Nouns are entered in their nominative singular form followed by the genitive singular and nominative plural endings. This became the standard format for nouns in Gaelic–English dictionaries. For irregular nouns these forms are written in full. For example:

> PIUTHAR, PEATHAR, PEATHRAICHEAN, *s. f.* A sister: soror. . . .

Verbs are listed under their root form (i.e., second person singular imperative) followed by the future tense ending and the past tense independent form:

> IOMCHAIR, -IDH, DH'-, *v. a.* 1. Carry, bear: fer, gesta. *C.S.*[37]
> Conduct, behave thyself: te gere, praebe.
> "Is *iomchaiream* mi féin gu glic."
> *Salm.* ci. 2.
> And let me conduct myself wisely. Et sapienter me ipsum geram.

Highland Society *Dictionarium* definitions are much more explanatory than those in previous dictionaries, suggesting analysis of the available evidence and consideration of the needs of the user. There are two Supplements to the Gaelic–English section: one for A–P at the end of volume 1, and one for R–U at the end of volume 2. These consist of short entries whose source is chiefly the spoken language.

Part II, English–Gaelic, contains around 37,000 headwords. Its word list is based on Todd's 1818 edition of Johnson,[38] which includes corrections and several thousand additional words. The semantic analysis is well developed and sense numbering is used to separate major strands of meaning, for example:

> RANGE, *v. a.* et *n.* 1. Place in ranks: eagaraich, cuir an sreathan.
> 2. rove over: siubhail thairis air, rach sios 's a suas, cuairtich.
> 3. separate the flour from the bran: criathair.

Nouns in this section are simply labelled '*s.*' (i.e. 'substantive'), and the Gaelic–English section must be consulted for gender and declension.

Part III is a Latin–Gaelic vocabulary giving main meanings for all its Latin entries and their Gaelic equivalents. There are roughly 14,500 headwords. Definitions are generally one-word equivalents, of which more than one can be given, for example:

> FLUXUS, *adj.* Silteach; sruthach; *instabilis*: diom-buan, neo-mhaireannach.

It was intended that Parts II and III should conduct the user to the Gaelic word in Part I, where fuller grammatical information was to be found.

The dictionary itself is prefixed by a Gaelic grammar, described as an abridged version of that published by Dr Alexander Stewart in 1801.[39]

Some Scots words are included in the Gaelic–English section:

> CUDAIG, -E, -EAN, *s. m.* A small fish called in Scotch cuddy, the young of the coal-fish: gadus carbonarius, *Linn. C.S. Scot.* Cooth, Cuth, and Cuddie. *Jam.*

These are mostly stated to be from Jamieson's *Etymological Dictionary of the Scottish Language* (i.e. '*Jam.*' in the case of CUDAIG) or its *Supplement.*[40] Sources such as 'Sibbald's glossary',[41] Skene's *De Verborum Significatione* (1597) (see Chapter 1) and *The Statistical Account of Scotland*[42] have also been drawn upon. Some Scots words are cited without a source, as happens regularly in the English–Gaelic section, where examples of Scots words appear as headwords, e.g., *cleg*, *flit*.

This project, like many others described in this chapter, faced many problems, not least the untimely death of Ewen MacLachlan.[43] Yet the admirable principles that underpinned the Highland Society's dictionary project were strong enough to withstand the buffets and permit the project to be brought to a successful conclusion. The articulation of sections I, II and III and the way they had been designed to be used together was a very considerable achievement. The resulting dictionary subscribes to Johnson's view that dictionaries should describe and not prescribe. The beneficial results of systematic organisation and teamwork are obvious in the final product, though these were not well understood or regularly practised in the nineteenth century. Considering that the editors were not working in the same place, and had none of the technological tools available to lexicographers working in multi-based projects today, the Highland Society's *Dictionarium* is a remarkable achievement.

The dictionary's publication in 1828 meant that Gaelic scholars could now consult two relatively large and authoritative dictionaries, independently produced and providing the user with a considerable level of access to what had been written in Gaelic hitherto. What was now needed was a distillation of the information provided by Armstrong's and the Highland Society's dictionaries, in the form of a small, moderately priced dictionary. This need was recognised and met by the Rev. Dr Norman MacLeod and the Rev. Dr Daniel Dewar. MacLeod (1783–1862) was born in Morvern and was one of the major figures in the history of Gaelic prose. He wrote voluminously on subjects as varied as history, geography, the natural sciences, current affairs and religious topics as well as descriptive essays and book reviews. His intention was to develop a formal standard Gaelic prose style for use in a wide variety of subjects previously only accessible through English. The standards that he set were to influence Gaelic writers for over a century. His years in the ministry took him to Campbeltown in 1808, Campsie in 1825 and St Columba's in Glasgow in 1838, where he remained until his death. He came to be known to Highlanders at home and abroad as 'Caraid nan Gàidheal' ('The Friend of the Gaels') in recognition of his work on education in the Highlands and for organising relief during the potato famines of 1836–7 and 1846–7. Dewar (1788–1867) was born in Glen Dochart, Perthshire. He studied at Edinburgh University, graduating MA in 1815. He was also awarded the Degrees of LLD (1815) and DD (1833) from the University of Glasgow. As a Church of Scotland minister, his charges included Strontian in Ardnamurchan and the College Church of Greyfriars, Aberdeen. In 1815, he was appointed Professor of Moral Philosophy at King's College, Aberdeen. He moved to the Tron Church in Glasgow in 1819, but returned to Aberdeen as Principal of Marischal College in 1832, becoming Professor of Church History in 1833.

In 1829 MacLeod and Dewar were encouraged to publish Gaelic prose material by the Very Rev. Dr Baird, Principal of the University of Edinburgh, who worked closely with MacLeod on Highland education and poverty relief in the 1830s and 1840s.[44] Amongst their many other commitments at the time, MacLeod brought out *An Teachdaire Gaelach* ('The Gaelic Messenger') between 1829 and 1831, and Dewar worked on selections of his Gaelic sermons with a view to publication. At this stage, if not before, they became aware of the need for a concise dictionary of Gaelic and at once began to compile one. *A Dictionary of the Gaelic Language* was published in 1831. In the Preface, the editors acknowledged their debt to the Gaelic Bible and the Gaelic *Ossian* as important sources of material. Armstrong's and the Highland Society's dictionaries had provided a solid lexicographical foundation on which to build, but MacLeod and Dewar claimed to have added further material and to have corrected some errors in these earlier works. The dictionary was seen through the press by Patrick MacFarlane, and MacLeod and Dewar acknowledge their considerable debt to his editorial skills.

In the Gaelic–English section there are an estimated 32,000 headwords. This comparatively high number can be accounted for partly by the conciseness of individual entries, and partly by the treatment of most compounds as separate entries. Entry structure largely follows that of the Highland Society's dictionary. Etymologies are included but are very basic. MacLeod and Dewar adhered to the recognised standard of orthography set by the Gaelic Bible.

Although definitions are concise they are explanatory and a few are quite encyclopaedic, for example:

> CRANN-TÀRA, } *pl.* CROINN-THÀRA.
> CRANN-TÀRAIDH, } *s. m.* (Crann and Tàra or Tàir,) A beam of gathering; a signal formerly used on occasions of insult or impending danger, to summon a clan to arms; being a piece of wood half burnt and dipt in blood, and handed from one clansman to another, so as to spread an alarm over a district in a short time; The same term is also applied to fires kindled on eminences for the purpose of notifying alarm, or danger. See Crois-tàra.

By contrast, the entry for *Crois-tàra* is very concise and cross-refers to the more informative entry:

> CROIS-TÀRA, } *s. f.* A signal for
> CROIS-TÀRAIDH, } arming; an alarm; a fiery cross. See Crann-tàra.

It is interesting to note that MacLeod and Dewar have chosen to retain comparisons with Scots mentioned in the Highland Society's dictionary in entries such as that for *cudaig*:

> CUDAIG, } -E, -EAN, *s. m.* A small fish.
> CUDAINN, } *Scot.* Cuddy: supposed the young of the coal-fish.

MacLeod and Dewar occasionally comment on spelling; often the orthographic challenges that existed in the nineteenth century are echoed by those of the present day:

> FACAL, -AIL, } *s. m.* for *Focal,*
> FACALL, -AILL, } which is the approved spelling, though *Facall* is more agreeable to the pronunciation.

The English–Gaelic section contains around 29,000 headwords. Its close correspondence with the English–Gaelic sections of the dictionaries on which it is based indicates that these were the sources being followed. The inclusion of headwords such as 'antitrinitarian' and 'salmagundi' must have presented a challenge to the compilers. There is positive evidence that MacLeod and Dewar translated their English sources directly. For example, the Gaelic–English section contains the entry:

> GEARRAN, -AIN, *s. m.* A gelding.

By contrast, the English–Gaelic section has:

> GELDING, *s.* Beathach spothta, gu h-àraidh each spothta.
> ['A gelded/castrated animal, especially a gelded horse.']

The lack of mention of Gaelic *gearran* at this point is telling.

As in the Highland Society's dictionary, nouns are labelled '*s.*' alone, and the user is supposed to consult the Gaelic–English section to establish gender and declension.

The quality of MacLeod's and Dewar's *Dictionary of the Gaelic Language* does great credit to its compilers, and its availability was a definite step forward for nineteenth-century Gaelic speakers. A second edition was published in 1832, only a year after the first, and a further twelve editions appeared between 1833 and 1910.

Sharpening the Focus

The early nineteenth-century dictionaries of Armstrong, the Highland Society and MacLeod and Dewar provided Gaelic with a sound, up-to-date and accessible lexicographical foundation. Questions could be raised about the breadth of that foundation, however. Of its twin pillars, the Gaelic Bible and the Gaelic

Ossian, the Gaelic Bible reflected the upper-register Gaelic of its mostly Perthshire and mainland Argyllshire translators; while the Gaelic of *Ossian* was thin gruel by comparison with the lexis of authentic Gaelic poetry as found in all parts of the Gàidhealtachd; and the spoken language of the many Gaelic dialect areas contained words and expressions which figured in neither the Bible nor *Ossian*. The next phase of Gaelic lexicography saw a series of attempts to address these perceived imperfections.

Neil MacAlpine (1786–1867) was born in Islay, and at the time of compiling his dictionary he was a schoolmaster and 'student of divinity' there. His work appeared first in 1832, bearing as its title *The Argyleshire Pronouncing Gaelic Dictionary*. A second edition was published in 1833, interestingly renamed *A Pronouncing Gaelic Dictionary*. It broke new ground by its inclusion of pronunciation – a considerable achievement when one considers that in the absence of anything like the International Phonetic Alphabet (which was not published until 1888) MacAlpine had to devise his own phonetic system from scratch. The recommended pronunciations show the intrusion of MacAlpine's own Islay dialect in places, e.g., in *aimhleasach* and other *aimh-* words, for which he gives characteristic Islay pronunciations in /ev/. His key to the symbols he uses to transcribe Gaelic pronunciation draws on English, Gaelic, Scots and French examples to arrive at approximations for the Gaelic. At the end of the key MacAlpine praises the acuteness and ingenuity of Gaelic orthography, dismissing any thought of altering it as an 'absurd whim'.[45]

Among the earlier lexicographic sources MacAlpine acknowledges are Armstrong, MacLeod and Dewar (described as 'Dr MacLeod's Glossary and Dictionary'), the Highland Society's dictionary and Shaw's dictionary. There are around 14,000 headwords with short, clear definitions, some combinations and a fairly generous ration of illustrative phrases. The gender of nouns is given but no principal parts, no sense numbers and no etymology.

A typical example is:

> IOMADACH, ēm'-ad-ach, *a.* many; *iomadach* uair, *often*; *iomadach* tè, *many a female*; *iomadach* fear, *many a man*.

Sometimes regional use is indicated:

> BORLUM, bôr'-llum, *n. m.* a sudden evacuation; a ridge of land. *Skye*.

Information about dialectal provenance, which includes many dialect areas, is of great interest when it occurs; one could wish it had been added more frequently. Amongst the dialect areas listed are Argyllshire, Harris, 'Islands', Islay, Lewis, Lochaber, Mull, Mainland (of Argyll), 'North Highlands', Perthshire, Skye,

Sutherlandshire and 'West Highlands'. It is also interesting to note the use of Scots in definitions, for example:

> BRAIGHLEAB, brī-gh''-lleb, *n. m.* wood-roof of a house; sarking. *Sc.*

Unpredictable forms of irregular nouns and verbs are given as separate entries, which would be a useful feature for learners of the language:

> RINN, róènn, *past. v.* dean; dean so, *do this; rinn* iad sinn, *they did that.*

MacAlpine stamps his own brand of individuality on the work, sometimes providing interesting cultural observations:

> COIN, kóén, *n. m. pl.* dogs; *coin*-fhodair, *fleas.* We must not tell the island where this word is used, otherwise our M______ friends would kill us.

Other entries give MacAlpine's own view, sometimes contradicting that of MacLeod and Dewar quite pointedly. For instance, where they had stated that *focal* was the most 'correct' form of the Gaelic for word for 'word', he retorts:

> FACAL, fachy'-al, *n. m.* word; . . . mispronounced and written in one county in Ireland *focal*, but never so in the Highlands; *fòcal* is a pole-cat.

MacAlpine also includes a substantial 'Rudiments of Gaelic Grammar', which has sections on orthography, parts of speech and syntax. As with the dictionary, he does not hold back in expressing his views:

> LABIALS. B has a simple sound somewhat harder than b or p in English; . . . at the end of words, it is very wickedly murdered, in some places u; as searbh, sheru, in place of shervv, as properly pronounced in the Islands. . . .[46]

The reader is left with the impression that MacAlpine feels much the better for putting his views in print.

Whilst MacAlpine's lexicographical analysis did not match that of MacLeod and Dewar, the simplicity of his dictionary meant that it was a very useful resource, not least for schools. Indeed, it was reproduced fourteen times, with very little change, between 1833 and 1973. Furthermore, MacAlpine's work inspired the first example of a linked resource in Gaelic lexicography, in the form of John MacKenzie's *An English–Gaelic Dictionary* (1847), which was created explicitly in response to MacAlpine's work, to the extent that its pagination ran on consecutively from that of MacAlpine's dictionary.

MacKenzie (1806–1848), who was born in Gairloch, showed an early interest in literature, and especially poetry. He also possessed musical ability and a talent for woodworking, and made himself a fiddle and a set of bagpipes. He was apprenticed to William Ross, an itinerant joiner, a position that gave him an ideal opportunity to note down Gaelic songs and tales from the areas in which he worked. His career was cut short when, at the age of seventeen, he sustained a head injury which meant he was no longer able to follow his trade. He then worked for the *Inverness Courier*, travelling through the Highlands and Islands collecting sums owed to the paper, before moving to Glasgow in 1833. In 1836, he became a book-keeper in Glasgow University's printing office, but moved to Edinburgh in 1845 to take up a post with the religious and Gaelic publishing house of MacLachlan and Stewart. His job here involved translation from English and the correction of Gaelic texts before they went to press. He himself was a prolific publisher of Gaelic texts, including the songs of William Ross (1830), a book of racy verse entitled *An Leobhar Liath* ('The Blue Book'), a new edition of Alexander MacDonald's Gaelic poems (1834) and the ground-breaking major anthology *Sàr-Obair nam Bàrd Gàelach* ('The Beauties of Gaelic Poetry') (1841).[47] *Sàr-Obair*, which contained works by all the major Gaelic poets, opened up the poetic vocabulary of Gaelic on a wide variety of topics, including clanship, war, praise, elegy, love, nature, satire and religion, from the sixteenth to the mid-nineteenth century, and itself became a frequently cited quarry for later lexicographers. MacKenzie also wrote a history of the 'Forty-five entitled *Eachdraidh a' Phrionnsa* (1844).[48] He seems to have spent some time in London and was an honorary member of the Gaelic Society of London. It is said that the stress of his work on his English–Gaelic dictionary brought on a stomach complaint, causing him to return to his father's home in Poolewe, where he died after a lingering illness.[49]

In the Preface to what he calls 'Part the Second' of his *English–Gaelic Dictionary*, MacKenzie pays a measured tribute to Neil MacAlpine. In his judgement, MacAlpine had made good use of the labours of his predecessors, building on their work with improved definitions, fuller examples of usage, more accurate specification of noun gender (apart from a few egregious exceptions), and more correct orthography. He praises MacAlpine for being the first to produce a dictionary without Irishisms and criticises the Gaelic Bible for retaining certain 'antiquated Irishisms'. He notes that there are still some omissions, and that various 'provincialisms' have been included (such as *driom* for *druim* 'back'). MacKenzie attributes the latter to MacAlpine's partiality for his own area and dialect. As to MacAlpine's omissions, MacKenzie claims to have inserted those he detected into the text of the English–Gaelic section, as additional Gaelic equivalents to the English headwords. As to his own original contribution, MacKenzie claims he has included many words not found in the first part of the dictionary, or indeed in any other vocabulary known to him. He also states that, having acquainted himself with the dialects of Gaelic, he has used only words which are generally understood, and avoided those which have different meanings in different areas.

As to orthography, MacKenzie claims (with typical equivocation, it has to be said) to have made a careful study of the arguments of all who have written on this vexed subject. On that basis and following the best authority, he has adopted a system which improves the received system in certain ways for which he, however, does not bear responsibility.

In practice, MacKenzie's English–Gaelic section contains roughly 22,500 headwords with a very simple entry structure containing definitions that are simple equivalents rather than explanations, and with no grammatical or etymological information. Some 'definitions' are in fact instances, e.g. 'constellation' is glossed as *An grigleachan*, which is the Gaelic term for the Pleiades. (MacAlpine has 'GRIOGLACHAN, . . . the plough *or* constellation of seven stars'.)

John MacKenzie's main aim seems to have been to give added value to what he saw as the best Gaelic–English dictionary available in terms of fidelity to the spoken language. He was not so concerned with improving lexicographical methodology. At all events, his dictionary was very popular. It was reproduced in its English–Gaelic form eight times between 1890 and 1973 with very little change to the original text, and in harness with MacAlpine's Gaelic–English dictionary seventeen times between 1847 and 1973.

Father Ewen MacEachen's *Faclair Gailig us Beurla* was published in 1842.[50] MacEachen (1769–1849) was born in Arisaig, Inverness-shire, and trained for the priesthood at Valladolid in Spain. Returning to Scotland, he took various charges: Arisaig; Badenoch, where he built the first chapel at Laggan; and as Professor at the Seminary of Lismore. In 1814, he took charge of the mission at Aigas in Strathglass. From 1818 until his retirement in 1838 he was priest in Braemar. He translated several works into Gaelic, most notably Thomas à Kempis' *De Imitatione Christi*. He died leaving an incomplete translation of the New Testament, which was completed by the Rev. Colin Grant of Strathglass, later bishop of Aberdeen, and published in 1875.[51]

MacEachen believed that a dictionary of 'pure' Gaelic words was the most pressing necessity. He complained that the Gaelic Bible, which was regarded as setting a standard, contained many errors. These included 'Irish' words and expressions (such as *àithne* for *fàithne* 'commandment'); there were a number of entries which he described as 'provincial' or 'impure' or 'improper' (such as *oilean* for *eilean* 'island'); and its spelling was inconsistent (e.g., *bleodhainn* was found beside *bleoghainn* for 'milking'). MacEachen also singled out for criticism the Englishisms that were often to be found in Gaelic prose. Dictionaries based on the Bible would perpetuate the errors in it, and so would future Gaelic authors unless they followed MacEachen's precept and took their expressions from the best Gaelic speakers. His aim in compiling a new dictionary was to rectify these errors, especially with regard to the propriety of words and the establishment of a satisfactory spelling system.

MacEachen took as his starting point MacLeod and Dewar's highly regarded *Dictionary of the Gaelic Language*. He read it over and over again, he tells us, marking the words that occurred in his own dialect and some terms that he classified as 'provincial'. Having regularised their orthography, he transcribed all the acceptable terms into his own dictionary, omitting some of the 'provincial' terms at that stage. Revision then took place, in which context some other words were added and further improvements and corrections were made. Regarding orthography, MacEachen's rule of thumb was that the spelling should correspond to the sound; and in instances where there was considerable orthographic variation, it was desirable to eliminate this by a principled decision. In practice, where established convention allowed two spelling options, such as *tarruing/tarraing* or *tighearn/tighearna*, MacEachen sometimes uses 'or' and sometimes selects one alternative as the preferred form.

Although his dictionary is smaller than that of MacLeod and Dewar, MacEachen claims it is nearly as comprehensive. Its reduced size is due to the fact that he has rejected some items, and because he gives fewer English terms and avoids explanations and repetitions. He claims to have included 10,500 headwords, though a rough calculation estimates there are approximately 11,500. Entry structure is simple and is explained in the Preface. The practice of giving principal parts of nouns and verbs, discontinued by MacAlpine, has been resumed. MacEachen's definitions are very short, consisting mainly of one-word equivalents rather than explanations. They are sometimes less informative than we might wish, for example:

> Mùtan, -ain, an, m. a muff, any short thing.
> Crann-tàraidh, m. an alarming beam.

Scots words are occasionally used in definitions and labelled as such:

> Bròthas, -ais, m. brose. [Scot.]
> Copag, -aig, f. the weed dock, docken, [Scot.] a. copagach.

MacEachen's dictionary appears to have been compiled with a view to inculcating more rigorous orthographical standards and as a contribution towards the establishment of a more settled diction, based on 'correct' Gaelic speech, for the purposes of educated discourse. His use of the term 'provincial', which would bear further scrutiny, seems to go beyond that of other writers and to include aspects of what would now be termed 'register'. It was for these qualities that MacEachen's dictionary was rescued from comparative neglect and given a new lease of life as an educational tool in the twentieth century, as we shall see below.

A New Era

As the nineteenth century drew to a close, Gaelic lexicography received a highly significant boost from the work of Alexander MacBain (1855–1907), who was quite recently described as 'the finest Professor of Celtic that Scotland never had'.[52] MacBain's *Etymological Dictionary of the Gaelic Language*, published in 1896, was undoubtedly his greatest work. Born in Glen Feshie, Badenoch, he began his career there as a pupil–teacher and then worked for a time in Wales with the Ordnance Survey. He studied at King's College, Aberdeen, and in 1880 became rector of Raining's School in Inverness, later holding a post in the High School of Inverness. His scholarly career lasted only twenty-four years but, in that time, he produced many learned papers on a wide range of topics, which included mythology, philology, history and onomastics. In collaboration with John Kennedy he edited the two volumes of *Reliquiae Celticae* (1892–4)[53] and, with John Whyte, he produced *How to Learn Gaelic* (1902) for schools and an edition of MacEachen's dictionary. In 1901 he was awarded the degree of LLD by the University of Aberdeen. He died suddenly in Stirling while making arrangements for the publication of the second edition of his dictionary.

In his Preface MacBain states that his is the first etymological dictionary of any modern Celtic language. To understand his achievement we should note that, while interest in etymology had a long history in connection with debates about the language of the Garden of Eden and suchlike, and these pre-scientific speculations had of course involved writers on the Gaels and Gaelic, the great edifice of comparative Indo-European philology, principally elaborated by German scholarship, had replaced these early constructions during the course of the nineteenth century. There was a continuing symbiosis between this rarefied study of the reconstructed parent language and the study of the earliest recorded phases of the Indic and European 'daughter languages', which provided material for the more abstract science and at the same time were illuminated by the latter's comparative insights. Celtic evidence and scholarship played its part in this ferment of activity, and Celtic evidence had its place in comparative works like Karl Brugmann's *Grundriss der Vergleichenden Grammatik der Indogermanischen*

Sprachen (1886–1916), while the groundwork for Holger Pedersen's *Vergleichende Grammatik der Keltischen Sprachen* (published in 1909–13) was still being elaborated in such journals as *Zeitschrift für Vergleichende Sprachforschung* and *Transactions of the Philological Society*. In order to create a Gaelic etymological dictionary, comparable to works that were now available for English, German and other languages, one had to master the rules for comparative philology and enough Indo-European languages to apply them confidently, and at the same time know the Celtic languages and understand how they had evolved in relation to each other and to their Germanic and other neighbours from prehistoric times to the present. MacBain was effectively the only Scottish Celtic scholar who was able to expound this learning authoritatively and exploit it creatively, though W.J. Watson and George Henderson could deploy it competently. MacBain's *Etymological Dictionary* thus represents the injection of up-to-date Celtic linguistic scholarship into the stream of Gaelic lexicography.

As MacBain explains, we owe this work to a promise he made, on the publication of *Reliquiae Celticae*, that he would provide such a dictionary as a companion volume to Dr Cameron's textual studies. He claimed to have produced a vocabulary of 'pure' Scottish Gaelic by eliminating numerous Irish words that appeared in the larger Scottish Gaelic dictionaries. It was also his aim to direct those interested in etymology along the correct path. With this in mind, he prefaced the work with an explanation of the principles of Gaelic philology.

Alexander MacBain.

MacBain based his dictionary on the Highland Society's *Dictionarium Scoto-Celticum*, supplemented by MacAlpine, MacEachen and other sources. In order to delete 'Irish' words included by earlier dictionary makers, he undertook detailed research using Irish dictionaries and authoritative works on Early Irish. In compiling etymologies, he recognised a special debt to the work of the Old Irish scholar and Indo-Europeanist Whitley Stokes.

The *Etymological Dictionary* contains approximately 6,900 headwords. Entries consist of basic definitions without the addition of grammatical or syntactic information. Sequences of securely dated linguistic developments for Early Gaelic were becoming available by this time; but the later stages of the Goidelic languages were not so well served, particularly in the case of Scottish Gaelic. This scarcity of linguistic signposting meant that MacBain's work had to be more comparative than historical in its presentation. For this reason, and as expected in an etymological dictionary, the major part of an entry is taken up with comparative material from other languages, for example:

> **mogul,** a husk, mesh (of a net), Ir. *mogal*, cluster, mesh of a net, husk, apple of the eye, E. Ir. *mocoll* (do.), O. Ir. *mocol*, subtel: **mozgu-*, I. E., *mozgho*, knot, mesh; Lit. *mázgas*, knot, mesh; O. H. G., *mascâ*, Ger. *masche*, Eng. *mesh*; Gr. *μόσχος*, sprout, calf. Lat. *macula*, a mesh, is not allied. Dialect G. **mugairle**, bunch of nuts (Glenmoriston).

MacBain's work charted new territory for Gaelic by hitching it securely to the framework of philological learning. Although much of the detail of that framework has been revised or superseded, MacBain's application of it to Gaelic retains validity and demands the respect of present-day scholars. His research was thorough and extensive, and drew on an impressive list of works and authorities. As a result, Gaelic was now located within the wider Indo-European context. MacBain was an excellent and outward-looking scholar whose work raised Gaelic, and indeed Celtic, lexicography to a new level.

After MacBain's death his dictionary was reprinted in 1911, with biographical notes on MacBain's career in teaching and scholarship, by Malcolm MacFarlane (see p. 236). This edition includes additions, amendments and corrections drawn from MacBain's 'Further Gaelic Words and Etymologies', the 'Addenda and Corrigenda' appended to the first edition, and from his notes. MacBain's Preface to 'Further Gaelic Words and Etymologies'[54] explains that this edition benefits from feedback on the first edition, as well as his own recent reading and further thinking. It is significant that MacBain's reference to the congratulations and criticisms he had received indicates that his work was accepted for its merits by some giants of European scholarship, and criticised for insignificant or imagined flaws by some commentators from nearer home.

MacBain's lexicographical endeavours were not restricted to his etymological dictionary. Along with John Whyte, he published a revised and enlarged edition of MacEachen's dictionary in 1902. There was a need for a small, cheap dictionary for schools and for ordinary purposes, and Gaelic scholars knew that MacEachen's work, now out of print, would, with some revision, fill this need. MacBain acknowledged MacEachen's remarkable achievement but suggested that the increase in philological understanding since MacEachen's day allowed the editors to improve upon his work considerably. In particular, spellings could now be determined on the basis of sound historical knowledge. Additionally, otiose derivatives and obsolete or provincial words, including some of the Scots words, had been deleted and several hundred new words added. The revised dictionary has approximately 12,300 headwords and claims to include all the words in ordinary literature. A two-page guide to Gaelic pronunciation has been added; it describes sounds chiefly in terms of approximate English equivalents. The editors express their confidence that this improved edition should meet the needs of students and readers of Gaelic; there is reason to suppose they were correct in this assumption, for the second edition sold out in approximately four years. A further revised edition appeared in 1906, and was recommended by the Education Department as supplying the orthography to be followed in the Leaving Certificate Examination in Gaelic; this was the last that MacBain had a hand in.[55]

While MacBain was completing his contribution to Gaelic lexicography, another very different work was under way: Edward Dwelly's *A Gaelic Dictionary*, which appeared in fascicules between 1902 and 1911. Dwelly's work is a remarkable monument to the achievement and commitment of one dedicated individual. Now 100 years old, it is still one of Gaelic's greatest lexicographical resources.

Edward Dwelly (1864–1939) was born in Twickenham, Middlesex. He originally intended to be an engineer but, at the age of seventeen, he joined his father on the staff of Cox & Company, a London bank. In his own words, Dwelly 'had a fancy for Gaelic, and began to learn it at school'.[56] The young Dwelly also had an interest in piping and, coming as he did from an English military family, he became a part-time soldier in the Queen's Westminster Rifle Volunteers. By the age of twenty-two he was keen to increase his competency in Gaelic by contact with native speakers, and in 1887 he became a piper in the 5th Volunteer Battalion Argyll and Sutherland Highlanders, spending his annual holiday leave of one month among them. It was here that he met Ronald Mackenzie, who was aware of Dwelly's desire to be a pipe major. He advised the young man to take the Scottish name of Ewen MacDonald in order to further his career, and the first edition of the *Gaelic Dictionary* was published under this pseudonym. Dwelly was in fact 'baptised' with this name by the grandfather of one of the authors of the present chapter using 'a splash of *uisge beatha*'.[57] Mackenzie said he would give Dwelly a 'note . . . to the pipe major of the 1st Ross'[58] and, in 1891, he joined the 1st Volunteer Battalion Seaforth Highlanders (Gairloch). It was in this year that Dwelly moved to the Highlands and his fluency in the language improved to such an extent that it was said that he was able to pass as a native speaker. In 1896, after resigning from the army, Dwelly married Mary MacDougall, a native Gaelic speaker from Ardchattan in Argyll. They lived in Perthshire for two years, moving in 1898 to Lentran, overlooking the Beauly Firth. They remained there until 1900 when the family moved to Lyminge in Kent apparently to be near to Dwelly's now widowed mother.[59]

Dwelly found that the lack of a reliable and up-to-date concise dictionary was an impediment to his study of Gaelic language and culture, and he resolved to provide such a resource himself.[60] In his opinion, MacLeod and Dewar's and Armstrong's dictionaries 'are, without doubt, the best all-round dictionaries hitherto available for students, especially when requiring to translate English into Gaelic'.[61] Dwelly's initial word list was in fact based primarily on MacLeod and Dewar. Words that were not in MacLeod and Dewar but could be found in other dictionaries were then added, together with many more which appear in print for the first time in Dwelly's dictionary. Specialist vocabulary, such as the names of plants, diseases, birds, etc, was gleaned from works on these subjects, and proverbs and idioms given in MacAlpine's dictionary were also included. Many additional examples came from Alexander Carmichael's *Carmina Gadelica* (1900) and other printed sources. Dwelly revealed in an interview that he had used sixteen informants from throughout Scotland who went through his material adding words. Consequently, his dictionary includes many words not in other dictionaries and many never previously in print.[62] At a rough estimate Dwelly's *Gaelic Dictionary* contains around 82,000 headwords; the aim of producing a 'concise' dictionary had been replaced by a more ambitious and wide-ranging project.

Dwelly had several advantages as he set about his task. He was an astute learner of Gaelic, and one who naturally possessed many of the qualities needed for lexicography. His wife, who was his constant helpmate, was a native speaker of Gaelic, and he had a network of native-speaker informants. He also received help of various sorts from several prominent Gaelic scholars, among whom was W.J. Watson, later to become Professor of Celtic at the University of Edinburgh.

At the end of the day, however, the *Gaelic Dictionary* bears the stamp, at all levels, of Dwelly's own unique and independent vision, and reflects his personal decisions on every sort of issue. Certain features of the dictionary exemplify this quality.

Dwelly did not provide pronunciations. He believed that the Gaelic language is practically phonetic in its own way, and that the learner should therefore learn the correct sounds not from a dictionary but from a good textbook, with the aid of a Gaelic speaker. On the other hand, the first entry for each letter of the alphabet gives a summary description of its sounds; to which is added – typically! – the Gaelic name of the tree traditionally associated with the letter in the old Ogham alphabet.[63] He did not provide etymological information either; we may infer that his concern was with the language as it existed, rather than with its origins and congeners.

Dwelly's entry structure is simple: he gives all the meanings that his sources have provided, without any obvious ordering or ranking principles, and without regard to overlaps or contradictions. Principal parts of nouns are listed in the standard format. In the case of verbs, the arrangement of root form and present participle is used for the first time. Definitions can take the form of explanations as well as the usual (mostly) one-word equivalents. For example, the entry for *sgrath* in MacLeod and Dewar is as follows:

> SGRATH, -A,-AN, *s.f.* The outer skin or rind of any thing; a turf, a green sod.

Dwelly's corresponding entry gives twelve senses:

> sgrath, -a, -an, *s.f.* Outer skin or rind of anything, husk, peel. 2 Bark of a tree. 3 Coat of an onion. 4 Turf, green sod, divot, as used for covering roofs of houses. 5†† Horror, dread. 6 Rust. 7 Scale. 8** Rough handling. 9** Long rhyme. 10 Pull, tug. 11* What covers the kiln of grain. 12** Green-sward.

The only indication of differing linguistic status is provided by daggers and asterisks (as here), and a few abbreviated names, which indicate that the following sense is taken from a specific source or is 'obsolete'.

Occasionally Dwelly refers to specific published works, for example to warn the reader that a word or sense is Ossianic. In the following example he refers to D.C. MacPherson's *An Duanaire* (1868) in order to correct an eccentric spelling:

> gearrastain, *Duanaire, 48,* is for gearasdan.

Somewhat more frequently there are references to dialect provenance or differences, for example in usage or in the gender of nouns. But for the most part

cuid 289 cuidheall-shniomha

came too; c. rium, *along with me;* theann i an lomairt c., *she squeezed the fleece together.*
cuideachd, -an, *s.f.ind.* Troop, company, throng. 2 Society, intercourse. 3 Friends, relations. 4**Private company. 'Nam ch., *in my company*; c. shaighdearan, *a company of soldiers*; a ch. a' chridhe, *my dear people*; bheir e e féin as gach c. le ceòl 's le conaltradh, *he would acquit himself well in any company in music or conversation*; ged a tha e math 'ga thoirt féin á c. tha e motha 's math 'ga chuir féin ann, *though he can acquit himself well in company, he is better at getting himself invited*—he is too forward or cheeky; cha'n ann de 'm ch. thù, *you are not of my flock*—an imitation of the cooing of a pigeon.
————aich, *v.a.* Accompany.
————ail, -e, *a.* Social, entertaining, sociable. 2 Assistant, helpful.
cuideag, -eig, -an, *s.f.* Small portion. 2†† Small effects. 3 Spider. 4(AC) see cuiteag.
cuideal, -eil, *s.m.* see cuidealas.
————ach, *a.* Proud, haughty.
————achd,** *s.f.* Pride.
————as, -ais, *s.m.* Pride, conceit, forwardness.
cuideam, *prov.* for cudthrom.
————ach, -aiche, *prov.* for cudthromach.
cuidear rium, *prov.* for cuide rium.
cuideil, -deala, *a.* Proud, conceited, forward, vain, prim.
cuide ri, *prep.* With, along with, C. rium, *along with me*; c. riut, *along with thee*; c. ris, *along with him*; c. rithe, *along with her*; c. rinn, *along with us*; c. ribh, *along with you*; c. riu, *along with them*; c. ri chéile, *with each other.*
cuidh,‡ -e, -ein, *s.f.* Enclosure. 2 Cattle-fold, pen—*Barra.* 3 Enclosed field—*Eigg.* 4(DC) Trench, hollow artificially formed as a sheltered place to milk cows in on the grazing ground, and save the trouble of driving them to and from the byre. This word enters largely into place-names—*Uist.*
†cuidhbheach, -eiche, *a.* see cubhaidh.
cuidhe, see cuithe.
†cuidheachd, *s.f.* Decency.

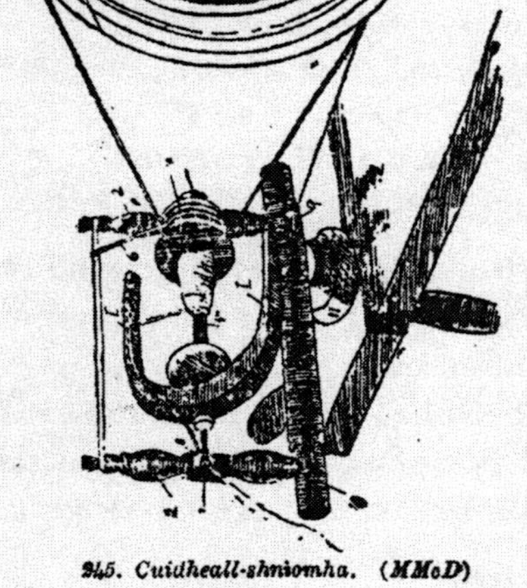

245. Cuidheall-shniomha. *(MMcD)*

cuidheall, -dhill [& cuidhle], -dhleachan, *s.f.* Wheel. 2 Coil. 3** Spinning-wheel, see cuidheall-shniomha. 4**Reel, yarn-windlass. 5**Whirl, whirling, reeling. 6** Cock of hay. 7 Circle. 8 Circular motion. Saor-chuidhleachan, *a wheelwright.*
————, *pr. pt.* a' cuidhleadh, *v.a.* Wheel. 2 Roll. 3 **Whirl, twirl. 4 Hurl. 5 Coil. 6 Gather into cocks, as hay.
————aireachd, *s.f.ind.* Wheeling. 2 Rolling. 3 Spinning.
———— -iarna, *s.f.* Hank-reel.
cuidheall-shniomha, *gen.* cuidhle-, *s.f.* Spinning-wheel.

PARTS OF A SPINNING-WHEEL:— (ill. 245.)
1 Teic, seic,†† *flyer.* Séicle—*Uist.*
2 Maighdeanan, gàirdeanan. *sing.* maighdeag & maideag.
3 Iuchair na ciche, *nave.*
4 Rolan, *wheel which turns the flyer.* Rathan—*Poolewe* (WC.)
5 Piorna, [pùirne,] *pirn, reel.*
6 Bann beag, *little band.* [A' bhann bheag, (*s.f.*) in *Poolewe* (WC.)]
7 Dealgan, *spindle.*
8 Cluas na cuidhle, *ears*, rests of leather fixed to maighdeanan, and through which dealgan-an-t-seic revolve. [A' chluasag—*Poolewe* (WC.)
9 Iuchair, *key.*
10 Beairt mheadhon, *bar.*
11 Stoc, *main body.*
12 Com, *body.*
13 Aisnean, aisnichean, *ribs* or *spokes* of large wheel.
14 Iuchair, *pin* for tightening bann beag.

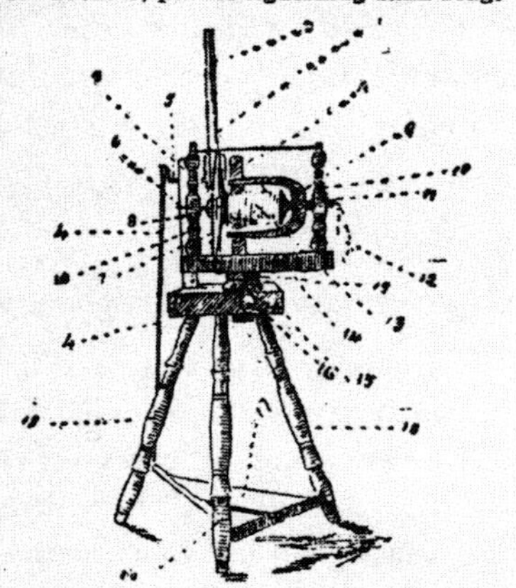

246. Cuidheall-shniomha. *(MMcD)*

Parts as shown in illust. 246:
1 Bann mór, *driving-belt* or *band* of large wheel. [A' bhann mhór (*s.f.*) in *Poolewe* (WC.)]
2 Réim, *rim of large wheel.*
3 Na h-eich, *supports of large wheel.*
4 Maide-siubhail, claidheamh, *connecting-rod*, one end of which is attached to the crank of the large wheel, and the other to the foot-board. An t-amadan—(WC.)
5 Deil, *crank.* Deil is aisil, *crank and axle* of large wheel.
6 Aiseil an-t-seic, *axle of flyer.*
7 Bann beag, *little band*, regulating string to prevent pirn from revolving. [*s.f.*—*Poolewe.*]

Page of *The Illustrated Gaelic–English Dictionary* by Edward Dwelly, showing some of the copious illustrations.

users are left to exercise judgement as to which of a set of multiple meanings is applicable in a given case. It would not be unfair to say that the more Gaelic one knows, the better use one can make of this uniquely valuable and uniquely challenging resource.

Dwelly has his own views on some of the issues that had exercised earlier Gaelic lexicographers. For instance, he has an answer to the complaint that many of the words in other dictionaries are Irish and not Scottish. He believes that some so-called 'Irishisms' have a place in Scottish Gaelic dictionaries, on the grounds that the difference between the Irish and Scots is merely geographical and not racial. He also points out that many so-called Irish words are in use in Kintyre, and criticises those who object to the use of 'Irish' words but have no compunction about using English or Scots words which they pronounce and write according to Gaelic rules. Regarding the latter, all such words identified by Dwelly are treated as follows in his *Gaelic Dictionary*:

> gàidsear, *s.m.* Gaelic spelling of *gauger*.

This strategy is used to highlight the fact that words of this sort are loan-words. Clearly, Dwelly has an agenda in this respect: in contrast to his tolerance of a Gaelic continuum linking Scotland and Ireland, he hopes that by 'naming and shaming' such words he can help to expel Anglicisms from the language.

Dwelly justifies the level of detail included in the dictionary by stating that one of his main objectives was to include all material liable to present difficulties to learners of the language. He is aware that his is the first dictionary of Gaelic to attempt to explain words with the help of specially drawn illustrations. These, in fact, add a great deal to the value of the dictionary entries and are an important expression of its encyclopedic dimension. For example, the entry for *bàta* 'boat', when one includes both the description and the illustration, takes up almost six pages. Dwelly's is also the first dictionary to include local terms, particularly the names of implements and their parts, many of which were no longer widely used. Here the ethnologist and antiquarian in Dwelly has – to our great advantage – reversed the tendency of earlier lexicographers to reject the rustic and 'provincial'. On the other hand, Dwelly also shows a desire to demonstrate that Gaelic is equal to English in his long entry on *coinneamh* 'meeting', which contains a comprehensive list of Gaelic words and expressions to cover procedural points and parliamentary conventions.

In addition to the riches contained in the dictionary itself, Dwelly includes a variety of expected and unexpected treasures in the preliminary and supplementary pages. There is a short essay entitled 'The Commercial Value of Gaelic', in which the benefits of learning another language, and Gaelic in particular, are outlined. He mentions the opinion of an acquaintance working in education which prefigures the findings of those involved in Gaelic-medium education today, with respect to the advantages of bilingualism: 'A well-known inspector of schools, who has examined bi-lingual children for thirty years, declares that Gaelic-speaking children are much more intelligent and brighter, and possess a better knowledge of English than the uni-lingual Lowland child.'[64]

Dwelly also provides an outline of the Gaelic language, presented in three sections: pronunciation, orthography and inflections. This outline, with the exception of the material on pronunciation, is intended for users who already have at least a basic knowledge of Gaelic. After the dictionary, we find a list of proper names ordered alphabetically according to the English form, with the Gaelic equivalent opposite. This lists place-names (including the names of countries) and personal names and surnames collected by Dwelly from newspapers, magazines, books and so on between 1880 and 1911. The list was revised and added to by W.J. Watson, whose additions are marked with an asterisk. There is also 'A Short Account of the Principal Persons and Places Mentioned in Old Gaelic Folk-Tales and Poetry', whose content is acknowledged to be drawn from Armstrong's dictionary. In the prefatory material there is also a reference to an appendix, in which users are advised to look if confronted with a word not included in the dictionary. This appendix did not appear during Dwelly's lifetime, but was rediscovered and published much later.

Finally, the subscribers to the dictionary are listed. Dwelly's wife and mother are included, along with seven others with the surname of Dwelly. Notable amongst the list of subscribers is Dr W.A. Craigie of Oxford, at that time the third editor of the *OED* (see Chapters 5 and 10).

The road to publication was long and arduous and every bit as challenging as the lexicography. Dwelly could not find a printer to produce the dictionary at a price he could afford. Nor could he find an artist to provide the illustrations. He set about doing both himself. The illustrations were probably the easier task, and most were drawn by Dwelly. The Stornoway artist Malcolm MacDonald drew the items for which Dwelly could not access examples in England, such as native implements. Publication, on the other hand, proved to be literally an uphill struggle. Stereotyping was done in Maidstone, and the journey to the railway station involved transporting 150 lb of type up and down steep hills, the highest of which was 600 feet above sea level, in a wheelbarrow. (Almost a century later in a different world, *DOST* copy in slip format was microfilmed before being flown to the Philippines for data capture (see Chapter 5)!) Eventually, Dwelly managed to buy a stereo foundry and cast the plates himself. As with all dictionary projects, the lack of financial support was a perennial problem.

Edward Dwelly at his printing press.

With the assistance of his family, he raised funds by producing Gaelic Pocket Books, postcards and Christmas cards. Such fundraising initiatives are still being practised in Scots lexicography. Publication of the dictionary was completed in 1911. Sadly, the work did not achieve its greatest level of esteem until after Dwelly's death, but he was given some recognition for his labours during his lifetime. He was made an honorary life member of the Gaelic Society of London and of An Comunn Gàidhealach (of which he was a founder member). He was also made a Fellow of the Society of Antiquaries of Scotland. Perhaps he would also have taken some satisfaction in the fact that, in the Gaelic world, the name of Edward Dwelly is probably as well known as that of Samuel Johnson and James Murray in English. In 1915 Dwelly's financial circumstances forced him to return to work for Cox & Company where he remained until 1919. In his spare time, he worked on many new projects, chiefly connected with genealogy, and he remained devoted to Scottish Gaelic.

The complete dictionary was reproduced, in a three-volume set, in 1911. This was described as a revised edition, but the text of the dictionary itself does not appear to have been altered. Given the effort required to reset type, it is probably safe to assume it was not. The frontispiece has a photograph of Dwelly with his bagpipes. The title page has been altered to read 'The Illustrated Gaelic Dictionary Specially designed for beginners and for use in schools, Including every Gaelic word in all the other Gaelic dictionaries and printed books, as well as an immense number never in print before. By Edward Dwelly, FSG. Vol. 1. Revised edition. Herne Bay: Printed and Published by the Author Singlehanded at his publishing office in Mill Lane. 1911.'

The Preface is titled thus with no equivalent title in Gaelic. Unlike the dictionary text, the Preface has been altered extensively, and these changes are of interest to the history of Gaelic lexicography. The overall tone has changed, and some of the passion of Dwelly's original Preface has disappeared. It is now written in the first person singular, not the first person plural as in the first edition. There are two new paragraphs at the beginning, in which Dwelly claims that the first edition 'has been carefully revised and no expense or labour spared to make this the most reliable and complete Gaelic Dictionary obtainable'.[65]

MacBain is now named as the principal authority on Gaelic orthography, and the commendation of MacLeod and Dewar and of Armstrong has been dropped. A reference to the appendix has also been omitted; by this time Dwelly would have known that he did not have sufficient funds to publish it. Dwelly goes on to thank the late King Edward profusely for awarding him a pension. He acknowledges the support and assistance of his wife and various scholars. (There are some changes in the list of scholars named.) There is a new paragraph about the difficulties faced by learners of Gaelic, including reference to the need to encourage native speakers to converse with them in Gaelic, and a further new paragraph advising users to use their own discretion when translating from English to Gaelic. Most notably, the paragraph in which he had talked about purging Gaelic of Anglicisms has been dropped.

A new final paragraph has been added which shows the extent of Dwelly's dedication to his work. It is worth reproducing here to show the magnitude of the debt the Gaelic language community owes to him:

> Every effort has been made to get the work finished as quickly as possible compatible with correct work and in consequence I worked long hours on many days when really too ill to do any work at all. The unique obstacles encountered in acquiring a fluent knowledge of Gaelic and compiling this dictionary, as well as the difficulty in not being able to pay the heavy expense of having it printed and published in the ordinary way and so being finally compelled to learn how to print and publish it myself, have been fully described by the Press from time to time and an epitome of these accounts will be found in my History of the Dwelly family. I have set up every letter of the type myself from beginning to end, and the only assistance I have had in connection with the printing of this book has been the occasional distribution of type by members of my family amounting to nearly 40 pages and by others 10 pages – in all under 50 pages. E.D. Herne Bay, June 1st 1911.

Although Dwelly's *Gaelic Dictionary* was published entirely within the twentieth century, it is to be regarded as the culmination of the labours of the nineteenth century, as a compendium and a summation. It fulfils that purpose admirably. It also reflects the attitudes of a younger generation of Gaelic speakers and sympathisers who had grown up in the days of Land Law reform, agitation, vocal émigré communities and the expansion of Gaelic education and scholarship. To them Gaelic could appear as a language with both a past and a future, both a rural and an urban presence, as a language that could be taught and learned, and as a language that could be spoken well or badly. All these ideas can be detected in the columns of Dwelly's dictionary, in his extra-linguistic editorial interventions, and in the prefatory pages where he has his say. His work has been justly esteemed; in a very real sense he rendered his lexical predecessors superfluous, at least in the Gaelic–English sphere. Another outstanding aspect of Dwelly's work is the rich vein of ethnological information it contains. His awareness of this level, in which he was well ahead of his time, was perhaps due to his roots in another culture; whatever its source, his work can be justifiably regarded as a major repository of Gaelic culture as well as Gaelic language.[66]

Considering nineteenth-century lexicography as a whole, it is important to remember that a number of profound and pervasive social, spiritual and intellectual developments were taking place, and can be seen as casting their shadow over the efforts of the dictionary-makers described above. By the end of the century the needs of users had expanded far beyond the Bible and sermons, and *Ossian* had been replaced by real Gaelic poetry in print. Gaelic itself had attained a certain prestige, and had shown that it could aspire to conquer new spoken and written domains, including higher education. The twin pillars of learning represented by MacBain and Dwelly were fitting end-pieces to the early history of Gaelic lexicography.

NINE

The Last Hundred Years

WILLIAM GILLIES AND LORNA PIKE

Edward Dwelly had responded to early developments in Gaelic education and the needs of a gradually expanding general readership, including learners of Gaelic like himself. But his work was compendious rather than analytic, interim rather than final. Continuing developments in Gaelic education, publishing and scholarship (including a new emphasis on the spoken Gaelic of the dialects and of oral tradition) called for new responses from dictionary-makers.

In 1912, a year after the completion of Dwelly's work, Malcolm MacFarlane (1853–1931) published *The School Gaelic Dictionary*. MacFarlane was born in Dalavich, Lochaweside, and was a native speaker of Gaelic. His family moved to Paisley when he was a young boy. A land surveyor by profession, he was a Gaelic editor, writer and translator, and an active promoter of the Gaelic language in education, literature and life. He was much concerned with the scholarly status of the language, and was the author of *Phonetics of the Gaelic Language: With an Exposition of the Current Orthography and a System of Phonography* (1889). His edition of the Fernaig Manuscript, *Làmh-sgrìobhainn Mhic Rath* (1923), is, in the absence of more scholarly editions, still an authority. He was also active in editing books for children to use in schools, and translated many Gaelic songs, both alone and in collaboration with others.

The Preface to the *School Gaelic Dictionary*, written only in English, states that Gaelic could not maintain its proper place in Highland schools without a graded series of elementary reading books supported by a dictionary of the vocabulary used in these books. The available books were *An Treòraiche, An Comh-threòraiche* and *Companach na cloinne*, all edited by MacFarlane. The dictionary, however, includes a wider vocabulary range than that. MacFarlane also excerpted material from Lachlan MacLean's popular historical sketches of the lives of Rob Roy, William Wallace and John Knox.[1] He also includes many other words in common use, though without any indication of sources. He felt that one of the great drawbacks to the increase of Gaelic literary output was ignorance of how to prepare writing for publication; accordingly, he provides instructions on the preparation of copy and the methods of correcting proofs.

The dictionary includes roughly 5,500 headwords. Definitions are simple and consist mostly of equivalents. Gaelic nouns are given in the standard format (see p. 214). Verbs are described as 'active' and/or 'neuter' (apparently equivalent to 'transitive' and 'intransitive' in more recent grammatical terminology), but with no further information than that. No etymological information is given. The degree of explanation and exemplification was designed to make the dictionary useful to the mostly Gaelic-speaking school pupils of the time. The quality of the information and the coverage of the vocabulary of standard Gaelic are good. MacFarlane's desire to raise the standards of written, and especially published, Gaelic was no doubt in response to the patchy quality of the editing of much nineteenth-century publishing and his own experience as editor of *An Deo-ghréine*, the official magazine of An Comunn Gàidhealach.

In over fifty instances MacFarlane gives the 'L. Sc.' (Lowland Scots) equivalent of the headword. Sometimes this is because the words are somehow related. For example:

> **spong,** nf. g.d. spuing ; pl. +an, tinder (L. Sc. spunk), sponge.

In other cases he seems to be simply pointing out a close Gaelic–Scots equivalence:

> **caileag,** nf. g.d. -eig; pl. +an, little girl (L. Sc. lassie).

The reasons why Gaelic lexicographers have included Scots terms in Gaelic dictionaries have clearly varied, and the subject would be worth investigating further as a linguistic and cultural–political phenomenon.

After MacFarlane's death his dictionary was reproduced twice: in 1948 and again in 1949. The reissue was retitled *Gaelic–English Dictionary*, perhaps with the aim of broadening its appeal.

When the Rev. Malcolm MacLennan (1862–1931) published *A Pronouncing and Etymological Dictionary of the Gaelic Language* in 1925, Gaelic had become a subject qualifying for graduation in arts courses in Scottish universities, and MacLennan's aim was to meet the needs of students taking such courses. Born in Cnip, Lewis, he went to Canada when quite young and was educated at McGill University. He became a minister in Glengarry and later Kirkhill, Ontario, before returning to Scotland in 1897, to the St Columba United Free Gaelic Church in Edinburgh, where he remained until his death. MacLennan was admired both as a pastor and as a scholar. He revised the Gaelic Bible,[2] published books of hymns, and edited the Gaelic pages of church magazines, as well as *An Deo-ghréine* (1906–8).

In his Preface, MacLennan explains that his dictionary contains all words given by MacAlpine, MacEachen and MacBain (see pp. 219, 222, 225). To meet the needs of students, the dictionary has both Gaelic–English and English–Gaelic sections, the former with pronunciation and etymology for some entries. To this core of vocabulary MacLennan has added words from contemporary and older literature, and more from spoken Gaelic. The scholars whom MacLennan enlisted to help him with this task consisted mainly of Gaels who, like himself, came from the North-West Highlands and Islands. As a result, MacLennan's dictionary contains many Hebridean words and meanings not recorded in earlier dictionaries.

MacLennan's Introduction includes a short treatise on Gaelic pronunciation in which he sets out to explain this in terms of English spelling. He realises this method has shortcomings, inasmuch as the same symbol in English orthography can represent a variety of sounds, and the same sounds can be represented by more than one English spelling; also, the English alphabet does not represent all the sounds of Gaelic. To help users of his dictionary, MacLennan gives a table of Gaelic vowel and consonant spellings, with their values expressed as phonetic symbols and by means of specimen words in English and, where English lacks an adequate counterpart, French and/or German examples. Unfortunately, he did not choose to use the phonetic symbols in the body of the dictionary, where the English-based pronunciations supplied are rebarbative and prone to misinterpretation.

The Gaelic–English section contains roughly 18,000 headwords. Declensional forms of nouns are not given unless they are unpredictable. Verbs seem to be labelled as in MacLennan's sources. Definitions consist mostly of equivalents, but some examples of usage are given, and these are occasionally attributed to authors. Etymologies are likewise sporadic in their occurrence. MacLennan acknowledges the help of a number of scholars, most notably W.J. Watson and Bruce Dickins, who were leading authorities on Gaelic and Scandinavian philology respectively. The English–Gaelic word list, containing approximately 21,500 headwords, is based on that of MacKenzie (see p. 221), and some entries unfortunately reproduce inconsistencies in the latter's labelling. Some definitions are more explanatory than MacKenzie's, but no exemplification of usage is given.

When it appeared, MacLennan's dictionary was probably most useful to students of Gaelic who already had a considerable knowledge of the language. This would have been especially true of Hebridean students and with regard to Hebridean literature and writing, since both were becoming increasingly important as the older Gaelic power bases of Argyllshire and Perthshire declined and contracted. While it contained no advances in semantic analysis, the format of MacLennan's dictionary was decidedly more user-friendly than others. That may explain its success in recent years, together with its more northerly *blas* and its attempt at all-round coverage, including pronunciation and etymology, in a one-volume dictionary.

Heinrich (later Henry) Cyril Dieckhoff (1869–1950) was born in Russia. His father was head of the Lutheran Church in Moscow. His parents separated after his mother's conversion to Catholicism, and she left Russia for Germany, taking

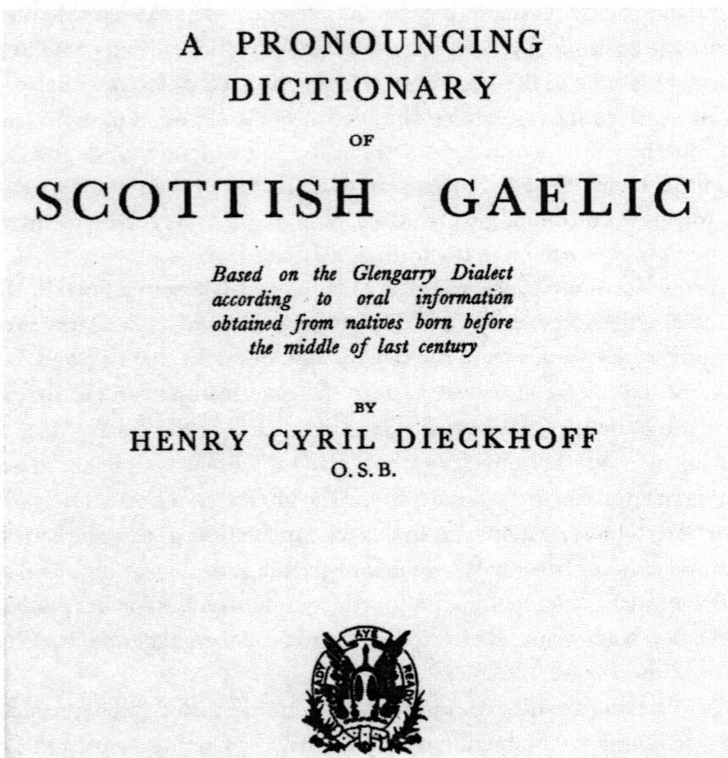

A PRONOUNCING
DICTIONARY
OF
SCOTTISH GAELIC

Based on the Glengarry Dialect according to oral information obtained from natives born before the middle of last century

BY
HENRY CYRIL DIECKHOFF
O. S. B.

Title page of *A Pronouncing Dictionary of Scottish Gaelic: Based on the Glengarry Dialect*... by Henry C. Dieckhoff.

Cyril with her. He went to school and university there and studied phonetics. The Russian army attempted to call him up and, following the advice of his mother's family in Germany, he left and went to Edinburgh. He studied at Edinburgh University before going to the abbey at Fort Augustus, where he became a priest, remaining there until his death.[3] Dieckhoff took a keen interest in Gaelic and took the opportunity to study dialect and collect words while assisting parish priests in Moidart, Lochaber and Glen Garry. He contributed scholarly articles on Gaelic linguistic matters to several learned journals.[4]

Dieckhoff's *A Pronouncing Dictionary of Scottish Gaelic* was published in 1932. In his Preface, Dieckhoff states that the dictionary owes its existence to his desire to capture the traditional pronunciation of Gaelic, which he had come to appreciate during his time in the Highlands. Having noticed differences between the speech of older people, in whose younger days Gaelic was the main language spoken, and the younger ones, who were losing some of the sounds and forms of the language, he had decided to keep an exact record of the traditional pronunciation for his own philological studies. Thinking this might be of interest to others, he now presented it in the form of a dictionary.

The pronunciation reflected is that of natives of Glengarry born in the first half of the nineteenth century. Dieckhoff defines the area of Glengarry as ending at Invergloy in the west, where the dialect marches with that of Lochaber, and Fort Augustus in the east, where eastern dialectal features are clearly discernible. For the benefit of the non-specialist reader, Dieckhoff, like MacLennan, devised his own set of phonetic symbols using the English alphabet in order to reproduce an approximate pronunciation. The interested reader is referred to the Introduction, which contains a more exact explanation of the phonetics; here International Phonetic Alphabet values are given beside Dieckhoff's own system and conventional Gaelic spellings. A fourth column supplies further guidance on pronunciation using examples from Gaelic and other languages, such as Spanish, Italian and French.

Dieckhoff also provides an innovative section entitled 'General Notes on Changes of Sound in Connection with Declensions, Conjugations, and Contact of Words', i.e., what we now call morphophonemics, including initial, internal and final mutations marking grammatical and syntactic alternations. Dieckhoff acknowledges the help of W.J. Watson and also that of John Fraser, Jesus Professor of Celtic at Oxford University, who was himself a native speaker of mainland Inverness-shire Gaelic. Fraser contributed a foreword warmly recommending Dieckhoff's work to Gaelic scholars.

The dictionary contains an estimated 9,000 headwords. In keeping with his commitment to traditional Gaelic, Dieckhoff omits words obviously borrowed from English, even those that had adopted Gaelic morphological traits. The entry structure is very simple and lacks detailed semantic analysis. Nouns are labelled as masculine or feminine; plurals and other forms are only given where unpredictable, for example:

> **croiteir,** *m.* kröh*d'*jer', *p.* -ean, -ən, a crofter.

Regular verbs are listed in the second singular imperative or 'root' form, with verbal noun forms mostly supplied. The several stem-forms of irregular verbs are given as separate entries linked by cross-references.

Although etymology as such is absent, related forms from other languages are occasionally given, for example:

> **ceile,** *m.* and *f.* k'*j***é**l'ə, a spouse, husband; a cheile, ə *c***é**l'ə, each other; le cheile, le *c***é**l'ə, together; troi-cheile, tr(oi)*c***é**l'ə, in disorder (compare Scottish "through other").
> **truis,** *v.* truS, *v.n.* trusadh, tr**u**səG, collect. (French trousser.)

Examples of usage are also occasionally given:

> **fiamhachd,** *f.* fi:a**w*ɐKg, resemblance; *e.g.* tha f. aig an duine so ris an duin'eile, this man resembles the other man.

An appendix lists proper names. Section 1 gives personal names, Section 2 gives names of places and their inhabitants sub-divided into part A (places in and near Glengarry) and part B (general names). Dieckhoff's dictionary is extensive enough to be regarded as a serious contribution to Gaelic lexicography, but it is best seen as a record of the conservative Glengarry dialect, comparable with Míchéal Ó Briain's collection of old words and phrases from Ballyvourney in Co. Cork or Archbishop Michael Sheehan's similar collection from the Decies of Co. Waterford.[5]

While based on the Glengarry dialect, Dieckhoff gives many comparisons with that of Moidart and, to a lesser extent, Lochaber, for example:

> **iomradh,** *m.* ümərаG, mention, a report (Moidart, imu:ra).

From a modern dialectological perspective, it is frustrating that Dieckhoff does not cite precise details of his sources for individual items. In general, they were presumably recorded in the same way as the Glengarry forms he collected in the mid-1920s.[6] While twenty-first century dialectologists may regret this degree of imprecision, Dieckhoff's work remains an important, if at times tantalising, resource. The dictionary was reproduced in a facsimile edition by Gairm publications in 1992.

The productivity of the early twentieth century was not to continue for Gaelic, however, in stark contrast to the decades of serious lexicographical activity that ensued with regard to English (see Chapter 10), Scots (see Chapters 5 and 6), Irish (the *Dictionary of the Irish Language* was published between 1913 and 1976),[7] and Welsh (collecting for *Geiriadur Prifysgol Cymru / Dictionary of the Welsh Language* began in 1921, editing ensued in 1948 and publication was completed in 2002).[8] This lack of progress in lexicography (and the same has been true of grammar) is especially regrettable when one considers the progress that has been made in other areas of Gaelic language maintenance and revitalisation. For the second half of the twentieth century has seen greatly increased literary activity, much expanded radio and television exposure, the development of bilingual and Gaelic-medium education, and a substantial increase in the number of serious learners of the language. All these would have benefited from the presence of authoritative versions of these fundamental supports of language.

But while there was no twentieth-century response comparable to that of the nineteenth century, in which a similar surge in enthusiasm for the language stimulated major lexicographical activity, there were some worthy and substantial advances, mostly stimulated by the needs of the Gaelic education system and by growth in the numbers of Gaelic learners. In 1979 *Abair Faclan!* – a pocket dictionary aimed primarily at learners – was published. Its compilers were John A. (Jake) MacDonald from the Isle of Skye, writer of the ground-breaking Gaelic course *Gàidhlig Bheò* for BBC TV, and Ronald Renton from Glasgow. Both were teachers of Gaelic in Glasgow, MacDonald having been lecturer in Gaelic in Jordanhill College of Education, and Renton a teacher of English and ultimately deputy head of St Aloysius' College.

With approximately 2,900 headwords in the Gaelic–English section and 2,600 in the English–Gaelic, the coverage of *Abair Faclan!* is very limited, but it aims nevertheless to provide an essential core of basic vocabulary. The entry structure is simple and semantic analysis is basic; some examples of usage are provided. Nouns are given together with the definite article. Verbs are given in standard style. The principal parts of nouns, verbs and adjectives are included in both Gaelic–English and English–Gaelic sections. This was not normal practice but was done by MacDonald and Renton, as good pedagogues, in order to reinforce the language structure for learners. Their dictionary also includes an appendix on irregular verbs. While limited in its content, *Abair Faclan!* proved a highly successful dictionary, particularly for beginners. It was renamed *Abair!* in 1993 and has been reprinted several times.

Abair Faclan! attempted to meet the needs of younger users in a changing world in which learners deserved to be properly catered for. This need was also clear to Derick Thomson, whose *New English–Gaelic Dictionary* was published in 1981. Thomson was born in Stornoway in 1921, the son of a schoolmaster. He had enjoyed a long and distinguished academic career before becoming Professor of Celtic at Glasgow University in 1963. He had been a co-founder of the periodical *Gairm* in 1952. He instituted the Historical Dictionary of Scottish Gaelic project in 1966 (see p. 251) and founded the Gaelic Books Council in 1968. He had already established himself as one of the major contemporary Gaelic poets of the twentieth century.

In his Preface, Thomson states the need for an up-to-date English–Gaelic dictionary. He refers to those currently in use (MacKenzie and MacLennan) as not adequate to meet the needs of learners in the late twentieth century. He acknowledges the improved quality of the coverage in MacDonald and Renton's *Abair Faclan!*, but criticises its limited range of vocabulary, which his work is designed to address. Thomson names his sources as existing dictionaries, literature and speech, without further specification.

At the time of its publication, Thomson's work represented an improvement in the vocabulary range of this new generation of English–Gaelic dictionaries. The dictionary was reprinted in 1986 and 1990, and a new edition was produced in 1994, with corrections and additions. New entries include 'computer', 'disk', 'job-centre', 'job description', 'keen' (v), 'maternity leave', 'Scottish National Party' and 'space-shuttle'. The *New English–Gaelic Dictionary* took account of the Scottish Certificate of Education Examination Board's revised Gaelic spelling recommendations, and likewise of such word lists as the board's 'List of Linguistic and Literary Terms'.[9] The dictionary is basic in lexicographical terms, but its vocabulary is extensive, at around 17,000 headwords. Its entries consist mostly of one-word Gaelic equivalents. The gender of nouns is given.

A new compact Gaelic–English dictionary appeared in 1993: Robert C. Owen's *Modern Gaelic–English Dictionary*, which was intended to be used in conjunction with Thomson's work. Owen also produced *Instant Gaelic* and *Gàidhlig le Gàire*.[10] Like the dictionaries of MacDonald, and Renton and Thomson, his dictionary was compiled to meet the needs of learners. Owen gives Gaelic pronunciations based on English spelling. His system suffers from the same weaknesses as other non-IPA-based systems, and also from excessive brevity. There are around 7,000 headwords, considerably fewer than in Thomson's dictionary, but the range and choice of vocabulary are suitable for learners.

In the year that Owen's dictionary appeared, the text of Thomson's English–Gaelic dictionary was reset to match the typography of Owen's Gaelic–English volume, and the two were chosen as a pair to be the standard Gaelic dictionaries for school use. Thomson's layout and vocabulary range is mirrored quite well in Owen, but there are many differences in detail. For example, Thomson gives *buaireaseach* for 'irksome', while Owen defines it as 'turbulent'. Thomson gives *comas* for 'possibility', while Owen defines it as 'power, ability, capacity'. Some of Thomson's entries are not represented at all. For example, Thomson gives *dotair bheathach* or *veat* for 'vet', while Owen gives neither.

MacDonald and Renton, Thomson and Owen can be seen as continuing a process of eliminating vocabulary irrelevant to a younger generation of Gaelic speakers and learners, and providing in its place up-to-date terminology to answer their practical needs. They were, however, largely innocent of the theoretical and methodological advances that characterised late twentieth-century language-learning tools for English and other languages. They were teachers of language and literature and, with the exception of Thomson, they were not professional Gaelic scholars. All had many involvements within the Gaelic language movement in addition to personal 'nine-to-five' commitments. It would also be true to say that the 'professional' lexicographical energies of the Gaelic world were concentrated on the Historical Dictionary project, which was ongoing from 1966; indeed, anticipation of its results created a sort of 'planning blight' as far as more ambitious schemes were concerned; and the urgent demands of the education system exerted ever greater pressure to provide short-term solutions. As a consequence, the Scottish Gaelic lexicographical tradition at the close of the twentieth century could be characterised as backward-looking or inward-looking, still feeding essentially on nineteenth-century exemplars with a greater or lesser degree of superficial adjustment based on personal introspection. Tomás de Bhaldraithe's *Foclóir Béarla–Gaeilge/English–Irish Dictionary* (first published in 1959) has been criticised for its use of the English–French section of Harrap's *Shorter French and English Dictionary* as its basis. But the benefits of allowing the fresh air of modern lexicographical standards into English–Irish dictionary-making (for example, in providing examples of usages and idioms involving the target word) far outweighed the drawbacks, to the advantage of Irish by comparison with Scottish Gaelic.[11]

One other development from this relatively fallow period deserves mention here. It has been explained in Chapter 8 how Edward Dwelly lacked the financial resources to publish the appendix of additional words that he had been collecting during the period when his dictionary was going through the press. The material, which appeared to have gone missing after his death, was rediscovered by Douglas Clyne, a medical practitioner with a strong interest in Gaelic, and the compiler of *Gaelic Verbs and their Prepositions* (1984) and *An English–Gaelic Dictionary of Expressions, Idioms and Phrases* (1985). He undertook to edit it, but died in 1989 before the editorial work was finished. This work was completed by

Derick Thomson, who published it in 1991 under the title *Appendix to Dwelly's Dictionary*.

The text of the appendix consisted of 500 sheets of dictionary entries, carefully written in Dwelly's hand, largely in alphabetical order. Most of the material related to the early part of the alphabet. The appendix is essentially Dwelly's compilation as he left it, though it should be recorded that Clyne compiled a detailed index, consisting of around 19,000 items, to go with the dictionary and maximise its continuing usefulness. Editing included some expansion of definitions, expansion of references to the published dictionary, expansion of syntax of Dwelly's explanations and review of translations of quoted verse, sometimes using editions published after Dwelly's death. The notes on Dwelly's manuscript show the extent and value of the network of contacts he built up during his years working on the dictionary. In many cases, considerable detail is added in the appendix, particularly with reference to usage in specific areas. It is clear that much of the fresh material was provided in response to the published fascicules of the dictionary. The positive reaction of so many Gaels to his dictionary, and their willingness to contribute additional material when invited to do so, indicates the great esteem in which Dwelly's work was held.

The authorities quoted are chiefly the same as in the main dictionary, but there are some additions, such as the *Celtic Magazine* and certain private individuals. Dwelly used special symbols to indicate some new key sources, such as MacBain's dictionary, and H. Cameron Gillies' names of diseases. Regrettably, for those with an interest in Dwelly's source material, not all of these have been reproduced in print.

The appendix contains approximately 5,500 headwords with the same entry structure as in the original dictionary. As before, items important to Gaelic culture have been well researched. Additional terms connected with boats extend over three columns under the heading *bàta*. There are also additional names for harness, parts of a byre, parts of a mill, a still, and a peat spade, and detailed definitions of words to do with weaving.

It is interesting to note that Dwelly uses some Scots terms, which may have been supplied by his informants. Some, but not all, of these attract a comment, for example:

> sriutan, (AH), *s. pl.* The "kinks" of whooping cough. [Scots *kink-hoast,* whooping cough].
>
> cas-arain, (AH), *s.f.* Toaster for drying and hardening oatmeal farls before the fire after being taken off the girdle.

Where new ground was genuinely broken, however, was in Richard Cox's *Brìgh nam Facal* (1991). This was the first, and regrettably is still the only, monolingual dictionary of Scottish Gaelic. Cox, a Gaelic learner originally from Croydon, graduated in Celtic Studies from the University of Glasgow and has published extensively on Gaelic and Scandinavian place-names. He is also a Gaelic publisher and a professor at Sabhal Mòr Ostaig UHI. The dictionary was published at a propitious time in the early years of Gaelic-medium education. It was asked for by the Primary Review Group for primary schools, and is therefore designed for the younger student. It has just over 8,000 headwords with a very simple entry structure, and sometimes includes examples of usage. A reprint was published with minor corrections in 2007. The pedagogical and symbolic value of the monolingual dictionary for a minority language cannot be overstated.

New ground of a different sort was broken by *Stòr-Dàta Briathrachais Gàidhlig* ('The Gaelic Terminology Database'), which was published by Sabhal Mòr Ostaig under the editorship of Fearchar MacGill'Fhinnein in 1993.[12] The *Stòr-Dàta* project (1987–92) had grown out of an original suggestion from Comunn na Gàidhlig, to the effect that public authorities and other agencies and bodies that used Gaelic in the discharge of their function should share Gaelic word lists they had created. The intention was to build up and circulate a lexicon of current educational, commercial and technical vocabulary and usage, including both neologisms and adaptations of traditional words and idioms. A further objective was to stabilise usage, share good practice and make it easier for such bodies to develop more ambitious policies in regard to their use of Gaelic. This publication was thought-provoking in the sense that it revealed divergences already present in terminological usage. Apart from the Examination Board's ad hoc committee, whose work underlay the Gaelic Orthographic Conventions (1981; see p. 243), Scotland had nothing comparable to the Irish Education Department's Standing Committee on Terminology (*Coiste Téarmaíochta*), with its specialist panels, for which such pioneering individual efforts as Derick Thomson's *Bith-eòlas* ('Biology'), published in 1976,[13] were a 'wake-up call' but no substitute. *Stòr-Dàta Briathrachais Gàidhlig* was valuable also in the way it captured and shared professional and other specialised sets of vocabulary, for example, for plant-names, weaving, and physical ailments and medical conditions. Although its practice of giving equivalents with no explanations rendered it fraught with pitfalls for learners, it incorporated two vital steps forward for Gaelic lexicography: first, it used the power of the computer to gather, organise and share the material; and second, it was actually based on material that was 'out there' in current use, as opposed to purging and embellishing the word-hoards of earlier dictionaries.

The importance of both these points will become clear in the ensuing discussion of Faclair Na Gàidhlig (see p. 251).

The first years of the new millennium have been productive ones for Gaelic lexicography. For one thing, three substantial and original contributions have already appeared. In 2001, Angus Watson's *Essential Gaelic–English Dictionary* was published. Watson is a Gaelic learner who received a training in Modern European Languages and Celtic, has a doctorate in Perthshire place-names, and writes Gaelic short stories and poetry. As a student he recognised the need for a detailed but accessible dictionary of Scottish Gaelic giving copious examples to illustrate the senses of Gaelic words and providing coverage of the major registers of the contemporary language, including formal, traditional, vulgar, familiar and colloquial speech. Accordingly, exemplification is central to the entries in Watson's dictionary; the examples are taken from a variety of genres, including modern poetry, administration, politics, journalism and information technology. Many entries cross-refer to related words and expressions to create additional learning paths and encourage browsing. Scots equivalents are given for a number of words, with the dual aim of reinforcing the understanding of those who know Scots, and at the same time 'building bridges' between the two languages in order to dispel the misconception that they are in some way in opposition.[14]

Watson accepts the view of the modern lexicographer that the dictionary must show the language as it is, and has therefore included material from new registers, such as that of public administration. Calques (or 'loan-translations') are also included on the grounds that they form part of the language as it is used today. Those items which only the reader of texts from earlier decades will encounter are marked '*trad.*', and the learner–user is advised (in the Introduction) that they may not fit easily into ordinary conversation.

There are just over 6,000 headwords, a relatively small number which reflects the fact that entries are in general more substantial than in earlier dictionaries on account of the relative wealth of examples given. Watson's dictionary lends itself more to browsing than to use as a reference tool. For example, the long entries for *air* 'on' and *mar* 'in the manner of, like' give an excellent overview of the range of usage of these words, but it might take time to identify the correct meaning of a given occurrence of *air* or *mar* in a text, even if it is there. In such cases, much more structured entries would be needed to render the content truly accessible.

A companion English–Gaelic volume, entitled *The Essential English–Gaelic Dictionary*, appeared in 2005, edited with the same guiding principles in mind and containing roughly 10,500 headwords. Some attempt is made to show distinctions of meaning in the source language, for example:

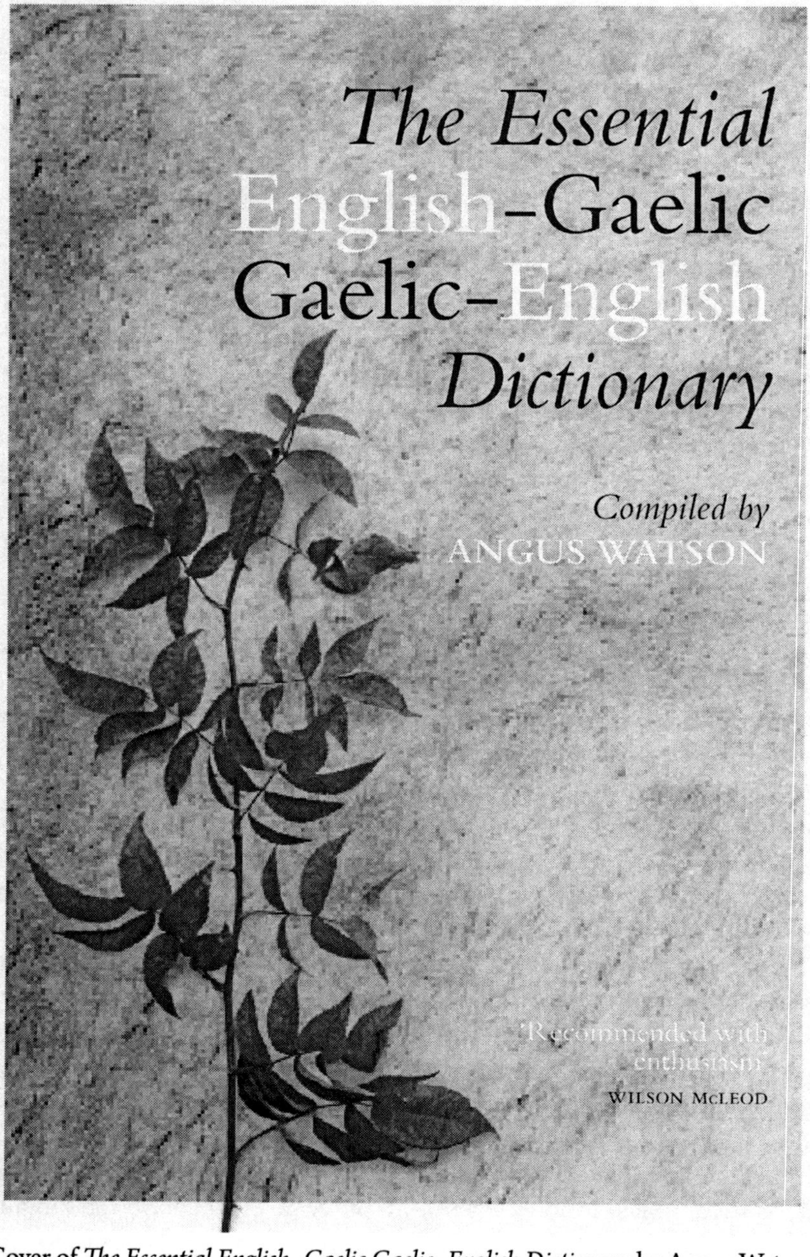

Cover of *The Essential English–Gaelic Gaelic–English Dictionary* by Angus Watson (reissued as one volume in 2010).

> **late** *adj & adv* **1** (*after appointed time &c*) air deireadh, fadalach . . . **2** (*advanced hour*) anmoch . . .

This is helpful for learners, since it reduces the need for them to use both volumes simultaneously in order to identify the correct Gaelic equivalent for an English word. However, this complication becomes unavoidable if one needs to know the forms of a noun or a verb, inasmuch as the principal parts of nouns and verbs are given only in the Gaelic–English volume. Scots words given as headwords are not marked as such, e.g., 'close', 'laird', 'machair', 'flit'. Both volumes include a helpful table on forms of the definite article.

Watson's readiness to include full examples, and to reflect the language as it is by including English calques, showed a new degree of awareness of the honesty and respect required of the lexicographer in his/her privileged position of describing and defining a language. Although justifiably hoping that his work would have something to offer Gaelic speakers, Watson has approached his task with the needs of the learner uppermost in his mind.

The needs of more advanced students of the language were foregrounded in Colin Mark's *The Gaelic Dictionary* (2003). Mark was born in Campbeltown in 1936 and brought up in the North-East. He was a school teacher for thirty-nine years, but for many years one of his main interests was Scottish Gaelic. His *Gaelic Verbs Systematised and Simplified* (1986) is a widely used work. He has also published Gaelic short stories and children's literature in Scots.

Mark's dictionary is firmly based on modern Gaelic literature, its chief source being the wide-ranging contents of the all-Gaelic periodical *Gairm* (1952–2002). Mark created a computer-based corpus of excerpts from this material. This means that his work was the first since the early nineteenth century to be based on raw data from the language.

Mark's priorities included clarity and ease of use. To this end, innovative layout features have been used, such as boxes to contain entries that involve a lot of explanation. This works well in entries such as *à* (preposition), but may cause problems in entries such as *a-* (prefix), where the box extends over six columns, particularly since alphabetical order is suspended within the box. The dictionary contains a detailed section on Gaelic spelling and pronunciation, which includes an explanation of the morphophonemics of initial mutation and consonant quality.

There are about 20,000 headwords. Mark uses the standard entry structure. Definitions are generally equivalents with little elaboration. On the other hand, the dictionary shows a strong and consistent interest in syntax. Not surprisingly, given his interest in Scots, Mark often uses Scots words in his definitions. For example:

gille, gillean *nm* boy, fellow, lad, loon . . .

Sometimes this has the effect of identifying the Scots origins of a word, though Mark does not make explicit reference to this:

glaoic, -ean *nf* buffoon (Scots glaik), fool . . .

Appendices dealing with the main parts of speech and other aspects of the language contain a treasure trove of information. But the greatest strength of Mark's dictionary lies in the volume and richness of the examples quoted. It would have been even stronger if these could have been referenced. Furthermore, the material is not presented in the clearest and most accessible way for the Gaelic learner. As a consequence, the dictionary has more to offer the intermediate and advanced learner, and the native speaker, than the beginner.

Another new dictionary, more suited to beginners, appeared in 2004: the one-volume *Gaelic Dictionary* compiled by Boyd Robertson and Ian MacDonald to complement the *Teach Yourself Gaelic* course produced by Robertson and Ian Taylor.[15] Robertson and MacDonald are both native speakers of Gaelic from North Uist. Robertson, a graduate in Celtic of the University of Aberdeen, was a teacher of Gaelic and subsequently a lecturer at Jordanhill College of Education and then Reader in Gaelic at the University of Strathclyde. He is now (2012) Principal of Sabhal Mòr Ostaig UHI. His research interests include Gaelic in education and the development and impact of Gaelic-medium education. MacDonald is a graduate of the University of Glasgow and worked as a civil servant before joining the Gaelic Books Council in 1976, where he remained until his retirement in 2010, having spent much of this time as director. He is an experienced editor and translator, and a leading authority on Gaelic orthography.

As their work was part of the *Teach Yourself* series, the compilers were required to adhere to strict limitations of space. Despite this, the coverage of everyday language is extensive. Layout is very clear and user-friendly. Robertson and MacDonald acknowledge their debt to existing Scottish Gaelic dictionaries, among them Dwelly's and MacBain's, and also to de Bhaldraithe's *English–Irish Dictionary* and Mac Mathúna and Ó Corráin's *Pocket Irish Dictionary*.

The Gaelic–English section contains an estimated 6,500 headwords with a standard entry structure. Definitions are generally one-word equivalents with very little explanation, but two to four equivalents are usually given. The meanings that the compilers believe to be the commonest are listed first.

Standard Scots words are used as equivalents without comment, usually alongside an English equivalent, for example:

caorann *n* **-ainn, -ainn/-ainnean** *m* rowan, mountain ash
imrich *n* **-e, -ean** *f* removal (*house*), flitting

The English–Gaelic section contains around 10,500 headwords. The vocabulary, selected from existing Gaelic–English and monolingual English dictionaries, is as wide-ranging as is attainable within the space requirements for the *Teach Yourself* series. The standard Gaelic–English entry structure is used. Gaelic equivalents (typically two) are given, the more common meaning appearing first. Some helpful examples of usage are included. Due to limitations of space, the principal parts of nouns and verbs are not given in this section, but have to be sought in the Gaelic–English section. Even there, not all are given.

Some Standard Scots words are included, in which case the English equivalent is usually given as a separate entry, for example:

oxter *n* achlais *f*
armpit *n* achlais *f*, lag na h-achlaise *f*

There is also a useful grammar section, which is clearly laid out to aid quick reference. The dictionary was reprinted in 2010, as part of the relaunch of the *Teach Yourself* series, with minor corrections and some additions, under the title *Essential Gaelic Dictionary* and incorporating the revised Gaelic Orthographic Conventions published in 2009.[16] In keeping with the new house style, 'Insight' boxes accompany each letter in both the Gaelic–English and English–Gaelic sections. These give small bites of information to aid understanding on a variety of levels, e.g. *fèis*, 'festival' (cultural), *Innse Gall* 'Hebrides' (historical), *làn* 'full, etc.' (semantic), 'asleep' (syntactic), 'in' (phonetic) and 'unappetizing' (morphological). Thus, Robertson and MacDonald's dictionary introduces some useful pedagogical and presentational innovations, drawing on current educational thinking and lexicographical practices from outside the Gaelic world.

The Birth of Historical Lexicography in Gaelic

Reference has already been made to the Historical Dictionary of Scottish Gaelic project, which was ongoing at Glasgow University between the 1960s and the 1990s. HDSG was designed to be not just bigger than all other Scottish Gaelic dictionaries, but constructed on a quite different principle. A historical dictionary cites its sources, ranks them in terms of their age, and classifies them chronologically according to the different discernible senses, including developments in senses through time. A portion of the language comes alive in the process, told in its own terms, three-dimensional, detailed, verifiable. Such a dictionary is based entirely on the words of the users of the language, and its output describes their view of the world: an enduring and unique linguistic and cultural truth. The ultimate value of a historical dictionary is of course dependent on the skill and diligence of the lexicographers whose historical detective work and semantic analysis constructs the entry. But because it is founded on a pre-defined corpus (or 'data-base') of texts, it provides an objective basis for whatever sort of ultimate purpose, from literary criticism to dialectology to language revitalisation, its users wish to pursue.

All this is well known to scholars and other users of English dictionaries, where the *Oxford English Dictionary*, 'based on historical principles', is recognised as an institution and as a national treasure and resource. It is well known in other countries, whose national academies typically oversee the recording and accessible preservation of the national language(s) as a pressing national priority. It is also well known in Scotland – partly because of the major input of Scottish lexicographers into the development of the *OED* (see Chapter 10), which led pretty directly to the setting up of the *DOST* and the *SND*, as explained in Chapters 5 and 6.

Like Scots, Gaelic is a language with a long literary history and a range of modern dialects. As such, it is a promising subject for a historical dictionary. Indeed, the prospect of such an evidence-based Scottish Gaelic dictionary, carrying on where the *Dictionary of the Irish Language* (see p. 242) left off, was prominent in the minds of Gaelic scholars at least back to the early years of the twentieth century. The reason is not hard to appreciate: the Gaelic literary heritage contains a lot of poetry, much of it being verbally showy or recondite or both: in short, difficult. In order to enjoy our inheritance we need to understand it as fully as may be. This requires a two-pronged attack. The meaning of a word can be elucidated by (1) close-range study of the specific textual context in which it appears, and (2) comparison of all the occurrences of the word in the different texts in which it appears. The former approach lies behind the scholarly editions of the Scottish Gaelic Texts Society, which was set up in 1934 and continues today;[17] the latter approach calls for a historical dictionary.

This was the intellectual scenario into which HDSG fitted. By the 1960s, historical dictionary projects were underway for English, Scots, Irish and Welsh, but not for Gaelic. Whereas the precursors of Scottish Gaelic lexicography, especially Edward Lhuyd, had placed Gaelic in European and Scottish perspectives of linguistic taxonomy and data-led ethnological collection, this bright scientific start had subsequently been overtaken by a mixture of extra-linguistic motives and aims (see Chapter 8). The field was therefore pretty clear, and the 1960s were a relatively propitious time for such ambitious projects to be set in motion.

With hindsight one can see that there was a lack of realism in some of HDSG's ground rules (e.g., the basis of coverage was not sufficiently tightly drawn) and methods (e.g., insufficient emphasis was placed on establishing a 'tradition' of appropriate lexicographical good practices), given the personnel and manpower available to the project. Additionally, one must remember that the project got under way at a time when computerisation was just beginning to be exploited for linguistic purposes, when the technologies were primitive by contemporary standards, and when their capabilities were as yet poorly understood. Furthermore, the senior members of staff were full-time academics whose efforts to sustain the project were limited by their many other commitments. As the 1960s were succeeded by the 1970s and 1980s, the times became less propitious, and the meagre arts funding available for university-based projects like HDSG was insufficient to sustain prolonged lexicographical activity. The fact that the HDSG personnel managed to continue to collect material for the dictionary throughout this period is in itself remarkable. The combined efforts of the staff and dedicated volunteers produced an archive of around 550,000 slips, chiefly excerpted from printed editions, dating from 1567 onwards, but also from manuscript sources. In addition, fieldwork was undertaken in Gaelic-speaking areas, including Nova Scotia.

In 1996 funding constraints, coupled with the retirement of key members of staff, meant that work on HDSG could not continue even to a limited degree, and the decision was taken to suspend the project. In the strict sense, it had no published output, for the reasons just given. Happily, a combination of fresh thinking, modern technology and a modicum of fresh funding has enabled the HDSG materials to be revisited in the last few years, and there are now better prospects for some of these becoming accessible in a twenty-first century online environment that also includes Faclair na Gàidhlig, to be mentioned next.

HDSG was not, of course, the only Scottish Gaelic lexicographical initiative that was data-led and computer-based. Both these features were, as we have seen, incorporated in *Stòr-Dàta Briathrachais Gàidhlig*. Shortly after the latter's initial appearance, one of the writers of this chapter presented a paper to the 1991 Languages of Scotland Conference entitled 'A Gaelic Thesaurus'.[18] This, as well as arguing for a new sort of lexicographical resource for Gaelic, contained proposals designed to exploit the potential that one could already see in *Stòr-Dàta Briathrachais Gàidhlig I*, and to bring on the undeveloped Gaelic lexicographical tradition by utilising the experience and expertise to be found in its well-developed Scots counterpart. The intention behind these proposals was to move Gaelic lexicography forward at a time when HDSG looked to be running out of steam but was still nominally functional, and *Stòr-Dàta Briathrachais Gàidhlig* had arguably not yet achieved its maximum potential for Gaelic.

Although nothing came of this at the time, what was in effect a highly significant response came in 2001 when the Director of Sabhal Mòr Ostaig, Dr Norman Gillies, invited the other writer of this chapter, who was then an editor of the *DOST*, to write a briefing paper on how to go about compiling a historical dictionary for Scottish Gaelic. In the meantime, HDSG had come to a halt, the *DOST* was winding up, and the project to create the online Dictionary of the Scots Language (digitising the *DOST* and the *SND*) was being set up (see Chapter 7). A broad-based initiative to create an Institute for the Languages of Scotland was also in the air at the time, one of whose prime aims was to secure continuing lexicographical support for Scotland's languages, such as exists in many other countries. Pike's paper was circulated to Celtic colleagues at the universities of Aberdeen, Edinburgh, Glasgow and Strathclyde, who recognised that there was now an opportunity – perhaps a last opportunity – to create this resource so essential to the preservation, understanding and revitalisation of Gaelic.

In May 2002 Norman Gillies, William Gillies, Donald Meek and Lorna Pike met to discuss the way forward. They agreed that there should be a historical dictionary project, that it should be called Faclair na Gàidhlig (Dictionary of the Scottish Gaelic Language), and that the universities of Aberdeen, Edinburgh, Glasgow and Strathclyde, and the then UHI Millennium Institute, now the University of the Highlands and Islands, should be invited to be partner institutions (the last mentioned through Sabhal Mòr Ostaig). All were eager to participate, and on 18 October 2002, the Strategy Committee for Faclair na Gàidhlig met for the first time at the University of Edinburgh under the convenership of Professor Meek. Members of this original committee were, in addition to Dr Gillies, Professor Gillies and Professor Meek: Professor Colm Ó Baoill, University of Aberdeen; Professor Cathair Ó Dochartaigh, University of Glasgow, and Boyd Robertson, Faculty of Education, University of Strathclyde. The relevant credentials of the committee were as strong as they could practically be. Norman Gillies, as the hugely successful Director of Sabhal Mòr Ostaig, was the overseer of many major Gaelic-related projects, including Sabhal Mòr Ostaig UHI's vital input to the archive digitisation project *Tobar an Dualchais* / Kist o Riches. William Gillies had overseen the revitalisation of the Linguistic Survey of Scotland (Gaelic) and the publication of *Survey of the Gaelic Dialects of Scotland*, volumes 1–5 (1994–7), and had managed the *DOST* from 1994 to its successful conclusion in 2001. Donald Meek had worked as an assistant editor on the HDSG from 1973–9, overseen the digitisation and implemented the revision of the Gaelic Bible, and edited and published many books and journals. Colm Ó Baoill had co-edited the Ulster and Scottish volume of Heinrich Wagner's *Linguistic Atlas and Survey of Irish Dialects*, was editor of *Scottish Gaelic Studies*, and an experienced Scottish Gaelic Texts Society author–editor. Cathair Ó Dochartaigh was the editor of the five published volumes of the Gaelic Linguistic Survey and an expert in the digitisation of Irish dictionaries. Boyd Robertson, in addition to wide experience in all aspects of Gaelic education, was the co-author of the *Teach Yourself* series' *Gaelic Dictionary* noted above. Lorna Pike, as the first employee, was a historical lexicographer with seventeen years' experience on the *DOST*.

The committee was under no illusions about the magnitude of the task; this project was going to take decades to complete, at a time when public and private funders were increasingly concentrating their resources on projects that showed results within a short to shortish timeframe. If Gaelic was to pull abreast of Irish, Welsh and Scots in lexicographical terms, some form of ongoing public commitment would be needed. Politicians and civil servants would need to be persuaded that an authoritative historical dictionary is not an optional extra but a necessity, one that plays a fundamental role in the sustainability and development of the language it covers. The message needed to be got across that this opportunity for Scottish Gaelic to 'catch up' could be a decisive factor in the long-term success of official policies for Gaelic to be a continuing element in Scottish life.

Lorna Pike, Project Co-ordinator of Faclair na Gàidhlig,
formerly one of the editors of the *Dictionary of the Older Scottish Tongue*.

The project was formally established in October 2003 with a research grant from the Carnegie Trust for the Universities of Scotland and additional funding from the Gaelic Language Promotion Trust. The committee was serviced by Lorna Pike, who was initially employed part-time. This became a full-time post in October 2004, supported by funding from the newly established Bòrd na Gàidhlig, which sustained the project until a major research award from the Leverhulme Trust came on-stream in February 2005. Bòrd na Gàidhlig has continued to support the project and currently (2012) co-funds it with the Scottish Funding Council. The Scottish government has also contributed directly.

Once the project was properly under way, the initial Strategy Committee gave way to a steering committee on which each participating university had one representative. It was inevitable that over the succeeding years, the composition of the managing body would alter due to the formal retirement of some members: Professor Norman Gillies was replaced in 2009 by Professor Boyd Robertson, now Principal of Sabhal Mòr Ostaig UHI, as the Sabhal Mòr Ostaig representative; Mona Wilson, Department of Curricular Studies, took his place as the University of Strathclyde representative; Professor Thomas Clancy replaced Professor Cathair Ó Dochartaigh for the University of Glasgow; and Professor Ó Baoill was replaced by Dr Moray Watson for the University of Aberdeen. Professor Susan Manning had assumed the role of Edinburgh representative in 2005 when Professors Meek and Gillies, as principal investigators and grant-holders, stood down from formal membership of the management committee to enable full involvement in the lexicographical aspects of the project. Fortunately, it has been possible to retain the management stability so vital to the development of a project of this nature in the form of Boyd Robertson, the only member of the original committee still involved in the running of the project, whose skilful management, steadfast commitment and firm leadership have steered the project so successfully in his role as convener. Thus, Faclair na Gàidhlig continues to be managed by experts from the field of language, and its governing body includes eminent Celtic scholars and strategists for Gaelic-medium education at every level. It was also felt that the project needed access to a sympathetic but objective forum of experts who could monitor progress and provide advice on general questions. At the end of 2005 an advisory board was set up. In addition to Professor Gillies and Professor Ó Baoill, it currently (2012) includes Dr Anthony Harvey, editor of the *Dictionary of Medieval Latin from Celtic sources*, Andrew Hawke, Managing Editor, *Geiriadur Prifysgol Cymru* (*Dictionary of the Welsh Language*) and Professor Roibeard Ó Maolalaigh, Professor of Gaelic at the University of Glasgow. Its main functions are quality assurance, especially in the early stages of dictionary construction and compilation, and advice on the project's progress and how to promote it.

Getting Faclair na Gàidhlig off the ground proved to be an object lesson in combining adaptability to shifting ground conditions with tenacity in pursuit of the ideal of transposing Sir James Murray's historical principles from English lexicography (see Chapter 10) to Gaelic via Scots, so as to provide Gaelic with a comparable resource. The journey to that goal is a long one. A historical dictionary is a project designed from first principles. With the exception of Colin Mark's *Gaelic Dictionary*, no Gaelic dictionary hitherto has been corpus-based. Nor are there 'ready-made' Gaelic-speaking historical lexicographers on whom one can call: this is a new discipline for Gaelic. Professor Meek's previous experience on the HDSG proved invaluable, when melded with Ms Pike's experience of implementing the principles applied to the *DOST* in the latter stages of the alphabet.

Central challenges included the problem of fitting the project's needs to current funding possibilities, and the task of building up what the present writers have called a 'lexicographical tradition' for Gaelic. After the initial phases of 'proof of concept' and feasibility studies, the Leverhulme-funded phase of Faclair na Gàidhlig was devoted to two distinct tasks: (1) the simultaneous investigation of entry structures and creation of a manual of methodology (based on the procedures used by the editors of the *DOST*) to instruct trainee lexicographers in every stage of the compilation of an individual dictionary entry; and (2) the identification of a selection of Gaelic texts representative of the major chronological phases, linguistic registers, literary genres and dialect bases of Scottish Gaelic, to form the digital corpus on which to base the dictionary, together with a Text Manual describing each of these sources in a standard way to aid lexicographers confronting a lemma from one of the core texts. The two tasks proceeded as follows.

The primary challenge has been the creation of the editorial foundation consisting of the agreed preferred entry structures and a manual of lexicographical methodology specific to the needs of Gaelic: simultaneously deciding what is to be done and providing the methodology for doing it. Work on this aspect of the project was expedited by access to the Historical Dictionary of Scottish Gaelic Archive (HDSG-A), which was generously made available to Faclair na Gàidhlig by the University of Glasgow. At the heart of this work is the compilation of a series of sample entries for different parts of speech. These are designed to expose new lexicographers to the categories of eventualities (e.g., orthographical, grammatical or semantic) that may confront them in their work. During the first year of the project, Pike compiled the very first sample entry, *craobh* n. 'a tree', using the slips from the HDSG-A. Although this would not be an adequate basis for a 'live' Faclair na Gàidhlig entry, the HDSG-A is sufficiently full and varied to permit instruction in the sort of analysis to be carried out on core material. Entries for other parts of speech have followed, and these are continually being developed. Each is accompanied by detailed instructions, which currently run to between eighteen and eighty-five pages, depending on the complexity of the entry. Pike's entries and instructions are reviewed by Margaret Dareau, former Editorial Director of the *DOST*, who acts as lexicographical consultant to Faclair na Gàidhlig. Professors Gillies and Ó Baoill scrutinise them in their role as language consultants, and provide scholarly input on the linguistic side throughout the compilation process. In this way authoritative, newly designed training materials are being created to guide the first historical lexicographers in Scottish Gaelic from the first read-through of excerpted quotations to the review of completed entries.

The first year of the project also saw the beginnings of the Faclair na Gàidhlig corpus on which the dictionary will be based. Professor Meek scrutinised the Gaelic catalogue of the National Library of Scotland (containing some 3,000 titles) and whittled it down to c.200 key texts. In the following three years the Leverhulme-funded research assistant, Dr Catriona Mackie,[19] assessed these texts in terms of their usefulness to the dictionary. The assessment of each text runs to 3–4 pages and focuses on such aspects as register, style, geographical origin, social context, language date and bibliographical details. These now form a Text Manual, in which information is presented in the order that lexicographers are most likely to wish to access it regularly, for example, to confirm language date or reference style to be used in the dictionary. This sort of textual knowledge becomes second nature to experienced lexicographers, but beginners are faced with a daunting amount to learn, and the Text Manual formalises this knowledge for them by providing instant information at a level of detail usually only acquired after years in post.

On the technical side, which is being conducted at the University of Glasgow, the digital corpus for Faclair na Gàidhlig, termed Corpas na Gàidhlig ('The Gaelic Corpus'), comprising the key texts in the Text Manual, is being compiled under the auspices of the separate Digital Archive of Scottish Gaelic (DASG) project directed by Professor Ó Maolalaigh. Corpas na Gàidhlig will provide the textual foundation for dictionary entries and will be electronically excerpted to provide the authoritative evidence for lexicographical analysis and illustrative quotations. Manuscript material from the twelfth century to the nineteenth will be included, and a citation database will be created to house interesting usages from oral sources and texts that do not qualify for inclusion in the full-text database. A systems developer will work on the specification for the database and the necessary software to enable lexicographers to search and excerpt from both the Corpas na Gàidhlig and DASG archives. As this technical foundation nears completion, training of the first historical lexicographers in Scottish Gaelic will begin. In the proposed timescale, always depending on the availability of sufficient funding, the compilation of the actual dictionary entries is scheduled to begin in 2016, a mere thirteen years after the establishment of the project. Overall progress in dictionary compilation will, as ever, be dictated by the level of funding. It follows from what has just been said that Faclair na Gàidhlig will be, in the first instance, an electronic resource with an entry structure similar to and compatible with that of the *DOST* in its present form as part of the Dictionary of the Scots Language (www.dsl.ac.uk). Definitions will be in English to maximise access to the language, but this in no way excludes the creation of 'spin-off' publications in traditional or other form, including all Gaelic derivatives.

In the twenty-first century, Gaelic, like Scots, has received greater support than at any other time in its history. Those involved in Faclair na Gàidhlig are endeavouring to provide what the twentieth century was, for perfectly understandable reasons, unable to achieve: a full-scale dictionary on historical principles which will stand beside its magnificent counterpart in Scots. The history and culture of the Gaels, as evidenced in their own words, and the integrity of the Gaelic language, will be described and defined, fixed in time, for all time. Future lexicographers will continue to add to, and update this work, which will inevitably provide the wherewithal to improve our understanding of obscurities in individual texts, as well as the perennial need to keep up with the development of new words and meanings in the language. Faclair na Gàidhlig will become a worthy addition to a proud lexicographical tradition, and add a currently missing dimension of accessibility and dignity to Scottish Gaelic as a properly respected language in the world.

Postscript

WILLIAM GILLIES AND LORNA PIKE

In Chapters 8 and 9 we have endeavoured to trace a principal stream of Gaelic lexicography from eighteenth-century and earlier sources down to the present day. The stream has sometimes threatened to dry up, but a current of conscious intellectual continuity can be traced, and it has been our aim to bring this out. Our account has not been exhaustive of word-gathering activities; and it is worth drawing attention to the existence of the following categories of material which have escaped our survey.

(1) A number of unpublished manuscript dictionaries have been preserved, some of which might have become influential and taken their place in our 'grand narrative' had they found a suitable publisher in good time: for example, Professor Donald Mackinnon's 'Gaelic–English Dictionary'[1] or Charles Loch's three-volume 'English–Gaelic Classified Dictionary of Technical and Modern Terms'.[2] A detailed study of these sources would doubtless refine many details of our picture.[3]

(2) We have omitted reference to a number of glossaries and vocabularies which are specialised or technical in their coverage, from the Rev. Duncan M Connell's *Reul-eòlas* (1857) on astronomy to Roy Wentworth's *Briathrachas Cànanach* (Gaelic Linguistic Terms) (2003). These also include works giving the Gaelic names for birds, animals or flowers. On a slightly different footing are those works which consciously set out to provide Gaelic equivalents for new areas of vocabulary, creating neologisms where necessary. An early example is Dwelly's long entry on *coinneamh* 'meeting' (see p. 231 above), and *Stòr-Dàta Briathrachais Gàidhlig* also incorporates some by-products of this sort of activity. A more recent example is provided by *Faclair na Pàrlamaid* (2001), which set out to supply Gaelic equivalents to parliamentary terminology for the Scottish Parliament.[4]

(3) We have confined our coverage to the interface between Gaelic and English, though there have been certain publications which do not fall within this

definition, including works whose main purpose is to give equivalents in different Celtic or other languages or (more germane to the present survey) in Gaelic and Scots, e.g. R.L. Cassie's *A Comparative Gaelic–Scots Vocabulary* (1930).

(4) We have excluded dialect word lists, with the exception of Fr. Dieckhoff's, which qualifies for treatment here by being extensive in coverage, lexicographical in presentation, and containing innovative pedagogical elements in its treatment of pronunciation. Admittedly, some of those excluded are well-known and substantial, e.g. Fr. Allan McDonald's *Gaelic Words and Expressions from South Uist and Eriskay* (c.1900, published 1958) and Roy Wentworth's *Faclan is Abairtean à Ros an Iar* (published online 2003). But contributions of this sort, both published and unpublished, exist for almost all parts of the Highlands and Islands, and form an important source for research by linguists and lexicographers alike.[5]

If we consider the Gaelic lexicographical tradition as it stands in 2012 and in prospect, two points stand out very clearly. First, the heroic labours of individuals continue to be relevant in the cyber age: for instance, the efforts of Mikael Bauer and Will Robertson have made Dwelly's dictionary fully searchable, as both a Gaelic–English and an English–Gaelic resource.[6] Given the costs and effort associated with traditional publishing, which have frustrated many Gaelic lexicographical endeavours in the past, the Internet and blogosphere will surely continue to be important, especially as traditional communities make room for virtual ones, and as the proportion of computer-literate Gaelic learners within the Gaelic community as a whole becomes more significant. These features are not unique to Gaelic, of course; but they are likely to be especially important to Gaelic for social and demographic reasons.

In the second place, Gaelic will need a normative agency or principle, as a counter-balance to the freedom and licence of the Internet and text-messaging, one that regulates or at least monitors language use. The point of this is not so much to tell people what is correct or incorrect *à l'Académie française* – though if Gaelic is going to be used for 'serious' purposes (e.g. in legal or similar contexts), there has to be a stratum of language that is exempt from the improvisatory tendencies of the language of chat-rooms and text-messaging; rather, it is needed to capture the boundaries between standard and innovative, and between standard and traditional speech.

PART III

The Scottish Contribution to English Dictionaries

TEN

The Scottish Contribution to the Lexicography of English

MARY O'NEILL

Introduction

From the Union of 1707, the Scottish contribution to the lexicography of English has been considerable. As Scots drove for betterment in post-Union Britain and anglicisation became part of that process, it could be argued that the potential loss to Scots lexicography became English lexicography's gain, as Scotland's skilled linguistic observers and educators concentrated their efforts on English.

Johnson's *Dictionary of the English Language*

The connections of Scotland and Scots with English-language lexicography can be traced to the eighteenth century, and one connection in particular is surprising. Samuel Johnson is widely believed to have despised Scotland and the Scots, although he is also known to have had a number of Scottish friends, including his biographer James Boswell (whom he encouraged in his compilation of a dictionary of Scots words;[1] see Chapter 3). It is less well known that the main London publisher of Johnson's *Dictionary of the English Language* (1755), viewed as Britain's pre-eminent dictionary until the publication of the *OED*, was William Strahan from Edinburgh (a friend of Johnson, who would later become King's Printer and a member of parliament). When the contract with Strahan was in place, five of the six amanuenses enlisted to assist Johnson in compiling his dictionary were Scots.

Perhaps this fact is less surprising when one considers that these amanuenses would be undertaking literary work of the most menial kind, possibly having relocated to London in order to find such work at all, and would have been poorly paid. Their job was to copy citations onto slips and sort them, while Johnson undertook the intellectual task of writing the definitions and etymologies. However, although they, rather than Johnson, were the real 'drudges' of lexicography, one is still compelled to look at Johnson's anti-Scottishness in another light. He could not have been without a fundamental trust in the work ethic and literary ability of these Scotsmen. The first-employed of these was Francis

Stewart, son of an Edinburgh bookseller, described posthumously by Johnson as 'an ingenious and worthy man'.[2] Employed later was Roxburghshire-born Robert Shiels, a journeyman printer and poet, who was also engaged to work on *The Lives of the Poets of Great Britain and Ireland: To the Time of Dean Swift* (1753), credited in its entirety to Theophilus Cibber (but credited by Johnson to Shiels). Also engaged as assistants on the dictionary were the Macbean brothers, William and Alexander, a man called Maitland (named only as 'Mr Maitland' by Boswell), and the Englishman V.J. Peyton. Alexander Macbean brought with him the useful experience of having worked as an amanuensis on Ephraim Chambers' *Cyclopaedia*, from which Johnson borrowed heavily, especially on the arts and sciences.

The relationship between Johnson and the men, who were reportedly given to occasional drinking and time-wasting, was not always smooth. Scottish words and variations suggested by the men on their slips were ignored by him when he prepared the final copy. Johnson was sometimes disappointed by what he perceived as a lack of quality in their work; they, in turn, may well have been frustrated by his frequent changes of method. However, Johnson appears to have regarded them with kindness, and describes them with seemingly genuine warmth. Although his own finances were in a precarious state, he supported both Stewart, who became ill and died during compilation, and Shiels, who died in 1853. After the dictionary was published, Johnson found Alexander Macbean a post as librarian for Archibald Campbell, duke of Argyll; after the death of Argyll in 1861, when Macbean was left in dire poverty, Johnson encouraged him to write *A Dictionary of Ancient Geography* (1773) and supplied the preface for it. He later used his influence to have Macbean admitted as a 'Poor Brother' to the Carthusian Charterhouse, where he died in 1784.

As a postscript, a further Scottish connection with Johnson's dictionary was made with the publication of one of its better-known editions in 1820, prepared by Aberdeen-born writer and editor Alexander Chalmers (1759–1834) of the Chalmers family, well known as newspaper proprietors in Aberdeen at that time. He also produced the 1798 revision of *A Complete and Universal Dictionary of the English Language* by Reverend James Barclay (first published 1774). Chalmers made studies of, and produced editions of, much of Johnson's work, and prepared the 1892 edition (as well as an acclaimed parody) of Boswell's *Life of Samuel Johnson LL.D.*

Post-Union English Reference Works by Scots

As Johnson worked on his comprehensive record of English vocabulary in London, in Enlightenment Scotland lists of Scotticisms were being produced in order to help Scots replace their native usages with English (see Chapter 2).

Reference books of English, including dictionaries, were another important part of this drive towards anglicisation. One of the English dictionaries produced by a Scot in this period[3] was schoolmaster James Buchanan's *Linguae Britannicae vera pronunciatio* [The True Pronunciation of the Language of Britain]*: or, a New English Dictionary* (1757). Not much is known about Buchanan's life; it is believed he moved to London at a young age, and ran a boarding school in the Camberwell area. His was the first published dictionary to have pronunciation guidance as its key feature: vowels in some headwords have diacritics designating length, and silent letters and primary stress are also indicated, while definitions are cursory. The suggested sounds do not seem specifically aimed at Scots aspiring to 'English' speech – indeed, the 'Scottishness' of some of the pronunciations was criticised in some quarters – but, judging by his introductory words, Buchanan is clearly aware of the social implications of a Scottish accent: 'The people of North Britain seem, in general, to be almost at as great a loss for proper accent and just pronunciation as foreigners . . . I therefore beg leave to recommend this book to . . . all teachers of youth in that part of the United Kingdom; by a proper application to which, they may in a short time pronounce as properly and as intelligibly as if they had been born and bred in London.'[4]

Buchanan had other involvement in general English dictionaries that did not emphasise 'correct' pronunciation: he edited the fifth edition (1760) of Nathan Bailey's *Universal Etymological English Dictionary* (first published 1720), the first edition to feature citations in the style of Johnson's dictionary. However, Buchanan continued to be an important figure in the drive throughout Britain to 'fix' the English language, and works with this aim included his 1766 *Essay Towards Establishing a Standard for an Elegant and Uniform Pronunciation of the English Language*. Presented by Buchanan as 'a work entirely new', it is a pronouncing dictionary in its purest sense: it provides a list of over 25,000 words, each with a phonetic respelling, but no definition. However, Buchanan's works did not impress some reviewers and lexicographers south of the border. In the preface to his 1773 *New Dictionary of the English Language*, William Kenrick makes reference to Buchanan and Irish elocutionist Thomas Sheridan (who was in the process of compiling a larger pronouncing dictionary, published in 1780) when he speaks of the 'ridiculous absurdity in the pretensions of a native of Aberdeen or Tipperary to teach the natives of London to speak and read'. Kenrick is even more forthright in his criticism of the system proposed in Buchanan's *Essay*, not least in his belief that it is comprehensible only to the people of 'Northern Britain'.

Another London-based Scot, William Johnston, published *A Pronouncing and Spelling Dictionary* (1764), 'in which, by distinguishing signs of the literal sounds, the proper sounds of English words are clearly intimated; and by which, both His Majesty's subjects, and foreigners, may correct an improper, or acquire a right pronunciation of the English language'. The elaboration of this aim in the Preface (written using the pronunciation system Johnston uses for his headwords) holds no surprises: 'I sincerely think, the youth of Cornwall and Cumberland, of Scotland and Ireland . . . may learn by themselves to pronounce English tolerably well; and by which, were they, after this, to reside for some time in London, their pronunciation might soon, become hardly distinguishable from that of the inhabitants.' Johnston's work comprises an alphabetical list of words with various pronunciation features indicated, with a very long introduction explaining the system in detail, and includes a discourse on English pronunciation in general.

Also compiling dictionaries at this time was William Perry, a schoolmaster in Kelso and Edinburgh and a navy surgeon. In his *Royal Standard English Dictionary* (first published in Edinburgh in 1775), he, as Kenrick had done, queries the representation of sounds used by Buchanan and attempts to impose his own. Perry is very much concerned with prescribing a spoken standard by showing the 'true pronunciation' of words, which is, once again, unapologetically identified as being 'according to the present practice of men of letters, eminent orators, and polite speakers, in London'.[5] It was a view that would be repeated by Perry in the dedication of his spelling guide for children, *The Only Sure Guide to the English Tongue: or, New Pronouncing Spelling Book* (1776). In 1788 the *Royal Standard* gained the distinction of becoming the first dictionary to be published in America rather than imported as printed copies from abroad, and Perry's works achieved popularity in the USA as well as at home.

Clearly, pronouncing dictionaries had come to be viewed as crucial tools in teaching 'pure' English usage. Englishman John Walker, in his popular *A Critical Pronouncing Dictionary* (1791), included a special section of 'rules to be observed by the Natives of Scotland for attaining a just Pronunciation of English' and so avoiding their 'native peculiarities'. Scots made numerous other contributions of their own to the canon of literature encouraging 'correct' English pronunciation. William Scott's *A New Spelling, Pronouncing and Explanatory Dictionary of the English Language* (1786),[6] was described by the author as 'particularly calculated for the Improvement of Natives and Foreigners in the Proper Speaking and Writing of the English Language'.[7] Like Buchanan and many of his contemporaries, Scott – a teacher of English and elocution in Edinburgh – produced a number of pedagogical spelling and usage guides, such as *An Introduction to Reading and Spelling* (1796). John Burn, a Glasgow English teacher who was best known for *A Practical Grammar of the English Language* (1766), had his

A Pronouncing Dictionary of the English Language published in 1777, also with the hope that it would 'enable one to read or deliver written language with so much propriety, as not to offend even an Englishman of the most delicate ear'. Edinburgh teacher Alexander Barrie's *A Spelling and Pronouncing Dictionary of the English Language for the use of Schools* (1794) has lists of words under headings representing different initial sounds, and William Angus' *A Pronouncing Vocabulary of the English Language* appeared in 1800, with systematic pronunciation for a long list of English words, as well as lists of homophones.

The *Encyclopaedia Britannica*

In post-Union Scotland, this drive to 'purify' spoken English may have had a detrimental effect on the status and health of the Scots tongue. But the Enlightenment also brought with it an explosion of knowledge and a strong impulse towards learning, represented in particular by the production of the *Encyclopaedia Britannica* in Edinburgh in 1768. *Britannica* was conceived by two Edinburgh men, printer Colin Macfarquhar and prominent engraver Andrew Bell (some of whose engraved plates are used as illustrations in the text to the present day), with the aim of producing a reference work that would truly reflect the breadth of learning of the time. They appointed William Smellie, then 28, as editor. Smellie, also an Edinburgh printer and editor of the *Scots Magazine*, would go on to put together the whole work and introduce it with the statement that 'utility ought to be the principal intention of every publication'. The first edition of *Encylopaedia Britannica* was published in instalments over three years, beginning in 1768, and a complete three-volume set was produced in 1771. The work grouped important concepts of the arts and sciences together, arranged them in alphabetical order and mixed concise entries with more discursive articles. Although its content borrowed heavily from other works and was not always entirely accurate, it broke new ground in the breadth of its coverage and scholarship, and in the usefulness of its presentation.

Having achieved enormous success with the first edition, the publishers produced a second edition, in ten volumes, between 1777 and 1784; it included articles on history and biography. Smellie had believed such content to be unsuitable for an encyclopedia of arts and sciences and resigned from the project, leaving Macfarquhar as editor. Macfarquhar died in 1793 during the editing of the third edition and Bell, the remaining proprietor, appointed George Gleig as editor. Gleig, a clergyman who would go on to become bishop of Brechin, began the practice of using learned contributors to compile specialist material. This practice would be extended throughout each new edition, and would secure the reputation of *Britannica* as a work of detailed and accurate scholarship.

After Bell's death in 1809, copyright was acquired by Archibald Constable, publisher of the *Scots Magazine*, the *Edinburgh Review*, and works of Sir Walter Scott. Constable engaged Scots lawyer and scholar Macvey Napier to edit a supplement, and it is with this that *Britannica* is considered to have become a truly international publication, with commissioned contributions from many of the great writers and thinkers of the day from Scotland and beyond, including Sir Walter Scott, Sir Humphry Davy and Thomas Malthus. Copyright was subsequently bought by A. & C. Black (a firm that relocated from Edinburgh to London in 1889), who issued the seventh edition (1830–42), edited by Napier, and the eighth edition (1853–60), which was under the editorship of Orcadian Thomas Stewart Traill. The firm also published the ninth edition (1875–9), although it was such an ambitious undertaking that Adam Black predicted dire failure and resigned from the company. The editors were Thomas Spencer Baynes, the first English-born editor of the work, and William Robertson Smith, a church minister and professor of divinity. Despite publisher Black's misgivings, the edition was to prove a huge success, with unprecedented levels of scholarship in its twenty-four volumes. Among the notable contributions was James Murray's twelve-page article on the English language, an essay still regarded as one of the finest pieces ever written on the subject. (A similar article proposed by Baynes on the Scots language was not to be, as Murray was very soon to be absorbed in the compilation of the *OED*.)

It was around this time that the connection with Scotland began to loosen further. In 1898 *The Times* of London sold a reprint of the ninth edition at half the original price, and in 1902 it issued an extensive supplement of eleven volumes which, along with the twenty-four volumes of the ninth edition, constituted a tenth edition. The eleventh edition (1910–11) was published in cooperation with the University of Cambridge, although by then *Encyclopaedia Britannica* was American-owned, and in the mid-1930s the company's headquarters was moved to Chicago. Today, only a thistle emblem and a dateline of 1768 on the covers testify to the Scottish origins of *Encyclopaedia Britannica*, but it remains a legacy of the Scottish Enlightenment. Its emergence in the eighteenth century marked the beginning of a whole world of reference in the nineteenth century in Scotland.

The Imperial Dictionary

Publisher Blackie & Son had its origin, as the partnership W. Sommerville, A. Fullarton & J. Blackie & Co., in Glasgow in 1809. The company sold bound sections of books known as 'Numbers', section by section, to subscribers (thus making them more affordable than a single bound volume). The earliest of these were often religious in theme, but in 1833 Blackie started to publish *The Popular Encyclopedia,*[8] an illustrated reference work that was edited by Alexander Whitelaw and, like the later *Chambers's Encyclopaedia,* was based on a German encyclopedia, the *Brockhaus Konversations-Lexikon* (or an American translation thereof).[9] Around the middle of the nineteenth century, the firm began to produce of a series of comprehensive, illustrated reference works under the title of 'Imperial'. As well as *The Imperial Family Bible* (1841–4), the company would go on to publish *The Imperial Gazetteer* (1850–5), *The Imperial Atlas of Modern Geography* (1859) and *The Imperial Bible Dictionary* (1863–5). Of great importance

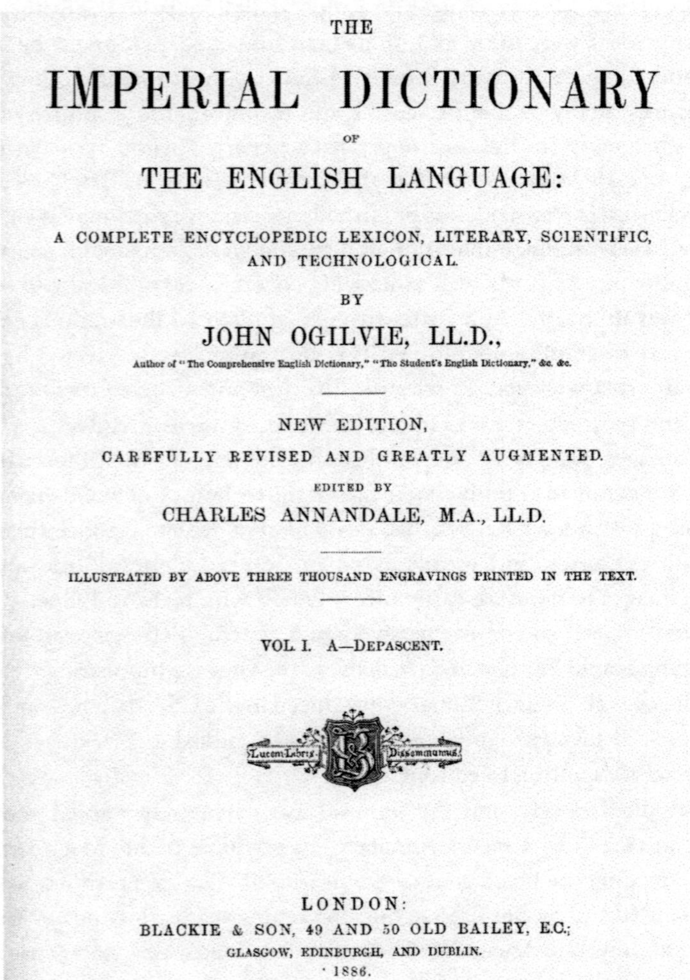

THE

IMPERIAL DICTIONARY

OF

THE ENGLISH LANGUAGE:

A COMPLETE ENCYCLOPEDIC LEXICON, LITERARY, SCIENTIFIC, AND TECHNOLOGICAL.

BY

JOHN OGILVIE, LL.D.,

Author of "The Comprehensive English Dictionary," "The Student's English Dictionary," &c. &c.

NEW EDITION,

CAREFULLY REVISED AND GREATLY AUGMENTED.

EDITED BY

CHARLES ANNANDALE, M.A., LL.D.

ILLUSTRATED BY ABOVE THREE THOUSAND ENGRAVINGS PRINTED IN THE TEXT.

VOL. I. A—DEPASCENT.

LONDON:
BLACKIE & SON, 49 AND 50 OLD BAILEY, E.C.;
GLASGOW, EDINBURGH, AND DUBLIN.
1886.

Title page of *The Imperial Dictionary* by John Ogilvie and Charles Annandale.

in the history of Scottish dictionary-making is *The Imperial Dictionary* (1847), edited by John Ogilvie, and its 1882 revision by Charles Annandale.

Ogilvie had been a farmworker at the family's farm in Aberdeenshire until an accident resulted in the amputation of his leg. He turned his attention to academic study, graduated with honours from Marischal College and became a schoolmaster, teaching mathematics at Robert Gordon's Hospital in Aberdeen. Ogilvie became known to Blackie when he sent contributions for an annotated Bible history being produced by the publisher, and in 1838, although he lacked lexicographical training, Blackie commissioned him to adapt Webster's *American Dictionary of the English Language* into a popular dictionary for the British market.

Ogilvie's ideas were more ambitious than simple adaptation of the Webster. He expanded, and also made some revisions to, the content, adding 15,000–20,000 words, many of them scientific and technical. The resulting work, *The Imperial Dictionary* (in full, *The Imperial Dictionary, English, Technological, and Scientific, Adapted to the Present State of Literature, Science, and Art; On the Basis of Webster's English Dictionary*), was published by Blackie in parts in 1847–9, came as a complete two-volume publication in 1850, and was reissued with supplements between 1855 and 1874. As well as its wide coverage of technical and scientific terms, it was innovative in its extensive use of pictorial illustrations integrated into the text to amplify definitions. The illustrations were selected by Robert Blackie, an artist who was a partner in the firm and a son of its founder John Blackie; and they depict, for example, plants and animals, architectural features, heraldic images, weaponry and machinery. The use of visual illustration in a dictionary was not an entirely new idea, but the technique of wood engraving, as popularised by Thomas Bewick, had developed in the late eighteenth and early nineteenth centuries, and woodcuts could be used alongside movable type, allowing images to be more easily incorporated with text. And illustration had never been utilised so comprehensively in a general dictionary: around 2,400 woodcuts appear in *The Imperial Dictionary*. Thus it was a pioneering work, more akin to the encyclopedic dictionaries produced in the USA than previous British publications. It brought commercial success to publisher Blackie, and further professional recognition to editor Ogilvie.

Ogilvie died in 1867, and the *Imperial* was extensively revised and greatly enlarged in 1882–3 by Charles Annandale, a graduate of Aberdeen University, who had become the firm's general editor in 1868. Blackie's printing works had been expanded and modernised in the intervening years, allowing more efficient book production, and Annandale's new edition gained even greater renown than the original. Now a four-volume work, it still included good-quality illustrations, this time, in Annandale's words, 'about four thousand in number',[10] and three full-page plates in each volume showing, for example, precious stones, decorations of honour, and mining terms. However, the improvements were not purely visual: new entries had been added, some 30,000 in all, not only from the arts and sciences but also 'Scotch words used by Burns, Sir Walter Scott, and other writers, together with numerous provincial English words; many Americanisms; and such foreign words as are frequently met with in English books'.[11]

Additional encyclopedic detail was included at a number of entries where it would be 'impossible to elucidate them satisfactorily by means of a bare definition',[12] for example by giving an account of the types and workings of a 'steam-engine' at that entry. Unlike Ogilvie, Annandale inserted pronunciations at every entry, using a simple respelling system. This dictionary also offered synonyms, for example, at the entry 'adroit' ('dexterous, skilful, ingenious, expert, ready').

The Scottish dictionary had an American work as its primary source, but the *Imperial* was destined to have an impact on the course of American dictionary-making. Many of the illustrations from Ogilvie's *Imperial* were used in the 1859 edition of Webster's *American Dictionary of the English Language* (known as the *Pictorial Edition*), which was hurriedly published in anticipation of a forthcoming illustrated dictionary from rival Joseph Worcester, with the illustrations in a section before the A–Z text. This supplement was successful to the extent that it would appear in every subsequent Webster dictionary up to 1934, even when the illustrations had also been integrated with the main text. US publisher Century reprinted Annandale's revision of the *Imperial* (1883), and later adapted it to create *The Century Dictionary and Cyclopedia* (1889–91), with William Dwight Whitney as editor-in-chief. This multi-volume dictionary is regarded by many as one of the best produced in the USA although, perhaps due in part to disputes over American copyright with the owners of Webster – G. & C. Merriam, who had originally permitted the use of Webster as the basis of the *Imperial* – Century did not become a widely recognised dictionary 'name'. Doubt has been expressed in some academic circles on the extent of the influence of *Imperial Dictionary* on the *Century Dictionary*. However, in Whitney's Preface to the latter text, while a debt is acknowledged to various sources, no doubt is left as to its provenance: 'This design originated early in 1882 in a proposal to adapt The Imperial Dictionary to American needs, made by Mr Roswell Smith, president of The Century Co., who has supported with unfailing faith and the largest liberality the plans of the editors as they have gradually extended far beyond the original limits.'[13]

The basis of the *Century* in the *Imperial* is even more apparent in the copyright notice, included in response to G. & C. Merriam's claims of copyright infringement:

> By permission of Messrs. Blackie & Son, the publishers of The Imperial Dictionary by Dr. Ogilvie and Dr. Annandale, material from that copyright work has been freely used in the preparation of THE CENTURY DICTIONARY, and certain owners of American copyrights having claimed that undue use of matter so protected has been made in the compilation of The Imperial Dictionary, notice is hereby given that arrangement has also been made with the proprietors of such copyright matter for its use in the preparation of THE CENTURY DICTIONARY.[14]

Later, Annandale produced concise versions of the *Imperial*, including *A Concise Dictionary of the English Language* (1886; also published by Blackie). The firm had already published, and continued to publish, a number of smaller dictionaries. Many of these, such as *The Student's English Dictionary* (1865) and *The School Dictionary* (1867), addressed the needs of the educational market, where the company – which had a strong ethic of making educational works widely available – would have an increasing presence, helped by the passing in 1872 of the Education (Scotland) Act, which introduced compulsory education for children aged between five and thirteen. But, despite the success of the *Imperial*, Blackie did not publish any other major dictionaries. Blackie & Son Ltd ceased publishing in 1991, and its lists were acquired by other publishers (Penguin, Thomas Nelson and Chapman & Hall).

John Boag's *A Popular and Complete English Dictionary*

Around the time of the appearance of the *Imperial*, other English dictionaries were being published under Scottish editorship. *A New Universal Etymological, Technological, and Pronouncing Dictionary of the English Language* (1848) was compiled by John Craig, an Airdrie-born lecturer in geology at Anderson's University in Glasgow. Craig's work is unashamedly based on the works of Johnson and John Walker and is dedicated to William and Robert Chambers for 'promoting the intellectual and moral improvement of all classes of society, particularly of the Working Class'. One of the more popular dictionaries to become available was John Boag's *A Popular and Complete English Dictionary*, published in 1847–8 by William Collins. Boag was a Congregationalist minister in Blackburn, West Lothian, where he also had a day school, and by the time of the publication of his dictionary, he was over seventy years old. Boag claimed his object 'was not to produce a dictionary entirely new' but to 'embody the many excellencies of the various standard Dictionaries already in use'.[15] Like the *Imperial*, however, the *Popular* had the word list of Webster as its basis. The dictionary includes pronunciations and etymologies, and definitions are concise and succinct. To the main text is appended 'A Popular English Grammar', which incorporates a history of the English language and style advice for composition. In 1852–3, the work was reissued by A. Fullarton in Edinburgh as *The Imperial Lexicon of the English Language*. Archibald Fullarton had, until 1831, been a partner of John Blackie; Fullarton also published *The Imperial Gazetteer of Scotland* and *The Imperial Gazetteer of England and Wales*, similar in name but different in content to Blackie's *Imperial* titles. This application of 'Imperial' to works of linguistic reference, and not just to atlases and gazetteers, does suggest that the notion held some appeal to a contemporary readership. Whether or not it indicates that an attitude of linguistic imperialism is inherent in the works or the publication of them is another question, although the use of the word and (in the case of the Blackie series) the printing of the books in the large Imperial format (Imperial octavo or quarto), suggests a preparedness to take advantage of the positive connotations of the word for the wider British public in the nineteenth century.

W. & R. Chambers

By the late nineteenth century, the firm of W. & R. Chambers was also in the vanguard of publishing in Scotland. The company was founded by brothers William and Robert Chambers, who were born in Peebles at the beginning of the nineteenth century. Their father moved the family to Edinburgh in 1813 after the collapse of his drapery business, and it was in Edinburgh that Robert Chambers, at the age of sixteen, set up a very modest bookselling operation. He was later joined in business by William, who began publishing short works of local interest, the first of which was 750 copies of *The Songs of Robert Burns*, printed about 1819. With further publications, the brothers pursued an objective of bringing affordable educational literature to as wide a readership as possible, so justifying the image they had created for the company as 'publisher for the people'. In 1832, the firm of W. & R. Chambers, founded that year, first published *Chambers's Edinburgh Journal*, later *Chambers's Journal of Popular Literature, Science, and Arts*, and finally just *Chambers's Journal*. This was a weekly sixteen-page journal featuring articles, many written by Robert Chambers himself, on history, language and science; and this, at the height of its popularity, achieved a circulation of 80,000 per week. Chambers' commendable educational aims were further attested by the publication of *Chambers's Information for the People* in 1834, a series of sheets on subjects such as science, mathematics, and literature, bound in sets. This was followed by *Chambers's Educational Course*, a series of works and schoolbooks on various subjects, in which over 100 titles were eventually produced.

The firm published the *Cyclopaedia of English Literature* in 1844, a chronological history of British authors and reviews of their works that became a standard history of English literature into the twentieth century. This was followed by an even more prestigious work of general encyclopedic coverage. *Chambers's Encyclopaedia* (in full *Chambers's Encyclopaedia: A Dictionary of Universal Knowledge for the People*) was based on a German encyclopedia, the *Brockhaus Konversations-Lexikon,* and published in 520 parts from 1859 to 1868. The editor of this ambitious title was Dr Andrew Findlater, who had in 1857 produced a revised edition of *Information for the People.* Findlater was born in 1810 in Aberdour, Aberdeenshire, the son of a small farmer. He had become a respected scholar since graduating MA from the University of Aberdeen, and was clearly highly regarded by Chambers; he edited some of the firm's other publications, including a revised edition of *Chambers's Etymological Dictionary* (see below). When he ended active involvement with Chambers in 1877, he was retained as consulting editor.

The publication might well have been prompted by the success of other encyclopedias; indeed, *Encyclopaedia Britannica* had been established in Edinburgh the century before (see above). It may also have been inspired in some part by Ephraim Chambers' influential *Cyclopaedia* of 1728, with which it was to become frequently confused, although there was no direct connection between the publications or any relation between the men lending their names to them. Shortly after the publication of *Chambers's Encyclopaedia,* William Chambers acknowledges that:

> When we entered on the undertaking, it was considerably more than a hundred years since Ephraim Chambers gave to the world his *Cyclopaedia or Universal Dictionary of Knowledge* [*sic*] – the prototype, as it proved to be, of a number of similar works in Britain as well as in other countries, which must have contributed in no small measure to increase the sum of general intelligence.[16]

It is perhaps no accident that Ephraim Chambers' work also had the word *Dictionary* in its full title: *Cyclopaedia: Or, An Universal Dictionary of Arts and Sciences.* William Chambers makes clear his view that, as a result of the tendency of subsequent encylopedic works to be 'aggregated in large and formal treatises', as opposed to having entries presented 'under a variety of specific heads', 'the serviceableness of the encyclopaedia as a dictionary of reference is greatly impaired'. Indeed, the Edinburgh work stayed true to the A–Z 'headword' structure of the earlier *Cyclopaedia,* so that the new encyclopedia was, like the *Brockhaus Konversations-Lexikon* on which it was based, close to what William describes as 'its original purpose of a dictionary'.[17]

It is unlikely that the success of Blackie's *Imperial Dictionary* had gone unnoticed by Chambers and, having made a success of the *Encyclopaedia,* the step into publication of more straightforwardly lexical dictionaries would be a logical one. However, Chambers first published a lexical dictionary in 1861, only two years after the publication of the *Encyclopaedia* had begun and several years before it was completed. This was *A Dictionary of the English Language*, in full *A Dictionary of the English Language Exhibiting the Orthography, Pronunciation and Definition of Words, According to the Prevailing Usage of Correct Writers and Speakers*, echoing the title of a previous Webster dictionary; it was edited by Arnold J. Cooley, a grammarian and pharmacist who was the author of reference works such as *The Cyclopaedia of Practical Receipts in all the Useful and Domestic Arts* (1841) and *The Pharmaceutical Latin Grammar* (1845). In the Preface to the work, Cooley acknowledges his publisher's principle of popular education, expressing confidence that the definitions are not 'so diffuse or complicated as to unfit them for the use of the "middle" and "upper" forms of schools, and for the general and humbler class of readers'.[18] The definitions themselves may be simple to follow, but the structure of the work is perhaps not quite so. The dictionary contains a compendious introduction of nearly seventy pages dealing in detail with pronunciation and orthography, with numbers in the entries linking them to details in the Introduction.

While Cooley's name was explicitly attached to the 1861 work, it was not until 1867 that the Chambers name appeared in the dictionary title, suggesting the company had published a dictionary about which it felt truly proprietorial. This was *Chambers's Etymological Dictionary of the English Language*, compiled by James Donald. It was not an etymological dictionary solely attempting to trace the development of the meaning of a word rather than defining it. It is not impossible that the term 'etymological' may have been used to give the work a degree of scholarly appeal at a time when comparative philology was having a huge influence on linguistics and lexicography. However, etymological principles did lie behind its organisation. Donald's aims are apparent from his description in its Preface: 'A Dictionary based on etymological relations of words, and exhibiting the results of the latest philological research' (and one which was 'at a price within the reach of even common schools').[19] It is clearly important to Chambers that, no matter how erudite the work, it maintains its reputation of bringing education to the people. Indeed, Donald does organise the dictionary by 'root word', nesting derived words below the root, so that (for example) 'adaptable', 'adaptability', and 'adaptation' are grouped under the root word 'Adapt', the root word having the upper-case initial conventional at the time. It is a system of 'nesting' still applied consistently in the *Chambers Dictionary* today. Also familiar from even the most recent edition is a pronunciation system that uses respelling with diacritic marks above vowel letters to distinguish the various vowel sounds (for example, ā represents the sound in 'fair'; ē the sound in 'me').

While Donald's 1867 system has not survived entirely intact, it is clearly at the basis of the expanded modern system.

It is worth noting that Donald was the first editor to put etymological detail *after* the definitions, now an accepted convention in general-purpose dictionaries. As for Donald's own credentials as a lexicographer, it has passed largely unremarked that he was highly regarded by Walter Skeat, acknowledged as one of the great etymologists. Skeat's indebtedness to the *Etymological Dictionary* in compiling his own seminal etymological dictionary, published by 1882, is acknowledged in the key to the plan of the latter work:

> The Word-list contains all the primary words of most frequent occurrence in modern literature . . . I have been chiefly guided in this matter by the well-arranged work known as *Chambers's Etymological Dictionary of the English Language*, edited by James Donald, F.R.G.S.[20]

The 1872 publication *Chambers's English Dictionary* was a larger version of the same dictionary, edited again by Donald. This time the text contained around 200 woodcuts, perhaps prompted by the success of the *Imperial* and other illustrated dictionaries. The *Imperial* remained unacknowledged in its list of sources, although a later edition in 1898, edited by the Reverend Thomas Davidson, has an acknowledgement in its preface of the *Century Dictionary* as one of the American dictionaries that 'still hold first place as works of reference', but how far either text was actually used in the editing is not clear. Davidson also acknowledges Jamieson's *Etymological Dictionary of the Scottish Language* (see Chapter 3) and Murray's 'magistral' *New English Dictionary* as sources of etymological information. He does not, however, acknowledge his predecessor James Donald.

Davidson was also editor of the 1901 *Chambers's Twentieth Century Dictionary*, a compact edition of *Chambers's English Dictionary*, and the new title was intended to reflect a new kind of dictionary. It could be argued that it was this dictionary that achieved the aim of creating a truly 'popular' dictionary, stripped of much scholarly philological detail yet still comprehensive and accurate. The aim had been to include the same number of entry words as the bigger book, but to compress and condense definitions and etymologies (the two-line etymology of 'amend', for example, was condensed to 'Fr. *amender*—L. *a* from, *menda* a mistake') to produce a more portable, convenient volume. Davidson's dictionary was a huge success; its sales of over 28,000 in 1901 were doubled the following year and, with some updating and occasional supplements with new words, the work continued to be published without major revision until 1952.

In 1914, Davidson took over a parish in Ayrshire, and was replaced by William and Liddell Geddie. The Geddies would be involved right up to the 1952 revision, a complete overhaul of the dictionary that saw every entry scrutinised, and many deleted. (They also expanded the feature of occasionally idiosyncratic definitions; the celebrated *Twentieth Century Dictionary* definition of 'éclair' as 'a cake long in shape but short in duration' was penned by Liddell Geddie.) It was an undertaking that would take ten years. The result went by the rather grand title of *New Mid-Century Version of the Twentieth Century Dictionary*, and was 150 pages longer than the previous dictionary. The Geddies had been joined in their efforts in 1944 by Agnes Macdonald, who went on to become the editor responsible for the 1972 edition of *Chambers Twentieth Century Dictionary*, which carried enough new material to make it one fifth longer than the 1952 edition. Macdonald was awarded OBE in 1973 for services to publishing. In subsequent years, many Scots lexicographers continued to contribute to and manage innovations in dictionary production at Chambers, including Betty Kirkpatrick, who supervised production of the 1983 *Chambers English Dictionary*, and Catherine Schwarz (née Collocott; 1933–2006), daughter of former Chambers editor and managing director Tom Collocott; she was editor-in-chief of two more editions of the dictionary.[21]

It could be said that Chambers English dictionaries have been lent unique character by the inclusion of many literary, rare and dialect words that may be sacrificed for pragmatic reasons by other dictionary publishers (for example, *mallemaroking*, 'carousing of seamen in icebound ships'), and the retention of such terms saw Chambers become the dictionary of choice for cruciverbalists and other word-puzzlers. Another notable feature of Chambers dictionaries from their inception has been the inclusion of more Scots vocabulary than other general-purpose dictionaries. This coverage is first made a feature of in the sub-title of the 1872 dictionary ('with Vocabularies of Scottish Words and Phrases, Americanisms, &c'), and words such as *clash-clash*, *dush* and *wanchancy* grace the pages to the present day. When asked to select a favourite word from the dictionary as part of a marketing campaign in 2008, Scottish personalities gravitated towards the Scots content: author Alexander McCall Smith selected *fantoosh*, fellow author Christopher Brookmyre favoured *shoogle*, while the then SNP leader Alex Salmond, who would go on to become Scotland's first minister, expressed a fondness for *sleekit*.

Such was the success of its publications, including English dictionaries, that by the end of the nineteenth century W. & R. Chambers was one of the biggest English-language publishers in the world. Fortunately, this focus on English did not mean the complete neglect of Scots language; in 1911 Chambers published Alexander Warrack's *Scots Dialect Dictionary*, later *Chambers Scots Dictionary* (see Chapter 7).

In 1992 Chambers was merged with London company Harrap, having itself been acquired by French company Groupe de la Cité in 1989, and in 2004 Chambers Harrap became part of another French group, Hachette Livre. In a sad postscript to the Chambers story, the immediate connection between Chambers and Edinburgh was ended on Hogmanay 2009, when the Chambers Harrap Edinburgh office was closed by its parent company, Hachette UK. It was announced that dictionaries of English, as well as other works bearing its name, would subsequently be produced from the offices of Hodder in London. Such was the dismay felt by many at this move – especially, it has to be said, in Scotland, where it was strongly felt that Chambers was part of the cultural fabric of the country – that an online petition against the closure garnered 1,600 signatures. The fact remains unaltered that a Scottish company had achieved the aim of bringing relatively inexpensive and accessible, yet meticulously researched and compiled, English dictionaries to a worldwide readership.

William Collins, Sons & Co.

While the goal of education inspired the foundation of Chambers, the origins of another Scottish publisher whose name would become closely linked with dictionaries were in the dissemination of religion. William Collins (Printers & Publishers) was set up in Glasgow in 1819 by William Collins, who was born in Eastwood, Renfrewshire, in 1789. It was established when Dr Thomas Chalmers, a renowned theologian and political economist, and later first moderator of the Free Church of Scotland, committed all his religious publishing work to Collins. To begin with, Chalmers' brother was involved and the company operated under the name Chalmers & Collins (Booksellers & Stationers); after five years Collins bought out Chalmers and the company became William Collins & Co. William Collins himself was a staunch Presbyterian and a leading member of the Scottish Temperance movement. The firm gained a licence to print and publish the Bible in 1842, in an effort to provide religious and moral education by publishing the 'Good Book' at a price many people could afford. It is a privilege the company still holds, with HarperCollins being one of few companies licensed to print the Bible today.

By the mid-1840s, despite difficult economic conditions, the business had flourished. It was now based in Glasgow's South Frederick Street, with distribution offices in London. By this time the company had taken a first step into dictionary publishing, and is reported as having produced a Greek and English lexicon as early as the 1820s. Boag's *Popular and Complete English Dictionary* was published in 1848. When steam presses were introduced to the firm in the 1850s, it was able to achieve production on a mass scale, and dictionaries constituted only part of an output that included works of Shakespeare, atlases, and the Bible. Further dictionary titles included *A Critical and Pronouncing Dictionary of the English Language* (1861), an edition of Joseph Worcester's *A Universal and Critical Dictionary of the English Language*. This was already a contentious work in that Worcester's dictionaries had caused a long-running feud known as the 'dictionary wars' in the US between former colleagues Thomas Webster and Joseph Worcester and their publishers, with Webster having directed accusations of plagiarism at Worcester. Although this work had been published in the US as the work of Worcester, and had included a statement by him that he had borrowed nothing from Webster, the Collins edition made the declaration in its subtitle that it was 'compiled from the materials of Noah Webster', as had another British edition the decade before. (Worcester responded to the British publication with a pamphlet entitled *A Gross Literary Fraud Exposed: Relating to the Publication of Worcester's Dictionary in London.*) The company also published a series of illustrated dictionaries, including *The Household Dictionary of the English Language* (?1869; 'founded on the labours of Johnson, Walker, Webster, Worcester, and other distinguished lexicographers'), containing 1,000 woodcuts, twenty full-page illustrations, and a fifteen-page supplement entitled 'A Glossary of Scottish Words and Phrases'. From this developed *The Illustrated National Pronouncing Dictionary of the English Language* (1869), a work with 250 engravings and pronunciations for every headword, intended for schools. Also in the series were *The Library Dictionary* (1871), again with 1,000 wood engravings, and *The Cabinet Dictionary* (1871), another comprehensive volume with 750 woodcuts. The firm educational aims characteristic of the wider Scottish publishing industry were, by this time, very much apparent in Collins' works; the Preface to this dictionary, published just before the passing of the Education Act, echoes Chambers prefaces in the hope that 'the price at which it is offered cannot fail to procure for it a speedy introduction and increasing employment even in our common schools'. *A Dictionary of the Derivations of the English Language, in Which Each Word is Traced to its Primary Root*, which is not illustrated, was published in 1872 with the stated intention of issuing a dictionary 'bearing more directly on the derivations of the language'. Like the *Chambers Etymological Dictionary* of 1867, it does not deal solely with etymology, and the etymologies are followed by concise definitions.

By the twentieth century, Collins had begun publishing a series of foreign-language dictionaries, and in the first decade of that century a number of English dictionary titles also appeared under the Collins name. These included *Collins' Graphic English Dictionary* (1903), edited by Alexander M. Williams, designated on the title page as Principal of the Church of Scotland Training College in

Glasgow. It is an impressive work of over 1,400 pages, incorporating fifteen full-page colour plates illustrating, for example, birds, buildings and flags, and with many appendices, again including a glossary of Scots words. Also published was *Collins' Home Dictionary* (1908), around half the size of the *Graphic* and with eight full-colour pages. The *Gem English Dictionary*, unprecedented in its small and portable size of approximately 3 × 4 inches, and containing 20,000 words, was first published in 1902 and brought great commercial success through the rest of the twentieth century, and into the twenty-first. The format proved so popular that many reference books, not just dictionaries, were, and still are, published in the *Gem* series.

Many other dictionaries emerged from the Collins stable throughout the twentieth century, some of them aimed at particular readerships; for example, *Everywoman's Dictionary* (1928), a small book with 'supplements of special interest to women', and the *National Dictionary and Encyclopedia* (1932), promising to be 'a highly efficient servant' to 'the business man' and offering him separate glossaries of business words, technical terms and facts and figures on countries of the world. Many titles of the 1920s and 1930s name English philologist and lexicographer Ernest Weekley as general editor; compilation of some titles is credited to D. Kermode Parr. Later works, such as *Collins New English Dictionary* (1956), with a 32-page colour atlas, appear under the editorship of A.H. (Alexander Hyndman) Irvine.

In the 1960s, the company took a new view on its dictionary publishing. Plans were put forward for a series of substantial bilingual dictionaries, and eventually titles were published for Spanish (1970), French (1978) and German (1980); they broke new ground, especially in meaning discrimination, and were compiled by teams of English speakers and speakers of the other language. One of the main compilers of the French dictionary was Sue Atkins, originally of Edinburgh, who later worked for Oxford University Press (OUP) and became a prominent member of EURALEX (the European Association for Lexicography), contributing especially to lexicographic theory and training of lexicographers.

In the late 1960s, Collins turned its attention to a new type of monolingual English dictionary, one that would include encyclopedic entries for people and places in the tradition of American college dictionaries. It would also follow their convention of ordering entries by placing the most modern, and what the editors regarded as the most generally useful, of the main senses of a word first. This was a radical departure from previous British one-volume dictionaries, which had traditionally been compiled on historical principles and shown the sense development of a word from the oldest to the newest. The dictionary had been envisioned by US lexicographer Laurence (Larry) Urdang, managing editor of the first *Random House Dictionary of the English Language* and founder of the language quarterly *Verbatim*, who, in liaison with Collins director Jan Collins, set up 'Laurence Urdang Associates' (later Market House Books) in Aylesbury, Buckinghamshire, in 1970. Urdang was given the role of editorial director. Patrick Hanks, another director of Laurence Urdang's company, was appointed as editor, and the Collins Urdang Project was born. From then, each entry was compiled from scratch, and although other dictionaries were relied upon for some reference, no one dictionary provided an identifiable source. The project suffered some vicissitudes, including the withdrawal of the American partner, Holt, Rinehart and Winston, which was to publish a US edition, and a temporary stoppage of the project by Collins. However, *Collins Dictionary of the English Language* was finally published in 1979, and within two years it had taken a large share of the general dictionary market.

Begun by Laurence Urdang's company, compilation and production of the *Collins Dictionary of the English Language* (*CED*) and its subsidiary volumes were subsequently undertaken largely from Glasgow. Later innovations included thesauruses in an A–Z rather than thematic arrangement, the first of these, *The New Collins Thesaurus*, published in 1984. The firm's first combined dictionary and thesaurus, with thesaurus entries placed alongside their dictionary equivalents, was published in 1987.

When the first *CED* was almost complete, John Sinclair, a Scotsman who was by then professor of Modern English Language at Birmingham University and a celebrated proponent of corpus linguistics, had been hired as consultant general editor at the suggestion of his sister, Sue Atkins. Later, he and Atkins put forward a plan for an entirely new and radically different monolingual dictionary for learners based on evidence of real, rather than perceived, usage. In 1980 a language research facility was set up at the University of Birmingham, led by Professor Sinclair and sponsored by Collins, with a view to producing such a dictionary. As with the *CED*, its gestation was not without difficulties but, following some changes in editorial personnel and intensive lexicographical labour, the *Collins COBUILD English Language Dictionary* was produced in 1987. It was progressive in its ordering of senses according to frequency, its full-sentence defining style and its presentation of detailed information on collocations, all based on evidence of usage. At the heart of the COBUILD ('Collins Birmingham University International Language Database') project had been the creation and analysis of a corpus of contemporary English, which was also used to develop the 'Bank of English', a balanced corpus that would subsequently inform all the company's English-language reference work. The Bank of English, which is still frequently augmented with new data, is held in both Glasgow and Birmingham. Sinclair, who died in 2007, is remembered as an outstanding linguist and scholar whose contribution to corpus linguistics and lexicography is immeasurable.

Collins remained in family hands until 1981, when the Collins' shares were sold to Rupert Murdoch's News Corporation; by 1989, the company had been acquired by News Corporation and merged with US firm Harper & Row to become HarperCollins. Although no longer a Scottish-owned company, the connection of Collins with Scotland endures. It continues to produce dictionaries under the Collins name from its base in Bishopbriggs, close to Glasgow, and still uses the services of many Scottish lexicographers.

The Oxford English Dictionary

While an abundance of reference works, including dictionaries, were being produced in Scotland in the late nineteenth century, in Oxford work was continuing on an English dictionary intended to be more meticulously researched and exhaustive in its coverage than any that had gone before. This was the *New English Dictionary*, now known as *The Oxford English Dictionary* (*OED*), and the man whose name is still most closely associated with it is James Augustus Henry Murray.[22] Born in Denholm, near Hawick, Roxburghshire in 1837, the son of a draper, Murray's remarkable intelligence and academic ability, evident from a very early age, fitted him for intellectual work. At seventeen, he was a teacher at The United School in Hawick and, just three years later, he was head teacher of Hawick Academy. By this time, while still feeding his voracious appetite for learning languages, Murray was pursuing various interests of his own, including archaeology, the natural sciences of botany and geology, and the dialects of the Lowlands of Scotland.

In 1864 he moved to London in the hope of finding a less harsh climate for his tubercular first wife, Maggie Scott; sadly, she died soon afterwards. He later married Ada Ruthven, and all of their eleven children helped in his dictionary work to some extent. In London he worked as a bank clerk but continued to pursue his interest in languages and linguistics. His studies included Hebrew and Syriac, as well as numerous European languages.

In 1857, Murray had attended a course given in Edinburgh by phonetician Alexander Melville Bell (the father of Alexander Graham Bell, the inventor of the telephone), who was then professor of Elocution at the University of Edinburgh. Bell introduced Murray to his phonetic notation system of 'Visible Speech', and Murray became a friend of the family. Bell also introduced Murray in London to mathematician and philologist A.J. Ellis, who would also become a lifelong friend. By this time, Murray was respected in intellectual, particularly philological, circles. He had worked on an (unfinished) pronunciation key for Jamieson's Scottish *Dictionary* and continued his collection of British dialects, making good use of Bell's Visible Speech system, to assist Ellis in his work. He also completed his own work, *The Dialect of the Southern Counties of Scotland* (see Chapter 4). By 1869 Murray had been elected to the council of The Philological Society, and the publication of *The Dialect of the Southern Counties of Scotland* by the society helped establish him as a leading philologist. He left his bank post in 1870 to become a teacher again, this time at Mill Hill School in London, and despite the demands of teaching there, coupled with his work in linguistics, he studied externally for a degree from London University, graduating BA in 1873.

In 1858, the Philological Society had begun work on an entirely new 'national dictionary', showing in detail the historical development in meaning and form of every word.[23] When the project required a new editor in the 1870s,[24] the society's Frederick Furnivall turned his attention to Murray,[25] prompted, it is said, by a chance remark of Murray's that he would like to have a go at the job himself. In 1877, negotiations began with Clarendon Press (Oxford University Press) to publish the dictionary. Murray prepared the specimens presented to OUP in support of the proposal and played a pivotal role in the discussions to the extent that, to secure their agreement to publish, it was understood by the Delegates to the Press that he would be in charge of the project as a whole. So, despite his initial reluctance (no doubt born of a knowledge of the immense nature of the task), Murray accepted the editorship to ensure that the dictionary itself might come, eventually, into existence. A formal contract was signed in 1879, with Murray agreeing that the dictionary should be a four-volume work, completed within ten years.

As a home for the work and for the many thousands of citation slips, Murray built what he humorously called a 'Scriptorium' in the garden of his London home. When the existing citation slips were forwarded to this new location, it was apparent that the task which Murray faced was enormous. The material he inherited was incomplete and often of poor quality, both in content and physical condition, giving the new editor little option but to virtually begin the project again. Murray made new calls for volunteer readers to gather citations, and despite a response that was initially less than overwhelming, even among the members of the Philological Society, as well as the unconscientious approach of some volunteers, enough readers were enlisted in Britain, the USA and throughout the world to provide around one million more citations in a relatively short time. Several million more would be collected during Murray's lifetime. However, even disregarding the bureaucratic aspects of the work, analysis of the material, sub-editing and proofreading were not done quickly, and in 1880

Murray changed his estimate of the time required to complete the dictionary from the publisher's stipulated ten years to a minimum of fifteen years,[26] itself an ambitious projection. In the course of his editorship, Murray was destined to come into frequent contention with the Delegates of the Clarendon Press over the content, scale and timing of the work.

The first fascicle of the dictionary, *A–Ant*, was not published until 1884 but, as Murray had anticipated, it was generally acclaimed. It was unlike any previous English dictionary in number of entries alone, and each of these entries was supported by numerous citations tracing sense development, etymology and pronunciation, all compiled from first principles. To the chagrin of the press and potential subscribers, however, it was desperately slow work: letter A was not completed it its entirety until 1885, and B in 1888. It had been increasingly clear that Murray could not complete such a comprehensive work on his own, and in 1888 a second editor, Henry Bradley, was appointed. Another Scot, William Alexander Craigie (see below and Chapter 5), was engaged as third co-editor in 1901 after working under Bradley since 1897; and a fourth editor, Charles Onions, was appointed in 1914. The necessity of these appointments was accepted with reluctance by Murray and did not speed up progress considerably; the rate of output steadied, but it was not completed until 1928.[27]

While Murray and Craigie are the Scots whose names are most closely associated with the *OED*, they were by no means the only Scots who contributed to this immense work. A number of the assistants to the main editors were Scottish. John Mitchell, the son of a Hawick clergyman, was appointed as an assistant by Murray in 1882, and was a highly valued member of the staff. He died in a climbing accident in 1894. Craigie took on John MacLean Ramsay in 1901, and he worked with Craigie for several years; he later became an esteemed statistician. Craigie's sister-in-law Isabella Hutchen worked with him on the *OED* from 1915 to 1921 before becoming heavily involved in the *DOST* (see Chapter 5). Several other assistants were engaged for shorter periods, including Ritchie Girvan, a Campbeltown-born scholar who was brought in by Murray in 1903 before being transferred to Craigie's staff, and who went on to become a lecturer, and later professor of English, at Glasgow University (1947–9). There is evidence to suggest that Scotland was considered a good source of potential assistants. In 1888, when Henry Bradley required an assistant, the Secretary to the Delegates wrote to him, noting that a colleague would 'write today to Aberdeen to see whether he can hear of any young Scotchman who would do'.[28] In addition, the contribution of the many Scots readers and sub-editors, who respectively identified then prepared citations for the assistants, should not be overlooked. The longest-serving of all the sub-editors was

William Bruce Robertson Wilson (b.1843), a Presbyterian minister from Dollar, Clackmannanshire.[29]

Murray died at home in Oxford in 1915, working on the dictionary right up to the final month of his life, and so did not see its completion in 1928. By then, his intellectual rigour, exacting editorial standards, tenacity and industry had given the project the impetus and organisation it required to succeed. For the *OED*, he had made physical, mental, social and financial sacrifices for most of his life – so much so that, in 1885, a 'Murray Indemnity Fund' was launched to help him meet some of the debts and expenses he had personally incurred. (One later appeal for funding for the project to Andrew Carnegie, which Murray had hoped would be viewed with sympathy by a fellow Scotsman, was met with rejection, because Carnegie was a proponent of spelling reform, and no reformed system had been used in the dictionary.[30]) The significance of the project in English linguistics, and the vastness of Murray's achievement as editor-in-chief, not only in editing almost half of the dictionary's content but in maintaining the momentum of the project, even in the frequent periods when it seemed destined for failure, had not gone unrecognised in his lifetime. He was presented with numerous honorary degrees, granted a founding membership of the British Academy, and knighted in 1908.

Of the surviving editors, Craigie was instrumental in producing the remainder of the work and establishing its future development, as well as editing *N, Q, R, Si–Sq, U, V,* and *Wo–Wy*. His relationship with Murray – from whom he largely worked separately, as he was based in the Old Ashmolean building at Oxford – had not been without conflict. Craigie had been appointed without the approval of Murray, who was given no opportunity to examine his work. Naturally, the approach of these two highly intelligent individuals would occasionally differ; in 1902 Murray wrote a long letter to Craigie in which he complained: 'No part of my work is so onerous and unpleasant to me as that of looking through your copy, which has consumed many many hours of this year.'[31] Despite these differences, a professional understanding apparently prevailed, and Craigie was widely recognised as a hard-working and skilled lexicographer. He became the senior editor on the death of Henry Bradley in 1925, and held this role when the final fascicle was published in 1928. It grew apparent during the course of publication that enough new material had become available to create a supplement, and again Craigie had a significant role in its compilation. The *OED* was reissued in 1933 with a one-volume supplement, of which Craigie had edited approximately one third.

Despite Craigie's hard work, progress towards completion of the *OED* in the later years had been slowed somewhat by his absences through academic work.

From 1925, Craigie carried out much of his work on the *OED* from Chicago, where he had been appointed as professor of English to edit *A Dictionary of American English on Historical Principles* (*DAE*), latterly in conjunction with American professor James R. Hulbert. Using the structure of the *OED* to plot the historical development of words, the aim of the *DAE* was to define usages particular to American English, from the earliest English settlers onwards, linking them to the culture and history of the country itself. It became part of his plans for a range of 'period dictionaries' in the style of and using source materials from the *OED* but intended to augment the information available there (see Chapter 5). He returned from Chicago in 1936 to concentrate on the *DOST*, but he continued to amass citations for the *OED*, for eventual use in a second supplement. Although his work on this dwindled, he continued to advise the Clarendon Press on dictionary policy. Craigie was recognised as one of the foremost lexicographers of his time.

It is worth noting that, especially during his absences on academic trips, Craigie was assisted greatly by two Scotsmen in particular: George Marr Watson (see also Chapters 4, 5 and 6) and J.M. Wyllie (see also Chapter 6). Watson, a printer from Jedburgh, did not receive a university education but took an interest in many subjects. He joined local societies, including the Hawick Archaeological Society, of which James Murray was a founding member. It may have been through Murray that Watson's abilities were made known to Craigie; Murray received a letter of recommendation for him from the secretary of the society in 1906. Watson joined the *OED* staff in 1907 to work under Craigie, and such was his dedication to the job that he corrected proofs during active service in the First World War. Watson took on increasing responsibility for work on the *OED* as Craigie made his trips, and when Craigie moved to his post in Chicago in 1925, he was heavily involved in completing the *U* section. Craigie decided that he should have responsibility for the stretch of text with words beginning *WR-*, but not everyone was happy with the prospect of his greater involvement. While not calling into question Watson's work rate, co-editor Charles Onions voiced concerns about his skills as a lexicographer.

Craigie clearly did not share Onions' concern, and in 1927 he invited Watson to Chicago to work as an assistant on the *DAE* and the *DOST*. Work on the supplement to the *OED* was also under way by this time, and Watson also contributed to this, although he was involved mainly with the American and Scots titles. Even so, Watson, who was given a mention in the acknowledgements in the published Supplement, believed that he and another editor, Mitford M. Mathews, had not received due credit for their efforts on the *OED* or the *DAE*. In 1958, Mathews submitted an essay to the journal *American Speech* emphasising the extent and value of Watson's contribution not just to the *OED* but to the *DOST* and, in particular, the *DAE*, and conveying Watson's crushing disappointment that he was not credited in the title page of the latter.[32] Watson did, however, receive an honorary degree from Oxford University in recognition of his contributions to lexicography.

Another Scotsman was also instrumental in the completion of the Supplement. James McLeod Wyllie was born in Glenbervie, Kincardineshire in 1907, and studied classics at Aberdeen University. He was employed in 1929 to work on the Supplement, taking a key role in Craigie's team in Oxford, processing the slips sent by Craigie from Chicago into dictionary copy. As well as being enlisted to work on the new *Oxford Latin Dictionary*, Wyllie continued to record corrections and possible additions after 1933, and acted in a consultative capacity for various other dictionary publications (see also Chapter 6). Although OUP recognised his lexicographical ability to the extent that he would be considered for the post of editor of the next Supplement, Wyllie suffered from mental health problems that would contribute to a deterioration of the relationship between the editor and the company over the years, and in 1954 he was dismissed.

Scots lexicographers continue to feature among the *OED* staff in more recent times. A number of Scots worked on the acclaimed second *Supplement to the Oxford English Dictionary* (published in four volumes 1972–86), among them Lesley Brown (née Burnett). Brown was editor-in-chief of *The New Shorter Oxford English Dictionary* (1993), the fourth edition and an entire revision of the two-volume *Shorter Oxford English Dictionary* first published in 1933. Others have been involved in the compiling of smaller Oxford dictionaries of English, among them Edward McIntosh, editor of the fourth (1951) and fifth (1964) editions of *The Concise Oxford Dictionary*.

It is natural to speculate whether the fact of Murray's, and later Craigie's, Scottishness had any influence on the coverage of Scots usage in the first edition of the *OED*. Both men had a strong interest in Scots, as evidenced by their studies and bodies of work. However, it had not been the stated intention, on the part of Murray at least, that the dictionary cover anything other than the English language. In a letter to a Greenock librarian in 1900 responding to the suggestion that he include words from more languages in the dictionary to create a 'Pan-Lexicon', Murray dismissed the idea with the words 'we find the language of little England enough for us'.[33] Murray was more explicit in his intention to exclude Scots in a letter to Craigie dated 10 May 1901, in which he discusses some of Craigie's copy:

> There are in it at least 60 slips which *I should naturally omit*, if editing it; i.e. 1/6 of the whole . . . I think it very necessary to reduce *Scotch* words to a bare minimum. Originally, we did not propose to include any modern Sc[ots] later than 1600, exc[luding] from one or two classical authors; but we have of late been rather laxer. I am now however excluding them rigidly in K. After all, we are making an *English* Dictionary, and must not allow purely Scotch words to take up the space wanted for English words.[34]

However, Murray's view that Scots was not a language in itself, and that Scots and Northern English were aspects of the same dialect, may have worked in favour of the inclusion of Scots usages to some extent; had Murray regarded Scots words as being from a distinct Scots tongue, he might have thought none worthy of inclusion in a dictionary of English. The *OED* included a substantial number of words in Scots usage, often labelled both 'Scots' and 'Northern English dialect'. As one might expect, given the *OED* had over 100 readers of (largely literary) Scottish texts, these words were largely historical, and found in literary citations. Examples of Older Scots in the *OED* include *artation* (compulsion; constraint), *dully* (doleful, gloomy), and *shoot (or play) nipshot* (to miss the mark). However, and despite Murray's determination to exclude most Modern Scots words, a number of words in current usage also found their way from printed sources on to the pages of the *OED*. Words treated in characteristic philological detail include *braw*, *fike*, and *paik*. As far as pronunciation was concerned, it had been suggested to Murray by a colleague that he should include two distinct forms of pronunciation, 'Northern' and 'Southern', with Murray providing the 'Northern' forms, but Murray did not take up this suggestion.[35]

Later Craigie, on proposing his 'period dictionaries', makes mention of the dictionary's Older Scots content (see Chapter 5). But while acknowledging the coverage is 'generous', he also takes the view that it is 'subject to accident', thus necessitating the separate work that would become the *DOST*. This would corroborate any evidence that there was no policy in place for the systematic inclusion of Scots words. Yet coverage of these words appears relatively plentiful in the *OED*, which might lead one to conclude that the main editors' Scots nationality and scholarship made the appearance of Scots in the *OED* far more likely, despite Murray's protestations.

At a dinner in honour of the publication of the first edition of the dictionary, prime minister Stanley Baldwin, recognising it as a landmark in British culture, delivered a speech lauding the book's editors.

> Our histories, our novels, our poems, our plays – they are all in this one book.
>
> . . .

> Every man and woman in this country whose gratitude and respect is worth having, will rise up and call you blessed for this great work.[36]

It is remarkable that two of the main protagonists in the story of the *OED* were Scots. Their contribution to English lexicography is incalculable and, without their input, the history of English lexicography would have been very different.

The *Historical Thesaurus of the Oxford English Dictionary*

Some vagaries of fortune aside, the Scottish connection with English lexicography remains strong. One of the most high-profile and ambitious examples of Scottish involvement in the recording of English in recent years has been the *Historical Thesaurus of the Oxford English Dictionary*. The project was presented to the Philological Society by Michael Samuels, then professor of English Language at the University of Glasgow, in 1965; his department was undertaking work on a historical thesaurus based on the content of the *OED* and a thorough analysis and classification of the senses therein. Also involved was Jane Roberts, who taught at Glasgow University, then Kings College, London, and who supplemented the Old English material from the *OED* with *A Thesaurus of Old English* (1995).[37] Christian Kay, who had been a lexicographer with Collins, and Irené Wotherspoon, who had studied at Glasgow under Professor Samuels, joined the project as research assistants in 1969; their editorial involvement would continue and increase until publication and beyond, with Christian Kay becoming its director.

While data collection from the *OED* progressed, a system of classification was devised to cover the wealth of material that would be presented. The historical nature of the work meant that changes in sense over centuries, and shifts in cultural perceptions, would have to be both accommodated and communicated by the system. The resultant system comprises three main headings: the external world; the mental world; and the social world, divided in turn into 354 major subcategories, with 236,000 categories and sub-categories in all.

The project was, like any other of its scope, beset by problems in the course of its completion. Not least of these was a fire in 1978 that seriously damaged the building housing the *Thesaurus* but which, because they were housed in metal cabinets, left the paper slips with data transcribed from the *OED* unscathed. To encourage funding, the project had to be divided into portions of work that could be covered by single grants. The decision to include material from the *OED* Supplements published between 1972 and 1986 and, later, from the second edition of 1989 and its Additions Series of 1993–7, ensured that the content was as full as was attainable; but it also broadened and prolonged the task, as material had to be cross-checked with information that had been included from the first edition. The classification system was redesigned as the project proceeded, but in July 2008 the process of print publication was started.

The print edition was published by Oxford University Press in October 2009, in two volumes and with a total of nearly 4,000 pages. The fruit of this 44-year task is the largest thesaurus in existence, comprising a database of almost every word in the second edition of the *OED* (800,000 meanings for 600,000 words), arranged semantically and chronologically. It won the Saltire Society Research Book of the Year award in 2009. In 2010, the content of the *Historical Thesaurus of the Oxford English Dictionary* was incorporated into the *OED* online, and its potential as an electronic resource is continually being explored and developed. The database behind it offers enormous possibilities for further academic use, for historical linguistics and in the analysis of historical texts.

Conclusion

The historical record shows that the contribution of Scotland and Scots to the lexicography of English has been, and continues to be, surprisingly – even disproportionately – great, taking into account the size of its population in relation to its English neighbour. However, it cannot be denied that dictionary publishing in Scotland is not quite as healthy as it once was, and HarperCollins is now the only publisher producing original English dictionary content from premises in Scotland to any significant degree. Nevertheless, a large number of lexicographers from Scotland still work in English lexicography, many in a freelance capacity and, despite a decline in the fortunes of 'traditional' print dictionary publishing, many Scottish lexicographers are thriving in related fields of English-language reference. There is no reason why their influence should not continue into the foreseeable future.

Acknowledgement

I am indebted to Anne Seaton for her valuable assistance, advice and encouragement in the writing of this chapter.

Notes

Introduction

1 Not the first translation of any kind into any vernacular language: the Middle Irish *Imtheachta Aeniasa* ('The Wanderings of Aeneas'), a prose rendering, is dated to the twelfth century (even earlier by some estimates), though its earliest surviving manuscripts are of the fourteenth.

Chapter 1

1 Nathan Bailey (c.1691–1742).
2 Charles Richardson (1775–1865).
3 James A.H. Murray (1900) *The Evolution of English Lexicography: The Romanes Lecture*, Oxford: Clarendon Press, p. 50.
4 B. Colombat (2005) 'Stephanus, Robertus (ca. 1503–1559)', in K. Brown (ed.) *Encyclopedia of Language and Linguistics*, 2nd edn, Oxford: Elsevier, p. 251.
5 P. Bogaards (2005) 'French Lexicography', in K. Brown (ed.) *Encyclopedia of Language and Linguistics*, pp. 638–41.
6 Hans Sauer (2009) 'Glosses, Glossaries, and Dictionaries of the Medieval Period', in A.P. Cowie (ed.) (2009) *The Oxford History of English Lexicography*, vol. 1, Oxford: Clarendon Press, pp. 17–40; p. 25.
7 Ibid.
8 Edinburgh, HM Register House, National Records of Scotland RH 6/72.
9 Balgarvie, PTH, 4 km NE Perth, 0.5 km NE New Scone (NO1426).
10 i.e. lands, buildings and any other adjuncts to land.
11 National Library of Scotland MSS Adv. MS 34.3.29 and Adv. MS 34.3.28.
12 William de Laudels, Bishop of St Andrews, 1342–1385. See D.E.R Watt (1969) *Fasti Ecclesiæ Scoticæ Medii Ævi*, St Andrews: University of St Andrews, Department of Medieval History, p. 294.
13 The identification of this entry in the 'Liber' as being in the same hand as the SG was first made by Dr Grant G. Simpson of the University of Aberdeen a number of years ago in joint research with Dr Margaret A. Mackay (University of Edinburgh) on the Scone Gloss (pers. comm., Dr Mackay). The results of Simpson and Mackay's work have not otherwise been published. I (re-)made the connection subsequently, unaware of the precise nature of the earlier work beyond the fact that a later date had been ascribed to the glosses cited in some fascicles of *DOST* from that given in earlier fascicles. My identification lends independent support to the earlier research.

14 Catherine R. Borland (1916) *A Descriptive Catalogue of the Western Medieval Manuscripts in Edinburgh University Library*, Edinburgh: Edinburgh University Press/T.A. Constable; and Gregory G. Smith (1902) *Specimens of Middle Scots*, Edinburgh: Blackwood.

15 The vernacular poems in the Makculloch MS and the glossary were edited for the Scottish Text Society by G. Stevenson (1918) *Pieces from the Makculloch and the Gray MSS*, Edinburgh: Scottish Text Society, 1st ser., no. 65, printed for the Society by W. Blackwood and Sons. More recently, the glossary has been re-edited along with a detailed linguistic analysis in Keith Williamson (2007) 'A Latin–Older Scots Glossary in Edinburgh University Library MS 205', *Spanish Society for Medieval English Language and Literature Journal*, 14, pp. 221–76.

16 For other problematic cases, see Williamson, 'A Latin–Older Scots Glossary', pp. 1234–42.

17 *Acts of the Parliament of Scotland*, iii, 614/1.

18 Perth Guildry MS f.193, 23 Jan. 1530/1. The original manuscript is held by Perth Museum and Art Gallery. For an edited edition, see Marion L. Stavert (ed.) (1993) *The Perth Guildry Book, 1452–1601*, Edinburgh: Scottish Record Society, new series, 19.

19 Definitions as in *DOST*, q.v. for references.

20 David Allan (2000) *Philosophy and Politics in Later Stuart Scotland*, East Linton: Tuckwell Press.

21 See especially David Murray (1905–6) 'On Some of Our Latin Grammars', *Transactions of the Glasgow Bibliographical Society*, Glasgow; and John Durkan (1990) 'Education: The Laying of Fresh Foundations', in John MacQueen (ed.) *Humanism in Renaissance Scotland*, Edinburgh: Edinburgh University Press, pp. 123–60.

22 Thomas M'Crie (1899) *Life of Andrew Melville*, Edinburgh and London, William Blackwood & Sons, p. 79.

23 'Index of words first which occur scattered in the etymologia, then added at the end [of which] are Scots interpretations.'

24 *A Latin Dictionary: Founded on Andrews' Edition of Freund's Latin Dictionary: Revised, Enlarged, and in Great Part Rewritten by Charlton T. Lewis, Ph.D. and Charles Short, LL.D.*

25 See article by James K. Cameron on James Carmichael (1542/3–1628) in *ODNB*.

26 See article by A.S. Wayne Pierce on David Wedderburn in the *ODNB*.

27 Ibid.

28 Edinburgh: Successors of Andrew Anderson, 1695 edition.

29 i.e. a trench or ditch: *DOST* s.v. gote.

30 Here 'dictionary' is to be considered a generic term, for such works might be termed 'glossary' or 'encyclopedia', for example. The basic structure is a term followed by an interpretation of its sense. Other information about the origins of the term, its pronunciation, provenance, date and relationship to cognates might also be provided.

31 See Luke Houwen (1994) *The Deidis of Armorie*, Edinburgh: Scottish Text Society, p. xiii.

32 Ibid., p. 22.

33 Ibid., p. 25.

34 See A.A.M. Duncan (1961), '*Regiam Majestatem*: A Reconsideration', *Juridical Review*, 6, pp. 199–217.

35 *Acts of the Parliament of Scotland*, iii, p. 89; John W. Cairns et al. (1990) 'Legal Humanism and the History of Scots Law: John Skene and Thomas Craig', in MacQueen (ed.) *Humanism in Renaissance Scotland*, pp. 48–74; p. 51.

36 See article by Atholl Murray on Skene of Curriehill, Sir James Skene, in the *ODNB*.

37 Gero R. Dolezalek (1996) 'Lexiques de droit et autres outils pour le *ius commune* (XIIe–XIXe

siècles)', in Jacqueline Hamesse (ed.), *Les manuscrits des lexiques et glossaires de l'antiquité tardive à la fin du moyen âge.* Publications de l'Institut d'Études Médiévales, Université Catholique de Louvain, Louvain-la-Neuve: Presses universitaires, pp. 353–76.

38 Cairns et al., 'Legal Humanism', p. 48.

39 Ibid.

40 Cairns et al., 'Legal Humanism', p. 52, claim that 'An examination of the intellectual background and methods of the leading members of the Scottish commissions strongly suggests that their work was inspired by the ideas of French humanism.'

41 OED s.v **farthing-man** n. defines it as 'some official of a guild' and cites 'Balfour *Practicks* 77 Quhen the Alderman, Thesurare, Farthing-man or Dene..convene the gild brether for the commoun affairis'. Balfour seems to make a distinction between farthing-man and thesaurer.

42 See article by Claire Jackson on Sir George Mackenzie of Rosehaugh in the *ODNB*.

43 Rosehaugh, Sir George Mackenzie of (1694) *The Institutions of the Law of Scotland, By Sir George Mackenzie of Rosehaugh, His late Majesty's Advocate, With an Alphabetical Explanation of the most difficult Scots Words*, London: Printed for Andrew Bell and Jonas Luntley, at the Pestle and Mortar over against the Horse-shoe-Tavern in Chancery Lane.

44 See, for example, John W. Cairns (1996) 'Andrew Bell, Jonas Luntley and the London Edition of Mackenzie's Institutions', *The Bibliotheck*, 21, pp. 7–11.

Chapter 2

1 On Ruddiman, see further Douglas Duncan (1965) *Thomas Ruddiman: A Study in Scottish Scholarship of the Early Eighteenth Century*, Edinburgh: Oliver & Boyd.

2 For the textual history of the poem see David F.C. Coldwell (ed.) (1951–64), *Virgil's Aeneid Translated into Scottish Verse by Gavin Douglas Bishop of Dunkeld*, Scottish Text Society Third Series, vols 25, 27, 28, 30, Edinburgh and London: Blackwood; vol. 1, 96–106.

3 For discussion of Ruddiman's precedents and much else germane to the present article, see A.J. Aitken (1989) 'The Lexicography of Scots Two Hundred Years Since: Ruddiman and his Successors', in J. Lachlan MacKenzie, and Richard Todd (eds.), *In Other Words: Transcultural Studies in Philology, Translation, and Lexicology Presented to Hans Heinrich Meier on the Occasion of his Sixty-fifth Birthday*. Dordrecht: Foris, 235–45.

4 These will be omitted in subsequent quoted definitions.

5 Aitken, 'The Lexicography of Scots': 'The reliability of his definitions is in consequence high: I counted some 28 erroneous or imprecise definitions [which he lists] (out of 3000).'

6 That of *The Tea-Table Miscellany* was not included in the first edition but added for the 1730 reprint.

7 *Sic*, in the poem text as printed: he uses the spelling *Gruntill* in the glossary. The word actually means a pig's snout, insultingly applied by Dunbar to Kennedy's features.

8 He is identified as its editor in the catalogue of the National Library of Scotland (I am indebted to Iseabail MacLeod for this information) and also in the British Library's English Short Title Catalogue.

9 According to *DOST*, but Bawcutt [full reference details needed here and in Bibliography – author to supply] 1998) conjectures that 'awppis' is an error for 'quhawppis'. Certainly her argument that whaups form a more likely pairing with owls that do bullfinches is a persuasive one.

10 Regrettably, North-Eastern writers with strongly local voices such as Ross, Forbes, Skinner and Shirrefs were succeeded in the nineteenth century by poets who wrote in an undifferentiated

Scots with few or no markedly local features, until the distinctive dialect re-emerged late in the century in the energetic hands of, among others, William Alexander and Charles Murray.

11 The full title of this edition is *Helenore, or the Fortunate Shepherdess, A Poem, in the Broad Scotch Dialect; by Alexander Ross, A.M. Schoolmaster at Lochlee. To Which are Added Songs, by the Same Author, and a Glossary. The Second Edition, Carefully Corrected.*

12 The phrase actually occurs not in any of Ross's own poems but in James Beattie's introductory verses, which appear for the first time in this second edition.

13 Definitions as in the Kilmarnock edition; the Edinburgh ones are given only if substantially different.

14 Cf. in the second stanza of Shirrefs' 'Invocation to Allan Ramsay' the rhyme sequence 'abuse it — refuse it — use it — *tease it*' (Andrew Shirrefs (1790) *Poems, Chiefly in the Scottish Dialect*, Edinburgh: privately printed).

15 I will leave this almost entirely out of the discussion. Predictably, the historical and philological arguments put forward contain hardly a single statement or postulate to which modern scholarship lends any credence; and the concluding section in which he discusses the metrical practices of early poets, though showing some insights, is not to our present purpose.

16 Sibbald, *Chronicle of Scottish Poetry*, vol. IV, xlv. A lesser degree of contempt for the spoken language of his own day might have saved him from such egregious errors as *Awmous* 'a fur cap. O.Fr. from Teut. *muts*' (*recte*, of course, 'alms, a charitable gift').

17 Sibbald, *Chronicle of Scottish Poetry*, vol. 4, lxii.

18 John Mactaggart (1824), *Scottish Gallovidian Encyclopedia*, original edn. (1824) London: printed for the author; reprinted (1981) Strath Tay, Perthshire: Clunie Press, 273–4. For further discussion of Mactaggart's *Encyclopedia*, see Chapter 4.

19 For more detailed discussion see J. Derrick McClure (1992), 'What, if anything, is a Scotticism?', in S.J. Bronner (ed.), *Creativity and Tradition in Folklore: New Directions*, Utah: State University Press, 205–21.

Chapter 3

1 'Thesaurus Paleo-Scoticus', published in *Auntran Blads* (1943).

2 George Watson (1916) 'The Story of Scottish Dictionary-making', *Transactions of the Hawick Archaeological Society*, pp. 7–12; p. 11.

3 The following chapter condenses the information in my book *Jamieson's Dictionary of Scots: The Story of the First Historical Dictionary of the Scots Language*, Oxford: OUP, 2012, which provides further details on the background, content, and publication history of Jamieson's work.

4 Frederick A. Pottle (ed.) (1952) *Boswell in Holland, 1763–1764*, London: Heinemann, p. 161.

5 The surviving manuscript materials of Boswell's dictionary have only recently been rediscovered: see Susan Rennie (2011) 'Boswell's Scottish Dictionary Rediscovered', *Dictionaries*, 32, pp. 94–110 and the Boswell's Scottish Dictionary website at <http://boswellian.com>.

6 Hailes compiled this work several years after his edition of the Bannatyne poems (see Chapter 2). For further discussion, see Rennie, *Jamieson, Dictionary of Scots*, pp. 40–1.

7 *Number First of a Dictionary of the Ancient Language of Scotland, with the Etymons* (1807) Edinburgh: printed by John Moir, Royal Bank Close.

8 Boucher died before his dictionary was finished, but the first part was published posthumously, as *A Supplement to Dr. Johnson's Dictionary of the English language: or, A Glossary of Obsolete and Provincial Words* (1807), Part I, London: printed for Longman, Hurst, Rees and Orme.

9 The Secession Kirk was formed after the first schism in the Church of Scotland in 1732. For a full history, see John M'Kerrow (1841) *History of the Secession Church*, rev. edn, Glasgow: A. Fullarton.

10 The work in question, *A Vindication of the Doctrine of Scripture*, published in 1794, was a refutation of Joseph Priestley's controversial views on the early Christian Church.

11 *The Sorrows of Slavery, A Poem* (1789), London: printed for J. Murray. The poem is reprinted in part in James G. Basker (2002) *Amazing Grace: An Anthology of Poems about Slavery, 1660–1810*, New Haven: Yale University Press, pp. 396–400.

12 For further discussion of this debate, see Colin Kidd (2002) 'Race, Theology and Revival: Scots Philology and Its Contexts in the Age of Pinkerton and Jamieson', *Scottish Studies Review*, 3:2, pp. 20–33; Marina Dossena (2008) 'When Antiquarians Looked at the Thistle: Late Modern Views of Scotland's Linguistic Heritage', *The Bottle Imp*, 4, November, available online at: <http://www.arts.gla.ac.uk/ScotLit/ASLS/SWE/TBI>.

13 *Caledonia, or, An Account, Historical and Topographic, of North Britain: from the Most Ancient to the Present Times* (1807–24), 3 vols, London: printed for T. Cadell and W. Davies.

14 For more on Dempster and Thorkelin, see John Evans (2005) *The Gentleman Usher: The Life and Times of George Dempster (1732–1818)*, Barnsley: Pen & Sword Military.

15 'Memoir of Dr. Jamieson' (1841), *Tait's Edinburgh Magazine*, 8:92, August, pp. 514–28; p. 525.

16 EUL, La.III.379, fols 889–90, Letter to Thorkelin, 12 Oct. 1787.

17 'Memoir of Dr. Jamieson', p. 525.

18 See H.J.C. Grierson (ed.) (1932–7) *The Letters of Sir Walter Scott*, 12 vols, London: Constable; vol. 1, pp. 38–9.

19 EUL, La.III.379, fols 897–8, Letter to Thorkelin, 18 January 1802.

20 See Andrew Somerville (1844) 'Memoir of the Rev. John Jamieson, D.D.', in John Jamieson, *Reality of the Gracious Influence of the Holy Spirit*, Glasgow: David Robertson, pp. xiii–cii; p. lxxiv.

21 EUL, La.III.379, fols 897–8, Letter to Thorkelin, 18 January 1802.

22 *The Bruce; and Wallace;Published from two Ancient Manuscripts Preserved in the Library of the Faculty of Advocates* (1820), 2 vols, Edinburgh: printed by James Ballantyne.

23 *Dictionary* (1808), Preface, p. vii.

24 Ibid., p. vi.

25 Richard Garnett (1859), 'English Lexicography', in *The Philological Essays of the Late Rev. Richard Garnett*, edited by his son, London: Williams and Norgate, pp. 1–40; p. 6.

26 Bodleian, MS Douce.d.23, fols 32–3, Letter to Douce, 18 November 1816.

27 Bodleian, MS Douce.d.22, fols 86–7, Letter to Douce, 14 April 1812.

28 *A Dictionary of the Scottish Language; Containing an Explanation of the Words Used by the Most Celebrated Ancient and Modern Scottish Authors* (1818) Edinburgh: printed for James Sawers, p. vii.

29 *A Description of the Isles of Orkney; by Master James Wallace, late Minister of Kirkwall* (1693) Edinburgh: printed by John Reid.

30 For further details, and a full transcription of the annotations which Jamieson used, see Rennie, *Jamieson's Dictionary of Scots*, Appendix C.

31 *Dictionary* (1840–1), Advertisement.

32 See Colin Milton (1995–6) 'Shibboleths of the Scots: Hugh MacDiarmid and Jamieson's *Etymological Dictionary of the Scottish Language*', *Scottish Language* 14/15, pp. 1–14.

33 'Thesaurus Paleo-Scoticus', published in *Auntran Blads* (1943).

34 W. M. Metcalfe (ed.) (1896) *Legends of the Saints in the Scottish Dialect of the Fourteenth Century*, 3 vols, Edinburgh: Scottish Text Society.

35 The glossary was appended to the third volume of *The Antiquary* (1816), Edinburgh: printed for Archibald Constable.

36 See Susan Rennie (2008) 'The *Electronic Jamieson*: Towards a Bicentenary Celebration', in M. Mooijaart and M. van der Wal (eds) (2008) *Yesterday's Words: Contemporary, Current and Future Lexicography*, Newcastle: Cambridge Scholars, pp. 333–40.

Chapter 4

1 Alexander Geddes (1792) 'Three Scottish Poems', *Archaeologica Scotica:Transactions of the Society of Antiquaries of Scotland*, 1, pp. 402–68. See also Charles Jones (1994) 'Alexander Geddes: An Eighteenth-Century Scottish Orthoepist and Dialectologist', *Folia Linguistica Historica*, 8, pp. 71–83.

2 He is sometimes confused with Thomas Edmondston, his first cousin and exact contemporary, a promising young botanist who was tragically killed at the age of twenty in an accident in South America during an expedition.

3 J. Laughton Johnston (2007) *Victorians 60 Degress North: The Story of the Edmondstons and Saxbys of Shetland*, Lerwick: Shetland Times Ltd, pp. 227–8.

4 Susan Rennie (2011) 'Boswell's Scottish Dictionary Rediscovered', *Dictionaries*, 32, pp. 94–110.

5 Jakob Jakobsen (1936) *The Place Names of Shetland*, London: David Nutt; Copenhagen: Vilhelm Prior; reprinted (1993) Lerwick: Shetland Library (preface by A. Hörsbol, intro by J. Fellows-Jensen).

6 E. Brooke-Freeman (2010) 'Putting Jakobsen on the Map: Collecting Shetland Place Names in the Twenty-First Century', in T. Sigurdardóttir and B. Smith (eds.), *Jakob Jakobsen in Shetland and the Faroes*, Lerwick: Shetland Amenity Trust, pp. 99–109.

7 Roy Grønneberg (1981) *Jakobsen and Shetland*, Lerwick: Shetland Publishing, p. 71.

8 See Caroline Macafee in Corbett et al. (eds.), *The Edinburgh Companion to Scots*, Edinburgh: Edinburgh University Press, p. 60.

9 Available online at:<http://sh.shetlanddictionary.com/index.php?title=Main_Page>.

10 Preface, p. ix.

11 Preface, p. viii.

12 Introduction, p. xxvii.

13 Preface, p. vii.

14 NLS Acc. 9448.395.

15 Earlier edition (1998) published as *Spik o the Place.*

16 Not Lionel, as in the *SND* Bibliography.

17 The Necropolis is a Victorian cemetery on a hill beside Glasgow Cathedral.

18 Reprinted (1981), Strath Tay: Clunie Press; (2008) Glasgow: Grimsay Press.

19 See also *Dictionary of Canadian Biography* online and J. Derrick McClure (2004) 'A Local Treasure Trove: John MacTaggart's *Scottish Gallovidian Encyclopedia*', *Transactions of the Dumfriesshire and Galloway Natural History and Antiquarian Society*, 3rd series, 78, pp. 131–8.

20 W.A.D. Riach (1979) 'A Dialect Study of Comparative Areas in Galloway 1st Report', *Scottish Literary Journal Supplement*, 9, pp. 1–16; 2nd Report (1980), 12, pp. 43–60; 3rd and Last Report (1982), *Scottish Language*, 1, pp. 13–22; (1984) 'Galloway Schools Dialect Survey' *Scottish Language* 3, pp. 49–59.

21 Third series, vol. 13 (1925–6), along with notes on Scott's lecture on the dialect to the society,

added as an introduction to this booklet.

22 Preface, p. vi.

23 Herein 'Ulster' refers to the historical nine-county province, not the present-day Northern Ireland of six counties.

24 For the broadest treatment of the planting and evolution of the Scots language in Ulster, see Michael Montgomery and Robert J. Gregg (1997) 'The Scots Language in Ulster', in Charles Jones (ed.) *The Edinburgh History of the Scots Language*, Edinburgh: Edinburgh University Press. pp. 569–622.

25 Robert Gregg (1985) *The Scotch-Irish Dialect Boundaries in the Province of Ulster*, [Port Credit, Ontario]: Canadian Federation for the Humanities. Originally a PhD thesis (1963) 'The Boundaries of the Scotch-Irish Dialects in Ulster', University of Edinburgh.

26 For a comparative survey of thirteen works published through 1991, see Michael Montgomery (1993) 'The Lexicography of Hiberno-English', *Irish Studies Working Papers*, 93–3, pp. 19–35.

27 The frequency with which the *SND* drew citations from other written sources was as follows: Traynor's *English Dialect of Donegal* (599), W.G. Lyttle (109), Robert Huddleston's 1844 *Poems* (63), Sam Hanna Bell (36), John Marshall (25), and William Carleton (14).

28 *Glossary of Words*, p. viii.

29 *Glossary of Words*, p. viii.

30 John J. Marshall (1904) 'The Dialect of Ulster. [Part 1]', *Ulster Journal of Archaeology*, new series, 10, pp. 121–30; p. 121.

31 Caroline Macafee (1996) *A Concise Ulster Dictionary*, Oxford: Oxford University Press.

32 John Braidwood (1965a) 'Towards an Ulster Dialect Dictionary', *Ulster Dialect Archives Bulletin*, 5, pp. 3–14.

33 J. Braidwood (1965b–87), 'Bird Names in Ulster: A Glossary', *Ulster Folklife*, 11 (1965b), pp. 98–135; 12 (1966), pp. 104–7; 17 (1971), pp. 81–4; 24 (1978), pp. 83–7; 33 (1987), 83–5.

34 For one of many such local items, see Jim Blaney (1985) 'Upper Ards Folk and Glossary of Words', *Journal of the Upper Ards Historical Society*, 9, pp. 6–7, which comments on the heritage and flavour of local speech in the Upper Ards Peninsula and compiles a glossary of 100 terms, many of Irish and Scots ancestry.

35 Caroline Macafee (1994) 'The Ulster Dictionary Project', *Belfast Working Papers in Language and Linguistics*, 12, pp. 177–93; p. 177.

36 Michael Montgomery (2010) 'Some Words with James Fenton', *Ullans: The Magazine for Ulster-Scots*, 11, pp. 13–27; p. 13.

37 Gero Dolezalek, *Scotland under Jus Commune: Census of Manuscripts of Legal Literature in Scotland, Mainly between 1500 and 1660*, Edinburgh: Stair Society, 3 vols, pp. 55–7.

38 Preface, p. viii.

39 Preface, p. v.

40 *The Laws of Scotland: Stair Memorial Encyclopaedia*, Service Volume, Glossary (1988), Edinburgh: Law Society of Scotland, Butterworths.

41 Preface, p. vi.

42 H.L. MacQueen (2004) *Studying Scots Law*, 3rd edn, LexisNexis UK, 217–20.

43 Preface, p. vii.

44 A transcription of the text is available on the Scottish Mining Website: <www.scottishmining.co.uk>.

45 Scottish Fisheries Information Pamphlet no. 17, Department of Agriculture and Fisheries for Scotland.

Chapter 5

1 *Scotsman*, 11 July 1981, p. 1.

2 Material from this section is included in Dareau (2002) '*DOST*: Its History and Completion', *Dictionaries: Journal of the Dictionary Society of America*, 23; and in *DOST* XII, pp. ix–xix.

3 'Craigie, Sir William Alexander', *ODNB*; J.M.Wyllie (1961) 'Sir William Craigie 1867–1957', *Proceedings of the British Academy* 47, pp. 273–91.

4 Published in *Transactions of the Philological Society*, 1925–32 (1930), pp. 6–11. The original handwritten text, written on the reverse of the galley proofs for the *OED* entries *Visory* to *Vitrial* is in the *DOST* Archives, Main Library, University of Edinburgh.

5 Ibid., p. 9.

6 *DOST*, vol. I, p. vii; available online: 'Craigie's Preface', *DOST* Prelims, *Dictionary of the Scots Language*, <www.dsl.ac.uk>.

7 *CSD*, p. xiii.

8 Preface and acknowledgements, Manual to the Corpus of Scottish Correspondence: <www.helsinki.fi/varieng/csc/manual/preface.html>.

9 Obituary in *Transactions of the Hawick Archaeological Society* (1950); P. Gilliver (2010) 'Walter Worrall and George Watson: The "nearly men" of the *Oxford English Dictionary*', Oxford University Research Archive, available online at <http://ora.ox.ac.uk/objects/uuid%3A6be52b97-aded-4de7-b42f-856c49f5dea5>.

10 By Hew Morrison, chief librarian of the Edinburgh Public Library.

11 In *Transactions of the Hawick Archaeological Society* (1916).

12 Gilliver, 'Walter Worrall', p. 4.

13 See M.M. Mathews (1985) 'George Watson and the Dictionary of American English', *Dictionaries*, 7, pp. 214–24.

14 *DOST* vol. I, p. viii.

15 See 'Introduction' (Section 1.4.2) to Angus McIntosh, Michael Samuels, Michael Benskin, et al. (1986), *Linguistic Atlas of Late Mediaeval English* (*LALME*): 'The attempt to infer information about the spoken language purely on the basis of documentary evidence is in fact a hazardous undertaking.'

16 'A re-editing of GIF' in Caroline Macafee and Iseabail Macleod (eds) (1987) *The Nuttis Schell: Essays on the Scots Language Presented to A J Aitken*, Aberdeen: Aberdeen University Press, pp. 25–57.

17 *DOST* vol. I, p. viii.

18 NLS Acc.9448.458.

19 Caroline Macafee, incorporating material by the late A.J. Aitken, 'A History of Scots to 1700', *DSL* <www.dsl.ac.uk>.

20 Later, Forum for Research in the Languages of Scotland and Ulster (FRLSU).

21 *DOST* Archives, University of Edinburgh.

22 Forbes Professor of English Language and General Linguistics in the University of Edinburgh.

23 *DOST* Archives.

24 At this time McIntosh was also actively involved in setting up both the School of Scottish Studies and the Linguistic Survey of Scotland.

25 *DOST* Prelims, *DSL* <www.dsl.ac.uk>.

26 *DOST* Archives.

27 See *DOST* Prelims, *DSL* <www.dsl.ac.uk>.

28 See 'The DOST Corpus', *DOST* Prelims, *DSL* <www.dsl.ac.uk>.

29 A.J. Aitken and Paul Bratley (1966) 'An Archive of Older Scottish Texts for Scanning by Computer', *English Studies,* 48, pp. 61–2; reprinted in *Studies in Scottish Literature,* 4 (1967), pp. 45–7. The texts are available in the Oxford Text Archive: <http://ota.oucs.ox.ac.uk>; A.J. Aitken (1971) 'Historical Dictionaries and the Computer', in R. A. Wisbey (ed.) (1971) *The Computer in Literary and Linguistic Research,* Cambridge: Cambridge University Press, pp. 3–17; N. Hamilton-Smith (1971) 'A Versatile Concordance Programme for a Textual Archive' in Wisbey, *Computer,* pp. 235–44.

30 *DOST* Archives.

31 Only one other member of the editorial staff had been designated 'associate' (Janet M. Templeton, associate editor (1970–5)), all others being 'junior assistant' or 'assistant editor'. In the 1980s the strict retention of 'editor' for the person in overall charge was lost sight of and the more senior editors were designated 'senior editor', the more junior now being called 'editor'. The administrative head was called 'editor-in-chief', then 'director'. In the final years the duties of the two senior editors were split and they were entitled, respectively, 'administrative director' and 'editorial director'. The earlier designation of 'clerical assistant' was in the 1980–90s replaced by the more accurate 'editorial assistant'.

32 Notes for a talk in the 1970s, *DOST* Archives.

33 Supposedly this has all changed since the beginning of the electronic age. But even if it is true that an online dictionary can be changed it is not so easy to find the staff capable of changing it for the better and the time to do it. At least that is how working lexicographers see it. My colleagues on Faclair na Gàidhlig are very clear that the first pass is still of the greatest importance.

34 A.J. Aitken '*DOST*: How we Make it and What's in it', in Roderick J. Lyall and Felicity Riddy (eds) (1981) *Proceedings of the Third International Conference on Scottish Language and Literature (Medieval and Renaissance)*, Stirling: University of Stirling; and Glasgow: University of Glasgow, pp. 33–51.

35 *Scotsman,* 11 July 1981, p. 1.

36 During the early stages of the crisis in 1994, Aitken's advice to me was to agree to whatever they wanted us to do but carry on in the way we were used to – it had worked in 1981, why not now? – but by 1994 the universities had become very different, and we were not Aitken.

37 *DOST*, vol. XII, Prelims.

38 William A. Craigie (1930), 'New Dictionary Schemes Presented to the Philological Society, 4 April, 1919', *Transactions of the Philological Society,* vol. 30 (1925–30), pp. 6–11.

39 'Review of *A Dictionary of the Older Scottish Tongue*' (1962) *English Studies,* 43, p. 445. Cf. Aitken's own comment on the 'encyclopedic' question quoted above: '[Aitken intended to supply] more detailed definitions, sometimes accompanied by brief notes of an encyclopaedic nature when the material for this lay to hand.'

40 Aitken, '*DOST*', pp. 41–2.

41 This policy had been criticised as early as 1962 in Dr Hans Meier's review in *English Studies* (1962, pp. 447–8): 'One disconcerting problem is the separate entry of spelling variants whenever these are numerous and/or can be interpreted to represent phonematic differences, i.e. separable morphemes. Since the order is strictly alphabetical, one may have to go to many different places for "the same word"'. This too was the aspect of the *DOST* most frequently complained of by colleagues in other fields.

42 See *DOST*, vol. VII, p. vi.

43 SPI (Technologies) Ltd, Manila, Philippines.

44 *DOST* Register of Titles: *Edinb. Test. 1514–32, 1567–1700.* MS NAS CC8/8/1–80, 80 manuscript volumes of the wills of residents of Edinburgh.

45 Private letter to Angus McIntosh, 27 Oct. 1980, *DOST* Archives.

46 Eileen M. Finlayson, Marjory B. McNeill, Heather G. Bree, M.A. Ruth Martin, Teresa A. Gribben, David Tugwell, and Gavin H.M. Miller.

Chapter 6

1 *Scottish National Dictionary*, vol. I, p. i.

2 R.L. Stevenson *Underwoods* (1887), Tusitala edition (1923) vol. 22, p. 99.

3 George Cowie, *Scotsman*, 29 January 1938.

4 Letter to *Scotsman*, 18 April 1942.

5 Lecture on 'The Limitations of Dialect' to the Scottish Association for the Speaking of Verse, reported in *Scotsman*, 18 November 1932.

6 Reported in *Dundee Courier, Scotsman*, 6 February 1956.

7 EUL E.2001.5 , minutes of meeting of English Association, Scottish Branch, 26 October 1907.

8 A new edition, with E.H.A. Robson, was published in 1925 under the title of *Speech Training for Scottish Students*, and the original was reprinted by an American reprint company in 1970. It was aimed at students in Scottish Training Colleges, who 'have peculiar difficulties to overcome in dealing with pupils whose everyday speech is Scottish Dialect or Gaelic. Such difficulties cannot be successfully tackled without some definite phonetic knowledge and practice such as we have set forth in this work.' (He also recommends 'some phonetic training in the early stages of the school curriculum', an ideal still a long way off.) This was part of an aim to encourage the use of English in schools at the expense of Scots and Gaelic, though it was 'the Scottish variety of Standard English' which was being encouraged, rather than RP.

9 NLS Acc. 9448.264 minutes of the Council of the English Association (Scottish Branch), 11 December 1907.

10 W. Grant, *What Still Remains to be Done for our Scottish Dialects*, published by the English Association as Leaflet No. 11 (1909); also reported in the *Scotsman*, 29 March 1909.

11 Ibid., p. 1.

12 Ibid., p. 3.

13 Ibid., p. 2.

14 Watson was one of the foremost Celtic scholars of the twentieth century, and his *History of the Celtic Place-Names of Scotland* (1926) remains the standard work on the subject.

15 Reported in the *Scotsman* and the *Glasgow Herald*, 1 October 1924.

16 NLS Acc.9448.245, letter from W.A. Craigie to W. Grant, 28 January 1916.

17 NLS Acc. 9448.230, letter from G. Watson to W. Grant, 12 January 1925.

18 NLS Acc.9448.266, 2nd AGM of SNDA 1931.

19 *Scotsman*, 10/11 December 1928.

20 He was also a staunch member of the Scots Vernacular Association.

21 NLS Acc. 9448. 245, notes attached to letter from W. A. Craigie to W. Grant, 7 January 1929.

22 NLS Acc. 9448. 245, as above, 14 May 1929.

23 NLS Acc. 9448.183, letter from W. Grant to Sir Joseph Dobbie, 22 October 1929.

24 The Dictionary ends with 'Zulu', a type of late nineteenth-century fishing boat, so called from the Zulu War of 1879.

25 NLS Acc.9448.246.

26 James Mather and Hans Henning Speitel (1975, 1977, 1986) *The Linguistic Atlas of Scotland: Scots Section*, 3 vols, London: Croom Helm. Material from the Gaelic section was published later, 1994–7; see Chapter 9.
27 NLS Acc. 9448.230, letter from G. Watson to W. Grant, 29 October 1929.
28 NLS Acc. 9448.481, 29 March 1909.
29 NLS Acc. 10873.2, SNDA Council minute, 13 January 1939; and minute 10 March 1939.
30 *Scotsman*, 9 February 1938.
31 NLS Acc. 10885.11.
32 NLS Acc. 10873.3. Quoted in minutes of the SNDA's sixth AGM, 7 December 1935.
33 Informal name for Glasgow, Edinburgh, Aberdeen and Dundee.
34 John McVie spent his entire career in Register House, becoming Keeper of the Registers of Scotland in 1946. A native of Ayrshire, he was long active in the Burns Federation, and its president 1950–1.
35 NLS Acc. 10873.4, Minutes of Executive Council, 23 June 1943.
36 NLS Acc. 9448.514-633.
37 *SND*, vol. I, p. i.
38 NLS Acc. 9448.511.
39 See chapter on dialect in A. Martin (1984) *Kintyre: The Hidden Past*, Edinburgh: John Donald; and several articles in the *Kintyre Magazine*, nos. 28, 29, 30, 37.
40 Wilson was a colonial administrator whose interest in language had been kindled by study of local languages in India; see Sheila Douglas (1998) 'Sir James Wilson and his Commonsense Approach to the Scots Language', *Scottish Language*, 17, pp. 16–21.
41 His manuscript, thought to have been destroyed by a Labrador dog, subsequently turned up in largely legible condition.
42 His word lists were published in the *Ulster Journal of Archaeology*, 10 (1904), pp. 121–30; 11 (1905) pp. 64–70, pp. 122–5 and pp. 175–9; and 12 (1906) pp. 18–21.
43 In a review of *SND*, vol. III, Part IV in the *Modern Language Review* (April 1953), 48:2, where he complains of the inadequacy of coverage of some dialect areas, including his native west mid Scots.
44 *SND*, vol. VII, p. i; *The New Testament in Scots*, 'Introduction', pp. xiv–xvi.
45 Grant, *What Still Remains*.
46 Ibid., p. 1.
47 NLS 9448.264, letter W. Grant to Carnegie Trust, 7 Oct. 1908.
48 Grant *What Still Remains*, p. 5.
49 Ibid., p. 6.
50 *SND*, vol. I, p. xxiv.
51 Ibid., p. xxv.
52 The term was used to describe a broad rural dialect and, following Allan Ramsay's use in 1721 in comparing his poetry in Scots with pastoral Greek verse, it later often referred to Scots dialects, before narrowing to those of the North-East in the twentieth century.
53 NLS Acc. 9448.245, letter from W.A. Craigie to D.D. Murison, 30 June 1947.
54 NLS 9448.230, letter from W. Grant to G. Watson, 14 November 1930.
55 *SND*, Preface.
56 J. Derrick McClure (ed.) (1983) *Scotland and the Lowland Tongue: Studies in the Language and Literature of Lowland Scotland in Honour of David D. Murison*, Aberdeen University Press, Preface, p. viii–ix.

57 *SND*, vol. I, p. xlvi.

58 *SND*, vol. I, p. xlvii.

59 *Glasgow Evening Citizen*, 4 March 1933.

60 A 1932 meeting of the Finance Committee felt that 'the Association would be well advised to enlist the help of ladies by way of getting up Bazaars or some such scheme as Lady Whitson's Diminishing Teas', as part of fundraising. NLS 9448.461.

Chapter 7

1 Such omission on space grounds was in fact suggested to William Grant for the *SND* by George Watson on the grounds that they already had Jakobsen, Edmondston and Marwick. NLS Acc. 9448.230, Letter from G. Watson, 30 October 1930.

2 Inaugural-Dissertation der Freien Universität Berlin (1970) (and, later, the STS edition (1980–4) of Barbour, edited by Matthew P. McDiarmid and James A. C. Stevenson).

3 *The Historie and Cronicles of Scotland . . . Written and Collected by Robert Lindsay of Pitscottie* (1899–1911), ed. Aeneas J.G. Mackay, vol. 3, Edinburgh, Scottish Text Society.

4 *CSD*, Introduction, pp. xx–xxviii; A.J. Aitken (1986) 'The Pronunciation Entries for the CSD' in Dietrich Strauss and Horst W. Drescher (eds), *Scottish Language and Literature, Medieval and Renaissance*, Frankfurt am Main: Peter Lang, pp. 35–45.

5 *CSD*, Introduction, pp. xxv.

6 See A.J. Aitken (1981) 'The Scottish Vowel-Length Rule', in Michael Benskin and Michael L. Samuels (eds) *So Meny People, Longages and Tonges: Philological Essays in Scots and Mediaeval English presented to Angus McIntosh*, Edinburgh: Edinburgh Middle English Dialect Project, pp. 131–57.

7 Republished in Charles King (ed.) (1971) *Twelve Modern Scottish Poets*, London: University of London Press, pp. 17–18.

8 *Scottish English: The Language Children Bring to School* (1980), published by The Scottish Committee on Language Arts in the Primary School (Falkirk Committee on Primary Education).

9 Now Learning and Teaching Scotland, part of Education Scotland.

10 See J. Robertson (forthcoming 2012) 'Pittin the wird(s) oot: the Itchy Coo Experience of Publishing in Scots in the Twenty-First Century', in John M. Kirk and Iseabail Macleod (eds) *Scots: The Language and its Literature: A Festschrift for J. Derrick McClure*, Amsterdam: Rodopi.

11 At that time 'Budget Line (B3-1006), Minority & Regional Languages & Cultures'.

12 See S. Rennie (2001) 'The Electronic Scottish National Dictionary (the *SND*): Work in Progress', *Literary and Linguistic Computing*, 16:2, pp. 153–60.

13 See S. Rennie (2000) 'Encoding a Historical Dictionary with the TEI', in *Proceedings of the Ninth Euralex International Congress, Euralex 2000*, Stuttgart, vol.1, pp. 261–71.

14 An online edition of the *EDD* is available, hosted by the University of Innsbruck: <www.uibk.ac.at/anglistik/projects/edd-online/>

15 In a letter to W. Grant (NLS Acc. 9448.245, 19 May 1909), Craigie noted that 'Mr Warrack is not a trained philologist or phonetician, but has a great interest in the subject, and has done an immense amount of reading in dialect books'.

16 The square brackets are Stevenson's.

17 Jarvie was Engineer Surveyor-in-Chief to the Marine Safety Division of the Ministry of War Transport.

18 Later (2003) titled *Collins Scots Dictionary*.

19 Jamieson's *Dictionary* is now available online: see Chapter 3.

Part II Introduction

1 From a letter from Walter MacFarlane, printed in Rev. David Malcolme (1738) *An Essay on the Antiquities of Britain and Ireland*, Edinburgh, pp. 6–7: 'Some more papers and some more Testimonies of the Learned', quoted by J.L. Campbell (1963) *Edward Lhuyd in the Scottish Highlands*, Oxford: Clarendon Press, p. xi.

Chapter 8

1 W. Stokes and J. Strachan (eds.) (1901) *Thesaurus Palaeohibernicus: A Collection of Old-Irish Glosses, Scholia, Prose, and Verse*, Cambridge: Cambridge University Press, vol. 1, 'Biblical Glosses and Scholia'.

2 See F. Kelly (1988) *A Guide to Early Irish Law*, Dublin: Dublin Institute for Advanced Studies; and cf. T. O'Neill (1984) *The Irish Hand: Scribes and their Manuscripts from the Earliest Times to the Seventeenth Century, with an Exemplar of Irish Scripts*, Portlaoise: Dolmen Press, for illustrations.

3 See the Cambridge Early Glossaries project led by Paul Russell, <http://www.asnc.cam.ac.uk/irishglossaries/>.

4 See D. Mackinnon (1912) *A Descriptive Catalogue of Gaelic Manuscripts in the Advocates' Library Edinburgh, and Elsewhere in Scotland*, Edinburgh: W Brown, pp. 178–80.

5 An instructive case is that of the group of Gaelic satires composed after the publication (1775) of Dr Johnson's *A Journey to the Western Islands of Scotland*; on these see R. Black (ed.) (2001) *An Lasair*, Edinburgh: Birlinn, pp. 292–9 and pp. 495–9. Those printed in the Gillies Collection (pp. 173–94) seem to have been deliberately glossed in such a way that a non-Gaelic speaking reader could pick up the (pretty virulent) gist of the poems by reading the glosses consecutively!

6 See the Prospectus attached to volume 1 of the SGTS (i.e. Watson (1937) *Scottish Verse from the Book of the Dean of Lismore*, Edinburgh: Oliver & Boyd, p. 328).

7 See J.L. Campbell (1938) 'An Early Scottish Gaelic Vocabulary', *Scottish Gaelic Studies*, 5:1, pp. 76–93.

8 See J.L. Campbell (1975) *A Collection of Rites and Customes etc.*, Cambridge: D.S. Brewer for the Folklore Society, 'Introduction'; J.L. Campbell and D.S. Thomson (1963) *Edward Lhuyd in the Scottish Highlands*, Oxford: Clarendon Press, pp. 91–7.

9 See Campbell and Thomson, *Edward Lhuyd*, p. 229.

10 Memorial to the Court of Police issued by the General Meeting of the SPCK, 2 June 1716, in J.L. Campbell (1937) 'The First Printed Gaelic Vocabulary', *Scots Magazine* 28.

11 Ibid., General Meeting Minutes, 6 June 1723.

12 Ibid., Report of the Sub-committee, 25 June 1725.

13 The first choice of compiler was the Rev. John MacLean (?c.1680–1756) minister of Kilninian in Mull. See C. Ó Baoill (ed.) (1979) *Eachann Bacach and Other MacLean Poets*, Edinburgh: The Scottish Academic Press, p. lxxi.

14 Derick Thomson (1990) 'MacMhaighstir Alasdair's Nature Poetry and its Sources', in D.S. Thomson, *Gaelic and Scots in Harmony: Proceedings of the Second International Conference on the Languages of Scotland (University of Glasgow, 1988)*, Glasgow: University of Glasgow, Department of Celtic.

15 *A New Vocabulary for the Use of Schools* (1720) Edinburgh: Mr. James McEuen. It has not been possible to access this edition.

16 In each dictionary examined for Chapters 8 and 9, the number of headwords has been estimated by selecting six pages at random and counting the headwords. The mean number of headwords for one page was calculated from the sample and multiplied by the total number of pages in the dictionary to give an estimated total number of headwords.

17 *A New Vocabulary English and Latin, for the Use of Schools* (1749) Edinburgh: T. & W. Ruddiman, 'To the Reader', pp. 1–2.

18 *A New Vocabulary English and Latine, for the Use of Young Scholars* (1702) has the same list of headings as the 1749 publication. The section 'To the Reader' is similar and contains the following statement: 'And because several *English* words are not understood by Children, and the generality of People, the *Scottish* names are join'd to as many of them as seem'd to need explanation.' (p. 2) There is no reference to an earlier edition, implying that this is the first edition.

19 Buchanan's letter, which was dated 31 January 1767, is quoted by D.E. Meek (2004) 'The Sublime Gael: The Impact of MacPherson's *Ossian* on Literary Creativity and Cultural Perception in Gaelic Scotland', in H. Gaskill (ed.), *The Reception of* Ossian *in Europe*, London: Thoemmes Continuum, pp. 44–5.

20 W. Shaw (1778) *An Analysis of the Galic Language*, London: W. and A. Strahan.

21 R. Mac Farlan (1795) *Nuadh Fhoclair Gaidhlig agus Beurla*, Edinburgh: John Moir, p. vi.

22 John Lorne Campbell concluded that one of Mac Farlan's sources was MacDonald's *Vocabulary* (1741); see J.L. Campbell (1949) 'Some Words from the Vocabulary of Alexander MacDonald', *Scottish Gaelic Studies*, 6, pp. 27–42.

23 Mac Farlan, *Nuadh Fhoclair*, p. 13.

24 J. MacPherson (ed.) (1807) *The Poems of Ossian in the Original Gaelic . . .*, London: W. Bulmer.

25 This is Patrick MacFarlane who saw MacLeod and Dewar (1831) through the press (see p. 217).

26 P. MacFarlane (1815) *Focalair Ùr Gaelig agus Beurla*, Edinburgh: A. Constable, 'To the Public'.

27 Jamieson, J. (1808) *An Etymological Dictionary of the Scottish Language*, Edinburgh: University Press for W. Creech, A. Constable and W. Blackwood; J. Jamieson (1825) *Supplement To the Etymological Dictionary of the Scottish Language*, Edinburgh: University Press, for W. & C. Tait, 78, Prince's Street; and Longman, Hurst, Rees, Orme, Brown and Green, London.

28 MacFarlane, *Focalair*, p. iv.

29 R. Armstrong (1825) *A Gaelic Dictionary . . .*, London: J. Duncan, 'Preface', p. vi.

30 J. O'Brien (1768) *Focalóir gaoidhilge-sax-bhéarla or an Irish–English Dictionary*, Paris.

31 E. O'Reilly (1817) *An Irish–English Dictionary*, Dublin: J. Barlow.

32 This presumably refers to W. Perry (1775) *Royal Standard English Dictionary*, Edinburgh.

33 Shaw, *Analysis of the Galic Language*; see note 20 above.

34 Possibly for (Thaddaeus) Connellan, whose *English–Irish Dictionary* was published in 1814 and whose *Irish–English Primer* was published in 1815; or perhaps for Conor Begley, whose *English–Irish Dictionary*, in collaboration with Hugh MacCurtin, was published in 1732.

35 R.I. Black (1986) 'The Gaelic Academy: The Cultural Commitment of The Highland Society of Scotland', *Scottish Gaelic Studies*, 14:2, pp. 1–38; and (1988) 'The Gaelic Academy: Appendix: The Ingliston Papers', *Scottish Gaelic Studies*, 15, pp. 103–21.

36 Highland Society (1828) *Dictionarium Scoto-Celticum: A Dictionary of the Gaelic Language*, Edinburgh: Blackwood and London: T. Cadell, p. xii.

37 'C.S.' = 'Common Speech'.

38 H.J. Todd (1818) *A Dictionary of the English Language: / by Samuel Johnson. With numerous*

corrections, and with the addition of several thousand words . . ., London: Longman, Hurst, Orme and Brown.

39 A. Stewart (1801) *Elements of Gaelic Grammar* Edinburgh: C. Stewart & Co..

40 Jamieson, *An Etymological Dictionary*; see note 27.

41 J. Sibbald (1802) *A Chronicle of Scottish Poetry*, Edinburgh: C. Stewart & Co.

42 Sir J. Sinclair (1791–9) *The Statistical Account of Scotland*, Edinburgh: William Creech.

43 See Black 'The Gaelic Academy', p. 26.

44 See the biographical sketch of Caraid nan Gàidheal (1867) by his son (also Rev. Dr Norman MacLeod) prefixed to *Caraid nan Gàidheal*, Glasgow: W. MacKenzie, pp. ix–xlviii.

45 N. MacAlpine (1832) *The Argyleshire Pronouncing Gaelic Dictionary*, Edinburgh, p. vi/2.

46 MacAlpine, *Argyleshire Pronouncing Gaelic Dictionary*, pp. x/1.

47 J. MacKenzie (1841) *Sàr-obair nam bàrd Gàelach; or, The Beauties of Gaelic Poetry and Lives of the Highland Bards* . . ., Glasgow: Macgregor, Polson & Co.

48 J. MacKenzie (1844) *Eachdraidh a' Phrionnsa; no, Bliadhna Theàrlaich*. Edinburgh: Thornton & Collie.

49 J.H. Dixon (1886) *Gairloch in North-west Ross-shire*, Edinburgh: Cooperative Printing Company, pp. 189–91.

50 Erroneously dated as 1862.

51 For MacEachen's scholarly career see A. Roberts (2006) 'Maighstir Eobhan Mac Eachainn and the Orthography of Scots Gaelic' *Transactions of the Gaelic Society of Inverness*, 63, pp. 358–95. For *Leanmhuin Chrìosd* and *An Cath Spioradail*, see D. Maclean (1915) *Typographia Scoto-Gadelica: Or Books Printed in the Gaelic of Scotland from the Year 1567 to the Year 1914 with Bibliographical and Biographical Notes*, Edinburgh: J. Grant, p. 212.

52 D.E. Meek (2001) '"*Beachdan Ura à Inbhir Nis*"/New Opinion from Inverness': Alexander MacBain (1855–1907) and the Foundation of Celtic Studies in Scotland' *Proceedings of the Society of Antiquaries of Scotland*, 131, pp. 23–39.

53 A. Cameron (1892–4) *Reliquiae Celticae: Texts, Papers, and Studies in Gaelic Literature and Philology Left by the Late Alexander Cameron; Edited by Alexander MacBain and John Kennedy*, 2 vols, Inverness: The Northern Counties Printing and Publishing Co.

54 A. MacBain (1911) *Etymological Dictionary of the Gaelic Language*, Stirling: E. Mackay, pp. xi–xii.

55 Fourth edition: E. MacEachen (1922) *Faclair Gaidhlic is Beurla*, Inverness: The Northern Counties Newspaper and Printing & Pub. Co. This edition was revised and enlarged by Dr D.J. Macleod and Mr R. Barron. Some literary words were added and some unimportant details omitted; the focus in this and in the fifth edition, also revised by Macleod and Barron, was clearly educational and pedagogical. Fifth edition: E. MacEachen (1936) *Faclair Gaidhlic is Beurla*, Inverness: The Northern Counties Newspaper and Printing & Pub. Co.

56 'Miracles of a Word Hunter', *Daily Express*, 25 August 1911.

57 W. Gillies (1991) 'Liam MacGill'Iosa: A Friend of the Gael', *Transactions of the Gaelic Society of Inverness* 56, p. 515.

58 'Miracles of a Word Hunter'.

59 Biographical details cited from 2001 edition.

60 As reported in an anonymous article entitled 'Some Notes on a Well-Known Work and its Little-Known Author', *The Celtic Review*, 15 January 1909, p. 195.

61 E. Dwelly (1911) *Faclair Gàidhlig* 3 vols, Herne Bay, vol. 1, p. iii.

62 In 'Miracles of a Word Hunter'.

63 See Dwelly, s.v. *oghum*. For the alphabet itself and the tree symbolism used in naming the letters, see D. McManus (1991) *A Guide to Ogam*, Maynooth: An Sagart, pp. 1–4 and 36–9.

64 E. Dwelly (1911) *Faclair Gàidhlig*, vol. 1, p. viii/1.

65 Ibid., vol. 1, p. i.

66 Volume 2 includes the same title page and a picture of Dwelly setting the type, while volume 3 has a picture of Dwelly printing. The third edition was published in 1918 in three volumes. It has 1,034 pages and does not include the lists of subscribers and Dwelly's complaint about lapsed subscribers. The fourth edition was published in 1930 in one volume, again with the full 1,037 pages. A further eight editions with 1,034 pages were published between 1941 and 1994. A new edition was published in 2001 by Birlinn, a reprint of the first edition, with the full 1,037 pages and a new biographical introduction by Peter Beresford Ellis. Dwelly's work is now available online, without illustrations, at 'Dwelly-d', 'The online version of Dwelly's great Scots Gaelic–English dictionary': <http://www.cairnwater.co.uk/gaelicdictionary/>.

Chapter 9

1 L. MacLean (1912) *Eachdraidhean-beatha nan Albannach iomraiteach ud: Uilleam Uallas, Iain Knox, agus Rob Ruadh*; fo laimh Chaluim Mhic Phàrlain, Struibhle: A MacAoidh.

2 See T.M. MacCalmain (1953) 'An t-Ollamh Urramach Calum MacGhillinnein', in *Turus a' Chriosduidh*, Lunnuinn: Comunn nan Trachdannan, p. 4.

3 Biographical information from radio programme 'Airidh air Urram – An t-Athair Cyril Dieckhoff', BBC Radio nan Gaidheal, 18 December 2000.

4 See H.C. Dieckhoff (1923) 'The Gaelic Dialect of Glengarry in Scotland', *Revue Celtique*, 40, pp. 391–5; (1926) 'Notes on Scottish Gaelic Dialects', *Scottish Gaelic Studies*, 1:2, pp. 188–94; (1941) 'Parallels in Gaelic and Russian Folk-Poetry', *Transactions of the Gaelic Society of Inverness*, 36, pp. 291–318.

5 For Ó Briain's collection see B. Ó Cuív (ed.) (1947) *Cnósach Focal ó Bhaile Bhúirne*, Dublin: Institiúid Ard-Léinn Bhaile Átha Cliath; for Sheehan's, see R.B. Breatnach (ed.) (1961) *Seanachaint na nDéise II, Studies in the Vocabulary and Idiom of Déise Irish Based Mainly on Material Collected by Archbishop Michael Sheehan (1870–1945)*, Dublin: Dublin Institute for Advanced Studies.

6 H.C. Dieckhoff (1923) 'The Gaelic Dialect of Glengarry in Scotland', *Revue Celtique* 40, pp. 391–5 and (1926) 'Notes on Scottish Gaelic Dialects', *Scottish Gaelic Studies*, 1, pp. 189–94.

7 M. Joynt, E.G. Quin, et al. (1939–1976) *Contributions to a Dictionary of the Irish Language: Based Mainly on Old and Middle Irish materials*, Dublin: Royal Irish Academy; compact edition (1983), Dublin: Royal Irish Academy. Now available online at the website Electronic Dictionary of the irish Language: <http://www.dil.ie/>.

8 R.J. Thomas, et al. (1950–2002) *Geiriadur Prifysgol Cymru / Dictionary of the Welsh Language*, Cardiff: Gwasg Prifysgol Cymru. A revised edition was started in 2002.

9 An Comunn Gàidhealach (n.d.), 'List of Gaelic Linguistic and Literary Terms Used in SCE Papers'.

10 R.C. Owen (1979) *Instant Gaelic: Gaelic and English in Parallel Texts, with a Complete Course of Drills for Grammar Practice*, Aberfeldy: Clò Chailleann; and (1982) *Gàidhlig le Gàire*, Aberfeldy: Clò Chailleann.

11 See T. de Bhaldraithe (1959) *Foclóir Béarla–Gaeilge/English–Irish Dictionary*, Oifig an tSoláthair, pp. v, x. Since then Niall Ó Dónaill's (1977) *Foclóir Gaeilge–Béarla*, Baile Átha Cliath: Oifig

an tSoláthair, has provided authoritative access to words and forms occurring in the Modern language, and the series of Irish dictionaries co-edited by Séamus Mac Mathúna and Ailbhe Ó Corráin have addressed the criticism levelled at de Bhaldraithe by taking on board contemporary thinking on layout, presentation and content, and at the same time the linguistic and sociolinguistic modalities specific to the Irish–English interface. See S. Mac Mathúna and A. Ó Corráin (1995) *Collins Gem Irish Dictionary*, (1997) *Collins Irish Dictionary*, express edn, and (1997) *Collins Pocket Irish Dictionary*, London: HarperCollins.

12 Also available online at <www.smo.uhi.ac.uk/gaidhlig/faclair/sbg/lorg.php>.

13 R. MacThomais (tr.) (1976) *Bith-eòlas: a'chealla, gintinneachd is mean-fhàs, le Raghnall MacLeòid*, Glasgow: Gairm.

14 A. Watson (2001) *The Essential Gaelic–English Dictionary*, Edinburgh: Birlinn, p. viii.

15 B. Robertson and I. Taylor (2003) *Teach Yourself Gaelic*, London: Teach Yourself.

16 *Gaelic Orthographic Conventions* (2009) Glasgow: Scottish Qualifications Authority.

17 See W.J. Watson (1937) *Scottish Verse from the Book of the Dean of Lismore*, Edinburgh: Oliver & Boyd, p. 328.

18 W. Gillies (1994) 'A Gaelic Thesaurus', in A. Fenton and D.A. MacDonald (eds.) *Studies in Scots and Gaelic: Proceedings of the Third International Conference on the Languages of Scotland*, Edinburgh: Canongate Academic.

19 Dr Mackie is now lecturer in Manx Studies at the Centre for Manx Studies, University of Liverpool.

Part II Postscript

1 The original is in the Special Collections of Edinburgh University Library. An attempt to prepare it for publication was made in the late 1950s under the auspices of the Linguistic Survey of Scotland; see Cathair Ó Dochartaigh (ed.) (1994–7) *Survey of the Gaelic Dialects of Scotland: Questionnaire Materials Collected for the Linguistic Survey of Scotland*, 5 vols, Dublin: Dublin Institute for Advanced Studies, vol. 1, p. 36.

2 The original is in Glasgow University Celtic Library. See A. Gunderloch (2002) 'The Quest for Gaelic: Charles Loch, Learner and Lexicographer', *Transactions of the Gaelic Society of Inverness*, 62 (2000–2), pp. 110–55 (pp. 134–40).

3 Some of these are mentioned by Kenneth MacDonald in his article 'Dictionaries, Scottish Gaelic', in D.S. Thomson (1983) *The Companion to Gaelic Scotland*, Oxford: Blackwell, pp. 61–3.

4 A critical evaluation of this by Dr Wilson McLeod (2001) can be retrieved from the 'Research on Language Policy and Language Planning' page for Celtic and Scottish Studies at the University of Edinburgh, at: <www.arts.ed.ac.uk/celtic/poileasaidh/faclairrep.pdf>.

5 References to these can be found in such sources as the NLS Gaelic MSS Catalogues, in the indexes to the *Transactions of the Gaelic Society of Inverness*, in the Bibliography of volume 1 of Ó Dochartaigh, *Survey of the Gaelic Dialects*, (see note 1 above), and in the ongoing 'Bibliography of Irish Literature and Linguistics', School of Celtic Studies, Dublin Institute for Advanced Studies, most easily consulted online at: <http://bill.celt.dias.ie/>.

6 See Chapter 8, note 66

Chapter 10

1 See James Boswell (1791; reprinted 2008) *The Life of Samuel Johnson*, London: Penguin, p. 307.

2 In a letter to James Boswell; see Boswell (2008 edn), p. 751.

3 There were earlier, small English dictionaries produced in Scotland, especially for schools; for example, MacEwing's *A New Vocabulary for the Use of Schools* (see Chapter 8).

4 James Buchanan (1757) *Linguae Britannicae vera pronunciatio*, London: printed for A. Millar, Preface, p. xii.

5 William Perry (1775) *Royal Standard English Dictionary*, Edinburgh: printed for the author, Preface.

6 The National Library of Scotland notes that this was first published in 1777, but no record of this edition exists.

7 William Scott (1786) *A New Spelling, Pronouncing and Explanatory Dictionary of the English Language*, Edinburgh: printed for C. Elliott, title page.

8 Michael Hancher suggests that the illustration of *The Popular Encylopaedia* and a subsequent Blackie publication, Oliver Goldsmith's *History of the Earth, and Animated Nature* (1840), created 'a climate of expectation' in that the illustration of any dictionary 'became virtually inevitable'. See Hancher (1998), 'Gazing at the Imperial Dictionary', *Book History*, 1, pp. 157–81.

9 Blackie had a more direct connection with Chambers, having published Robert Chambers' *Lives of Eminent Scotsmen* (1832 and 1834).

10 John Ogilvie (1883) *The Imperial Dictionary*, ed. Charles Annandale, Glasgow, Edinburgh, London: Blackie and Son, Preface, p. viii.

11 Ibid., p. vi.

12 Ibid., p. vii.

13 William Dwight Whitney (ed.) (1889) *The Century Dictionary and Cyclopedia*, New York: The Century Co, vol. 1, Preface, p. v.

14 Ibid., p. ii.

15 John Boag (1848) *A Popular and Complete English Dictionary*, Glasgow: William Collins, Preface.

16 William Chambers (1872) *Memoir of Robert Chambers*, Edinburgh: W. & R. Chambers, pp. 267–8.

17 Ibid., p. 268.

18 Arnold J. Cooley (1861) *A Dictionary of the English Language*, Edinburgh: W. & R. Chambers, Preface, p. iii.

19 James Donald (1867) *Chambers's Etymological Dictionary of the English Language*, Edinburgh: W. & R. Chambers, Preface, p. v.

20 Walter W. Skeat (1882) *An Etymological Dictionary of the English Language*, Oxford: The Clarendon Press, p. 2.

21 Obituary in *The Scotsman*, 17 January 2006, also available online at: <http://news.scotsman.com/obituaries/Catherine-Schwarz.2742792.jp>.

22 For a full biography, see K.M. Elisabeth Murray (1977) *Caught in the Web of Words*, New Haven and London: Yale University Press.

23 In 1857, Richard Chevenix Trench, a member of the Philological Society's 'Unregistered Words Committee', delivered a two-part paper, 'On Some Deficiencies in our English Dictionaries'. The original aim of the committee had been to identify words and meanings not recorded in contemporary English dictionaries and collect these in a separate work; by 1858, the society had

passed a proposal to produce an entirely new, complete dictionary.

24 Work on the dictionary had begun briskly, with a reading programme for word collection using over seventy volunteers, a practice borrowed from the *Deutsches Wörterbuch* of the Grimm brothers in Germany. By 1871, however, work had stalled.

25 Murray was not recognised as a lexicographer and was not first choice. Phonetician Henry Sweet had already turned the job down when Murray was approached; Sweet's cousin Henry Nicol agreed to take on the role but was prevented by ill-health from doing so. Early in 1876 a Scot, William Johnston Anderson, from Markinch in Fife, offered to take on the editorship of the dictionary, but his offer was declined. Anderson was, however, a reader for the *OED* and later involved in its sub-editing.

26 OUP archives, ref. OED/B/3/1/4: 'Report of Work done and Progress made in connexion with the New English Dictionary to 1st March 1880'.

27 The first parts were published under the title *A New English Dictionary on Historical Principles, Founded Mainly on Materials Collected by the Philological Society*. In 1895 the title *Oxford English Dictionary* began to appear on the covers and wrappers of the fascicles, though not on the title pages. It was not until 1933 that the whole was reissued as the *Oxford English Dictionary*.

28 OUP archives, secretary's letterbooks: letter from P. L. Gell, Secretary to the Delegates, to H. Bradley 12 April 1888.

29 With thanks to Peter Gilliver for the information on assistants and readers.

30 Murray, *Caught in the Web*, p. 292.

31 OUP archives: letter from J.A.H. Murray to W.A. Craigie, 3 December 1902.

32 See M.M. Mathews (1985) 'George Watson and the Dictionary of American English', *Dictionaries*, 7, pp. 214–24.

33 NLS MS 3219.f158; quoted in Richard W. Bailey, 'National and Regional Dictionaries of English', in A.P. Cowie (ed.) (2009) *The Oxford History of English Lexicography*, 2 vols, Oxford: Clarendon Press, vol. 1, p. 284.

34 OUP archives, ref. OED/B/3/8/5

35 This and other aspects of pronunciation are discussed in Michael K.C. MacMahon, 'Pronunciation in the *OED*', in Lynda Mugglestone (ed.) (2000) *Lexicography and the OED: Pioneers in the Untrodden Forest*, Oxford: Oxford University Press, p. 174.

36 See Stanley Baldwin (1928) *The Oxford English Dictionary, 1884–1928*, Oxford: Clarendon Press, an address delivered in Goldsmiths' Hall, 6 June 1928 by the Rt. Hon. Stanley Baldwin. Available online in facsimile form at: <http://oed.hertford.ox.ac.uk/main/content/view/275/351/>.

37 The *Thesaurus of Old English* was co-authored by Jane Roberts and Christian Kay with Lynne Grundy, and published by the Centre for Late Antique and Medieval Studies, King's College, London in 1995.

Bibliography

Dictionaries and Word Lists

[Anon.] (1827) *A Dictionary of the Scottish Language; Founded upon that of John Jamieson*, Edinburgh: Archibald Allardice.

Allan, Robert (1807) *Number First of a Dictionary of the Ancient Language of Scotland*, Edinburgh: printed by John Moir.

Angus, James Stout (1914) *A Glossary of the Shetland Dialect*, Paisley: A. Gardner.

Angus, William (1814) *A Pronouncing Vocabulary of the English Language, 5th edn*, Glasgow: printed for the author, Brash and Reid.

Annandale, Charles (1886) *A Concise Dictionary of the English Language*, London: Blackie and Son.

Armstrong, Robert (1825) *A Gaelic Dictionary in Two Parts . . .*, London: J. Duncan.

Ayton, William (1811) *General View of the Agriculture of the County of Ayr*, Glasgow.

Bailey, Nathan (1760) *Universal Etymological English Dictionary*, 5th edn, London: printed for W. Johnston.

Barclay, Hugh (1852) *A Digest of the Law of Scotland, with Special Reference to the Office and Duties of a Justice of the Peace*, Edinburgh.

Barclay, James (1774) *A Complete and Universal Dictionary of the English Language*, London.

Barrie, Alexander (1794) *A Spelling and Pronouncing Dictionary of the English Language for the Use of Schools*, Edinburgh: printed for the author.

Barrowman, James (1886) *Glossary of Scotch Mining Terms*, Hamilton: printed at the *Advertiser* office.

Beaton, John Angus (1982) *Scots Law Terms and Expressions*, Edinburgh: W. Green.

Beattie, James (1779) *Scoticisms, Arranged in Alphabetical Order, Designed to Correct Improprieties of Speech and Writing*, Aberdeen.

Bell, Robert (1807) *Dictionary of the Law of Scotland Intended for the Use of the Public at Large, as Well as of the Profession*, 3rd edn (1826) revised by William Bell, Edinburgh: John Anderson.

Bell, William (1838) *Dictionary and Digest of the Law of Scotland*, Edinburgh.

Bell, William (1882) *Bell's Dictionary and Digest of the Law of Scotland / adapted to the present state of the law and in great part re-written by George Watson*, Edinburgh.

Bhaldraithe, Tomás de (1959) *Foclóir Béarla–Gaeilge/English–Irish Dictionary*, Oifig an tSoláthair.

Boag, John (1848) *A Popular and Complete English Dictionary*, Glasgow: William Collins.

Boucher, Jonathan (1807) *A Supplement to Dr. Johnson's Dictionary of the English Language: or, A Glossary of Obsolete and Provincial Words*, part I, London: printed for Longman, Hurst, Rees, and Orme.

Braidwood, J. (1965b–87) 'Bird Names in Ulster: A Glossary', *Ulster Folklife* 11 (1965b), pp. 98–135; 12 (1966), pp. 104–7; 17 (1971), pp. 81–4; 24 (1978), pp. 83–7; 33 (1987), pp. 83–5.

Brown, Captain Thomas (1845) *A Dictionary of the Scottish Language*, London: Simpkin & Marshall.

Brown, Lesley (ed.) (1993) *The New Shorter Oxford English Dictionary*, Oxford: Oxford University Press.

Buchan, Peter and Toulmin, David (1989) *Buchan Claik: The Saut an the Glaur o't: A Compendium of Words and Phrases from the North-East of Scotland*, Edinburgh: Gordon Wright.

Buchanan, James (1757) *Linguae Britannicae Vera Pronunciatio: Or, a New English Dictionary*, London: printed for A. Millar.

Buchanan, James (1766) *Essay towards Establishing a Standard for an Elegant and Uniform Pronunciation of the English Language*, London: printed for Edward and Charles Dilly.

Burn, John (1777) *A Pronouncing Dictionary of the English Language*, Glasgow: printed by Rob Chapman and Alex Duncan.

Burness, Lawrence R. (1997) *A Scottish Historian's Glossary*, Aberdeen: Scottish Association of Family History Societies.

Burns, Robert (1786) *Poems, Chiefly in the Scottish Dialect*, Kilmarnock: John Wilson.

Burns, Robert (1787) *Poems, Chiefly in the Scottish Dialect*, Edinburgh: William Creech.

Cabinet Dictionary of the English Language, The (1871), Glasgow: William Collins.

Carmichael, James (1587) *Grammaticae Latinae, de Etymologia, Liber Secundus*, Cambridge: Thomas Thomas, printer to the University.

Christie-Johnston, Alastair and Adaline (2010) *Shetland Words: A Dictionary of the Shetland Dialect*, Lerwick: Shetland Times.

[Cleishbotham the Younger] (1858) *A Handbook of the Scottish Language*, Edinburgh: J. L. Smith; reissued (1975) as *The Old Scots Tongue: 5,000 Scottish Words and their Meanings*, Lang Syne.

Clyne, Douglas (1985) *An English–Gaelic Dictionary of Expressions, Idioms and Phrases*, Glasgow: Gairm.

Collins Gem Scots Dictionary (1995), reissued as *Collins Scots Dictionary* (2003), Glasgow: Collins.

Collins' Home Dictionary of the English Language (1908), Glasgow: William Collins.

Collins' National Dictionary and Encyclopedia (1932), Glasgow: William Collins.

Cooley, Arnold J. (1861) *A Dictionary of the English Language*, Edinburgh: W. & R. Chambers.

Cox, Richard A.V. (1991, 2007) *Brìgh nam Facal: Faclair ùr don bhun-sgoil*, Glaschu: Roinn nan Cànan Ceilteach, Oilthigh Ghlaschu.

Craig, John (1848) *A New Universal Etymological, Technological, and Pronouncing Dictionary of the English Language*, London: Henry George Collins.

Craigie, W. A., Aitken, A. J., et al. (eds) (1931–2001) *A Dictionary of the Older Scottish Tongue: From the Twelfth Century to the End of the Seventeenth*, 12 vols, London: Oxford University Press; available online at: <http://www.dsl.ac.uk/>.

Craigie, William A. and Hulbert, James R. (1938–44) *A Dictionary of American English on Historical Principles*, Chicago: University of Chicago Press.

Dalrymple, David, Lord Hailes (1770) *Ancient Scottish Poems, Published from the MS. of George Bannatyne*. Edinburgh: John Balfour.

Davidson, R. (1872) *Chambers's English Dictionary*, London and Edinburgh: W. & R. Chambers.

Davidson, R. (1901) *Chambers's Twentieth Century Dictionary*, London and Edinburgh: W. & R. Chambers.

Dictionary of the Derivations of the English Language, in which Each Word is Traced to its Primary Root, A (1872), Glasgow: William Collins.

Dictionary of the Scots Language, available online at: <www.dsl.ac.uk>.

Dieckhoff, Henry C. (1932) *A Pronouncing Dictionary of Scottish Gaelic: Based on the Glengarry Dialect . . .*, Edinburgh: W. & A.K. Johnston; reprinted (1992), Glasgow: Gairm Publications.

Donald, James (1867) *Chambers's Etymological Dictionary of the English Language*, Edinburgh: W. & R. Chambers.

Donald, Janine (2009) *The Cromarty Fisherfolk Dialect, Dualchainnt Iasgairean Chrombaidh*, Inverness: Am Baile.

Duncan, Andrew (1595) *Latinae Grammaticae pars prior, sive Etymologia Latina in usum rudiorum*, Edinburgh: printed by Robert Waldgrave.

Dwelly, Edward (1902–11) *A Gaelic Dictionary . . .*, Herne Bay: E. Macdonald; reissued (1911) as *The Illustrated Gaelic–English Dictionary . . .*, Herne Bay: E. Dwelly; reprinted (2001), Edinburgh: Birlinn.

Dwelly, Edward (1991) *Appendix to Dwelly's Gaelic–English Dictionary: Compiled by Edward Dwelly; Edited by Douglas Clyne, Completed by Derick Thomson*, Glasgow: Gairm.

Edmondston, Thomas (1866) *An Etymological Glossary of the Shetland and Orkney Dialect*, London: The Philological Society.

Fenton, James (1995, 2000, 2006) *The Hamely Tongue: A Personal Record of Ulster-Scots in County Antrim*, 1st edn, Newtownards, Ulster-Scots Academic Press for the Ulster-Scots Language Society); 2nd and 3rd edns Belfast, Ullans Press.

Flaws, Margaret and Lamb, Gregor (1996) *The Orkney Dictionary*, Kirkwall: Orkney Language and Culture Group.

Forbes, Robert (1755) *Ajax his Speech to the Grecian Knabbs, from Ovid's Metam. Lib. XIII. . . . Attempted in Broad Buchans. To which are Added A Journal to Portsmouth, and a Shop-Bill, in the Same Dialect. With a Key. By R— F— Gent.*, Glasgow.

Gem English Dictionary (1902), Glasgow: William Collins.

Gibb, Andrew Dewar (1946) *Students' Glossary of Scottish Legal Terms,* new edn (1982) (ed.) A.G.M. Duncan, Edinburgh: W. Green.

Glossary: Scottish Legal Terms and Latin Maxims and European Community Legal Terms (1992), Edinburgh: Law Society of Scotland: Butterworths; reissued (2003) as *Glossary of Scottish and European Union Legal Terms and Latin Phrases,* Edinburgh: Law Society of Scotland: LexisNexis UK.

Graham, John (1979, 1984, 1993, 1999) *The Shetland Dictionary,* Lerwick, Shetland Times.

Graham, William (1977) *The Scots Word Book,* Edinburgh: Ramsay Head Press.

Grant, William and Murison, David D. (eds) (1931–76) *The Scottish National Dictionary,* 12 vols, Edinburgh: Scottish National Dictionary Association.

Gray, Adam (1997) *A Scots Agricultural Glossary,* Dumfries: Dumfries & Galloway Family History Society.

Gregor, Walter (1866) *The Dialect of Banffshire with a Glossary of Words not in Jamieson's Scottish Dictionary,* London: The Philological Society.

Hanks, Patrick (ed.) (1979) *Collins Dictionary of the English Language,* London and Glasgow: Collins.

Harper, Norman (1998) *Spik o the Place,* Edinburgh: Canongate.

Harper, Norman (2009) *Spikkin Doric: A Doric Word Book,* Edinburgh: Birlinn.

Household Dictionary of the English Language, The (?1869) Glasgow: William Collins.

Hume, David (1760) 'Scoticisms', *Scots Magazine,* vol. 22, pp. 686–7.

Illustrated National Pronouncing Dictionary of the English Language, The (1869) Glasgow: William Collins.

Imperial Lexicon of the English Language, The (1852–3), Edinburgh: A. Fullarton.

Irvine, A.H. (1956) *Collins New English Dictionary,* Glasgow: William Collins.

Jakobsen, Jakob (1908–21) *Etymologisk Ordbog over det Norrøne Sprog på Shetland,* Copenhagen: Vilhelm Prior. Translated (1928–32) as *An Etymological Dictionary of the Norn Language in Shetland,* 2 vols, London: David Nutt; reprinted (n.d.) New York: AMS Press; and (1985) Shetland Folk Society.

Jamieson, John (1808) *An Etymological Dictionary of the Scottish Language,* 2 vols, Edinburgh: printed at the University Press.

Jamieson, John (1818) *An Etymological Dictionary of the Scottish Language . . . Abridged from the Quarto Edition,* Edinburgh: Archibald Constable & Co., and Alexander Jameson.

Jamieson, John (1825) *Supplement to the Etymological Dictionary of the Scottish Language* 2 vols, Edinburgh: printed at the University Press for W. & C. Tait.

Jamieson, John (1840–1) *An Etymological Dictionary of the Scottish Language . . . The Second Edition, Carefully Revised and Collated, . . . by John Johnstone,* 2 vols, Edinburgh: William Tait.

Jamieson, John (1846) *A Dictionary of the Scottish Language . . . Abridged from the Dictionary and Supplement . . . by John Johnstone,* Edinburgh: William Tait.

Jamieson, John (1867) *Jamieson's Dictionary of the Scottish Language . . . Abridged by John*

Johnston [sic]. A New Edition, Revised and Enlarged, by John Longmuir, A.M., LL.D., Edinburgh: W. P. Nimmo.

Jamieson, John (1879–82) *An Etymological Dictionary of the Scottish Language . . . A New Edition, Carefully Revised and Collated . . . by John Longmuir, A.M., LL.D., and David Donaldson, F.E.I.S.*, 4 vols, Paisley: Alexander Gardner.

Jamieson, John (1910) *Jamieson's Dictionary of the Scottish Language, Abridged . . . with Supplement to which is Prefixed an Introduction by W. M. Metcalfe*, Paisley: Alexander Gardner.

Jarvie, James Nicol (1947) *Lallans: A Selection of Scots Words Arranged as an English–Scots Dictionary with Pronunciation and Examples*, London.

Johnson, Samuel (1755) *A Dictionary of the English Language*, London: printed by W. Strahan for J. and P. Knapton, et al.

Johnston, A.H. (ed.) (1928) *Everywoman's Dictionary*, Glasgow: William Collins.

Johnston, William (1772) *A Pronouncing and Spelling Dictionary*, 2nd edn, London: printed for W. Johnston.

Joynt, M, Quin, E.G. et al. (1939–1976) *Contributions to a Dictionary of the Irish Language: Based Mainly on Old and Middle Irish Materials*, Dublin: Royal Irish Academy. Compact edition (1983), Dublin: Royal Irish Academy. Available online at <http://www.dil.ie/>.

Kay, Christian and Roberts, Jane with Grundy, Lynne (1995) *A Thesaurus of Old English*, London: King's College.

Kay, Christian, Roberts, Jane, et al. (2009) *Historical Thesaurus of the Oxford English Dictionary*, Oxford: Oxford University Press.

Kenrick, W. (1773) *New Dictionary of the English Language*, London: printed for John and Francis Rivington.

Kerr, R.D. (ed.) (1980) *A Glossary of Mining Terms Used in Fife*, Kirkcaldy: Fife Colleges.

Kirkpatrick, Betty (2006) *The Concise Dictionary of Scottish Words and Phrases*, Edinburgh: Crombie Jardine.

Kurath, Hans et al. (eds) (1952–2001) *Middle English Dictionary*, Ann Arbor: University of Michigan Press.

Kynoch, Douglas (1996, 2004) *A Doric Dictionary. Two-way Lexicon of North-East Scots. Doric–English, English–Doric*, Dalkeith: Scottish Cultural Press.

Lamb, Gregor (1988, 1995) *Orkney Wordbook. A Dictionary of the Dialect of Orkney*, Birsay: Byrgisey.

Leslie, William (1811) *General View of the Agriculture in the Counties of Nairn and Moray*, London: Richard Phillips.

Library Dictionary of the English Language, The (1871), Glasgow: William Collins.

Macafee, Caroline (1996) *A Concise Ulster Dictionary*, Oxford University Press.

MacAlpine, Neil (1832) *The Argyleshire Pronouncing Gaelic Dictionary . . .*, Edinburgh; reissued (1833) as *A Pronouncing Gaelic Dictionary . . .*, Edinburgh: Stirling & Kenney; Glasgow: Reid & Co.; London: James Duncan; Dublin: John Cumming. Second edition with numerous improvements and additions; many subsequent reprints.

MacBain, Alexander (1896) *An Etymological Dictionary of the Gaelic Language*, Inverness: The Northern Counties Printing and Publishing Co.; 2nd edn (1911), Stirling: E. Mackay; 2nd revised edn (1982), Glasgow: Gairm.

McCluskey, Mick (1990, 2005) *Dundonian for Beginners*, Edinburgh: Mainstream (2005); London: Intro2 Publishing.

MacDonald, Alexander (1741) *A Galick and English Vocabulary/Leabhar a theagasc ainminnin . . .*, Edinburgh: Robert Fleming.

McDonald, Allan (1958, 1991) *Gaelic Words and Expressions from South Uist and Eriskay*, Dublin: Dublin Institute for Advanced Studies.

MacDonald, J.A. and Renton, R. (1979) *Abair Faclan!* Glasgow: Mingulay Publications.

MacEachen, Eobhan (1842) *Faclair Gailig us Beurla*, Peirt: R. Morison; reissued as *Faclair Gaidhlic is Beurla*, 2nd (1902) and 3rd (?1906) editions revised and enlarged by A. MacBain and J. Whyte, Inverness: Taylor & Bain; 4th (1922) and 5th (1936) editions revised and enlarged by D.J. Macleod and R. Barron, Inverness: The Northern Counties Newspaper and Printing & Pub. Co.

Mac Farlan, R. (1795) *Nuadh Fhoclair Gaidhlig agus Beurla . . .*, Edinburgh: E. Moir.

MacFarlane, Malcolm (1912) *The School Gaelic Dictionary . . .*, Stirling: E. Mackay; reissued (1948) as *Gaelic–English Dictionary*, Stirling: E. Mackay.

MacFarlane, Patrick/Peter (1815) *Focalair Ùr Gaelig agus Beurla . . .*, Edinburgh: A. Constable.

MacGill'Fhinnein, F. (1993) *Stòr-Dàta Briathrachais Gàidhlig/The Gaelic Terminology Database*, An Teanga: Clò Ostaig.

McInnes, L. (1936) *The Dialect of South Kintyre*, Campbeltown: *Campbeltown Courier*.

McIntosh, E. (1951, 4th edn; 1964, 5th edn) *The Concise Oxford Dictionary*, Oxford: Oxford University Press.

Mackay, Charles (1888) *A Dictionary of Lowland Scotch*, London: Whittaker and Co.

Mackay, Charles (1882) *The Poetry and Humour of the Scottish Language*, Paisley: Alexander Gardner .

MacKenzie, John (1847) *An English–Gaelic Dictionary; Being Part Second of the Pronouncing Gaelic Dictionary*, Edinburgh: Maclachlan, Stewart and Company.

Mackenzie, Sir George (1694) *The Institutions of the Law of Scotland . . . With an Alphabetical Explanation of the Most Difficult Scots Words*, 3rd edn, London: printed for Andrew Bell and Jonas Luntley.

Mackie, Albert (1978) *Talking Glasgow*, Belfast: Blackstaff.

Mackie, Albert (1984) *The Illustrated Glasgow Glossary: Awra Words Awragirra*, Belfast: Blackstaff.

MacKinnon, Iain (1966) *Lowland Scots Glossary*, Stirling.

MacLennan, Malcolm (1925) *A Pronouncing and Etymological Dictionary of the Gaelic Language*, Edinburgh: J. Grant.

Macleod, Iseabail and Cairns, Pauline (1993) *The Concise English–Scots Dictionary*, Edinburgh: Chambers.

Macleod, Iseabail and Cairns, Pauline (1996) *The Scots School Dictionary: Scots–English,*

English–Scots, Edinburgh: Chambers; later reissued as *The Essential Scots Dictionary*, Edinburgh: Edinburgh University Press.

Macleod, Iseabail, Cairns, Pauline, Macafee, Caroline and Martin, Ruth (1990) *The Scots Thesaurus*, Aberdeen: Aberdeen University Press.

Macleod, Iseabail, Martin, Ruth and Cairns, Pauline (1988) *The Pocket Scots Dictionary*, Aberdeen: Aberdeen University Press.

Macleod, John et al. (1828) *Dictionarium Scoto-Celticum: A Dictionary of the Gaelic Language; . . . Compiled and Published under the Direction of the Highland Society of Scotland*, Edinburgh: Blackwood; London: T. Cadell.

MacLeod, Norman, and Dewar, Daniel (1831) *A Dictionary of the Gaelic Language*, Glasgow: W.R. M'Phun.

McLeod, William T. (1984) *The New Collins Thesaurus*, Glasgow: Collins.

MacTaggart, John (1824) *The Scottish Gallovidian Encyclopedia*, London: printed for the author; reprinted (1981), Strath Tay: Clunie Press.

Malzahn, Manfred (2005) *Scots die Sprache der Schotten*, 4th printing, Bielefeld: Peter Rump.

Mark, Colin (2003) *The Gaelic–English Dictionary*, London and New York: Routledge.

Marwick, Hugh (1929, 1992) *The Orkney Norn*, Dunfermline: W.I.A. Murray; originally published (1929), London: Oxford University Press.

Miller, James (2001) *A Caithness Word Book*, Wick: North of Scotland Newspapers.

Mitchell, James (1799) *Scotticisms, Vulgar Anglicisms and Grammatical Improprieties Corrected, with Reasons for the Corrections*, Glasgow: Falconer and Willison.

Montgomerie-Fleming, J.B. (1899) *Desultory Notes on Jamieson's Scottish Dictionary*, Glasgow and Edinburgh: William Hodge & Company.

Motherby, Robert (1826) *Taschen-Wörterbuch des Schottischen Dialekts, or, Pocket Dictionary of the Scottish Idiom*, Königsberg: printed for Brothers Borntraeger.

Munro, Michael (1996, 2006) *The Complete Patter*, Edinburgh: Birlinn (incorporating *The Patter: A Guide to Current Glasgow Usage* (1985), Glasgow District Libraries, and *The Patter. Another Blast* (1988), Edinburgh: Canongate.)

Murray, James A.H., et al. (eds) (1884–1928) *A New English Dictionary on Historical Principles*, Oxford: The Clarendon Press.

Murray, James A.H., et al. (eds) (1933) *The Oxford English Dictionary*, being a corrected reissue with Supplement, Oxford: The Clarendon Press.

New Vocabulary English and Latine, for the Use of young scholars, A (1702) Edinburgh: Andrew Symson; reissued (1720) as *New Vocabulary English & Latin, A: for the Use of Schools, To which is added a collection of the most common adjectives and adverbs*, Edinburgh: Mr James McEuen; and (1749) Edinburgh: T. & W. Ruddiman.

O'Brien, John (1768) *Focalóir gaoidhilge-sax-bhéarla or an Irish–English Dictionary*, Paris: printed by Nicolas-Francis Valleyre, for the author.

Ó Dónaill, Niall (1977) *Foclóir Gaeilge-Béarla*, Baile Átha Cliath: Oifig an tSoláthair.

O'Kane, William (1991) *You Don't Say: The Tyrone Crystal Book of Ulster Dialect*, Dungannon: Irish World.

O'Reilly, Edward (1817) *An Irish-English Dictionary . . .*, Dublin: J. Barlow.

O'Rourke, Stephen E. (2009) *Glossary of Legal Terms*, Edinburgh: W. Green.

Ogilvie, John (1847–8) *The Imperial Dictionary*, Glasgow; Edinburgh; London: Blackie and Son.

Ogilvie, John (1865) *The Student's English Dictionary*, London: Blackie and Son.

Ogilvie, John (1883) *The Imperial Dictionary*, revised, augmented and edited by Charles Annandale, Glasgow, Edinburgh, London: Blackie and Son.

Owen, Robert C. (1993) *The Modern Gaelic–English Dictionary*, Glasgow: Gairm.

Patterson, William H. (1880) *A Glossary of Words in Use in the Counties of Antrim and Down*, London: Trübner for the English Dialect Society.

Perry, William (1775) *Royal Standard English Dictionary*, Edinburgh: printed for the author.

Perry, William (1776) *The Only Sure Guide to the English Tongue: or, New Pronouncing Spelling Book*, Edinburgh: printed by Gavin Alston for the author.

[Picken, Ebenezer] (1818) *A Dictionary of the Scottish Language*. Edinburgh: printed for James Sawers; 4th edn (1827), Edinburgh: printed for John Dick & Co.

Pride, Glen L. (1975) *Glossary of Scottish Building*, Glasgow: Scottish Civic Trust.

Pride, Glen L. (1996) *Dictionary of Scottish Building*, Edinburgh: Rutland Press, Historic Scotland

Ramsay, Allan (1721) *Poems*, Edinburgh: Thomas Ruddiman.

Ramsay, Allan (1724) *The Ever Green, being a Collection of Scots Poems, Wrote by the Ingenious before 1600*, Edinburgh: Thomas Ruddiman.

Ramsay, Allan (1727) *Poems*, Edinburgh: Thomas Ruddiman.

Ramsay, Allan (1730) *The Tea-Table Miscellany, or Allan Ramsay's Collection of Scots Sangs*, London: J. Watson.

Ray, John (1675) *Dictionariolum Trilingue*, London: Burrel.

Rennie, Susan (1998) *CannieSpell: An Electronic Scots Spellchecker*, Edinburgh: SNDA.

Rennie, Susan (1998) *Electronic Scots School Dictionary*, Edinburgh: SNDA.

Rennie, Susan (1999) *Grammar Broonie: A Guide tae Scots Grammar*, Edinburgh: SNDA.

Riach, W.A.D. (1988) *A Galloway Glossary*, Glasgow: Association for Scottish Literary Studies, Occasional Papers 7.

Robertson, Boyd and MacDonald, Ian (2004) *Gaelic Dictionary*, London: Hodder Headline; reissued with minor corrections and some additions (2010) as *Essential Gaelic Dictionary*, London: Hodder Education.

Robinson, Mairi (1985) *The Concise Scots Dictionary*, Aberdeen University Press.

Ross, Alexander (1778) *Helenore, or, The Fortunate Shepherdess, a Poem in the Broad Scotch Dialect; By Alexander Ross, A. M. Schoolmaster at Lochlee. To which are Added, Songs by the Same Author, and a Glossary.* Aberdeen: J. Chalmers & Co.

Ross, David and Smith, Gavin D. (2007) *Scots–English, English–Scots Dictionary*, New Lanark: Geddes & Grosset.

Ruddiman, Thomas (1710) *Virgil's Aeneis, Translated into Scottish Verse, By the Famous Gawin Douglas Bishop of Dunkeld.* Edinburgh: Printed by Mr Andrew Symson and

Mr Robert Freebairn.

School Dictionary, The (1867), London: Blackie and Son.

Scots Dictionary Online (*Scots-Online: Pittin the Mither Tongue on the Wab*), <www.scots-online.org/dictionary/>.

Scots Travelmate: a Wordbook for Scotland, The (2005) Glasgow: Lexus.

Scott, W.A. and Anderson, I.G. (1998) *A Mid-Nithsdale Glossary: Dumfriesshire Dialect Seventy Years Ago*, Thornhill: Addendum Books; originally published (1925/6) in the *Transactions of the Dumfriesshire and Galloway Natural History and Antiquarian Society*.

Scott, William (1786) *A New Spelling, Pronouncing and Explanatory Dictionary of the English Language*, Edinburgh: printed for C. Elliott, Edinburgh.

Scott, William (1796) *An Introduction to Reading and Spelling*, Edinburgh: printed by Alex Chapman and Company.

Shaw, Rev. William (1780) *A Galic and English Dictionary . . .*, London: W. and A. Strahan.

Shirrefs, Andrew (1790) *Poems, Chiefly in the Scottish Dialect*. Edinburgh, Printed for the author, by D. Willison.

Sibbald, James (1802) *Chronicle of Scottish Poetry from the Thirteenth Century to the Union of the Crowns, to which is Added a Glossary*, Edinburgh: Sibbald.

Sinclair, Sir John (1782) *Observations on the Scottish Dialect*. London.

Sinclair, J.M. (1987) *Collins COBUILD English Language Dictionary*, London and Glasgow: Collins.

Skeat, Walter W. (1882) *An Etymological Dictionary of the English Language*, Oxford: The Clarendon Press.

Skene, Sir John (1681; first published 1597) *De Verborum Significatione. The exposition of the termes and difficill wordes, conteined in the foure buikes of Regiam Majestatem, and uthers, in the Acts of Parliament, infestments, and used in the practique of this realme, with diverse rules, and common places, or principalles of the lawes. Collected and exponed be M. John Skene, clerke of our Soveraine Lordis register, councell and rolles. And now re-printed by His Majestie's special command*, Edinburgh: printed by David Lindsay, anno Dom. M.D.C. LXXXI, 2nd edn, 1599.

Stein, J. and Urdang, L. (1966) *The Random House Dictionary of the English Language, Unabridged*, New York: Random House.

Stevenson, David (1963) *En Liten Skotsk–Norsk Ordliste: A Short Scots–Norwegian Wordlist*, Fort Johnston.

Stevenson, James A.C. (1989) *Scoor-oot: A Dictionary of Scots Words and Phrases in Current Use*, London: Athlone Press.

Sutherland, Iain (1992) *The Caithness Dictionary*, Wick: published by the author.

Thomas, Richard J. et al. (1950–2002) *Geiriadur Prifysgol Cymru/Dictionary of the Welsh Language*, Cardiff: Gwasg Prifysgol Cymru.

Thomson, Derick S. (1981, new edns 1994, 2004) *The New English–Gaelic Dictionary*, Glasgow: Gairm.

Transactions of the Scottish Dialects Committee (1914–21), Aberdeen: The Committee.

Trayner, John (1861) *Latin Maxims and Phrases Collected from the Institutional and Other Writers on Scotch Law with Translations and Illustrations*, Edinburgh: Patterson.

Traynor, Michael (1953) *The English Dialect of Donegal: A Glossary Incorporating the Collections of H.C. Hart, etc.*, Dublin: Royal Irish Academy.

Walker, John (1791) *A Critical Pronouncing Dictionary*, London: sold by G.G.J. and J. Robinson.

Wallace, J. (1693) Description *of the Isles of Orkney*, Edinburgh.

Warrack, Alexander (1911) *Scots Dialect Dictionary*; later *Chambers Scots Dictionary*, Edinburgh: Chambers.

Watson, Angus (2001, 2004) *The Essential Gaelic–English Dictionary*, Edinburgh: Birlinn.

Watson, Angus (2005) *The Essential English–Gaelic Dictionary*, Edinburgh: Birlinn; both reissued as one volume (2010), *The Essential Gaelic–English/English–Gaelic Dictionary*, Edinburgh: Birlinn.

Watson, George (1923) *The Roxburghshire Word-Book, Being a Record of the Special Vernacular Vocabulary of the County of Roxburgh with an Appendix of Specimens*, Cambridge: Cambridge University Press.

Watt, Robert (1989) *A Glossary of Scottish Dialect Fish and Trade Names*, Scottish Fisheries Information Pamphlet No.17, Department of Agriculture and Fisheries for Scotland, Marine Laboratory, Aberdeen.

Webster, Noah (1859) *An American Dictionary of the English Language*, Springfield, MA: G. & C. Merriam.

Wedderburn, David (1685) *Vocabula, Cum aliis nonnullis Latinae Linguae Subsidiis. In eorum gratiam, qui prima Latini Sermonis tyrocinia faciunt*, Edinburgh: Heirs of Andrew Anderson.

Wentworth, Roy (1993) *Gaelic Words and Phrases from Wester Ross*, Inverness: Comhairle nan Sgoiltean Araich; reissued (2003) Inbhir Nis: CLÀR.

West Lothian Broadly Scots Group (2008) *Scots Words and Their Meanings as Used in West Lothian*, 2nd edn, West Lothian: The West Lothian Broadly Scots Group.

Whitney, William Dwight (ed.) (1889–91) *The Century Dictionary and Cyclopedia*, New York: The Century Co.

Williams, A.M. (1903) *Collins' Graphic English Dictionary*, Glasgow: William Collins.

Wilson, Sir James (1915) *Lowland Scotch as Spoken in the Lower Strathearn District of Perthshire*, Oxford University Press.

Wilson, Sir James (1923) *The Dialect of Robert Burns as Spoken in Central Ayrshire*, London.

Wilson, Sir James (1926) *The Dialects of Central Scotland*, London.

Wilson, William Morrice (1993) *Speak o' the North-East*, Dundee: NES Publications.

Worcester, Joseph E. (1846) *A Universal and Critical Dictionary of the English Language*, Boston: Wilkins, Carter and Co.

Worcester, Joseph E. (1861) *A Critical and Pronouncing Dictionary of the English Language*, Glasgow: William Collins.

Wright, Joseph (1896–1905) *English Dialect Dictionary*, London: Henry Frowde.

Other References

Periodicals have not been listed separately. The main international journals in the field are the *International Journal of Lexicography* and *Dictionaries: Journal of the Dictionary Society of North America*. *Scottish Language* covers both Scots and Gaelic, and contains articles on dictionaries and word lists.

Aitken, A.J. (1981) 'The Scottish Vowel-Length Rule', in Benskin and Samuels, pp. 131–57.

Aitken, A.J. (1985) 'The Pronunciation Entries for the *CSD*', *Dictionaries*, 7, pp. 134–150.

Aitken, A.J. (1986) 'The Pronunciation Entries for the *CSD*', in Strauss and Drescher, pp. 35–45.

Aitken, A.J. (1964) 'Completing the Record of Scots', *Scottish Studies*, 8, pp. 129–40.

Aitken, A.J. (1971) 'Historical Dictionaries and the Computer', in Wisbey, pp. 3–17.

Aitken, A.J. (1980) 'On Some Deficiencies in our Scottish Dictionaries', in Pijnenburg and de Tollenaere, pp. 33–56.

Aitken, A.J. (1981) '*DOST*: How we Make it and What's in it', in Lyall and Riddy, pp. 33–51.

Aitken, A.J. (1987) 'The Extinction of Scotland in Popular Dictionaries of English', in Bailey, Richard W., *Dictionaries of English*, pp. 99–135.

Aitken, A.J. (1987) 'The Period Dictionaries', in Burchfield, pp. 94–116.

Aitken, A.J. (1988) 'The Lexicography of Scots: The Current Position' in Hyldegaard-Jensen, pp. 323–33.

Aitken, A.J. (1989) 'The Lexicography of Scots Two Hundred Years Since: Ruddiman and his Successors', in Mackenzie and Todd, pp. 235–45.

Aitken, A.J. (1990) 'The Lexicography of Scots', in Hausmann et al, pp. 1983–7.

Aitken, A.J. (1992) 'Scottish Dictionaries', in McArthur, pp. 901–3.

Aitken, A.J. (1993) 'Lexicography', in Daiches, pp. 182–3.

Aitken, A.J. and Bratley, P. (1967) 'An Archive of Older Scots Texts for Scanning by Computer', *English Studies*, 48, pp. 60–1.

Allan, David (2000) *Philosophy and Politics in Later Stuart Scotland*, Phantassie, East Linton: Tuckwell Press.

Bailey, Richard W. (ed.) (1987) *Dictionaries of English: Prospects for the Record of our Language*, Cambridge: Cambridge University Press.

Bawcutt, Priscilla (ed.) (1988) *The Poems of William Dunbar* 2 vols., Glasgow: Association for Scottish Literary Studies.

Benskin, Michael and Samuels, Michael L. (eds) (1981) *So Meny People, Longages and Tonges: Philological Essays in Scots and Mediaeval English Presented to Angus McIntosh*, Edinburgh: Edinburgh Middle English Dialect Project.

Black, Ronald (ed.) (2001) *An Lasair*, Edinburgh: Birlinn.

Blaney, Jim (1985) 'Upper Ards Folk and Glossary of Words', *Journal of the Upper Ards Historical Society*, 9, pp. 6–7.

Boswell, James (2008; first published 1791) *The Life of Samuel Johnson*, London: Penguin.

Braidwood, John (1965a) 'Towards an Ulster Dialect Dictionary', *Ulster Dialect Archives Bulletin*, 5, pp. 3–14.

Bronner, Simon J. (ed.) (1992) *Creativity and Tradition in Folklore: New Directions*. Utah: State University Press.

Brown, K. (ed.) (2005) *Encyclopedia of Language and Linguistics*, 2nd edn, Oxford: Elsevier.

Bryce, T.G.K and Humes, W.M. (eds) (2008) *Scottish Education Third Edition: Beyond Devolution*, Edinburgh: Edinburgh University Press.

Buchan, David and Olson, Ian A. (1997) 'Walter Gregor (1825–97): A Life and Preliminary Bibliography', *Folklore*, 108, pp. 115–17.

Burchfield, R.W. (ed.) (1987) *Studies in Lexicography*, Oxford: Oxford University Press.

Byers, John W. (1903) *Humour of Ulster*, Belfast: Strain and Sons.

Cairns, John W. (1992) 'John Spotswood, Professor of Law: A Preliminary Sketch', *Stair Society Miscellany*, 3, pp. 131–59.

Cairns, John W. (1996) 'Andrew Bell, Jonas Luntley and the London Edition of Mackenzie's Institutions', *The Bibliotheck*, 21, pp. 7–11.

Cairns, John W. (2001) 'The Moveable Text of Mackenzie: Bibliographical Problems for the Scottish Concept of Institutional Writing', in John W. Cairns and O. F. Robinson (eds) *Critical Studies in Ancient Law, Comparative Law and Legal History*, Oxford: Hart Publishing.

Cairns, John W., Fergus, T. David and MacQueen, Hector L. (1990) 'Legal Humanism and the History of Scots Law: John Skene and Thomas Craig', in MacQueen, pp. 48–74

Campbell, J.L. (1937) 'The First Printed Gaelic Vocabulary', *Scots Magazine* 28.

Campbell, J.L. (1938) 'An Early Scottish Gaelic Vocabulary' *Scottish Gaelic Studies*, 5:1, pp. 76–93.

Campbell, J.L. (ed.) (1975) *A Collection of Rites and Customes Copied by Edward Lhuyd from the Manuscript of James Kirkwood (1650–1709) and Annotated by him with the Aid of John Beaton; . . .*, Cambridge: D.S. Brewer for the Folklore Society.

Campbell, J.L. and Thomson, Derick S. (1963) *Edward Lhuyd in the Scottish Highlands*, Oxford: Clarendon Press.

Carmichael, Alexander (1900) *Carmina Gadelica: Hymns and Incantations . . .*, 2 vols, Edinburgh: T. & A. Constable; reprinted (1928) Edinburgh: Oliver & Boyd; J.C. Watson, (ed.) (1940, 1941) vols 3 and 4, Edinburgh: Oliver & Boyd; A. Matheson, (ed.) (1954) vol. 5, Edinburgh: Oliver & Boyd; A. Matheson, (ed.) (1971) vol. 6, Edinburgh: Scottish Academic Press; facsimile edition (2006), Edinburgh: Floris Books.

Chambers, Ephraim (1728) *Cyclopaedia*, London: printed for James and John Knapton.

Chambers, Robert (1844) *Cyclopaedia of English Literature*, Edinburgh: W. & R. Chambers.

Chambers, William (1872) *Memoir of Robert Chambers, With Autobiographic Reminiscences of William Chambers*, Edinburgh: W. & R. Chambers.

Clyne, Douglas (1984) *Gaelic Verbs and their Prepositions/Gnìomhairean Gàidhlig leis na Roimheirean aca*, Glasgow: Gairm.

Coldwell, David F.C. (ed.) (1951–64) *Virgil's Aeneid Translated into Scottish Verse by Gavin Douglas Bishop of Dunkeld*, Edinburgh: Scottish Text Society, 3rd Series, vols 25, 27, 28, 30, and London (Blackwood).

Corbett, John, McClure, J. Derrick and Stuart-Smith, Jane (eds) (2003) *The Edinburgh Companion to Scots*, Edinburgh: Edinburgh University Press.

Cowie, A.P. (ed.) (2009) *The Oxford History of English Lexicography*, 2 vols, Oxford: Clarendon Press.

Craigie, William A. (1926) 'New Dictionary Schemes Presented to the Philological Society, 4 April, 1919', *Transactions of the Philological Society* (1925–30), pp. 6–13.

Daiches, David (ed.) (1993) *The New Companion to Scottish Culture*, Edinburgh: Polygon.

Dareau, Margaret G. and Macleod, Iseabail (2009) 'Dictionaries of Scots', in Cowie, vol. 1, pp. 303–25.

Dieckhoff, Henry C. (1923) 'The Gaelic Dialect of Glengarry in Scotland', *Revue Celtique*, 40, pp. 391–5.

Dieckhoff, Henry C. (1926) 'Notes on Scottish Gaelic Dialects' *Scottish Gaelic Studies*, 1, pp. 188–94.

Dieckhoff, Henry C. (1941) 'Parallels in Gaelic and Russian Folk-Poetry' *Transactions of the Gaelic Society of Inverness*, 36, pp. 291–318.

Douglas, Sheila (1998) 'Sir James Wilson and his Commonsense Approach to the Scots Language', *Scottish Language*, 17, pp. 16–21.

Duncan, Douglas (1965) *Thomas Ruddiman: A Study in Scottish Scholarship of the Early Eighteenth Century*, Edinburgh: Oliver & Boyd.

Durkan, John (1990) 'Education: The Laying of Fresh Foundations', in MacQueen, pp. 123–60.

Encyclopaedia Britannica (1771) 1st edn, Edinburgh: printed for A. Bell and C. Macfarquhar.

Eunson, Karen (2003) 'James Stout Angus – Our First Dialect Poet', *New Shetlander*.

'Examining the OED', project website: <http://oed.hertford.ox.ac.uk>.

Fenton, A. and MacDonald, D.A. (eds) (1994) *Studies in Scots and Gaelic: Proceedings of the Third International Conference on the Languages of Scotland*, Edinburgh: Canongate Academic

Findlater, A. (1859–68) *Chambers's Encyclopaedia*, London and Edinburgh: W. & R. Chambers.

Forte, A.D.M. (2005) 'Law and Lexicography: *DOST* and Late Medieval and Early Modern Scottish Shipping Law' in Kay and Mackay, pp. 61–72.

Gaelic Orthographic Conventions (2009) Glasgow: Scottish Qualifications Authority.

Geddes, Alexander (1792) 'Three Scottish Poems', *Transactions of the Society of Antiquaries of Scotland*, 1, pp. 402–40.

Gillies, Hugh C. (1898) *Gaelic Names of Diseases and of Diseased States*, Glasgow: Printed by Alex MacDougall, reprinted from the Caledonian Medical Journal.

Gillies, William (1991) 'Liam MacGill'Iosa: A Friend of the Gael' *Transactions of the Gaelic Society of Inverness*, 56, Inverness, pp. 503–33.

Gillies, William (1994) 'A Gaelic Thesaurus' in Fenton and MacDonald (eds), pp. 149–62.

Gillies, William (2001) 'Gaelic Dictionaries', in M. Lynch (ed.), *The Oxford Companion to Scottish History*, Oxford: Oxford University Press, pp. 251–2.

Grant, Colin (1875) *Tiomnadh Nuadh ar Tighearna agus ar Slanair Iosa Criosta; air a thionndadh as an Laidinn gu Gaidhlig le aonta Easbuigean na h-Alba*, Aberdeen: A. King. [Translation by Colin Grant, based on the MS by Ewen MacLachlan.]

Grant, William (1909) *What Still Remains to be Done for the Scottish Dialects*, English Association Leaflet No. 11.

Grant, William (1912) *The Pronunciation of English in Scotland*, Cambridge: Cambridge University Press.

Grant, William and Dixon, James Main (1921) *Manual of Modern Scots*, Cambridge: Cambridge University Press.

Grønneberg, Roy (1981) *Jakobsen and Shetland*, Lerwick: Shetland Publishing.

Hamilton-Smith, N. (1971) 'A Versatile Concordance Program for a Textual Archive', in Wisbey (1971), pp. 235–44.

Hancher, Michael (1998) 'Gazing at the Imperial Dictionary', *Book History*, 1, pp. 157–81.

Hausmann, F.J., et al. (eds) (1990) *Wörterbücher/Dictionaries/Dictionnaires*, vol. 2, Berlin: de Gruyter.

[Hickes, G.] (1678) *Ravillac Redivivus being a Narrative of the late Tryal of Mr. James Mitchel, a conventicle-preacher . . .*, London: Henry Hills.

'History of Encyclopaedia Britannica and Britannica Online', Encyclopaedia Britannica Corporate Site: <http://corporate.britannica.com/company_info.html>.

Hüllen, Werner (1999) *English Dictionaries 800–1700: The Topical Tradition*, Oxford: Clarendon Press.

Hyldegaard-Jensen, Karl (ed.) (1988) *Symposium on Lexicography III: Proceedings of the Third International Symposium on Lexicography . . .*, Tübingen: Niemeyer.

Jakobsen, Jakob (1936) *The Place Names of Shetland*, London: David Nutt; Copenhagen: Vilhelm Prior; reprinted (1993) Lerwick: Shetland Library (preface by A. Hörsbol, intro by J. Fellows-Jensen).

[Johnstone, Christian] (1841) 'Memoir of Dr. Jamieson', *Tait's Edinburgh Magazine*, 8:92 (August), pp. 514–28.

Jones, Charles (1994) 'Alexander Geddes: An Eighteenth-Century Scottish Orthoepist and Dialectologist', *Folia Linguistica Historica*, 8, pp. 71–83.

Jones, Charles (ed.) (1997) *The Edinburgh History of the Scots Language*, Edinburgh: Edinburgh University Press.

Kay, Christian J. and Mackay, Margaret A. (eds) (2005) *Perspectives on the Older Scottish Tongue*, Edinburgh: Edinburgh University Press.

Kay, John (1838) *A Series of Original Portraits and Caricature Etchings, by the Late John Kay*, 2 vols, Edinburgh: Hugh Paton, Carver and Gilder.

Kelly, Fergus (1988) *A Guide to Early Irish Law*, Dublin: Dublin Institute for Advanced Studies.

Kidd, Colin (2002) 'Race, Theology and Revival: Scots Philology and its Contexts in the Age of Pinkerton and Jamieson', *Scottish Studies Review*, 3:2, pp. 20–33.

Kirk, John M. and Macleod, Iseabail (forthcoming, 2012) *Scots: The Language and its Literature: A Festschrift for J. Derrick McClure*, Amsterdam: Rodopi.

Kirk, Rev. R. (1690) *An Biobla Naomhtha, iona bhfuil leabhair na Seintiomna ar na ttarruing as . . ., le R.K. M.A.*, Lunnduin: R. Ebheringhtham.

Kist/a' Chiste Anthology, The (1995), Walton-on-Thames: Thomas Nelson for Scottish Consultative Council on the Curriculum.

Leabhraiche an t-Seann Tiomhnaidh, air an tarruing o'n cheud chanain chum Gaelic Albannaich (1783–1801). Dun-eidin: U. Smellie.

Lhuyd, Edward (1707) *Archaeologia Britannica: Giving some account additional to what has been hitherto publish'd, of the languages, histories, and customs of the original inhabitants of Great Britain: From collections and observations in travels through Wales, Cornwal, Bas-Bretagne, Ireland and Scotland*, vol. 1: *Glossography*, Oxford.

Linguistic and Literary Terms: Revised List for Use in Examinations in Gaelic (Native Speakers) in and after 1982 (1979), Dùn Èideann: Scottish Certificate of Education Examination Board.

Lorimer, William Laughton (1983) *The New Testament in Scots*, Edinburgh: Southside (Publishers).

Lounsbury, Thomas R. (1904) *The Standard of Pronunciation in English*, New York and London: Harper & Brothers.

Lyall, Roderick J. and Riddy, Felicity (eds) (1981) *Proceedings of the Third International Conference on Scottish Language and Literature (Medieval and Renaissance)*, Stirling: University of Stirling, and Glasgow: University of Glasgow.

Macafee, Caroline (1994) 'The Ulster Dictionary Project', *Belfast Working Papers in Language and Linguistics*, 12, pp. 177–93.

Macafee, Caroline and Macleod, Iseabail (eds) (1987) *The Nuttis Schell: Essays on the Scots Language Presented to A J Aitken*, Aberdeen: Aberdeen University Press.

McArthur, Tom (ed.) (1992) *The Oxford Companion to the English Language*, Oxford: Oxford University Press.

MacBain, Alexander and Whyte, John (1902) *How to Learn Gaelic: Orthographical Instructions, Grammar and Reading Lessons*, Inverness: The 'Northern Chronicle' Office.

Macbean, Alexander (1773) *A Dictionary of Ancient Geography*, London: printed for G. Robinson.

McClure, J. Derrick (1992) 'What, if Anything, is a Scotticism?', in Bronner (ed.), pp. 205–21.

McClure, J. Derrick (2004) 'A Local Treasure Trove: John MacTaggart's Scottish Gallovidian Encyclopedia', *Transactions of the Dumfriesshire and Galloway Natural History and Antiquarian Society*, 3rd series, 78, pp. 131–38.

McClure, J. Derrick (ed.) (1983) *Scotland and the Lowland Tongue: Studies in the Language and Literature of Lowland Scotland in Honour of David D. Murison*, Aberdeen: Aberdeen University Press.

M'Crie, Thomas (1899) *Life of Andrew Melville*, Edinburgh and London: William Blackwood & Sons.

MacDhomhnuill, A. (1834) *Aiseiridh na sean chànain Albannaich; no, 'N nuadh òranaiche Gàelach*, ed. J. MacKenzie. Glascho: Muir, Gobhan agus an Cuideachd.

MacDonald, Alasdair A., et al. (eds) (1994) *The Renaissance in Scotland: Studies in Literature, Religion, History, and Culture Offered to John Durkhan*, Leiden, New York: E.J. Brill.

Macdonald, Angus (1941) *The Place-Names of West Lothian*, Edinburgh: Oliver and Boyd.

MacDonald, J.A. (1976) *Gàidhlig Bheò: A Course Leading to the Scottish Certificate of Education 'O' Grade (Learners) Examination*, Cambridge: National Extension College in association with An Comunn Gàidhealach.

MacDonald, K. D. (1983) 'Dictionaries, Scottish Gaelic', in Thomson, pp. 61–3.

Mac Eachainn, E. (1826) *Leanmhuinn Chriost'; air a thionnadh o Laidinn gu Gàidhlig le Eoghan Mac Eachainn*, Peirt: Morisons.

MacFarlane, Malcolm (1889) *Phonetics of the Gaelic Language: With an Exposition of the Current Orthography and a System of Phonography*, Paisley: J. and R. Parlane; Edinburgh: J. Menzies; London: Houlston.

MacFarlane, Malcolm (1903) *An treòraiche: Leabhran sgoil air son na cloinne*, Struibhle: A. MacAoidh.

MacFarlane, Malcolm (1911) *An Comh-threòraiche: Leabhran sgoil a chum feum na cloinne*, Stirling: Aonghas Mac Aoidh.

MacFarlane, Malcolm (1923) *Làmh-sgrìobhainn Mhic Rath . . ./The Fernaig manuscript . . .*, Dun-dé: C.S. MacLeoid.

MacFarlane, Malcolm (ed.) (1912) *Companach na cloinne*, le Iain Mac Phaidein, Struibhle: A. Mac Aoidh.

MacFarlane, Patrick (tr.) (1812) *Aireamh thaghta de shearmoinibh E. Blair*, Dun-eudainn: S. Cléireach.

MacFarlane, Patrick (1812) *Cuairt an oilthirich: No turus a Chriosduidh . . .*, Dun-eudainn: T. Stiùbhart.

McIntosh, Angus, Samuels, Michael L., Benskin, Michael, et al. (eds) (1986) *Linguistic Atlas of Late Mediaeval English*, Aberdeen: Aberdeen University Press.

McIntyre, Rae (ed.) (1990) *Some Handlin': The Dialect Heritage of North Ulster, Collected by Pupils and Friends of Ballyrashane Primary School*, 2nd edn, Limavady: North-West Books.

MacKenzie, J. Lachlan and Todd, Richard (eds) (1989) *In Other Words: Transcultural Studies in Philology, Translation, and Lexicology Presented to Hans Heinrich Meier on the Occasion of his Sixty-Fifth Birthday*, Dordrecht: Foris.

MacKenzie, John (1841) *Sàr-obair nam bàrd Gàelach: or, The Beauties of Gaelic Poetry and Lives of the Highland Bards; . . .*, Glasgow: Macgregor, Polson & Co.

MacKenzie, John (1844) *Eachdraidh a' Phrionnsa; no, Bliadhna Theàrlaich*, Duneideann: Thornton agus Collie.

MacKenzie, John (ed.) (n.d., c.1845) *An Leabhar Liath*, Paisley: n.p.

Mackinnon, Donald (1912) *A Descriptive Catalogue of Gaelic Manuscripts in the Advocates' Library Edinburgh, and Elsewhere in Scotland*, Edinburgh: W. Brown.

Maclean, Donald (1915) *Typographia Scoto-Gadelica: or Books Printed in the Gaelic of Scotland from the Year 1567 to the year 1914 with Bibliographical and Biographical Notes*, Edinburgh: J. Grant.

MacLean, Lachlan (1912) *Eachdraidhean-beatha nan Albannach iomraiteach ud: Uilleam Uallas, Iain Knox, agus Rob Ruadh; fo laimh Chaluim Mhic Phàrlain*, Struibhle: A. MacAoidh.

MacLeod, Rev. Norman (1867) *Caraid nan Gàidheal: Àireamh taghta de sgrìobhaidhnean an Ollaimh Urramaich Tormoid MacLeòid . . .*, Glasgow: W. MacKenzie.

MacLeod, Rev. Norman (ed.) (1829–31) *An Teachdaire Gaelach*, Glasgow: W.R. M'Phun.

McManus, Damian (1991) *A Guide to Ogam*, Maynooth: An Sagart.

MacPherson, Donald C. (1868) *An Duanaire . . .*, Dun-Eidin: MacLachluinn agus an Stiùärtach.

MacPherson, James (ed.) (1807) *The Poems of Ossian in the Original Gaelic . . .*, London: W. Bulmer.

MacQueen, H (1994) '*Glanville* Resarcinate: Sir John Skene and the *Regiam majestatem*', in MacDonald et al., pp. 382–403.

MacQueen, John (ed.) (1990) *Humanism in Renaissance Scotland*, Edinburgh: Edinburgh University Press.

Malcolme, Rev. David (1738) *An Essay on the Antiquities of Britain and Ireland*, Edinburgh: T. & W. Ruddiman.

Mark, C. (1986) *Gaelic Verbs Systematised and Simplified*, Glasgow: Roinn nan Cànan Ceilteach, Oilthigh Ghlaschu; 2nd edn, 2006, 2007, London: Steve Savage.

Marshall, John J. (1904–6) 'The Dialect of Ulster [Part 1]', *Ulster Journal of Archaeology*, (1904) new series, 10, pp. 121–130; (1905) 11, pp. 64–70, 122–5, 175–9; (1906) 12, pp. 18–22.

Mather, James and Speitel, Hans Henning (1975, 1977, 1986) *The Linguistic Atlas of Scotland: Scots Section*, 3 vols, London: Croom Helm.

Mathews, M.M. (1985) 'George Watson and the Dictionary of American English', *Dictionaries*, 7, pp. 214–24.

Meek, Donald E. (1992) *Am Bìoball Gàidhlig: Air a tharraing o na ciad chànainean a-chum Gàidhlig na h-Alba*, Dùn Èideann: Comann-Bhioball Dùthchail na h-Alba.

Meek, Donald E. (2001) '"Beachdan Ura à Inbhir Nis"/New Opinions from Inverness: Alexander MacBain (1855–1907) and the Foundation of Celtic Studies in Scotland', *Proceedings of the Society of Antiquaries of Scotland*, 131, pp. 23–39.

Meek, Donald E. (2004) 'The Sublime Gael: The Impact of MacPherson's *Ossian* on Literary Creativity and cultural perception in Gaelic Scotland', in H. Gaskill (ed.), *The Reception of Ossian in Europe*, London: Thoemmes Continuum.

Meier, Hans H. (1962) 'Review of *A Dictionary of the Older Scottish Tongue*', *English Studies*, 43, pp. 444–5.

Montgomery, Michael (1993) 'The Lexicography of Hiberno-English', *Irish Studies Working Papers*, 93–3, pp. 19–35.

Montgomery, Michael (2010) 'Some Words with James Fenton,' *Ullans: The Magazine for Ulster-Scots*, 11, pp. 13–27.

Montgomery, Michael and Gregg, Robert J. (1997) 'The Scots Language in Ulster', in Jones, pp. 569–622.

Mooijaart, M. and van der Wal, M. (eds) (2008) *Yesterday's Words: Contemporary, Current and Future Lexicography*, Newcastle: Cambridge Scholars.

Mugglestone, Lynda (ed.) (2000; reprinted 2002) *Lexicography and the OED: Pioneers in the Untrodden Forest*, Oxford: Oxford University Press.

Muir, Willa (1938) 'Dr John Jamieson', BBC radio script (broadcast 12 July), Scottish Theatre Archive, Glasgow University Library Special Collections, STA Kc 5/1.

Murison, David D. (1977) *The Guid Scots Tongue*, Edinburgh: Blackwood.

Murison, David D. (1981) *Scots Saws*, Edinburgh: James Thin.

Murison, David D. (1987) 'Scottish Lexicography', in Macafee and Macleod, pp. 17–24.

Murray, James A.H. (1873) *The Dialect of the Southern Counties of Scotland*, London: The Philological Society.

Murray, James A.H. (1900) *The Evolution of English Lexicography: The Romanes Lecture*, Oxford: Clarendon Press.

Murray, K.M. Elisabeth (1977) *Caught in the Web of Words: James A.H. Murray and the Oxford English Dictionary*, New Haven and London: Yale University Press.

Nicolson, William (1702) *The Scottish Historical Library: Containing a short view and character of most of the writers, records, registers, lawbooks, &c. which may be serviceable to the undertakers of a general history of Scotland, down to the union of the two kingdoms in K. James the VI*, London: T. Childe.

Ó Cuív, Brian (ed.) (1947) *Cnósach Focal ó Bhaile Bhúirne i gCunndae Chorcaí*, Dublin/Baile Átha Cliath: Institiúid Ard-Léinn Bhaile Átha Cliath.

Ó Dochartaigh, Cathair (ed.) (1994–7) *Survey of the Gaelic Dialects of Scotland: Questionnaire Materials Collected for the Linguistic Survey of Scotland*, 5 vols, Dublin: Dublin Institute for Advanced Studies.

O'Neill, Timothy (1984) *The Irish hand: Scribes and their Manuscripts from the Earliest Times to the Seventeenth Century, with an Exemplar of Irish Scripts*, Portlaoise: Dolmen Press.

Pedersen, Holger (1909–13) *Vergleichende Grammatik der Keltischen Sprachen*, Göttingen: Vandenhoeck und Ruprecht.

Pijnenburg, W. and de Tollenaere, F. (eds) (1980) *Proceedings of the Second International Round Table Conference on Historical Lexicography*, Dodrecht: Foris.

Pokorny, Julius (1948–69) *Indogermanisches Etymologisches Wörterbuch*, Bern: Francke.

Popular Encyclopedia, The (1833), Glasgow: Blackie & Son.

Rennie, Susan (2008) 'The *Electronic Jamieson*: Towards a Bicentenary Celebration', in Mooijaart and van der Wal, pp. 333–40.

Rennie, Susan (2011) 'Boswell's Scottish Dictionary Rediscovered', *Dictionaries*, 32.

Rennie, Susan (forthcoming, 2012) *Jamieson's Dictionary of Scots: The Story of the First Historical Dictionary of the Scots Language*, Oxford: Oxford University Press.

Riach, W.A.D. (1979) 'A Dialect Study of Comparative Areas in Galloway 1st report', *Scottish Literary Journal Supplement*, 9, pp. 1–16; 2nd report (1980), 12, pp. 43–60; 3rd and last report (1982), *Scottish Language*, 1, pp. 13–22.

Riach, W.A.D. (1984) 'Galloway Schools Dialect Survey', *Scottish Language*, 3, pp. 49–59.

Roberts, A. (2006) 'Maighstir Eobhan Mac Eachainn and the Orthography of Scots Gaelic', *Transactions of the Gaelic Society of Inverness*, 63, Inverness: The Society, pp. 358–95.

Robertson, Boyd and Taylor, Iain (2003) *Teach Yourself Gaelic*, London: Teach Yourself.

Robertson, T.A. and Graham, John. J. (1952, 1991) *Grammar and Usage of the Shetland Dialect*, Lerwick: Shetland Times.

Robinson, M. (1986) '*The Concise Scots Dictionary*', in Strauss and Drescher (1986), pp. 19–33.

Ros, Uilleam (1830) *Orain Ghae'lach le Uilleam Ros air an sgriobadh, agus air an co'-chruinneachadh ri cheile le Iain Mac-Coinnich*, Inverness: R. Carruthers.

Sauer, Hans (2009) 'Glosses, Glossaries, and Dictionaries of the Medieval Period', in Cowie, vol. 1, pp. 17–40.

Shaw, Rev. William (1778) *An Analysis of the Galic Language*, London: W. and A. Strahan.

Starnes, De Witt T. and Noyes, Gertrude E. (1991; first published 1946) *The English Dictionary from Cawdrey to Johnson 1604–1755*, Amsterdam, Philadelphia: John Benjamins.

Stein, Gabriele (1985) *The English Dictionary before Cawdrey*, Tübingen: Max Niemeyer Verlag.

Stewart, Alexander (1801) *Elements of Gaelic Grammar*, Edinburgh: C. Stewart & Co.

Stokes, Whitley and Strachan, J. (eds) (1901) *Thesaurus Palaeohibernicus: A Collection of Old-Irish Glosses, Scholia, Prose, and Verse*, Cambridge: Cambridge University Press, vol. 1, *Biblical Glosses and Scholia*.

Strauss, Dietrich and Drescher, Horst W. (eds) (1986) *Scottish Language and Literature, Medieval and Renaissance*, Frankfurt am Main: Peter Lang.

Thomson, Derick S. (1990) 'MacMhaighstir Alasdair's Nature Poetry and its Sources', in Thomson, D.S. (ed.) *Gaelic and Scots in Harmony: Proceedings of the Second International Conference on the Languages of Scotland (University of Glasgow, 1988)*, Glasgow: University of Glasgow, Department of Celtic.

Thomson, Derick S. (ed.) (1983; reissued 1994) *The Companion to Gaelic Scotland*, 2nd edn, Glasgow: Gairm.

Tiomnadh Nuadh ar Tighearna agus ar Slanuigh-Fhir Ios Criosd (1767), Dun-eidain: Balfour, Auld agus Smellie.

Tiomnadh Nuadh ar Tighearna agus ar Slanuighir Iosa Criosd. Eadar-theangaichte o'n ghreugais chum gaelic albannaich (1796), Dun-eidin: E. Paterson.

Tobar an Dualchais/Kist o Riches website: <http://www.tobarandualchais.co.uk/>.

Wagner, Heinrich and Ó Baoill, Colm (1958–69) *Linguistic Atlas and Survey of Irish Dialects*, Dublin: Dublin Institute for Advanced Studies.

Watson, George (1916) 'The Story of Scottish Dictionary-Making', *Transactions of the*

Hawick Archaeological Society, pp. 7–12.

Watson, William J. (1926) *The History of the Celtic Place-Names of Scotland*, Edinburgh and London: Blackwood.

Watson, William J. (1937) *Scottish Verse from the Book of the Dean of Lismore*, Edinburgh: Oliver & Boyd.

Williamson, Keith (2007) 'A Latin–Older Scots Glossary in Edinburgh University Library MS 205', *Spanish Society for Medieval English Language and Literature Journal*, 14, pp. 221–76.

Williamson, Keith (unpublished) 'A Linguistic Study of the "Scone Gloss"', University of Edinburgh: Institute for Historical Dialectology.

Wisbey, R.A. (ed.) (1971) *The Computer in Literary and Linguistic Research*, Cambridge: Cambridge University Press.

Index